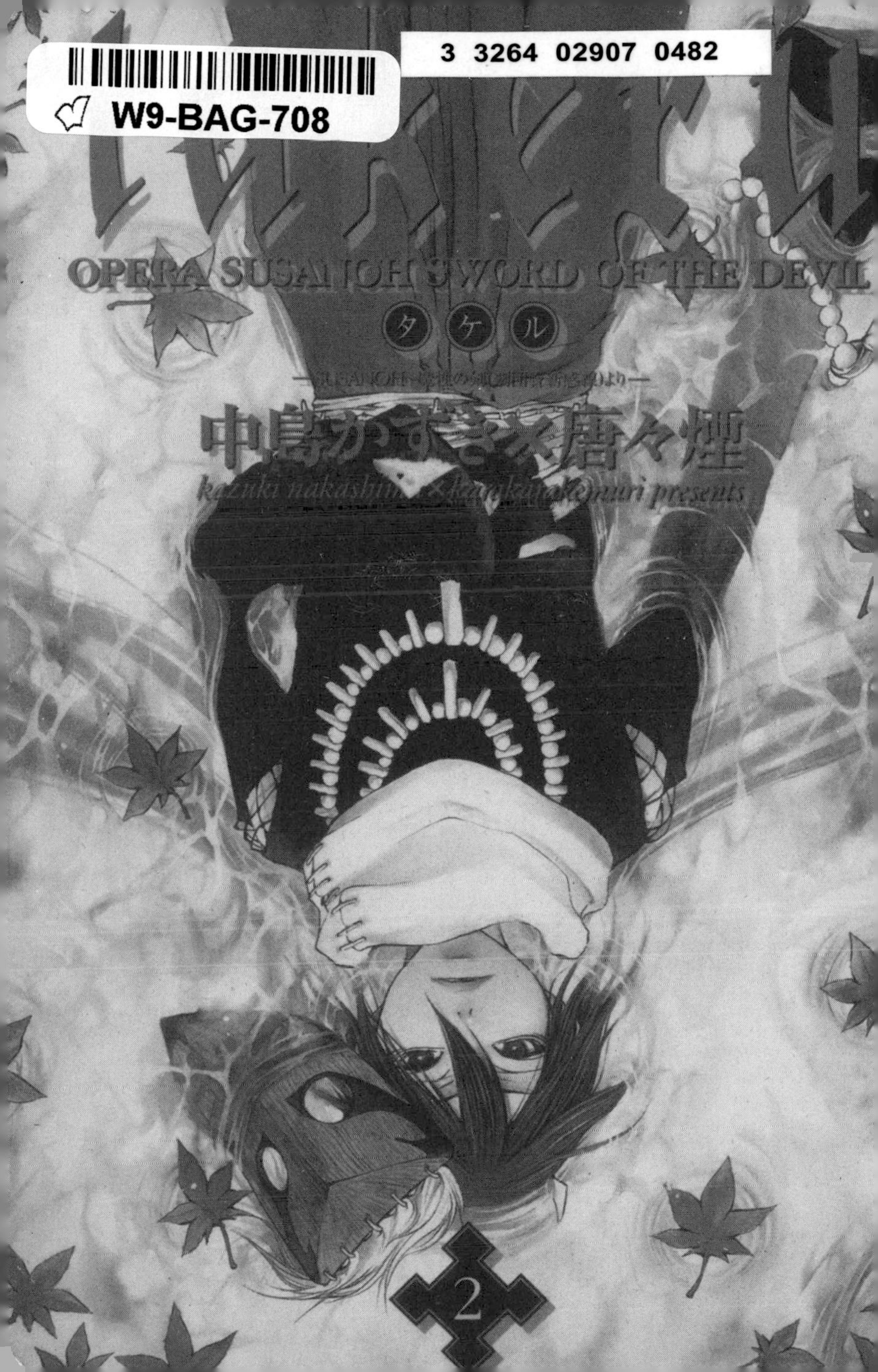
OPERA SUSANOH 3 WORD OF THE DEVIL
タケル
中島かずき×唐々煙
kazuki nakashima×karakarakemuri presents
2

takeru: OPERA SUSANOH SWORD OF THE DEVIL 2
Created by Kazuki Nakashima X Karakarakemuri

Translation - Stephen Paul
English Adaptation - Tim Beedle
Retouch and Lettering - Star Print Brokers
Production Artist - Rui Kyo
Graphic Designer - Louis Csontos
Cover Layout - Jessica Yun

Editor - Lillian Diaz-Przybyl
Print Production Manager - Lucas Rivera
Managing Editor - Vy Nguyen
Senior Designer - Louis Csontos
Director of Sales and Manufacturing - Allyson De Simone
Associate Publisher - Marco F. Pavia
President and C.O.O. - John Parker
C.E.O. and Chief Creative Officer - Stu Levy

A  Manga

TOKYOPOP and 🐸 are trademarks or registered trademarks of TOKYOPOP Inc.

TOKYOPOP Inc.
5900 Wilshire Blvd. Suite 2000
Los Angeles, CA 90036

E-mail: info@TOKYOPOP.com
Come visit us online at www.TOKYOPOP.com

akeru -OPERA SUSANOH SWORD OF THE DEVIL- Volume 2
©2006 KAZUKI NAKASHIMA/KARAKARAKEMURI
©KAZUKI NAKASHIMA/GEKIDAN☆SHINKANSEN
All Rights Reserved. First published in Japan in 2006 by
ag Garden Corporation. English translation rights arranged
with MAG Garden Corporation.
English text copyright © 2009 TOKYOPOP Inc.

All rights reserved. No portion of this book may be
reproduced or transmitted in any form or by any means
without written permission from the copyright holders.
This manga is a work of fiction. Any resemblance to
actual events or locales or persons, living or dead, is
entirely coincidental.

ISBN: 978-1-4278-1571-2

First TOKYOPOP printing: September 2009
10 9 8 7 6 5 4 3 2 1
Printed in the USA

Takeru

Opera Susanoh
Sword of the Devil™

SUSANOH～魔性の剣（劇団☆新感線）より

HAMBURG // LONDON // LOS ANGELES // TOKYO

CONTENTS

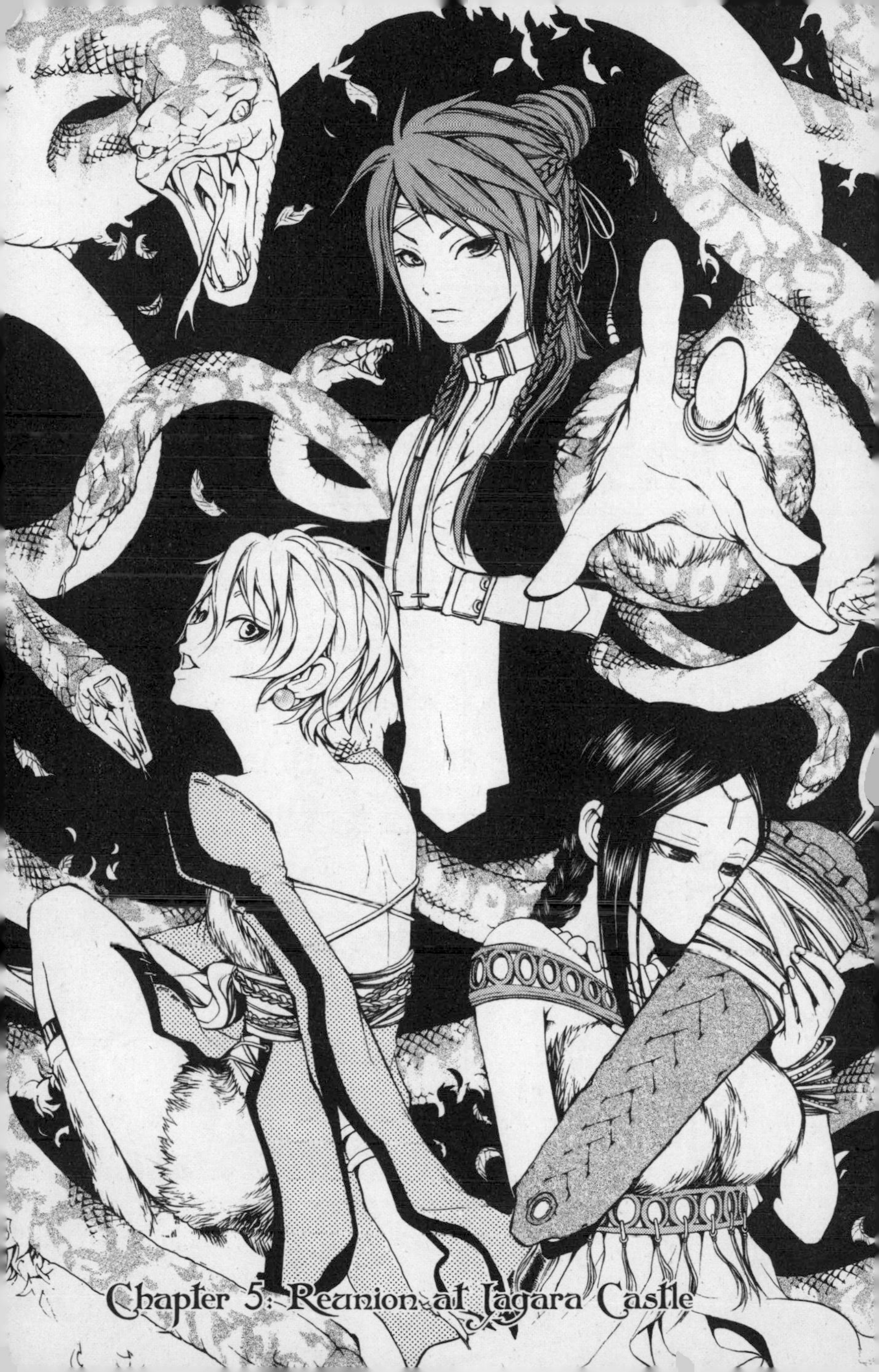
Chapter 5: Reunion at Jagara Castle

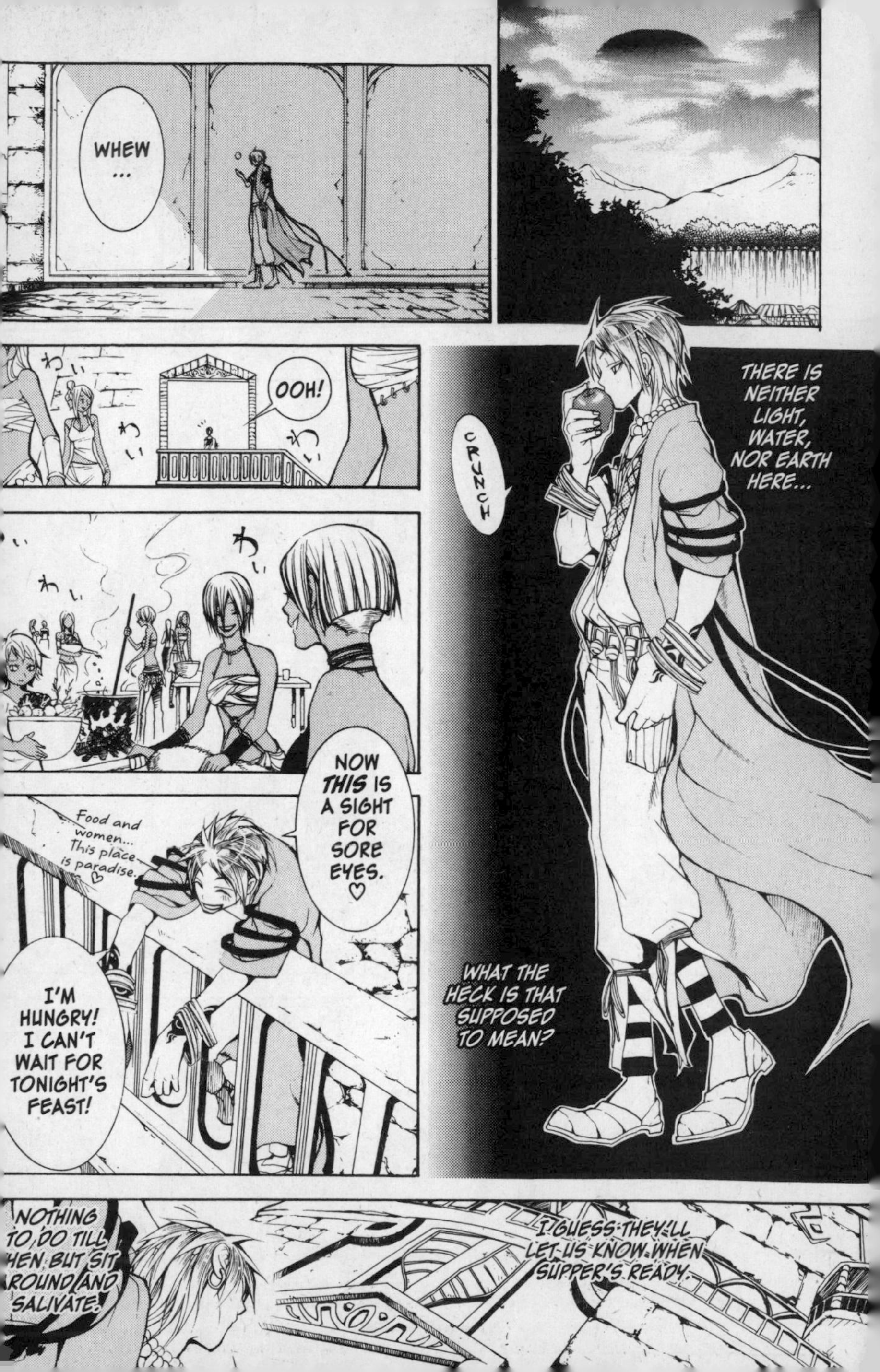
WHEW ...
THERE IS NEITHER LIGHT, WATER, NOR EARTH HERE...
CRUNCH
WHAT THE HECK IS THAT SUPPOSED TO MEAN?
OOH!
NOW THIS IS A SIGHT FOR SORE EYES. ♡
Food and women... This place is paradise. ♡
I'M HUNGRY! I CAN'T WAIT FOR TONIGHT'S FEAST!
I GUESS THEY'LL LET US KNOW WHEN SUPPER'S READY.
NOTHING TO DO TILL THEN BUT SIT AROUND AND SALIVATE!

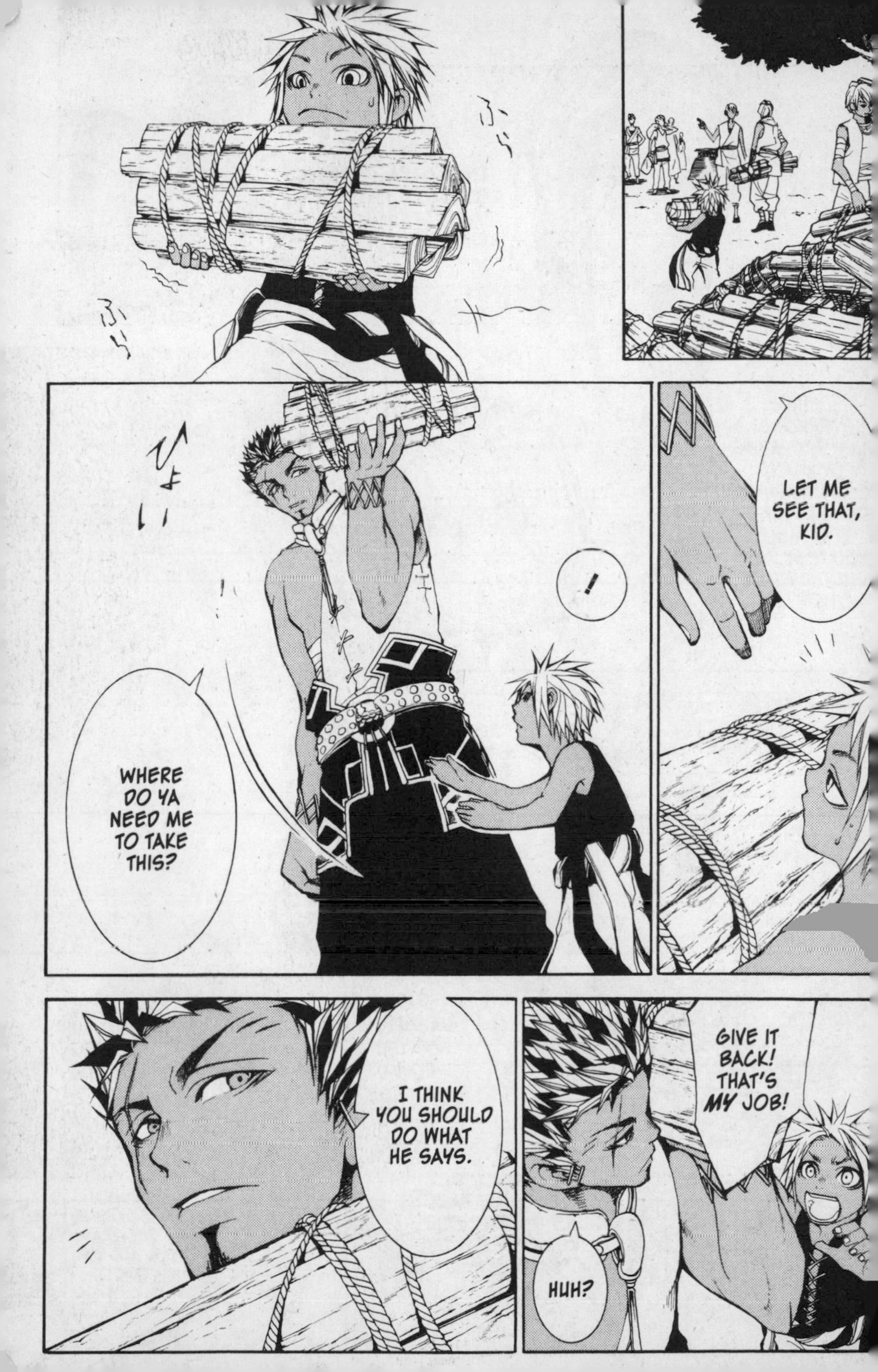
ふら
ふら
LET ME SEE THAT, KID.
ひょい
!
WHERE DO YA NEED ME TO TAKE THIS?
GIVE IT BACK! THAT'S *MY* JOB!
HUH?
I THINK YOU SHOULD DO WHAT HE SAYS.

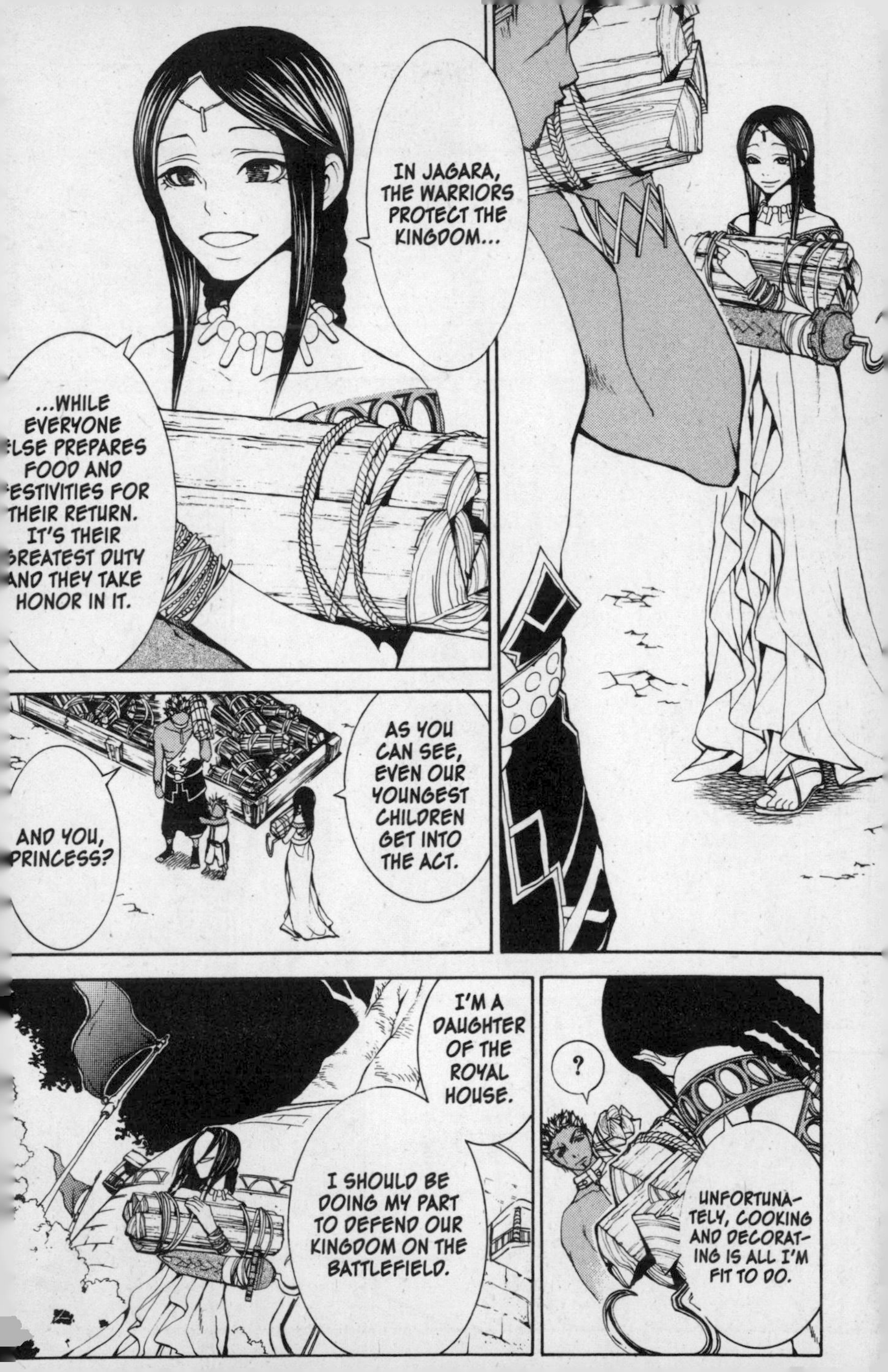
IN JAGARA, THE WARRIORS PROTECT THE KINGDOM...
...WHILE EVERYONE ELSE PREPARES FOOD AND FESTIVITIES FOR THEIR RETURN. IT'S THEIR GREATEST DUTY AND THEY TAKE HONOR IN IT.
AS YOU CAN SEE, EVEN OUR YOUNGEST CHILDREN GET INTO THE ACT.
AND YOU, PRINCESS?
?
UNFORTUNATELY, COOKING AND DECORATING IS ALL I'M FIT TO DO.
I'M A DAUGHTER OF THE ROYAL HOUSE.
I SHOULD BE DOING MY PART TO DEFEND OUR KINGDOM ON THE BATTLEFIELD.

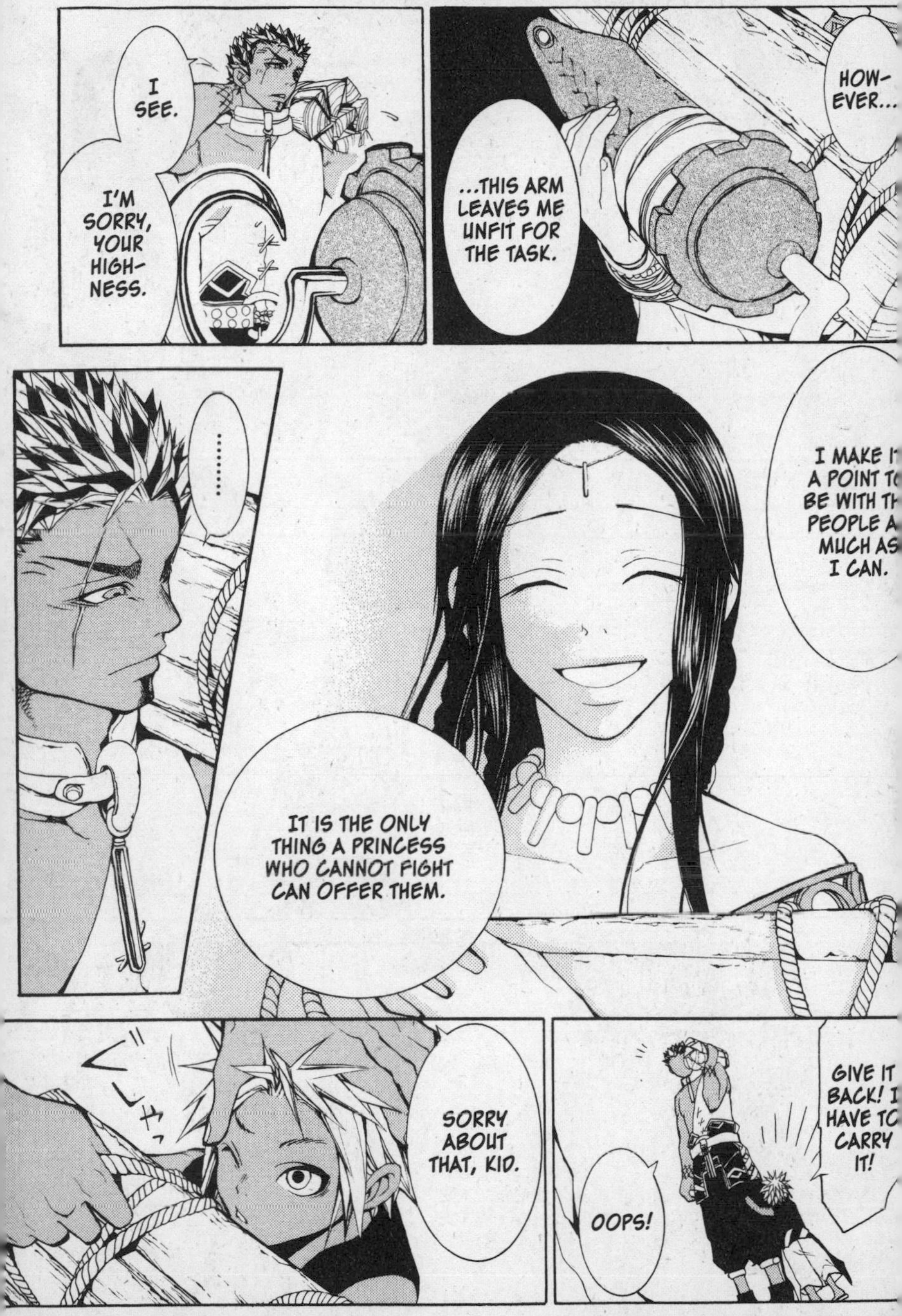
HOW-EVER...
...THIS ARM LEAVES ME UNFIT FOR THE TASK.
I SEE.
I'M SORRY, YOUR HIGHNESS.
I MAKE IT A POINT TO BE WITH THE PEOPLE AS MUCH AS I CAN.
IT IS THE ONLY THING A PRINCESS WHO CANNOT FIGHT CAN OFFER THEM.
......
GIVE IT BACK! I HAVE TO CARRY IT!
OOPS!
SORRY ABOUT THAT, KID.

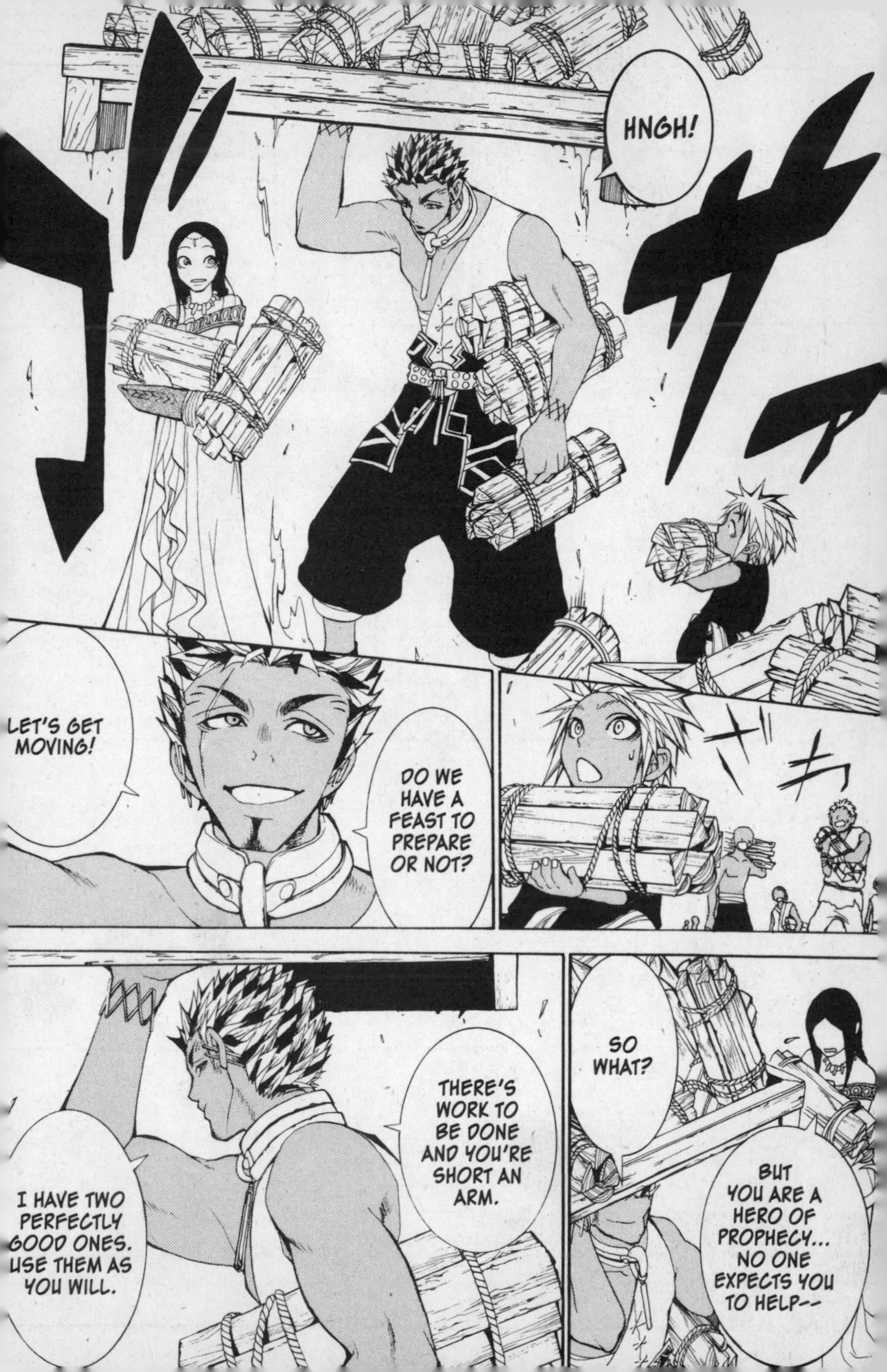
HNGH!
DO WE HAVE A FEAST TO PREPARE OR NOT?
LET'S GET MOVING!
BUT YOU ARE A HERO OF PROPHECY... NO ONE EXPECTS YOU TO HELP--
SO WHAT?
THERE'S WORK TO BE DONE AND YOU'RE SHORT AN ARM.
I HAVE TWO PERFECTLY GOOD ONES. USE THEM AS YOU WILL.

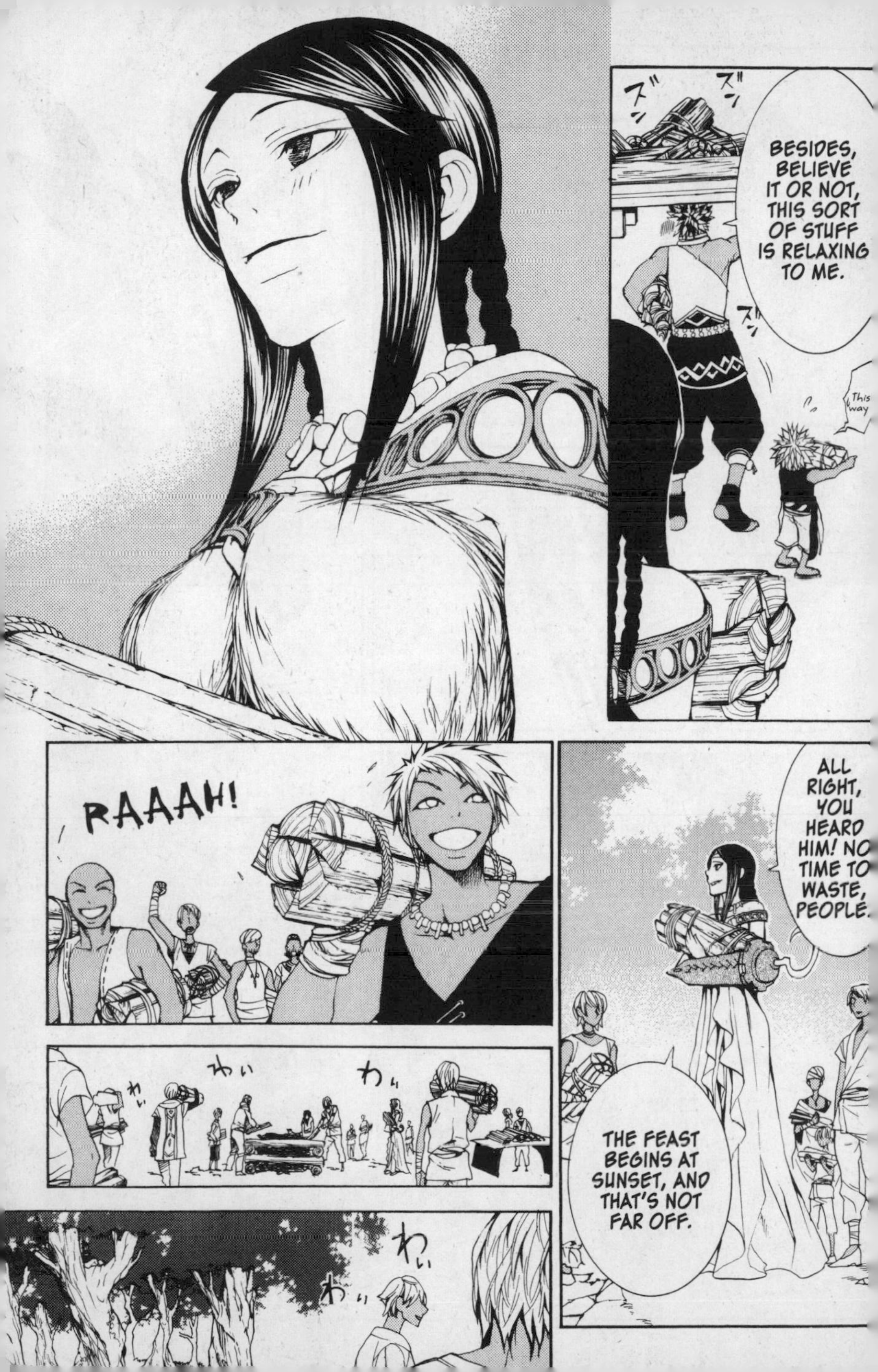
ズン
ズン
BESIDES, BELIEVE IT OR NOT, THIS SORT OF STUFF IS RELAXING TO ME.
ズン
This way
ALL RIGHT, YOU HEARD HIM! NO TIME TO WASTE, PEOPLE.
THE FEAST BEGINS AT SUNSET, AND THAT'S NOT FAR OFF.
RAAAH!
わい
わい
わい
わい
わい

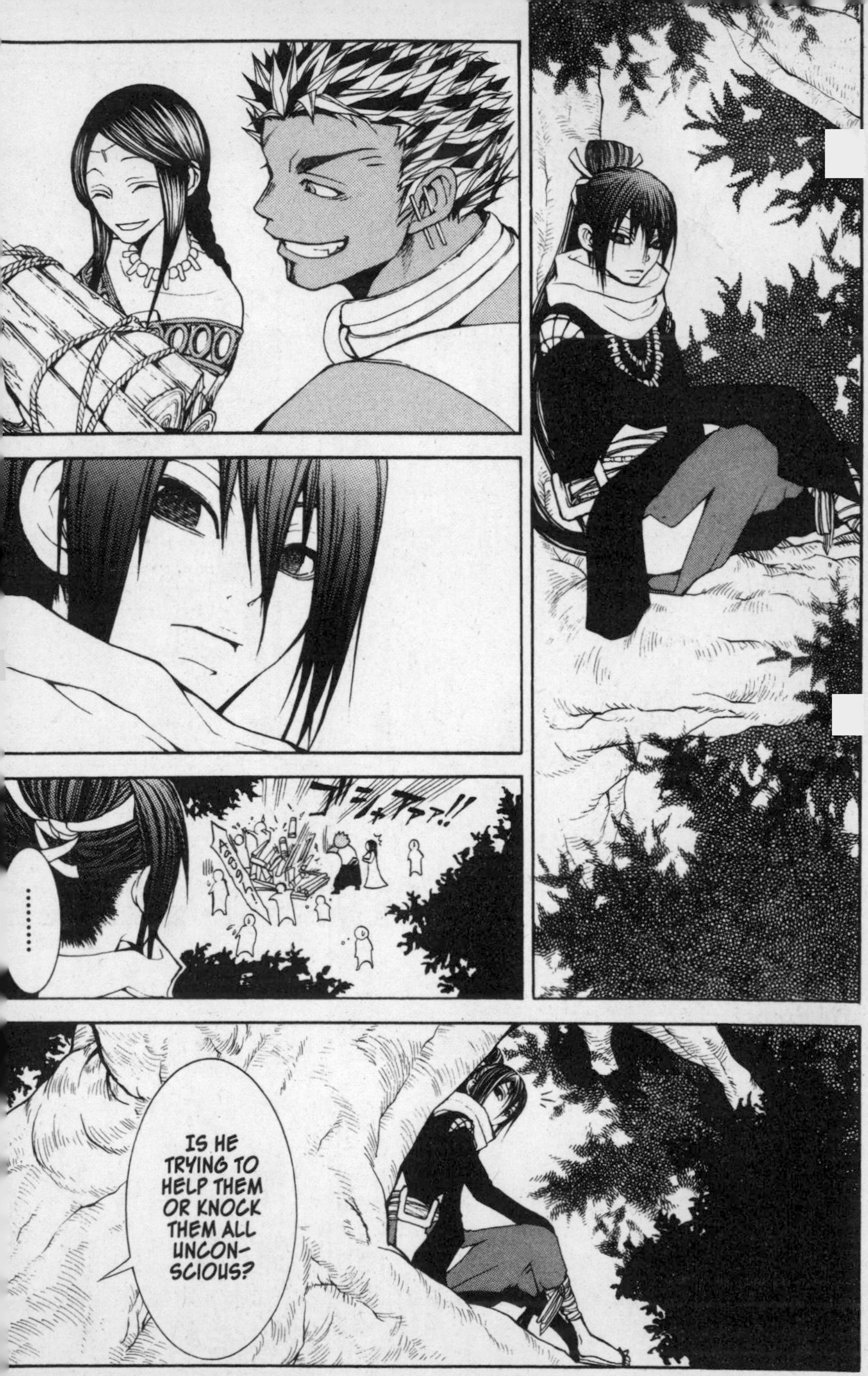

ゴシャアァァ!!
Aaaagh!!
......
IS HE TRYING TO HELP THEM OR KNOCK THEM ALL UNCON-SCIOUS?

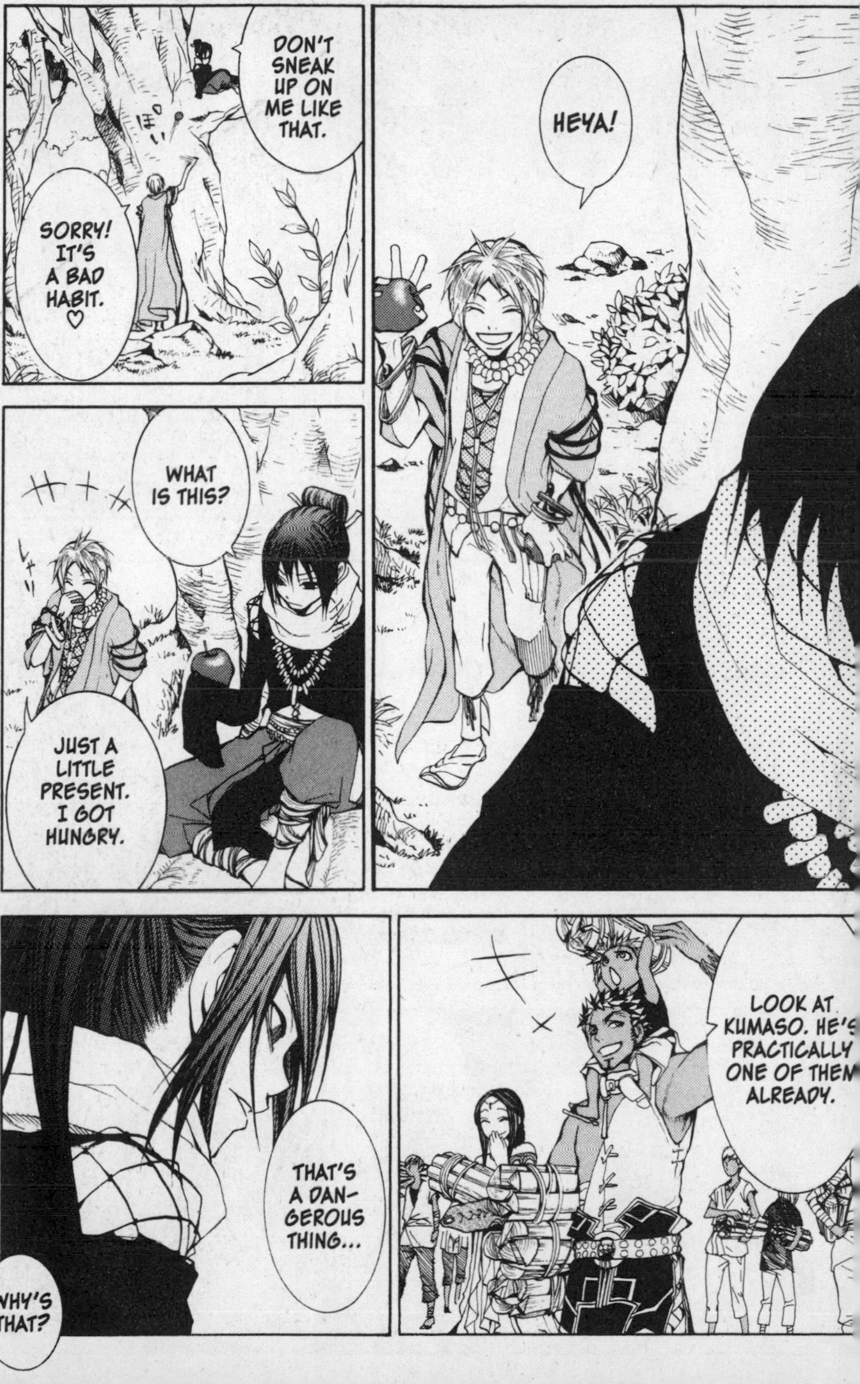
HEYA!
DON'T SNEAK UP ON ME LIKE THAT.
SORRY! IT'S A BAD HABIT. ♡
WHAT IS THIS?
JUST A LITTLE PRESENT. I GOT HUNGRY.
LOOK AT KUMASO. HE'S PRACTICALLY ONE OF THEM ALREADY.
THAT'S A DAN-GEROUS THING...
WHY'S THAT?

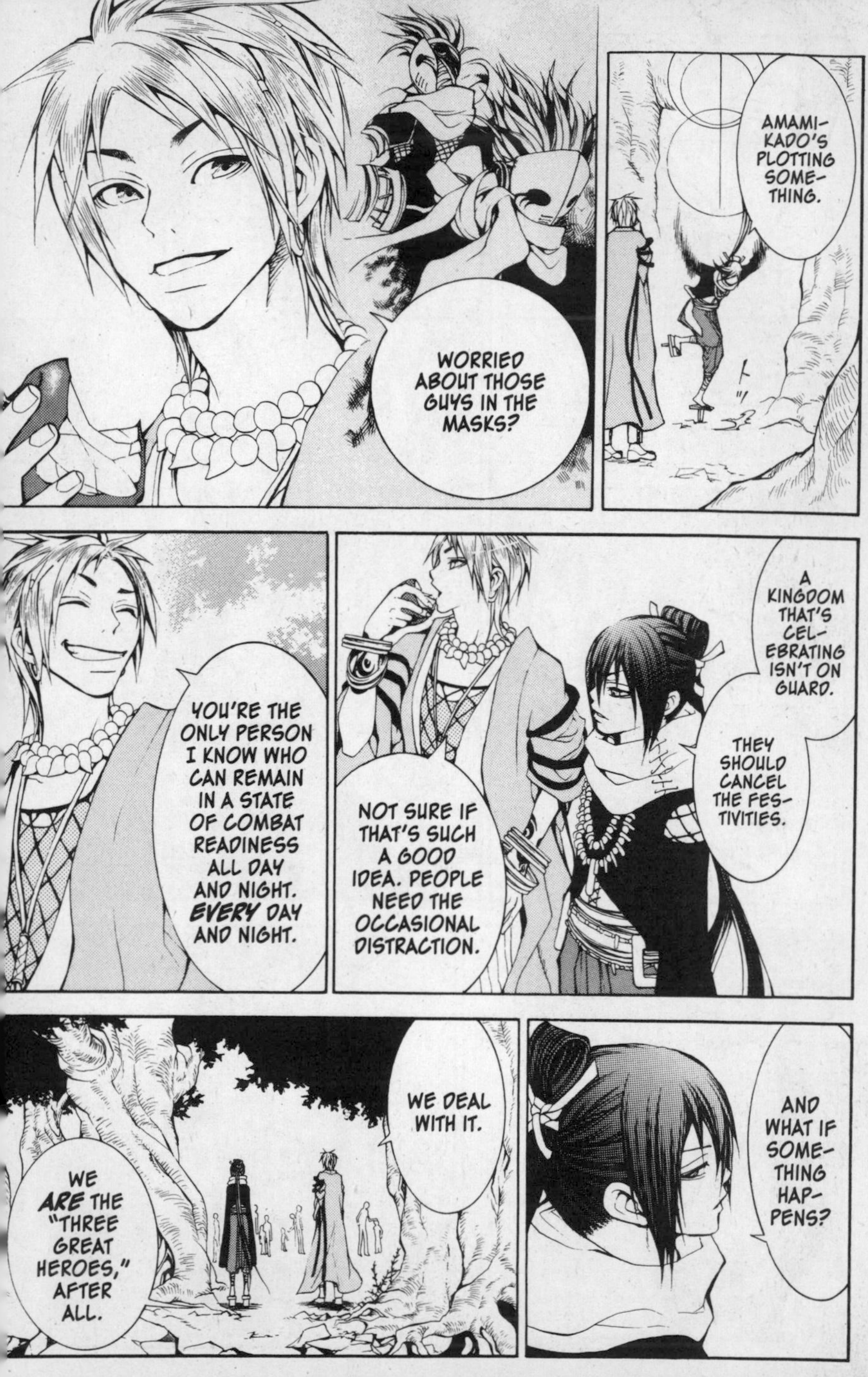
AMAMI-KADO'S PLOTTING SOME-THING.
WORRIED ABOUT THOSE GUYS IN THE MASKS?
A KINGDOM THAT'S CEL-EBRATING ISN'T ON GUARD.
THEY SHOULD CANCEL THE FES-TIVITIES.
NOT SURE IF THAT'S SUCH A GOOD IDEA. PEOPLE NEED THE OCCASIONAL DISTRACTION.
YOU'RE THE ONLY PERSON I KNOW WHO CAN REMAIN IN A STATE OF COMBAT READINESS ALL DAY AND NIGHT. *EVERY* DAY AND NIGHT.
AND WHAT IF SOME-THING HAP-PENS?
WE DEAL WITH IT.
WE *ARE* THE "THREE GREAT HEROES," AFTER ALL.

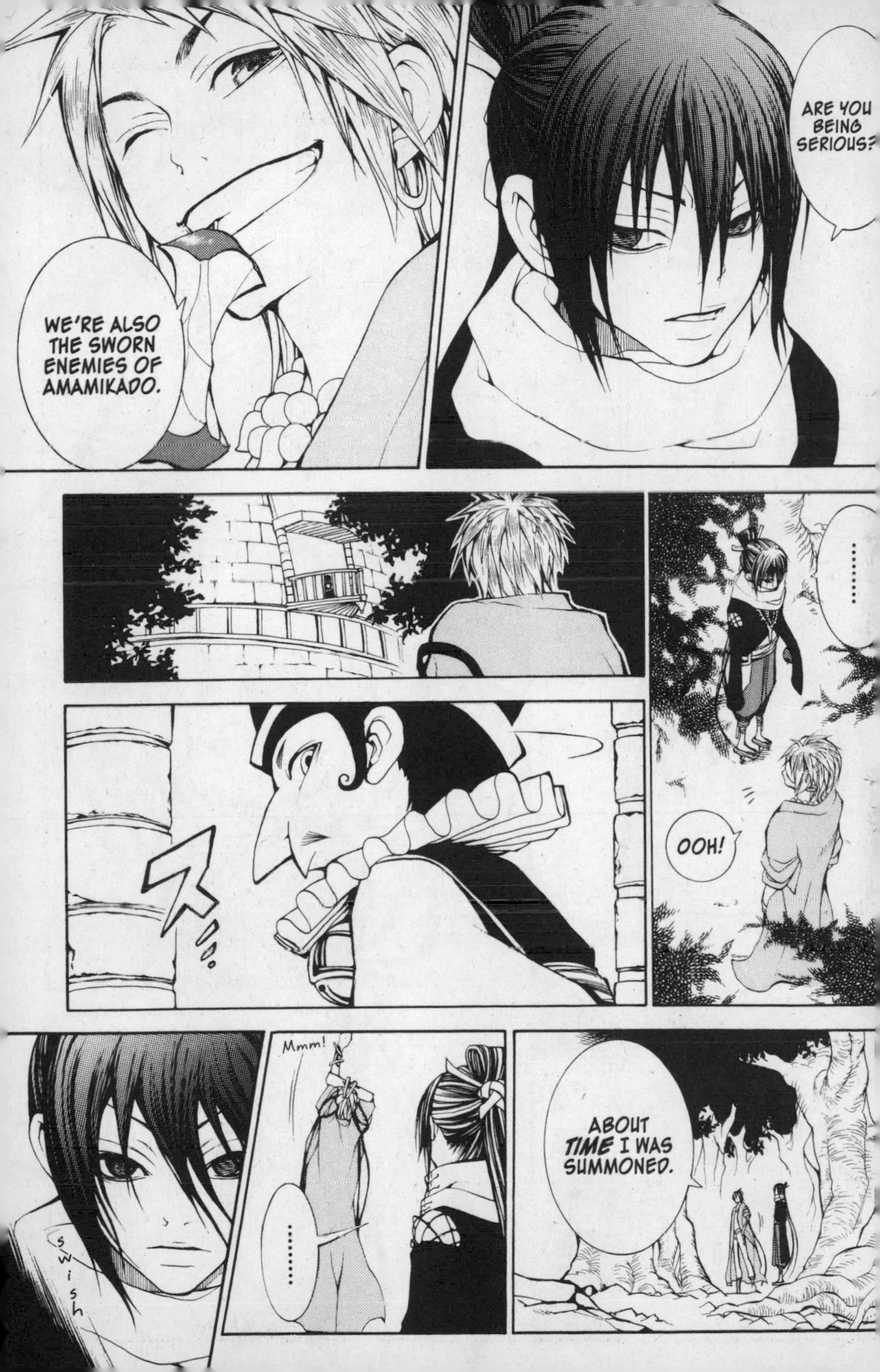
ARE YOU BEING SERIOUS?
WE'RE ALSO THE SWORN ENEMIES OF AMAMIKADO.
......
OOH!
ABOUT *TIME* I WAS SUMMONED.
Mmm!
......
swish

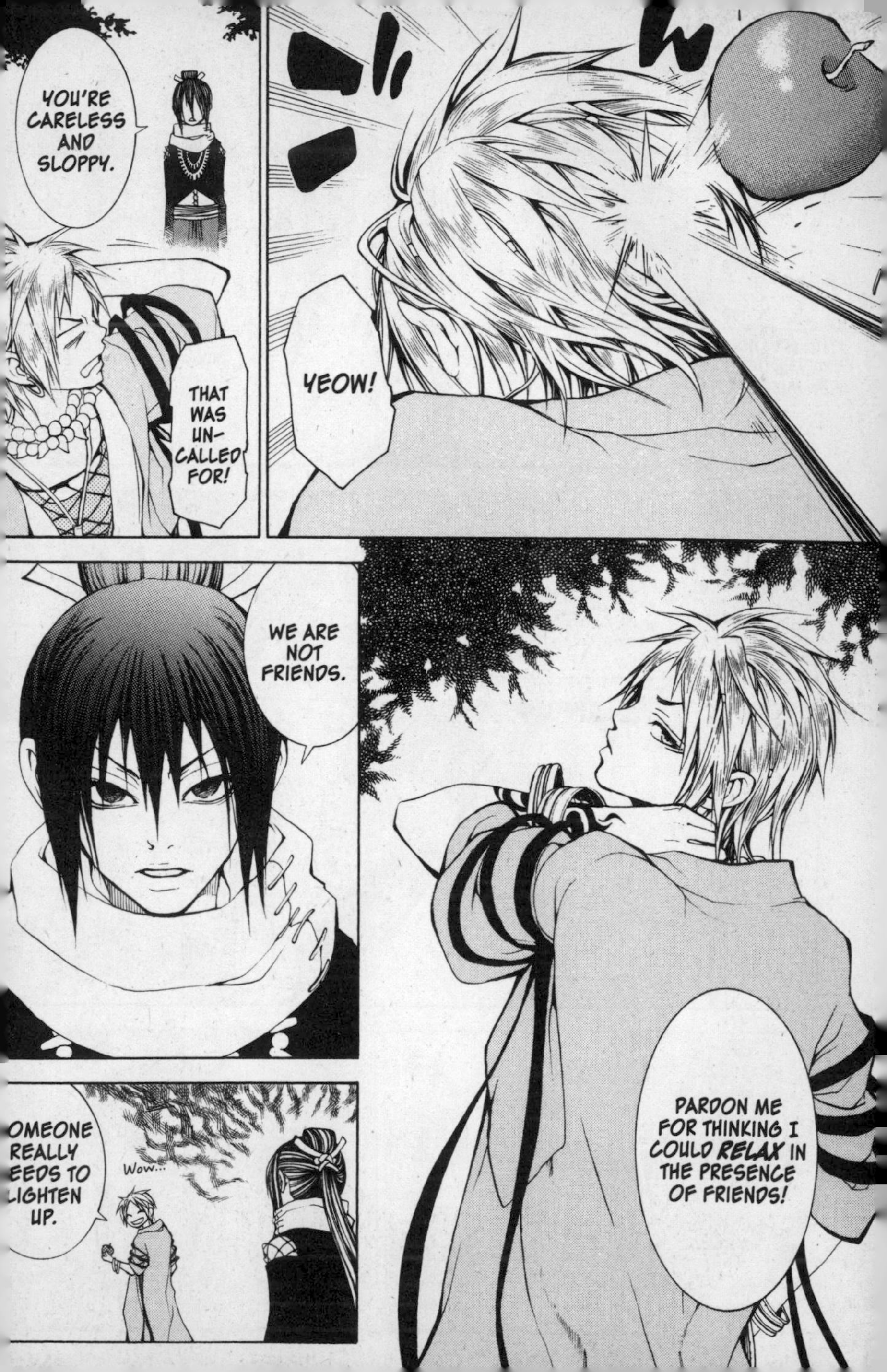
YEOW!
YOU'RE CARELESS AND SLOPPY.
THAT WAS UN-CALLED FOR!
PARDON ME FOR THINKING I COULD **RELAX** IN THE PRESENCE OF FRIENDS!
WE ARE NOT FRIENDS.
OMEONE REALLY EEDS TO LIGHTEN UP.
Wow...

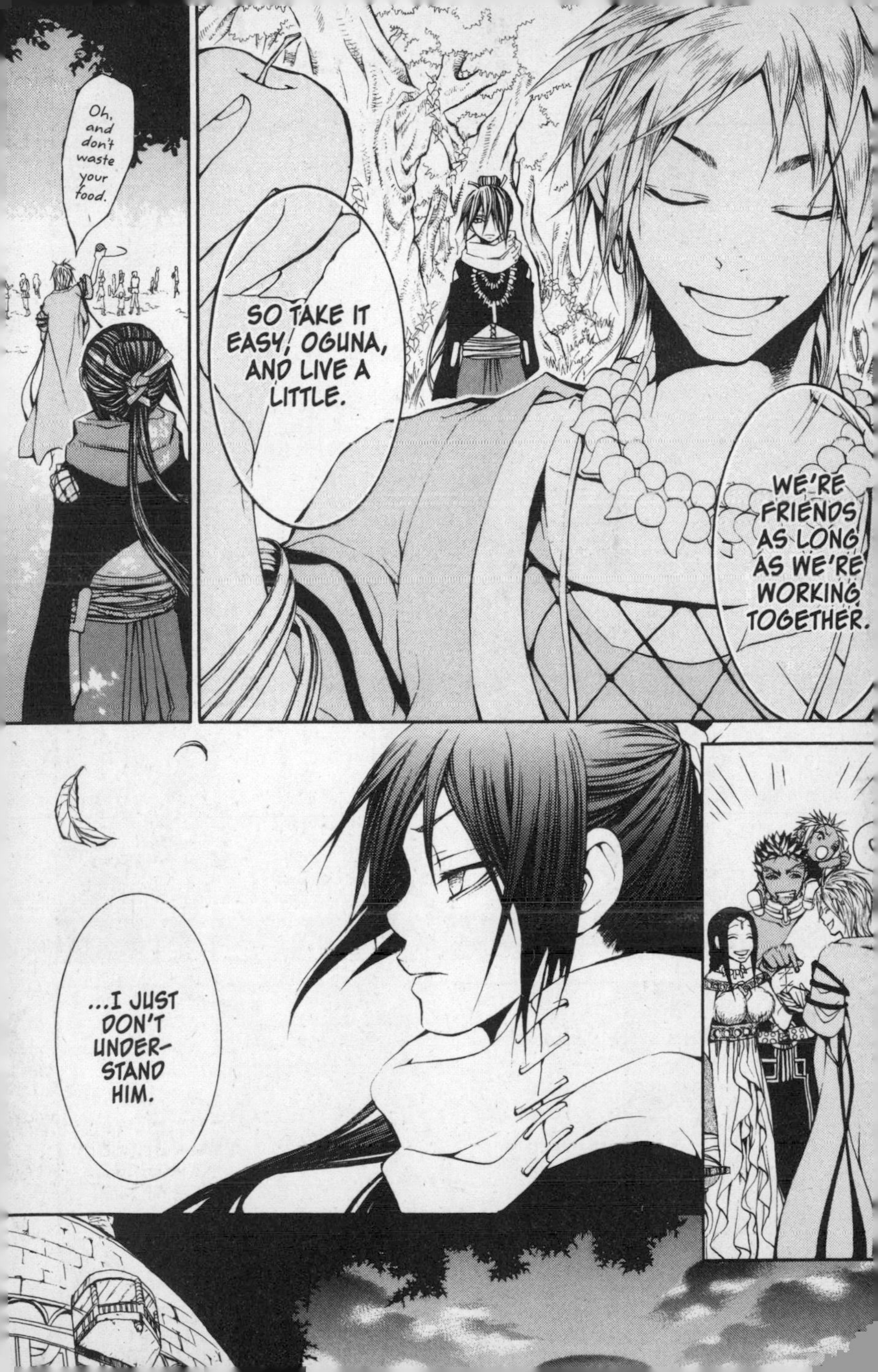
SO TAKE IT EASY, OGUNA, AND LIVE A LITTLE.
WE'RE FRIENDS AS LONG AS WE'RE WORKING TOGETHER.
Oh, and don't waste your food.
...I JUST DON'T UNDER-STAND HIM.

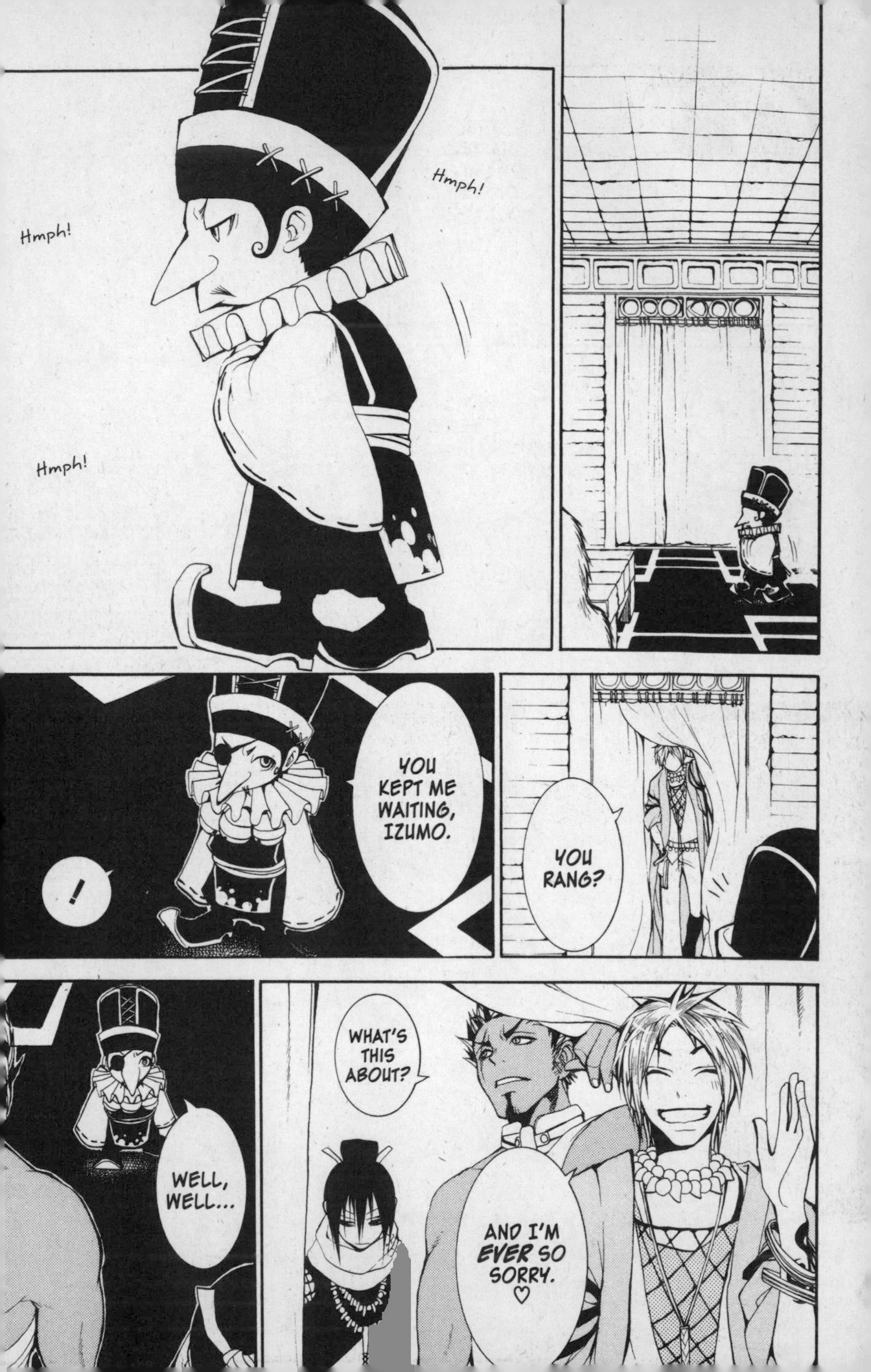
Hmph!
Hmph!
Hmph!
YOU RANG?
YOU KEPT ME WAITING, IZUMO.
!
WHAT'S THIS ABOUT?
AND I'M EVER SO SORRY. ♡
WELL, WELL...

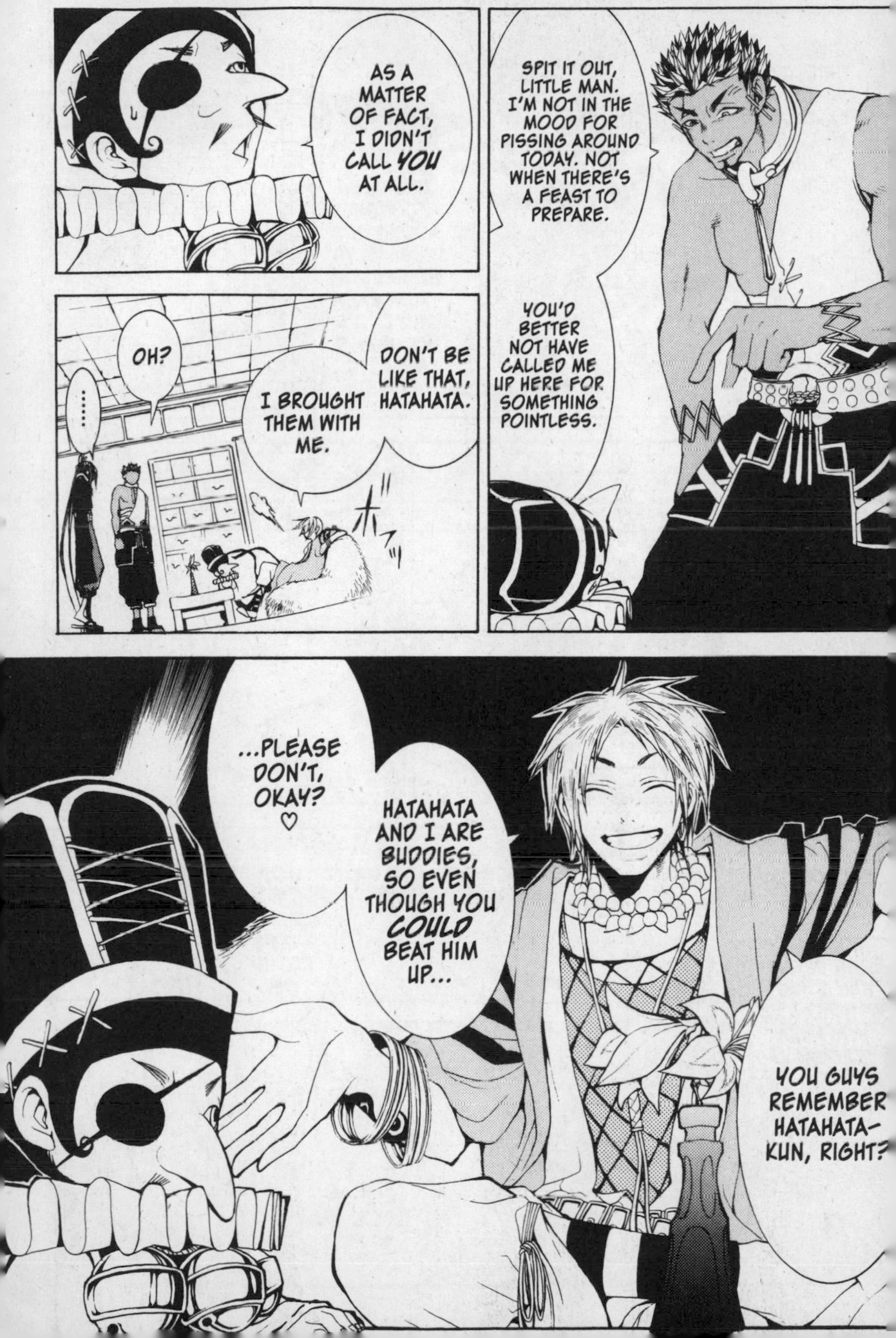
SPIT IT OUT, LITTLE MAN. I'M NOT IN THE MOOD FOR PISSING AROUND TODAY. NOT WHEN THERE'S A FEAST TO PREPARE.
YOU'D BETTER NOT HAVE CALLED ME UP HERE FOR SOMETHING POINTLESS.
AS A MATTER OF FACT, I DIDN'T CALL *YOU* AT ALL.
DON'T BE LIKE THAT, HATAHATA.
I BROUGHT THEM WITH ME.
OH?
......
YOU GUYS REMEMBER HATAHATA-KUN, RIGHT?
HATAHATA AND I ARE BUDDIES, SO EVEN THOUGH YOU *COULD* BEAT HIM UP...
...PLEASE DON'T, OKAY? ♡

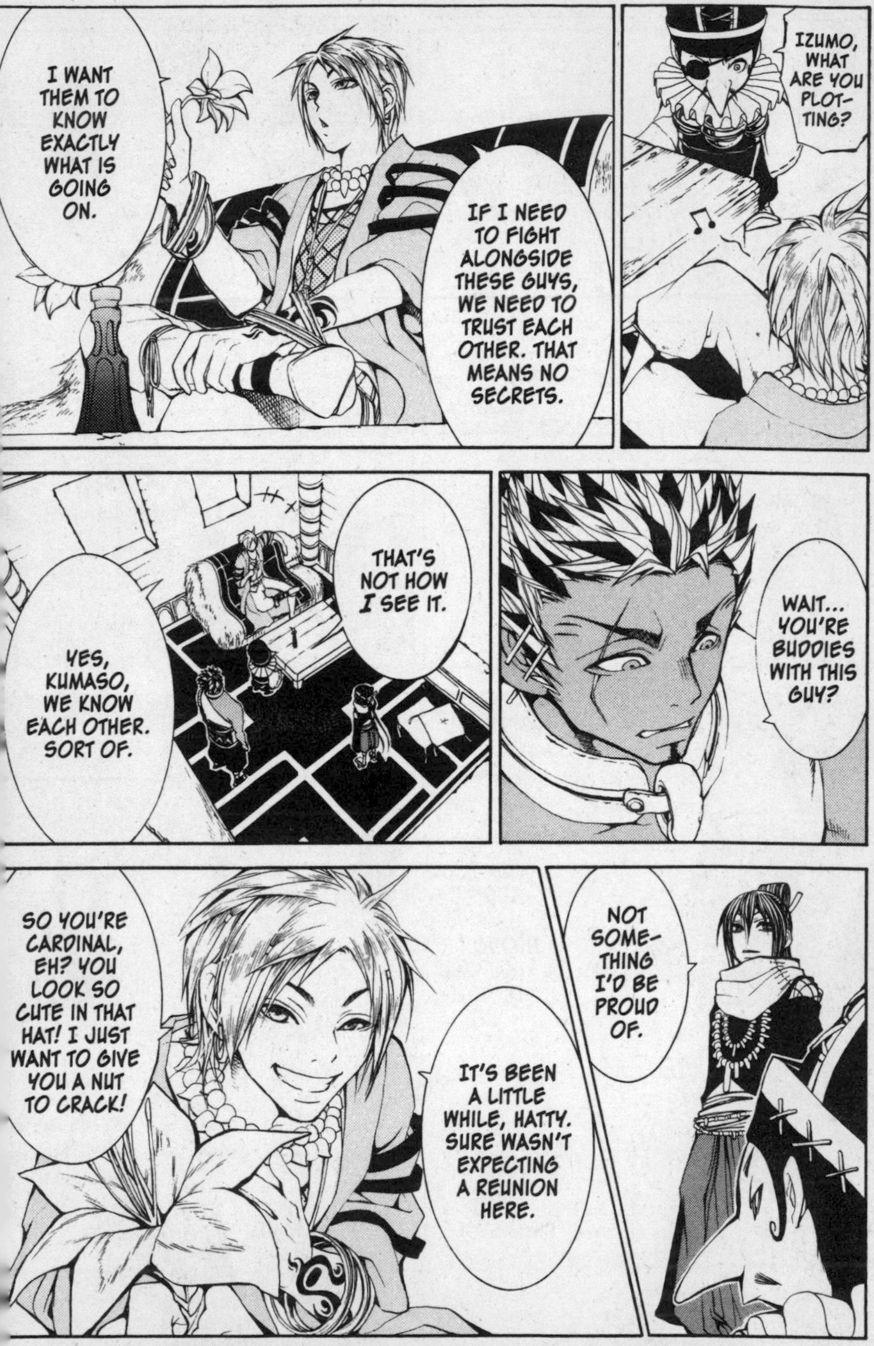
IZUMO, WHAT ARE YOU PLOT-TING?
I WANT THEM TO KNOW EXACTLY WHAT IS GOING ON.
IF I NEED TO FIGHT ALONGSIDE THESE GUYS, WE NEED TO TRUST EACH OTHER. THAT MEANS NO SECRETS.
WAIT... YOU'RE BUDDIES WITH THIS GUY?
YES, KUMASO, WE KNOW EACH OTHER. SORT OF.
THAT'S NOT HOW *I* SEE IT.
NOT SOME-THING I'D BE PROUD OF.
IT'S BEEN A LITTLE WHILE, HATTY. SURE WASN'T EXPECTING A REUNION HERE.
SO YOU'RE CARDINAL, EH? YOU LOOK SO CUTE IN THAT HAT! I JUST WANT TO GIVE YOU A NUT TO CRACK!

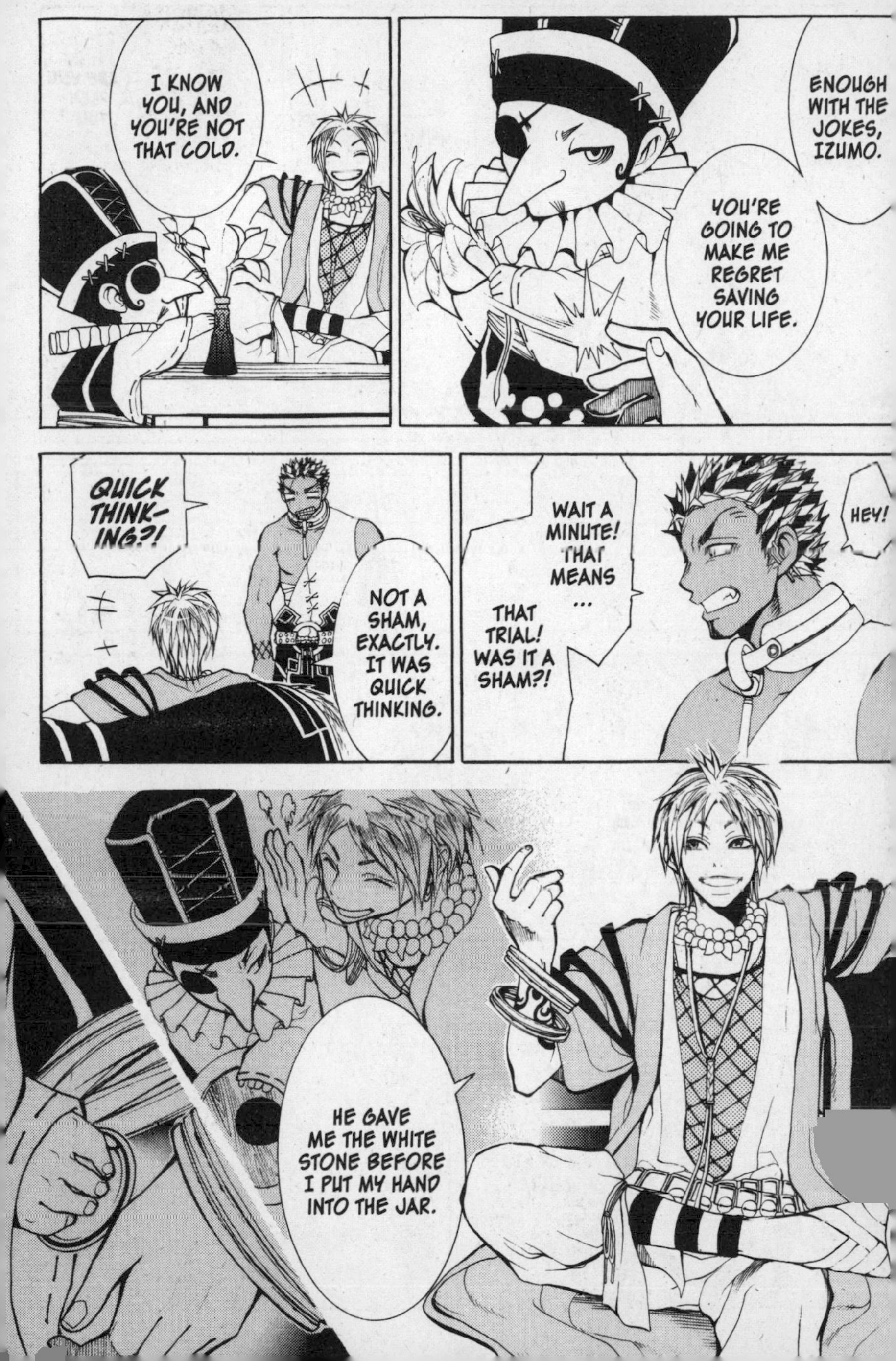
ENOUGH WITH THE JOKES, IZUMO.
YOU'RE GOING TO MAKE ME REGRET SAVING YOUR LIFE.
I KNOW YOU, AND YOU'RE NOT THAT COLD.
HEY!
WAIT A MINUTE! THAT MEANS ...
THAT TRIAL! WAS IT A SHAM?!
NOT A SHAM, EXACTLY. IT WAS QUICK THINKING.
QUICK THINKING?!
HE GAVE ME THE WHITE STONE BEFORE I PUT MY HAND INTO THE JAR.

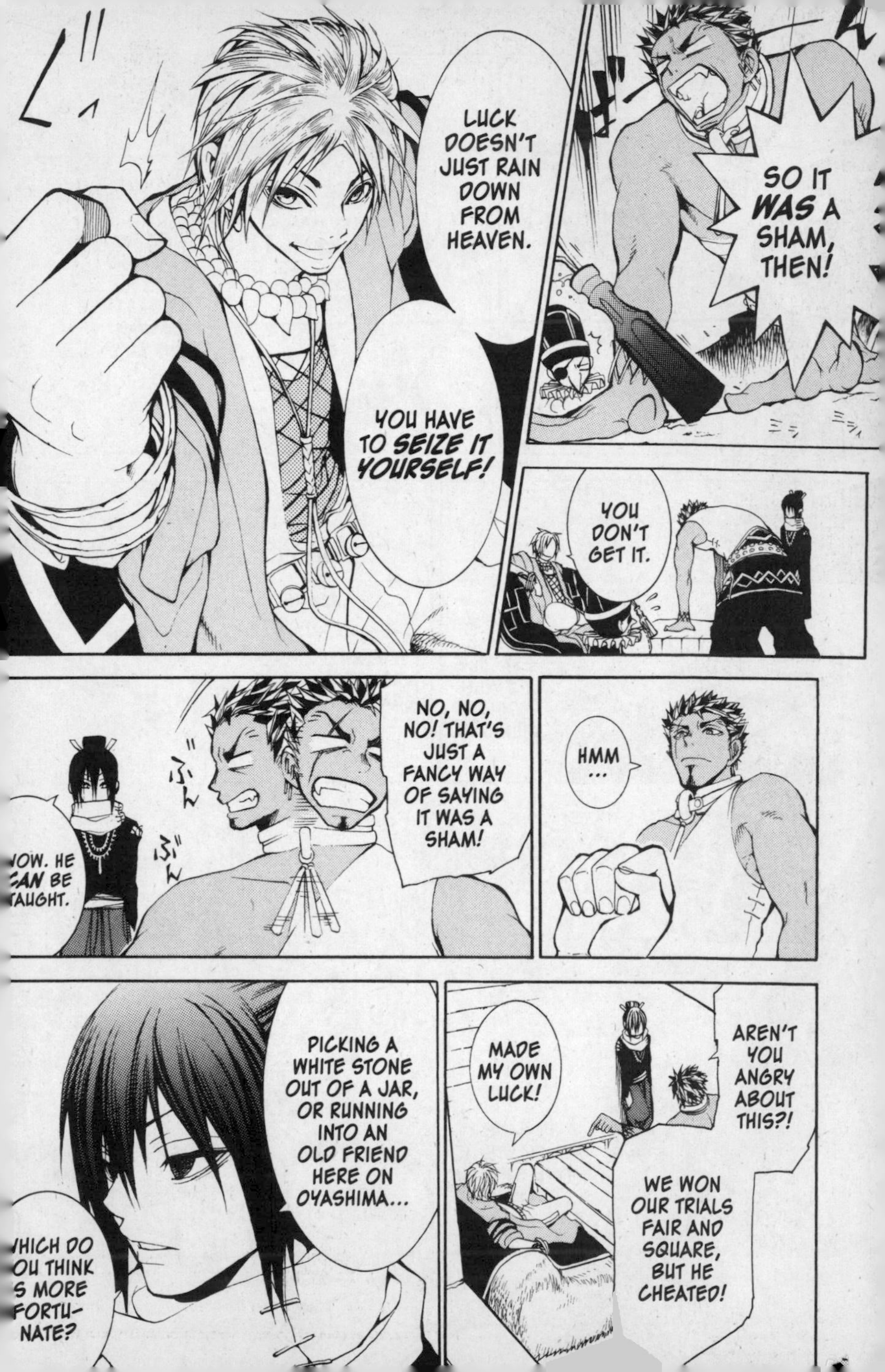
SO IT WAS A SHAM, THEN!
YOU DON'T GET IT.
LUCK DOESN'T JUST RAIN DOWN FROM HEAVEN.
YOU HAVE TO SEIZE IT YOURSELF!
HMM ...
NO, NO, NO! THAT'S JUST A FANCY WAY OF SAYING IT WAS A SHAM!
OW. HE CAN BE TAUGHT.
AREN'T YOU ANGRY ABOUT THIS?!
WE WON OUR TRIALS FAIR AND SQUARE, BUT HE CHEATED!
MADE MY OWN LUCK!
PICKING A WHITE STONE OUT OF A JAR, OR RUNNING INTO AN OLD FRIEND HERE ON OYASHIMA...
HICH DO OU THINK S MORE FORTU-NATE?

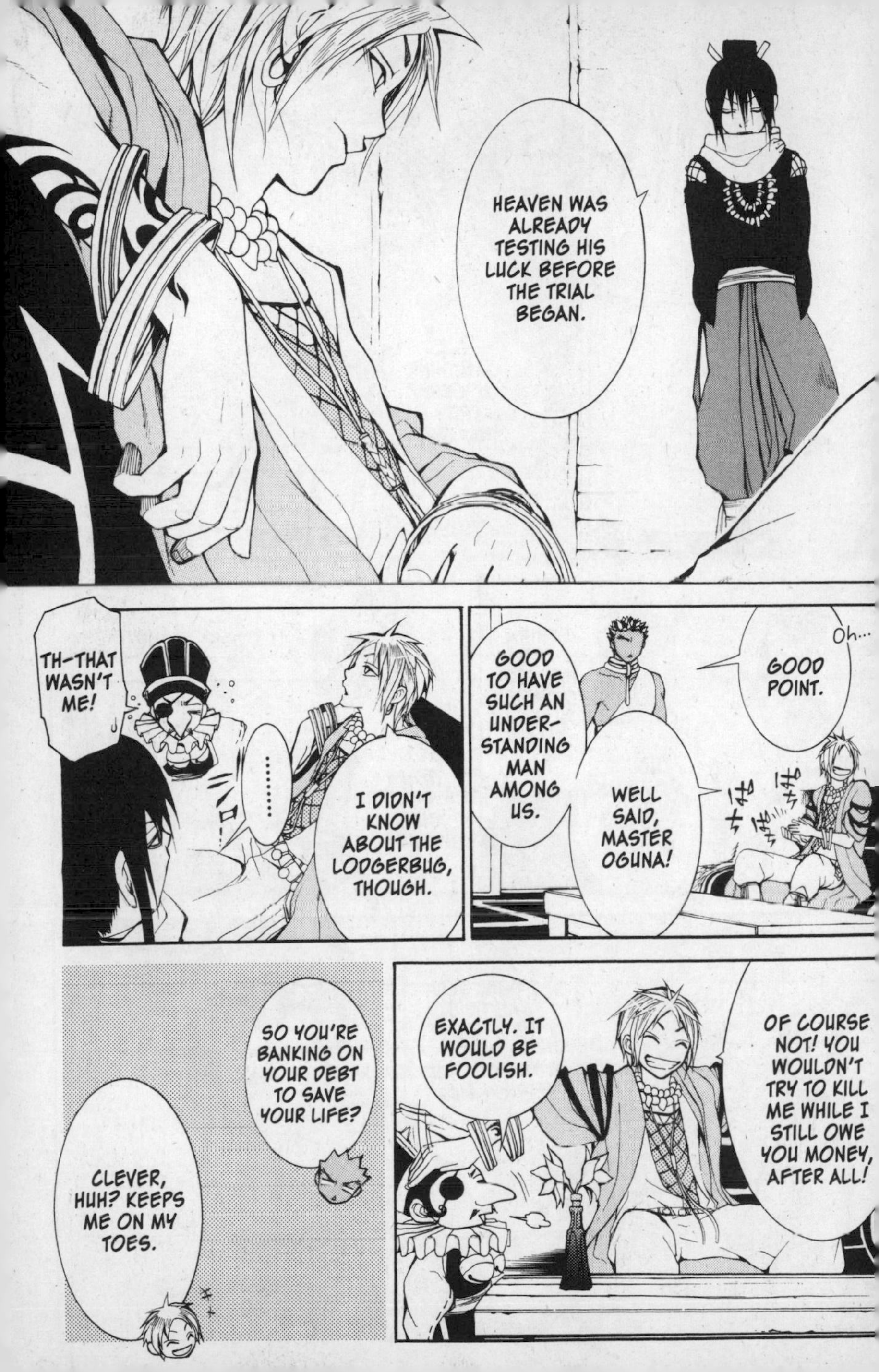
HEAVEN WAS ALREADY TESTING HIS LUCK BEFORE THE TRIAL BEGAN.
Oh...
GOOD POINT.
GOOD TO HAVE SUCH AN UNDER-STANDING MAN AMONG US.
WELL SAID, MASTER OGUNA!
I DIDN'T KNOW ABOUT THE LODGERBUG, THOUGH.
......
TH-THAT WASN'T ME!
OF COURSE NOT! YOU WOULDN'T TRY TO KILL ME WHILE I STILL OWE YOU MONEY, AFTER ALL!
EXACTLY. IT WOULD BE FOOLISH.
SO YOU'RE BANKING ON YOUR DEBT TO SAVE YOUR LIFE?
CLEVER, HUH? KEEPS ME ON MY TOES.

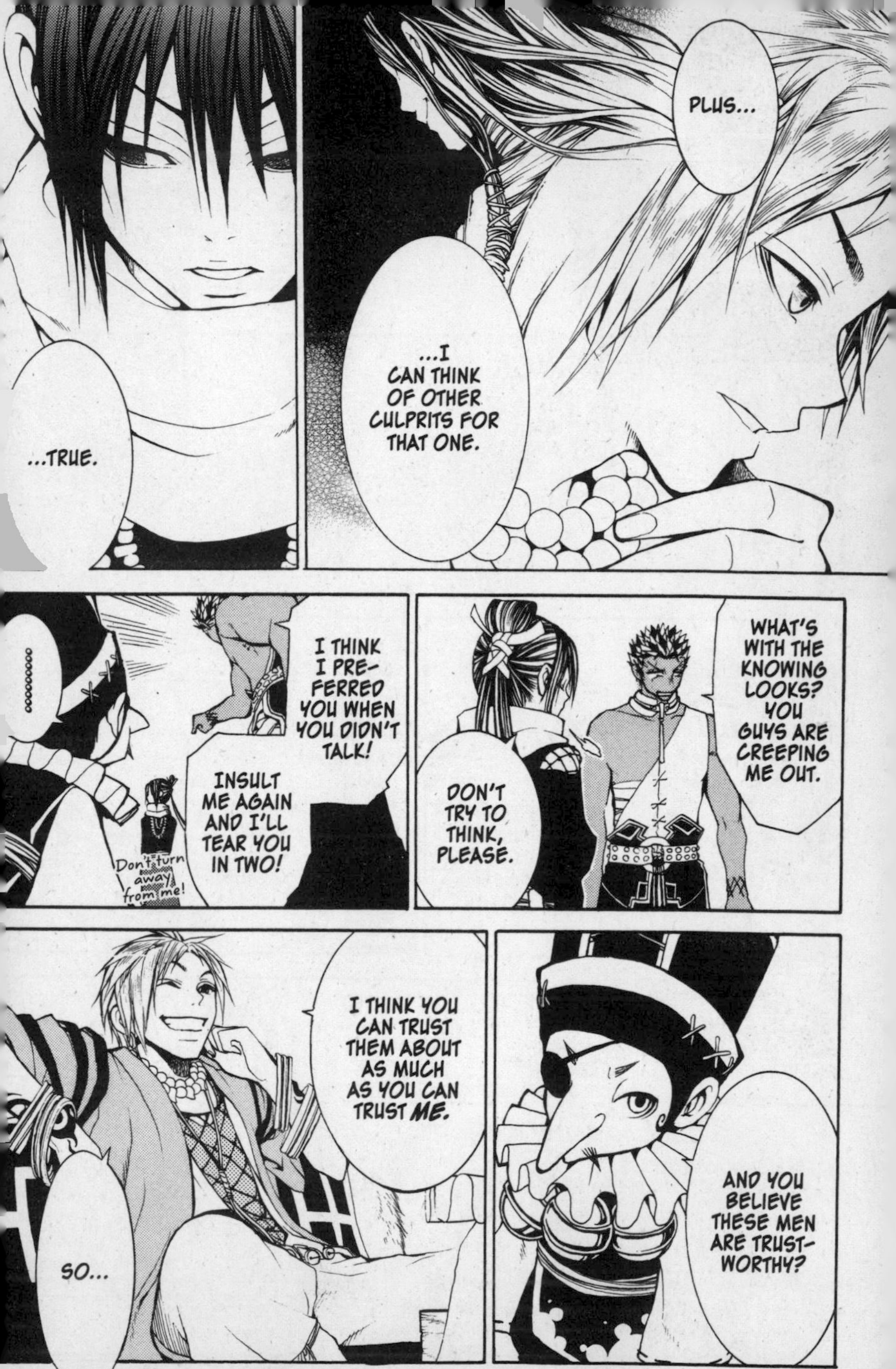
PLUS...
...I CAN THINK OF OTHER CULPRITS FOR THAT ONE.
...TRUE.
WHAT'S WITH THE KNOWING LOOKS? YOU GUYS ARE CREEPING ME OUT.
DON'T TRY TO THINK, PLEASE.
I THINK I PRE-FERRED YOU WHEN YOU DIDN'T TALK!
INSULT ME AGAIN AND I'LL TEAR YOU IN TWO!
Don't turn away from me!
....
AND YOU BELIEVE THESE MEN ARE TRUST-WORTHY?
I THINK YOU CAN TRUST THEM ABOUT AS MUCH AS YOU CAN TRUST *ME*.
SO...

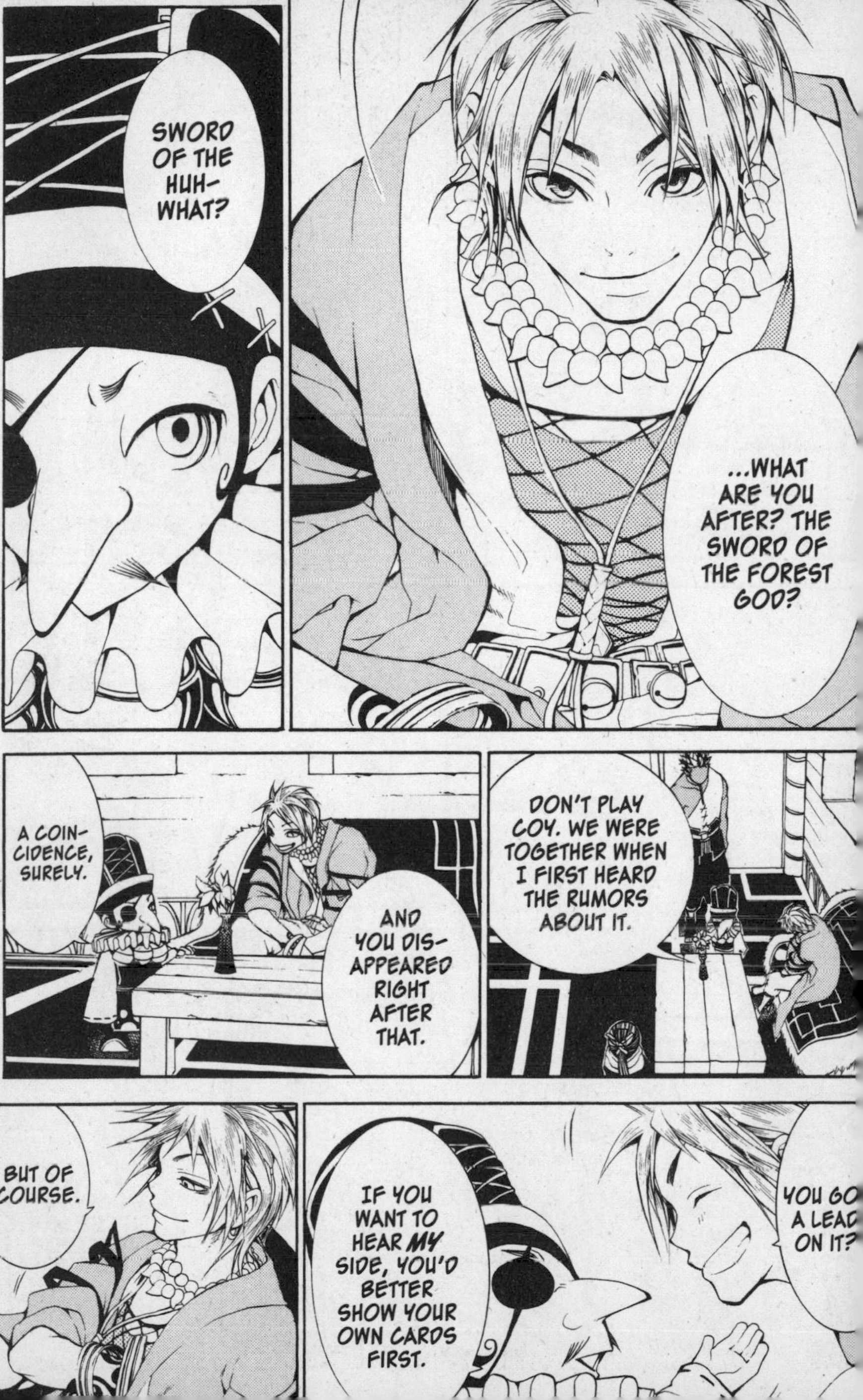
...WHAT ARE YOU AFTER? THE SWORD OF THE FOREST GOD?
SWORD OF THE HUH- WHAT?
DON'T PLAY COY. WE WERE TOGETHER WHEN I FIRST HEARD THE RUMORS ABOUT IT.
AND YOU DIS- APPEARED RIGHT AFTER THAT.
A COIN- CIDENCE, SURELY.
YOU GO A LEAD ON IT?
IF YOU WANT TO HEAR *MY* SIDE, YOU'D BETTER SHOW YOUR OWN CARDS FIRST.
BUT OF COURSE.

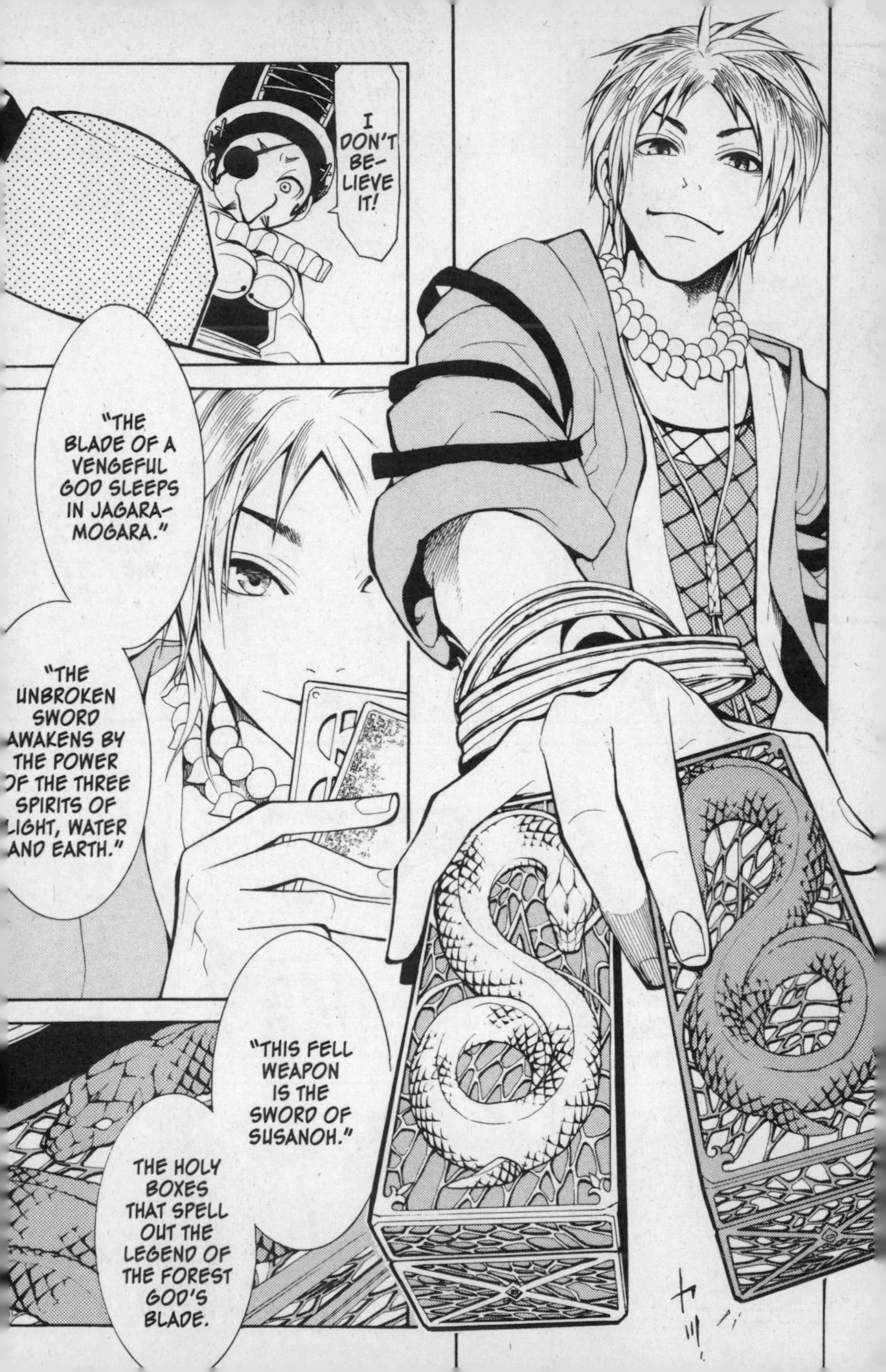
I DON'T BE-LIEVE IT!
"THE BLADE OF A VENGEFUL GOD SLEEPS IN JAGARA-MOGARA."
"THE UNBROKEN SWORD AWAKENS BY THE POWER OF THE THREE SPIRITS OF LIGHT, WATER AND EARTH."
"THIS FELL WEAPON IS THE SWORD OF SUSANOH."
THE HOLY BOXES THAT SPELL OUT THE LEGEND OF THE FOREST GOD'S BLADE.

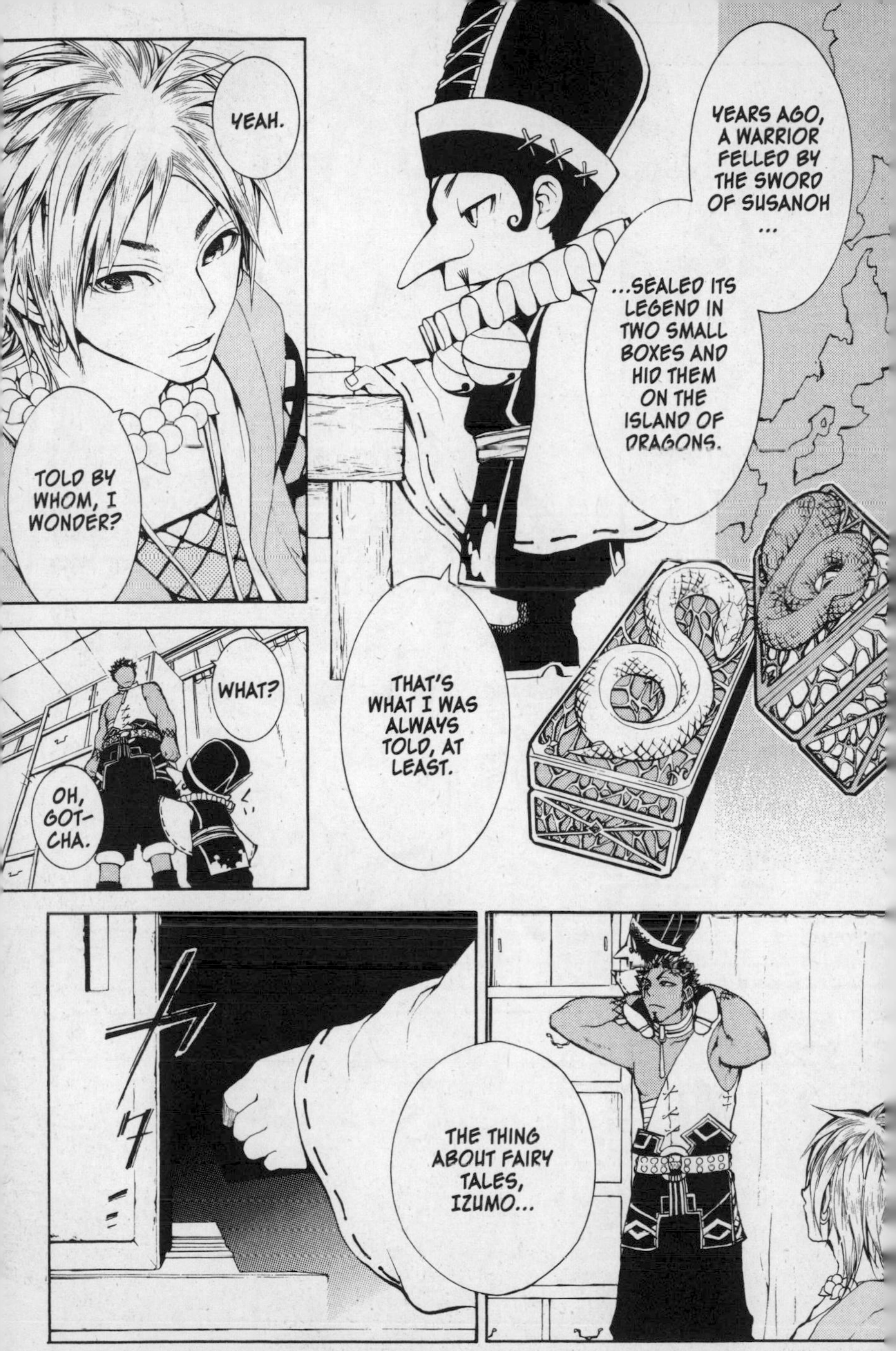
YEARS AGO, A WARRIOR FELLED BY THE SWORD OF SUSANOH ...
...SEALED ITS LEGEND IN TWO SMALL BOXES AND HID THEM ON THE ISLAND OF DRAGONS.
THAT'S WHAT I WAS ALWAYS TOLD, AT LEAST.
YEAH.
TOLD BY WHOM, I WONDER?
WHAT?
OH, GOT-CHA.
THE THING ABOUT FAIRY TALES, IZUMO...

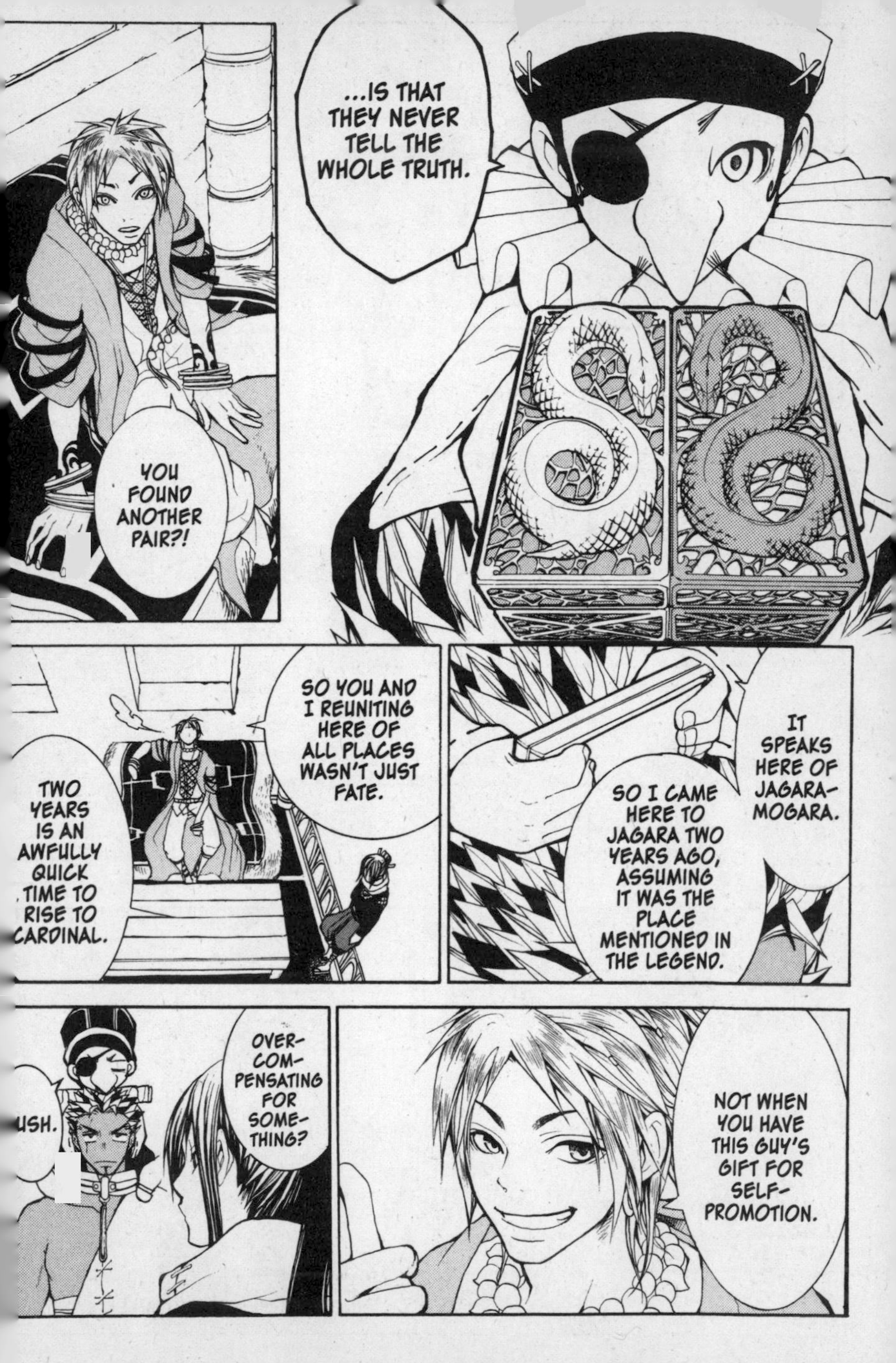
...IS THAT THEY NEVER TELL THE WHOLE TRUTH.
YOU FOUND ANOTHER PAIR?!
IT SPEAKS HERE OF JAGARA-MOGARA.
SO I CAME HERE TO JAGARA TWO YEARS AGO, ASSUMING IT WAS THE PLACE MENTIONED IN THE LEGEND.
SO YOU AND I REUNITING HERE OF ALL PLACES WASN'T JUST FATE.
TWO YEARS IS AN AWFULLY QUICK TIME TO RISE TO CARDINAL.
NOT WHEN YOU HAVE THIS GUY'S GIFT FOR SELF-PROMOTION.
OVER-COMPENSATING FOR SOME-THING?
USH.

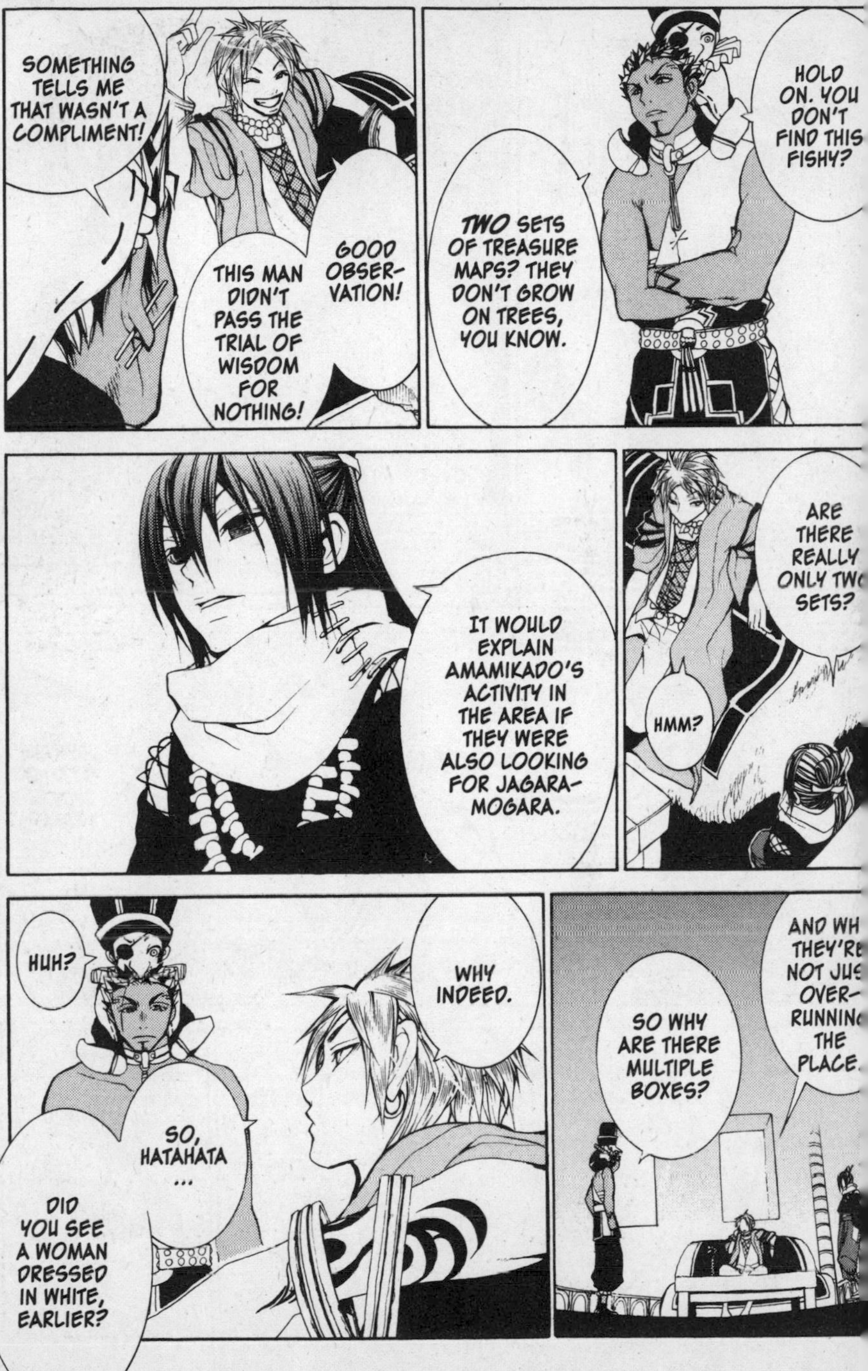
HOLD ON. YOU DON'T FIND THIS FISHY?
TWO SETS OF TREASURE MAPS? THEY DON'T GROW ON TREES, YOU KNOW.
GOOD OBSER-VATION!
THIS MAN DIDN'T PASS THE TRIAL OF WISDOM FOR NOTHING!
SOMETHING TELLS ME THAT WASN'T A COMPLIMENT!
ARE THERE REALLY ONLY TW SETS?
HMM?
IT WOULD EXPLAIN AMAMIKADO'S ACTIVITY IN THE AREA IF THEY WERE ALSO LOOKING FOR JAGARA-MOGARA.
AND WH THEY'RE NOT JUS OVER-RUNNIN THE PLACE.
SO WHY ARE THERE MULTIPLE BOXES?
WHY INDEED.
HUH?
SO, HATAHATA ...
DID YOU SEE A WOMAN DRESSED IN WHITE, EARLIER?

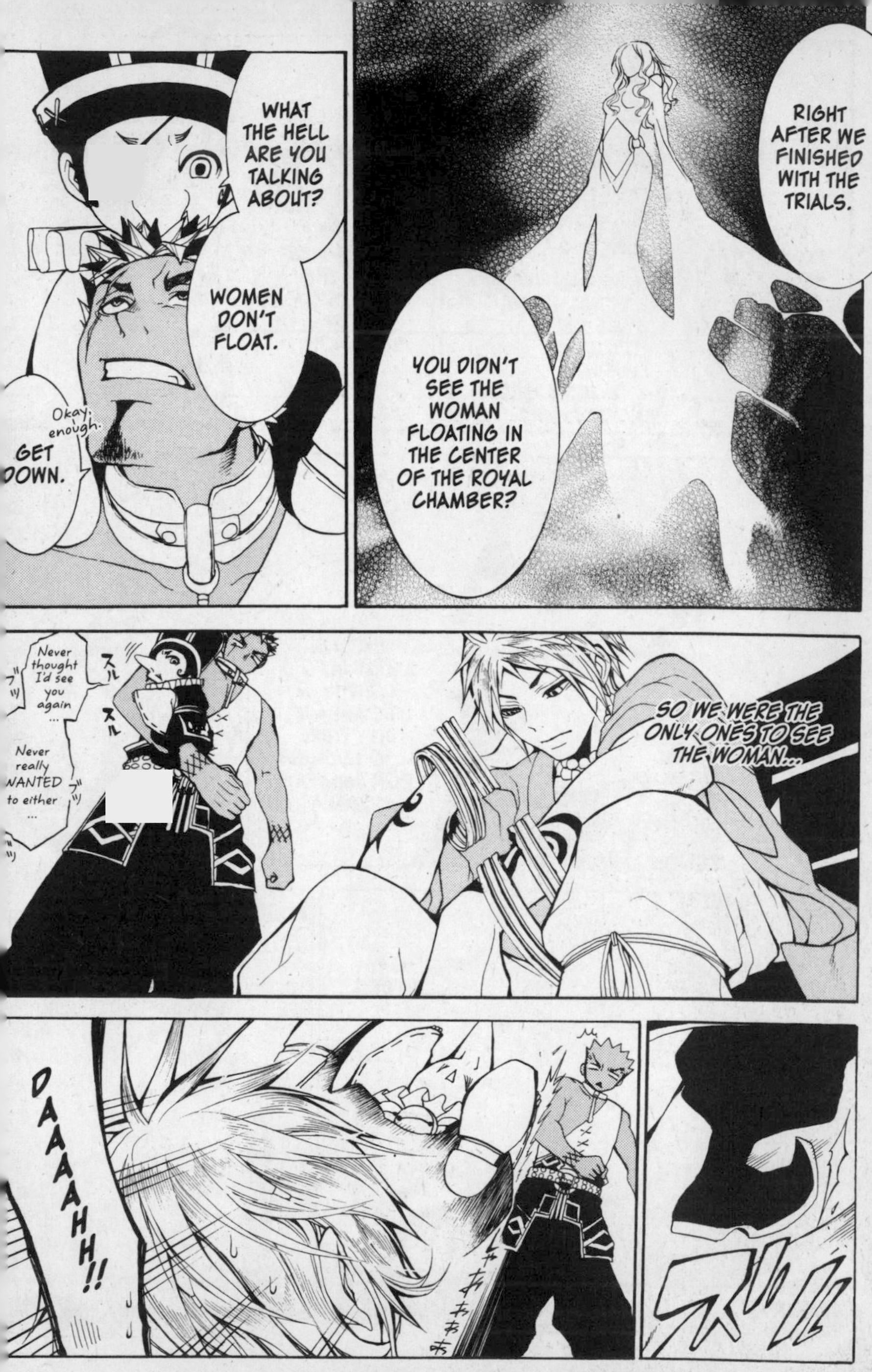
RIGHT AFTER WE FINISHED WITH THE TRIALS.
YOU DIDN'T SEE THE WOMAN FLOATING IN THE CENTER OF THE ROYAL CHAMBER?
WHAT THE HELL ARE YOU TALKING ABOUT?
WOMEN DON'T FLOAT.
Okay, enough.
GET DOWN.
SO WE WERE THE ONLY ONES TO SEE THE WOMAN...
スル
スル
Never thought I'd see you again ...
Never really WANTED to either ...
DAAAAHH!!

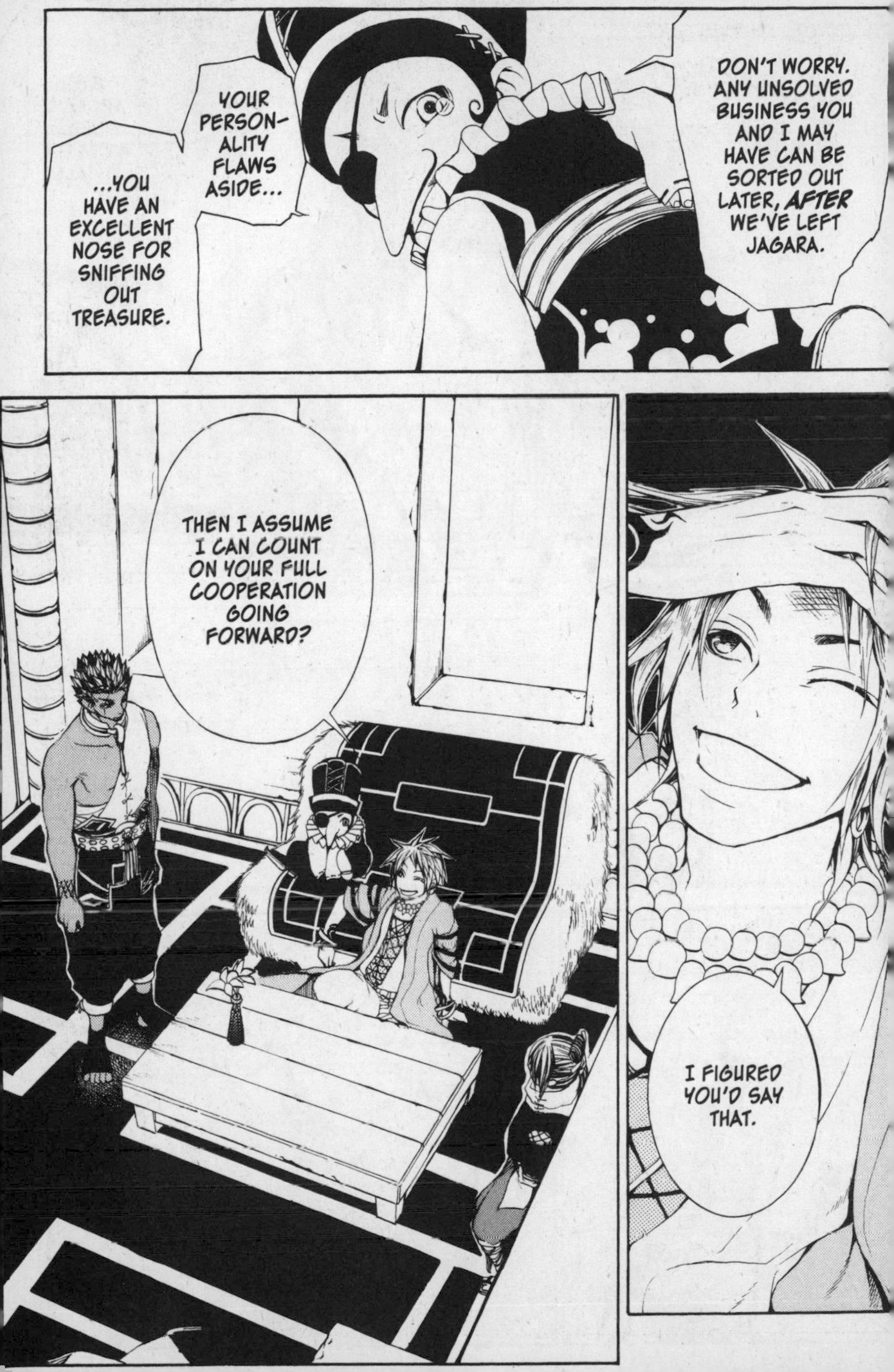
DON'T WORRY. ANY UNSOLVED BUSINESS YOU AND I MAY HAVE CAN BE SORTED OUT LATER, AFTER WE'VE LEFT JAGARA.
YOUR PERSON-ALITY FLAWS ASIDE...
...YOU HAVE AN EXCELLENT NOSE FOR SNIFFING OUT TREASURE.
I FIGURED YOU'D SAY THAT.
THEN I ASSUME I CAN COUNT ON YOUR FULL COOPERATION GOING FORWARD?

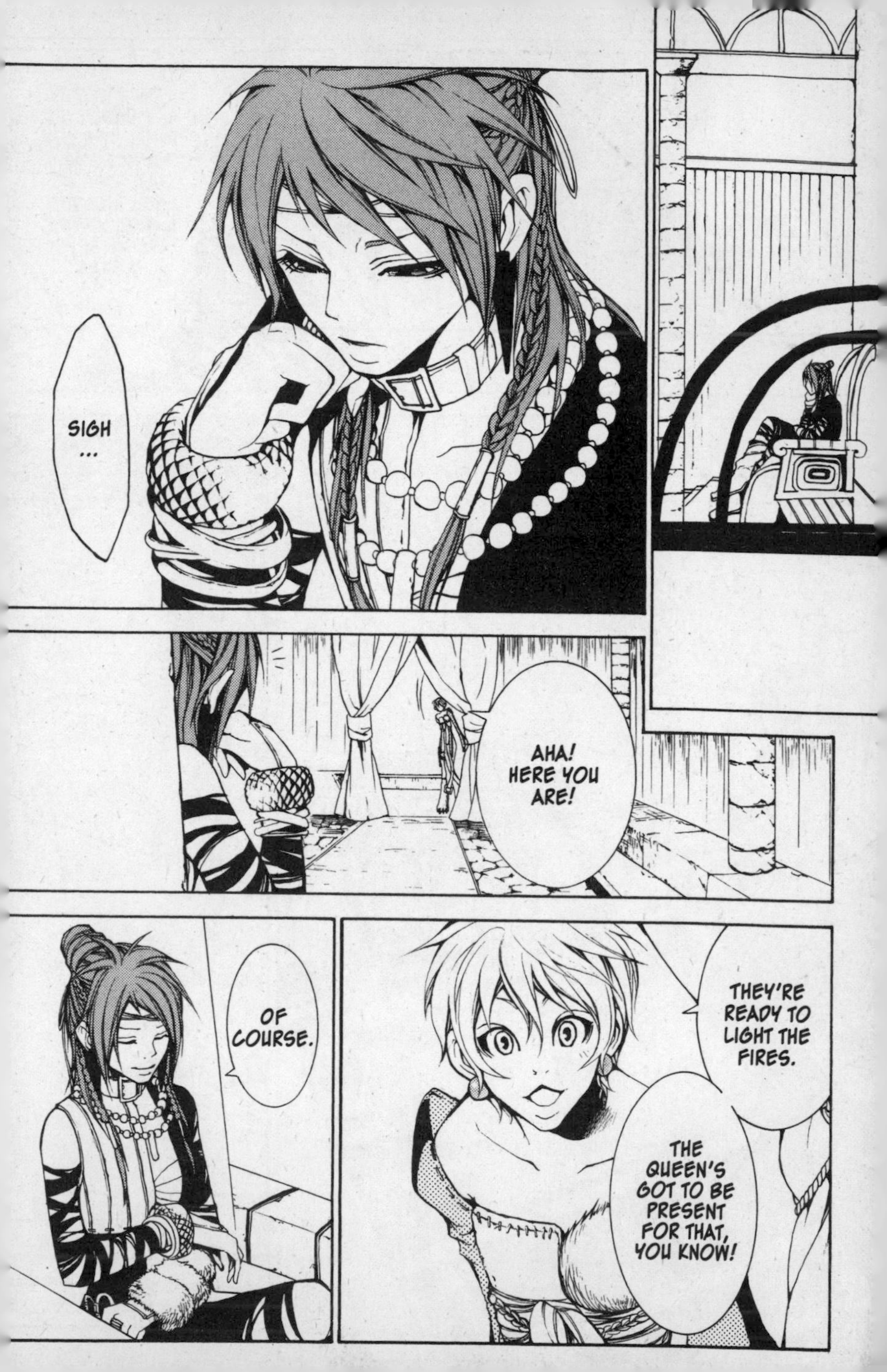
SIGH ...
AHA! HERE YOU ARE!
THEY'RE READY TO LIGHT THE FIRES.
THE QUEEN'S GOT TO BE PRESENT FOR THAT, YOU KNOW!
OF COURSE.

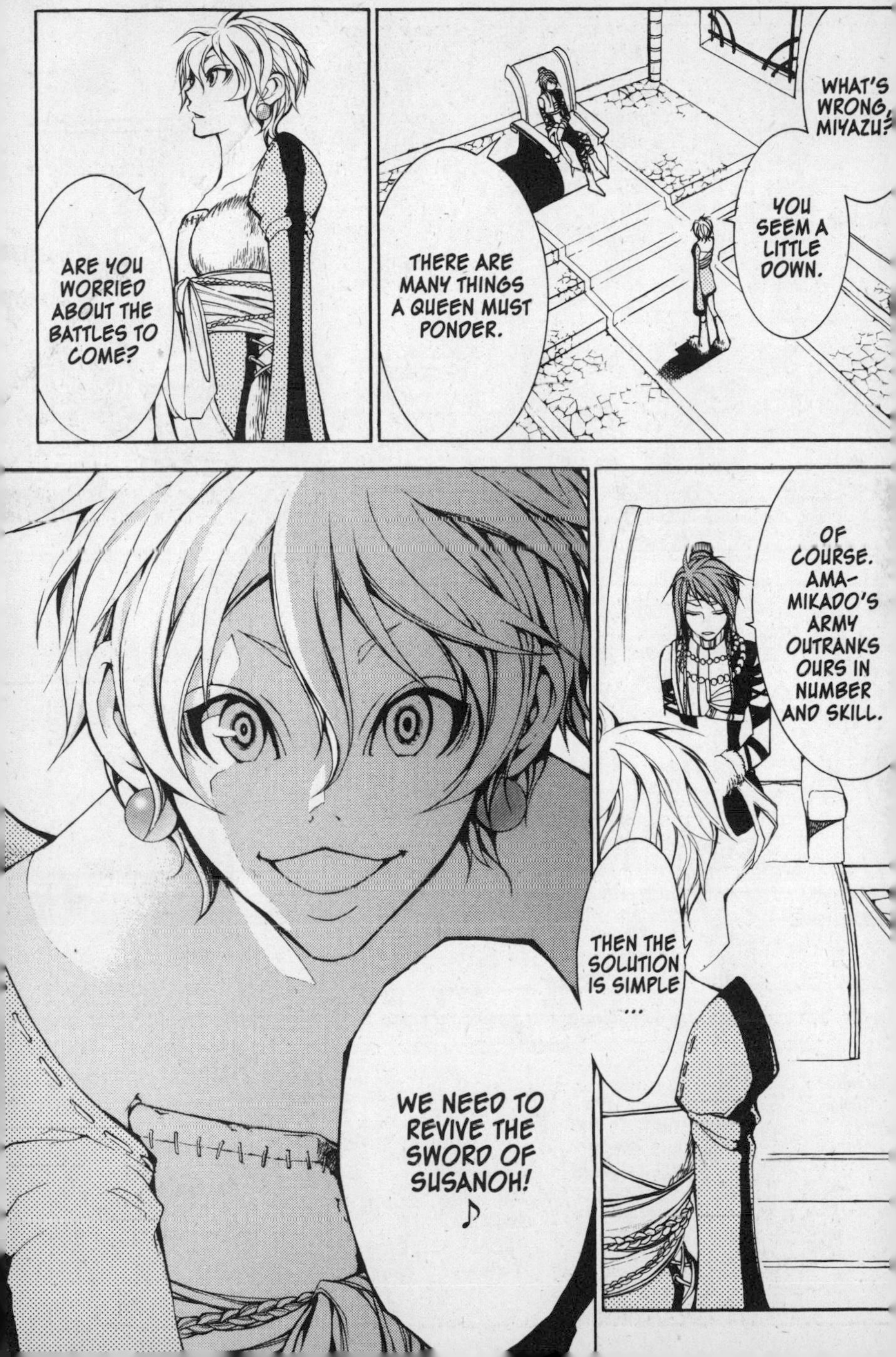
WHAT'S WRONG, MIYAZU?
YOU SEEM A LITTLE DOWN.
THERE ARE MANY THINGS A QUEEN MUST PONDER.
ARE YOU WORRIED ABOUT THE BATTLES TO COME?
OF COURSE. AMA-MIKADO'S ARMY OUTRANKS OURS IN NUMBER AND SKILL.
THEN THE SOLUTION IS SIMPLE ...
WE NEED TO REVIVE THE SWORD OF SUSANOH! ♪

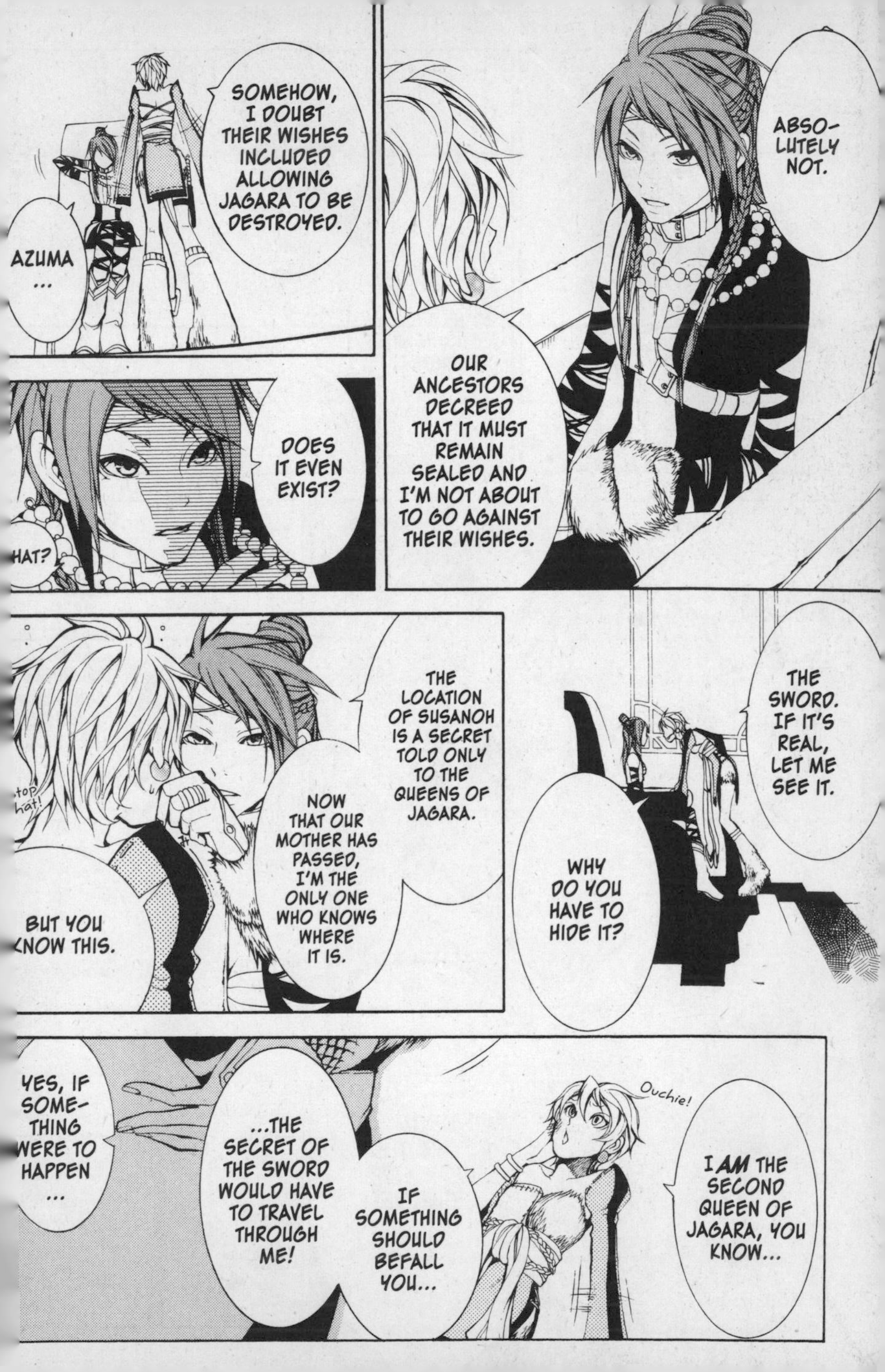
ABSO-LUTELY NOT.
OUR ANCESTORS DECREED THAT IT MUST REMAIN SEALED AND I'M NOT ABOUT TO GO AGAINST THEIR WISHES.
SOMEHOW, I DOUBT THEIR WISHES INCLUDED ALLOWING JAGARA TO BE DESTROYED.
AZUMA ...
DOES IT EVEN EXIST?
HAT?
THE SWORD. IF IT'S REAL, LET ME SEE IT.
WHY DO YOU HAVE TO HIDE IT?
THE LOCATION OF SUSANOH IS A SECRET TOLD ONLY TO THE QUEENS OF JAGARA.
NOW THAT OUR MOTHER HAS PASSED, I'M THE ONLY ONE WHO KNOWS WHERE IT IS.
top hat!
BUT YOU KNOW THIS.
I AM THE SECOND QUEEN OF JAGARA, YOU KNOW...
Ouchie!
IF SOMETHING SHOULD BEFALL YOU...
...THE SECRET OF THE SWORD WOULD HAVE TO TRAVEL THROUGH ME!
YES, IF SOME-THING WERE TO HAPPEN ...

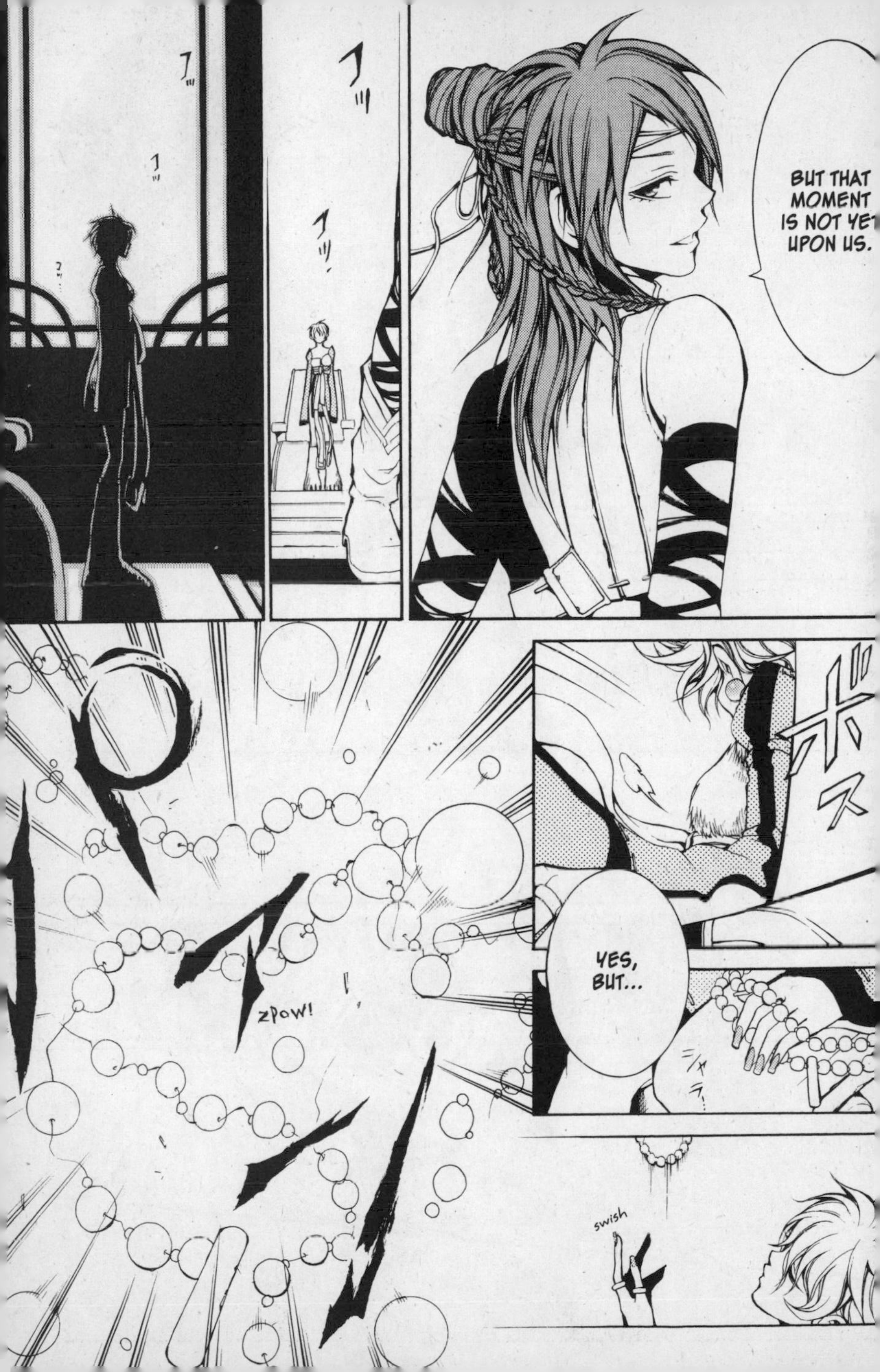
BUT THAT MOMENT IS NOT YET UPON US.
YES, BUT...
ZPOW!
swish

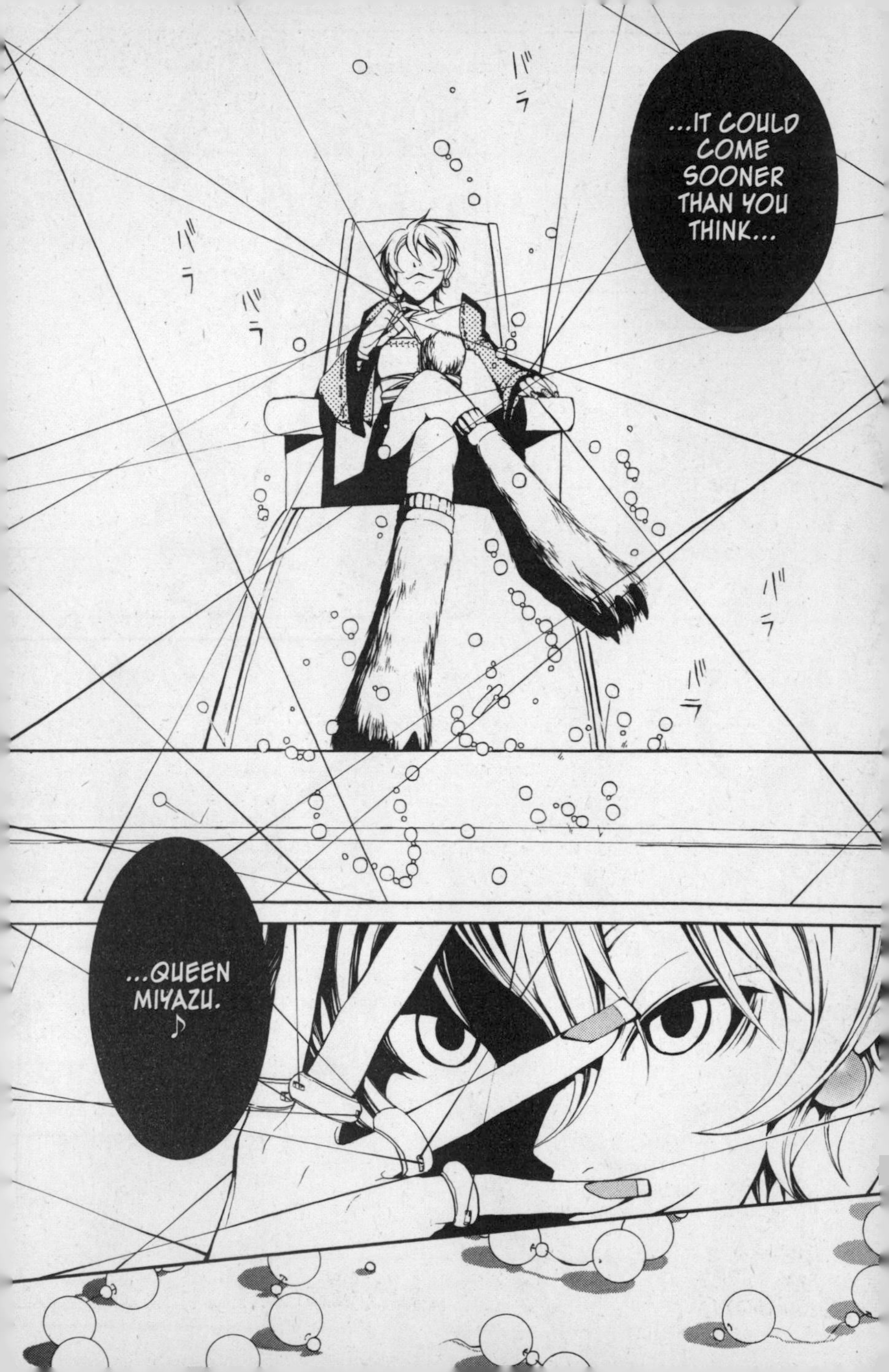
...IT COULD COME SOONER THAN YOU THINK...
バラ
バラ
バラ
バラ
バラ
...QUEEN MIYAZU. ♪

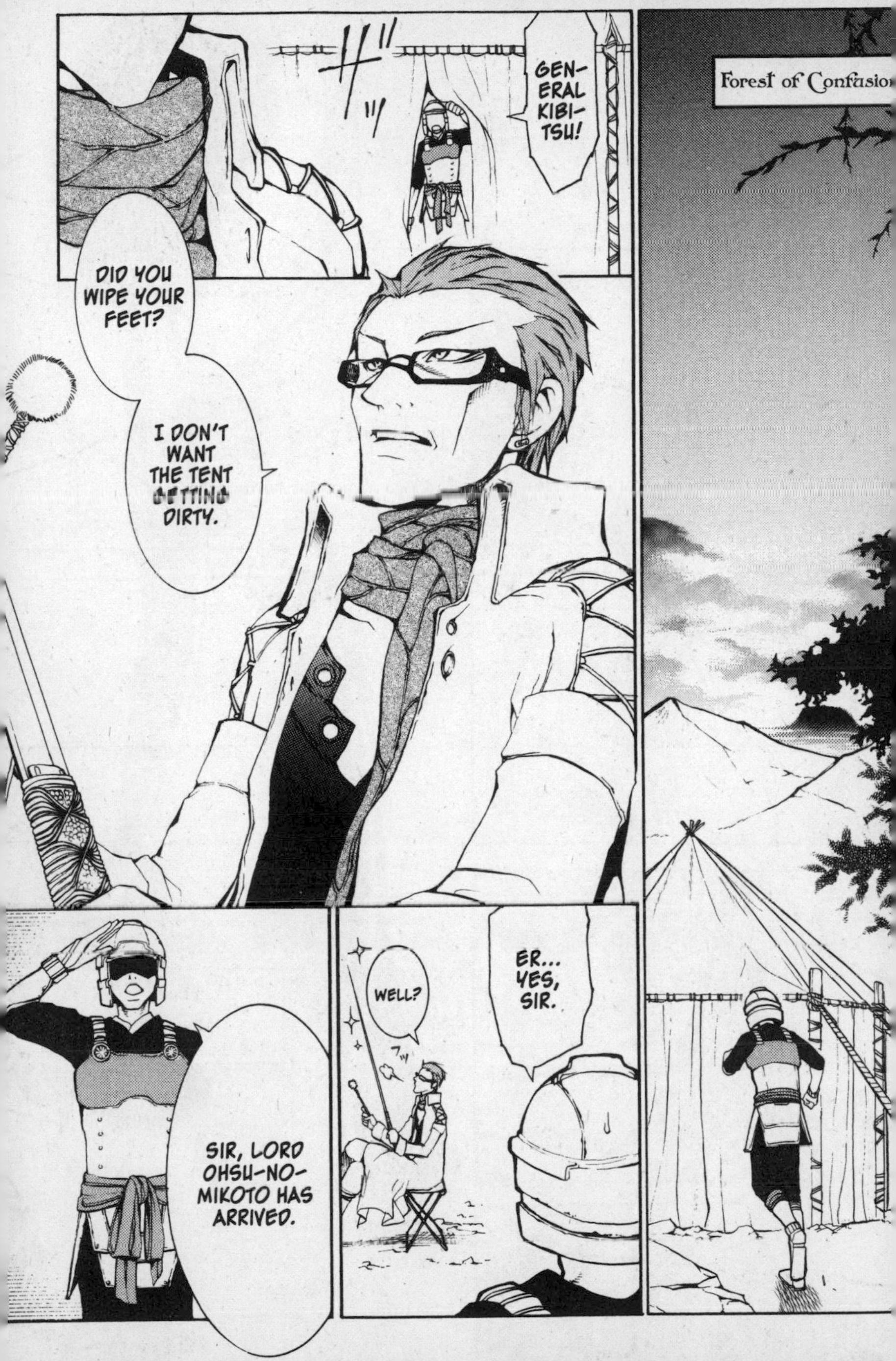
Forest of Confusion
GEN-ERAL KIBI-TSU!
DID YOU WIPE YOUR FEET?
I DON'T WANT THE TENT GETTING DIRTY.
ER... YES, SIR.
WELL?
SIR, LORD OHSU-NO-MIKOTO HAS ARRIVED.

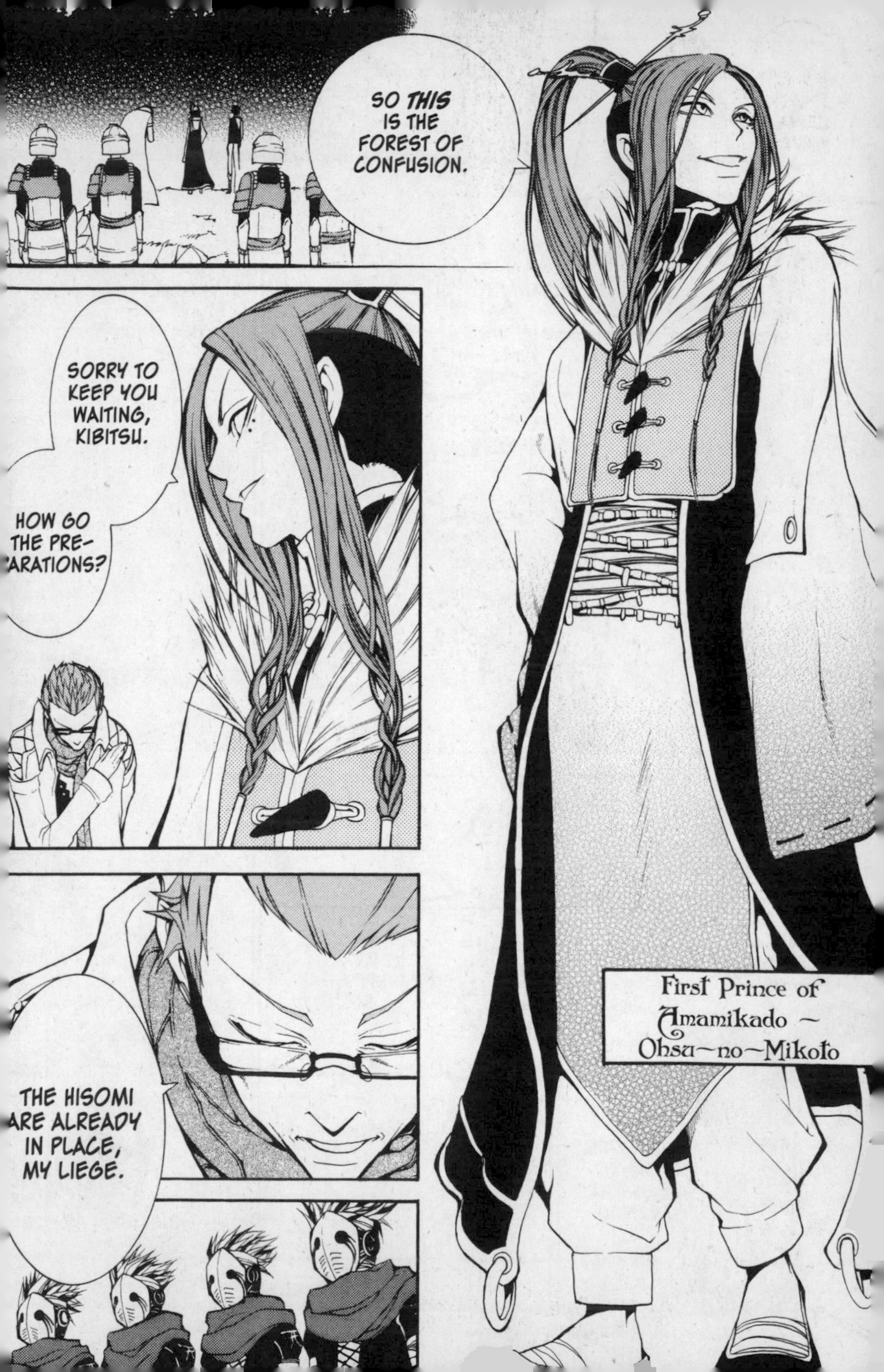
SO THIS IS THE FOREST OF CONFUSION.
First Prince of Amamikado ~ Ohsu~no~Mikoto
SORRY TO KEEP YOU WAITING, KIBITSU.
HOW GO THE PRE-PARATIONS?
THE HISOMI ARE ALREADY IN PLACE, MY LIEGE.

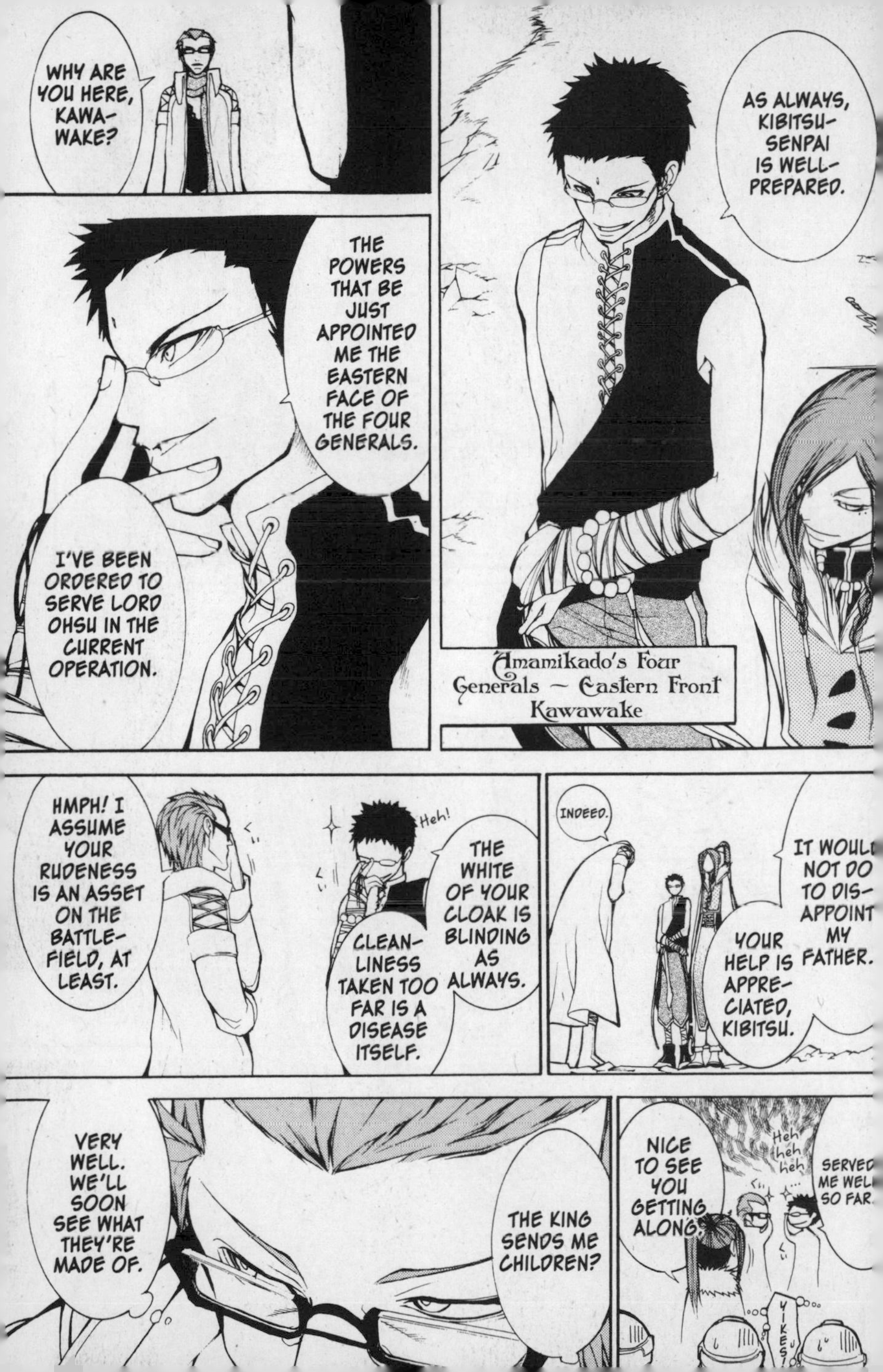
AS ALWAYS, KIBITSU-SENPAI IS WELL-PREPARED.
Amamikado's Four Generals ~ Eastern Front Kawawake
WHY ARE YOU HERE, KAWAWAKE?
THE POWERS THAT BE JUST APPOINTED ME THE EASTERN FACE OF THE FOUR GENERALS.
I'VE BEEN ORDERED TO SERVE LORD OHSU IN THE CURRENT OPERATION.
IT WOULD NOT DO TO DISAPPOINT MY FATHER.
INDEED.
YOUR HELP IS APPRECIATED, KIBITSU.
Heh!
THE WHITE OF YOUR CLOAK IS BLINDING AS ALWAYS.
CLEANLINESS TAKEN TOO FAR IS A DISEASE ITSELF.
HMPH! I ASSUME YOUR RUDENESS IS AN ASSET ON THE BATTLEFIELD, AT LEAST.
SERVED ME WELL SO FAR.
Heh heh heh
NICE TO SEE YOU GETTING ALONG.
YIKES!
THE KING SENDS ME CHILDREN?
VERY WELL. WE'LL SOON SEE WHAT THEY'RE MADE OF.

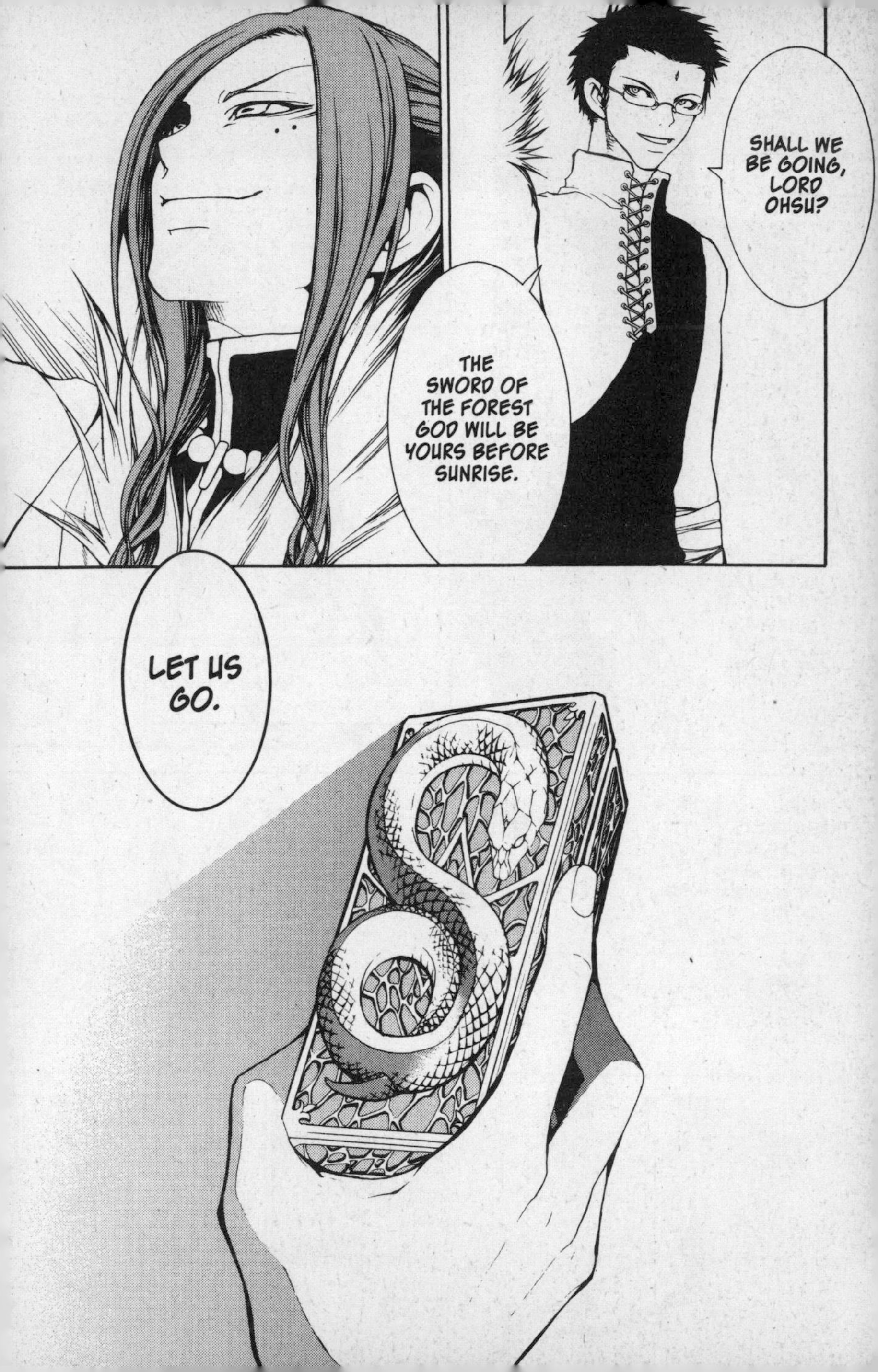
SHALL WE BE GOING, LORD OHSU?
THE SWORD OF THE FOREST GOD WILL BE YOURS BEFORE SUNRISE.
LET US GO.

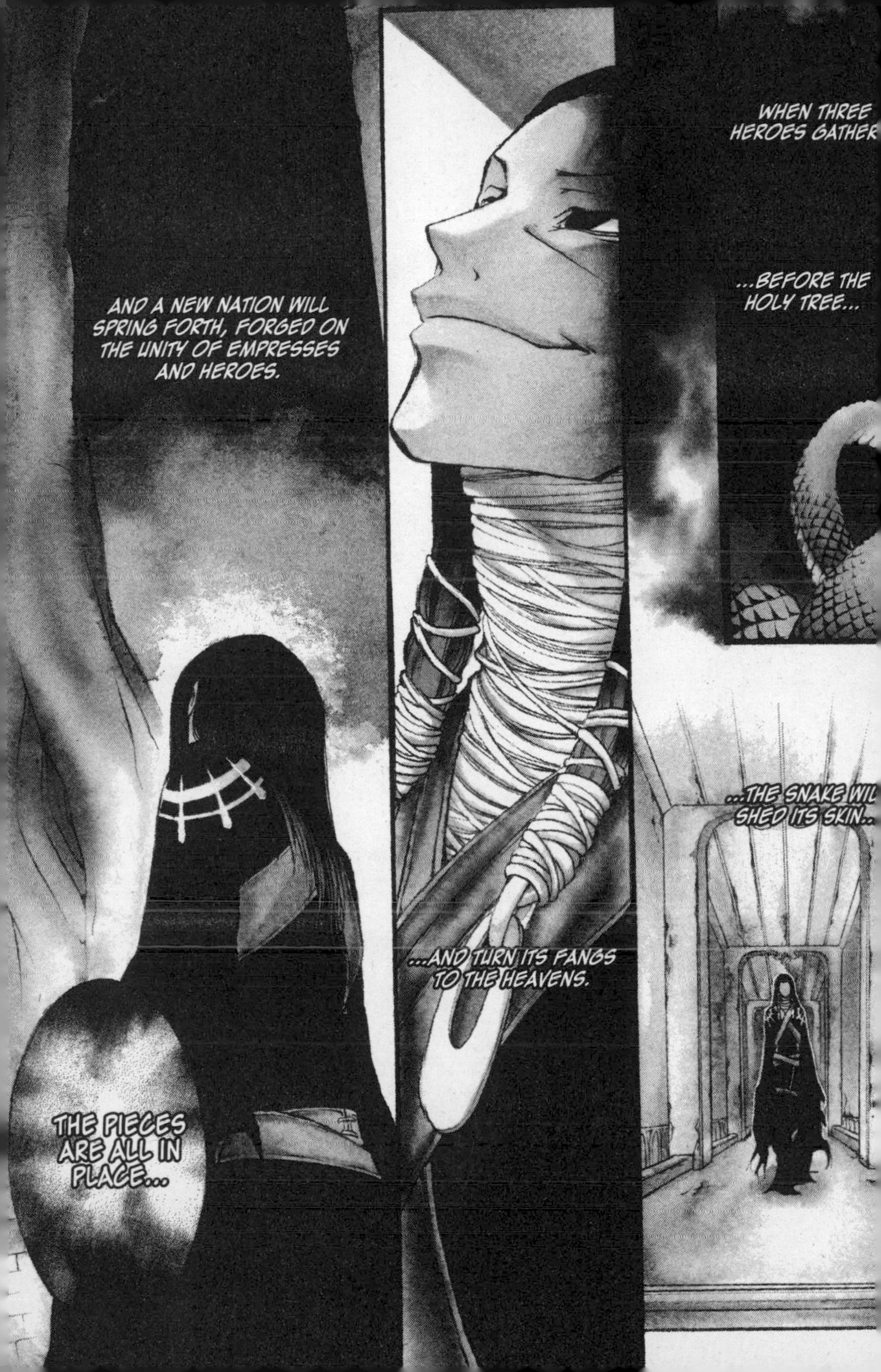
WHEN THREE HEROES GATHER
...BEFORE THE HOLY TREE...
...THE SNAKE WIL SHED ITS SKIN...
...AND TURN ITS FANGS TO THE HEAVENS.
AND A NEW NATION WILL SPRING FORTH, FORGED ON THE UNITY OF EMPRESSES AND HEROES.
THE PIECES ARE ALL IN PLACE...

Chapter 6: Amamikado Attacks

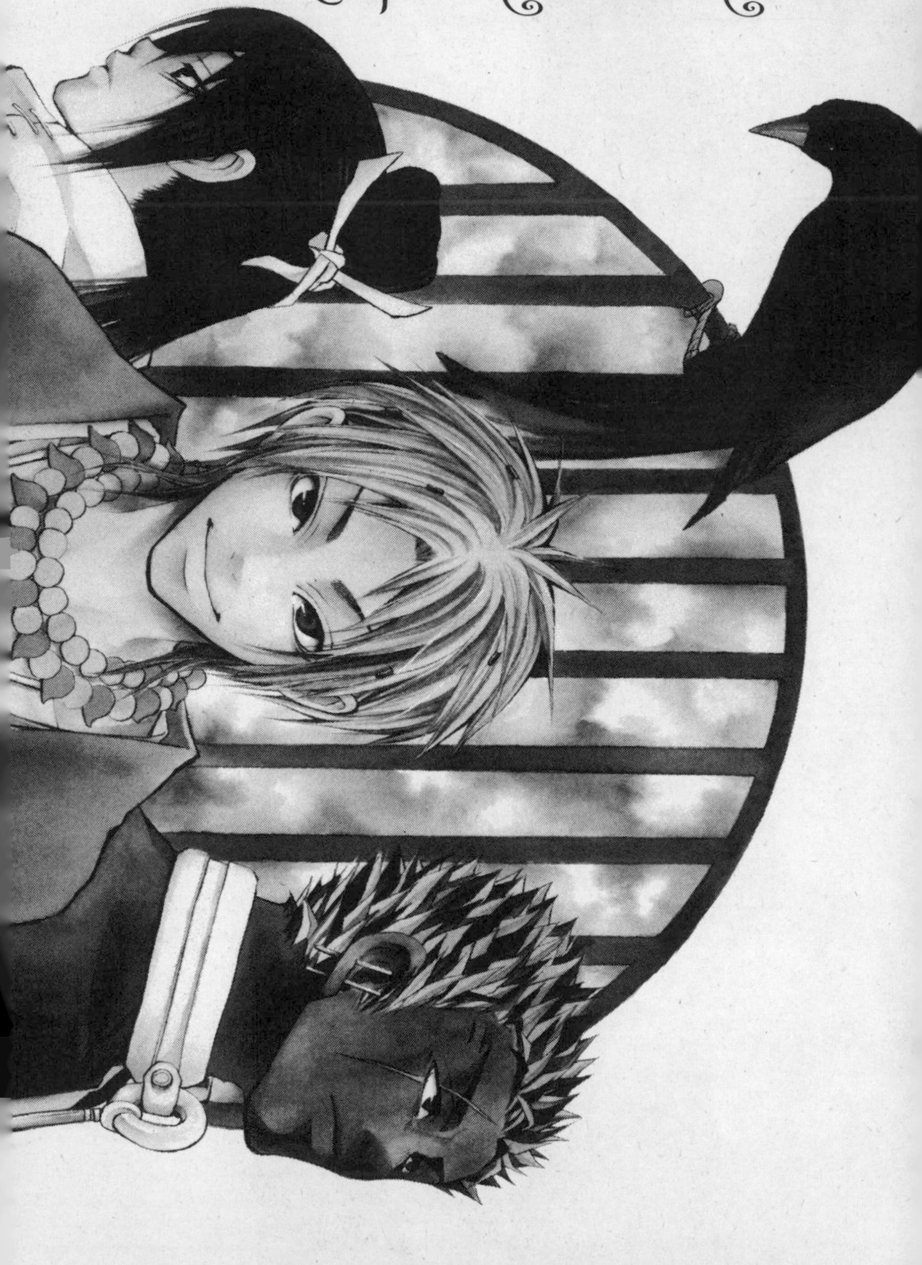

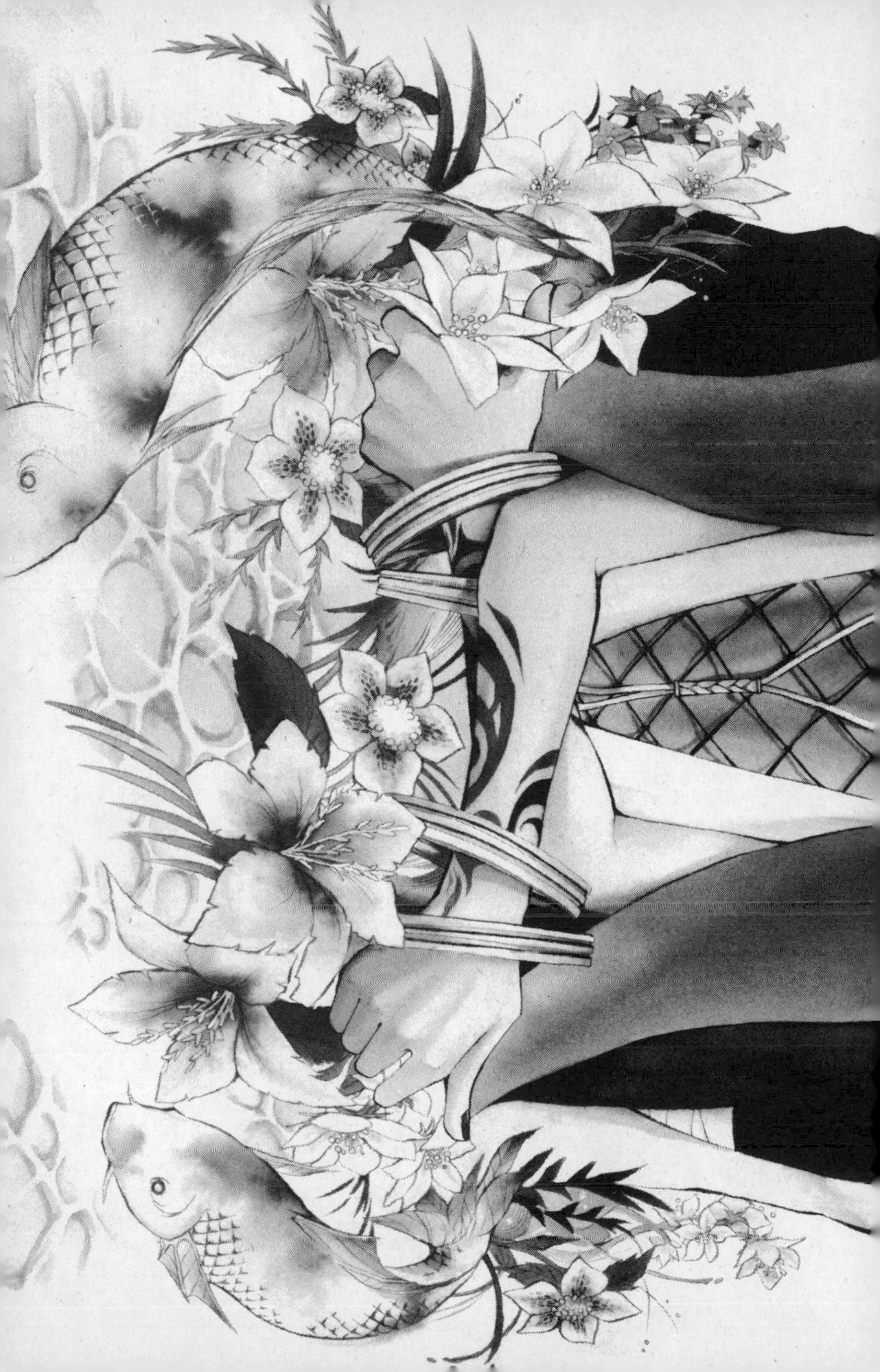

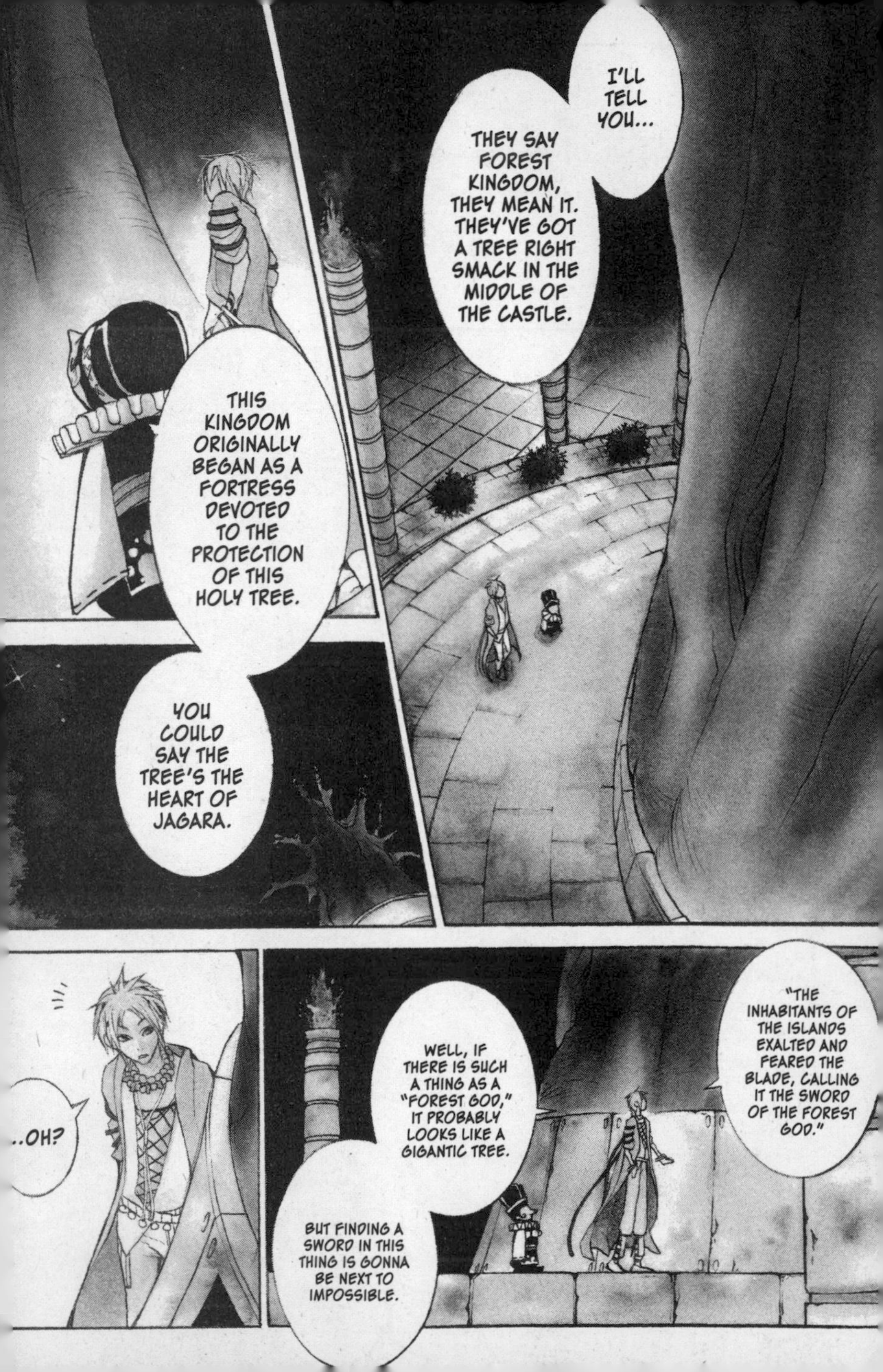
I'LL TELL YOU...
THEY SAY FOREST KINGDOM, THEY MEAN IT. THEY'VE GOT A TREE RIGHT SMACK IN THE MIDDLE OF THE CASTLE.
THIS KINGDOM ORIGINALLY BEGAN AS A FORTRESS DEVOTED TO THE PROTECTION OF THIS HOLY TREE.
YOU COULD SAY THE TREE'S THE HEART OF JAGARA.
"THE INHABITANTS OF THE ISLANDS EXALTED AND FEARED THE BLADE, CALLING IT THE SWORD OF THE FOREST GOD."
WELL, IF THERE IS SUCH A THING AS A "FOREST GOD," IT PROBABLY LOOKS LIKE A GIGANTIC TREE.
BUT FINDING A SWORD IN THIS THING IS GONNA BE NEXT TO IMPOSSIBLE.
...OH?

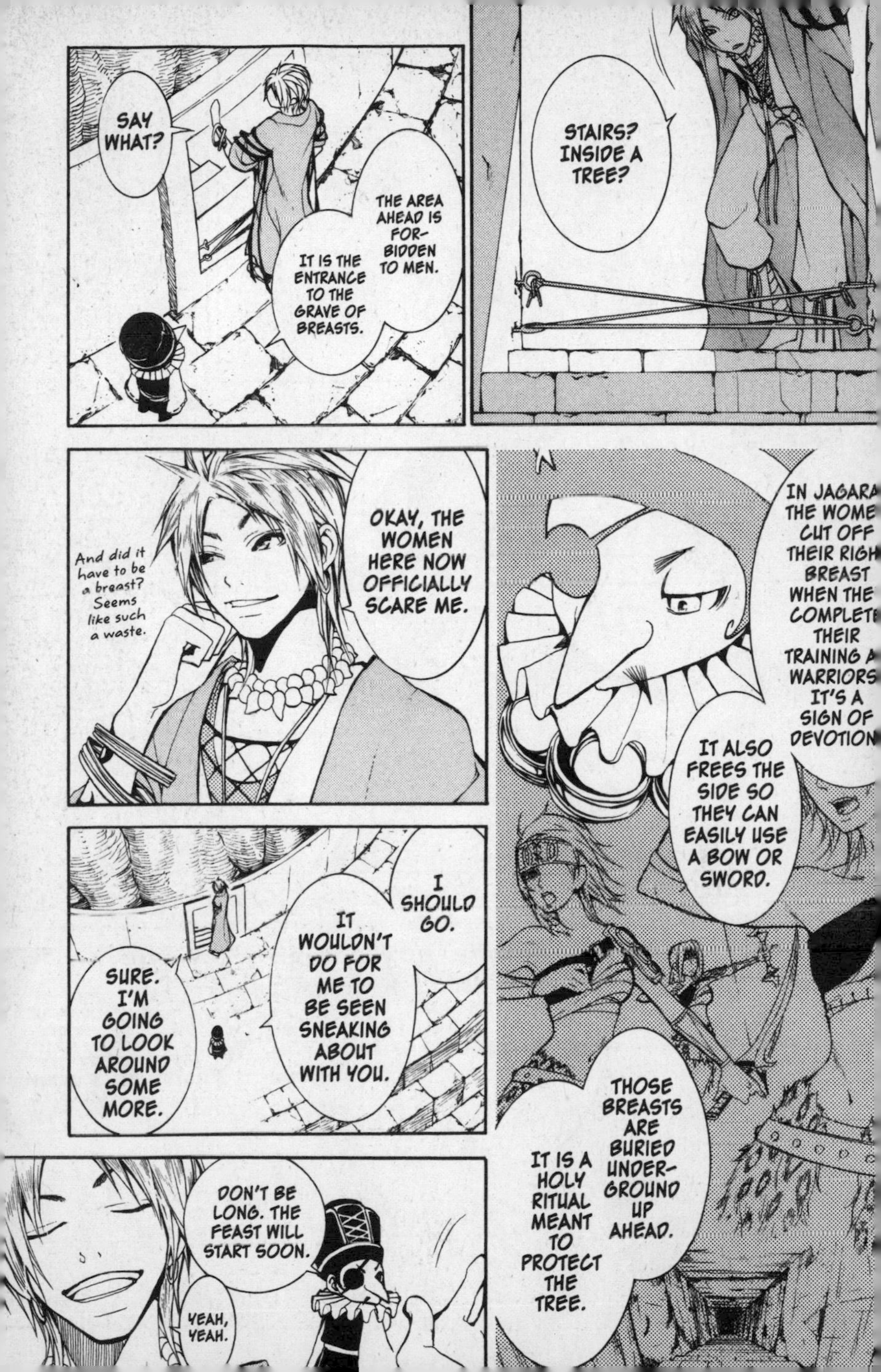
STAIRS? INSIDE A TREE?
THE AREA AHEAD IS FOR-BIDDEN TO MEN.
IT IS THE ENTRANCE TO THE GRAVE OF BREASTS.
SAY WHAT?
IN JAGARA THE WOME CUT OFF THEIR RIGH BREAST WHEN THE COMPLETE THEIR TRAINING A WARRIORS IT'S A SIGN OF DEVOTION
IT ALSO FREES THE SIDE SO THEY CAN EASILY USE A BOW OR SWORD.
THOSE BREASTS ARE BURIED UNDER-GROUND UP AHEAD.
IT IS A HOLY RITUAL MEANT TO PROTECT THE TREE.
OKAY, THE WOMEN HERE NOW OFFICIALLY SCARE ME.
And did it have to be a breast? Seems like such a waste.
I SHOULD GO.
IT WOULDN'T DO FOR ME TO BE SEEN SNEAKING ABOUT WITH YOU.
SURE. I'M GOING TO LOOK AROUND SOME MORE.
DON'T BE LONG. THE FEAST WILL START SOON.
YEAH, YEAH.

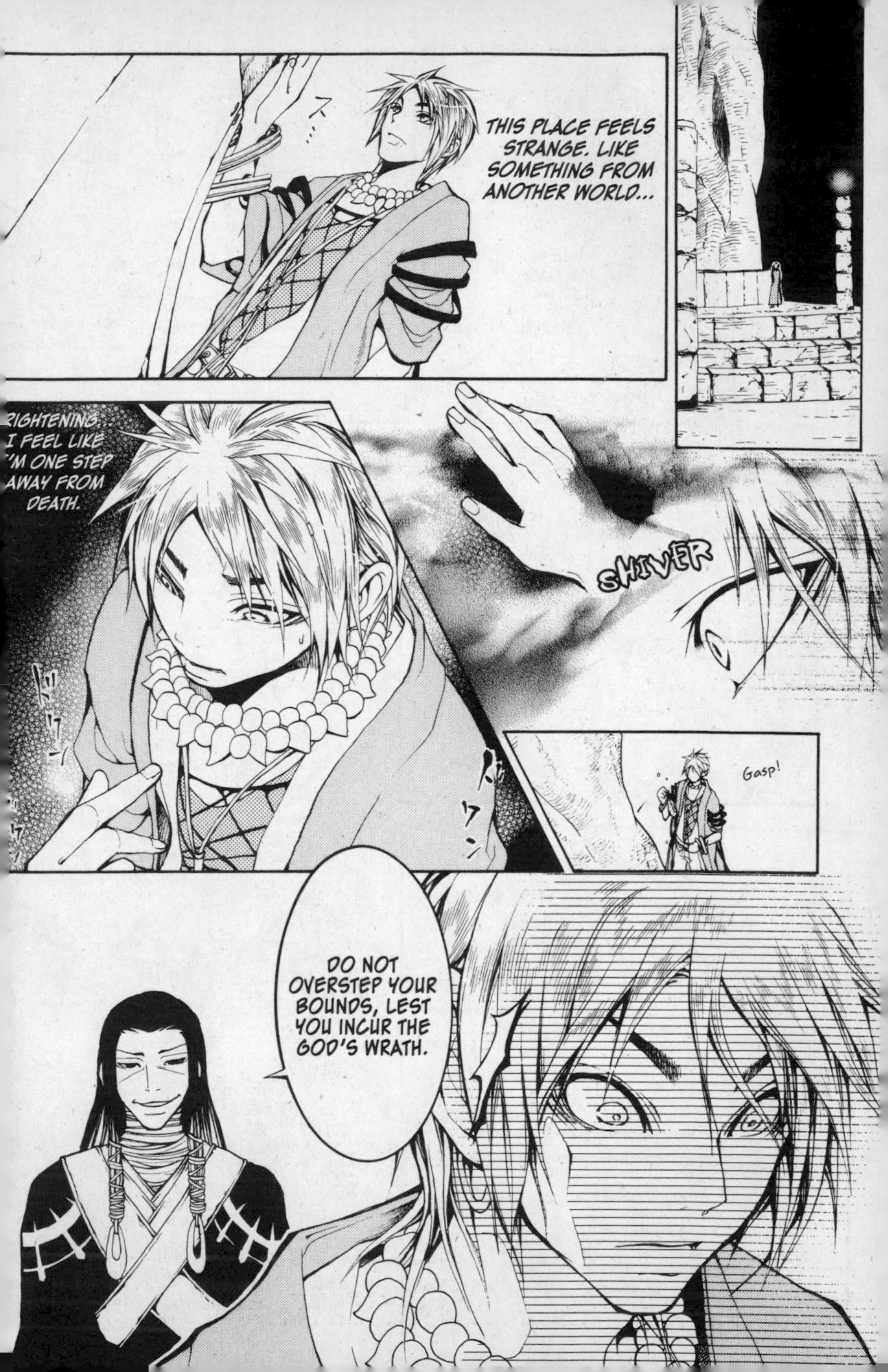
THIS PLACE FEELS STRANGE. LIKE SOMETHING FROM ANOTHER WORLD...
SHIVER
Gasp!
RIGHTENING. I FEEL LIKE 'M ONE STEP AWAY FROM DEATH.
DO NOT OVERSTEP YOUR BOUNDS, LEST YOU INCUR THE GOD'S WRATH.

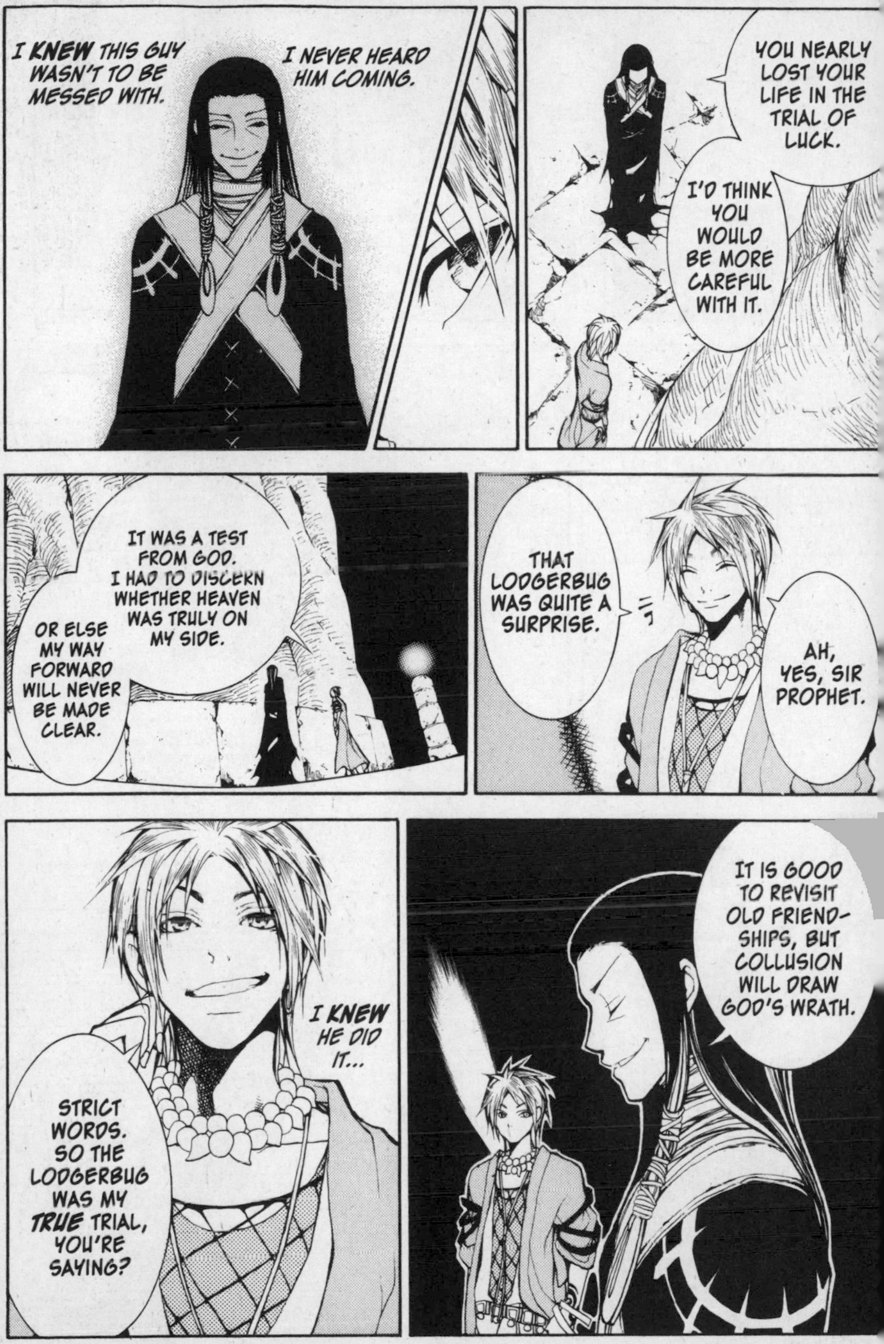
YOU NEARLY LOST YOUR LIFE IN THE TRIAL OF LUCK.
I'D THINK YOU WOULD BE MORE CAREFUL WITH IT.
I NEVER HEARD HIM COMING.
I KNEW THIS GUY WASN'T TO BE MESSED WITH.
AH, YES, SIR PROPHET.
THAT LODGERBUG WAS QUITE A SURPRISE.
IT WAS A TEST FROM GOD. I HAD TO DISCERN WHETHER HEAVEN WAS TRULY ON MY SIDE.
OR ELSE MY WAY FORWARD WILL NEVER BE MADE CLEAR.
IT IS GOOD TO REVISIT OLD FRIEND-SHIPS, BUT COLLUSION WILL DRAW GOD'S WRATH.
I KNEW HE DID IT...
STRICT WORDS. SO THE LODGERBUG WAS MY TRUE TRIAL, YOU'RE SAYING?

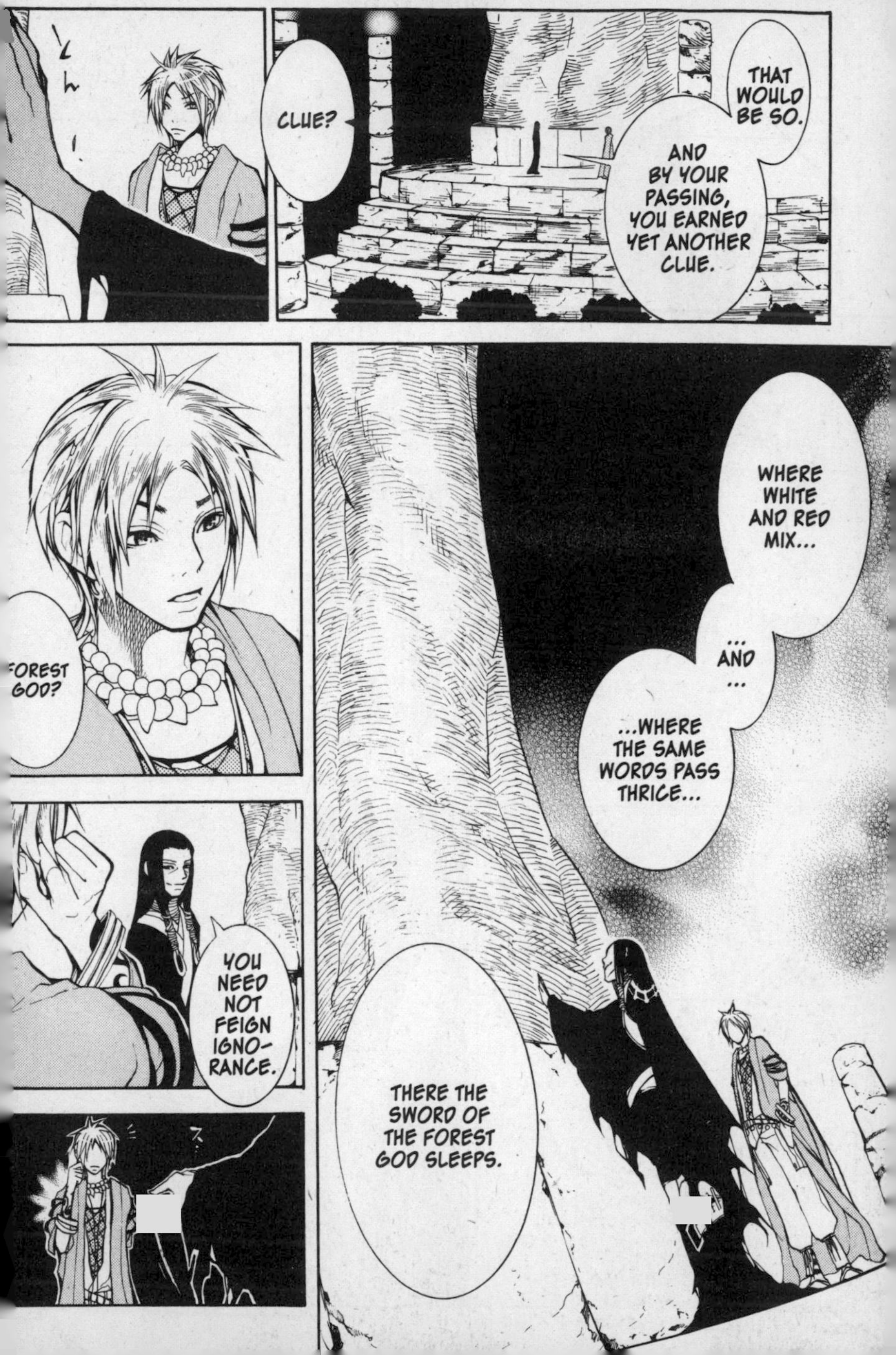
THAT WOULD BE SO.
AND BY YOUR PASSING, YOU EARNED YET ANOTHER CLUE.
CLUE?
WHERE WHITE AND RED MIX...
... AND ...
...WHERE THE SAME WORDS PASS THRICE...
THERE THE SWORD OF THE FOREST GOD SLEEPS.
FOREST GOD?
YOU NEED NOT FEIGN IGNO-RANCE.

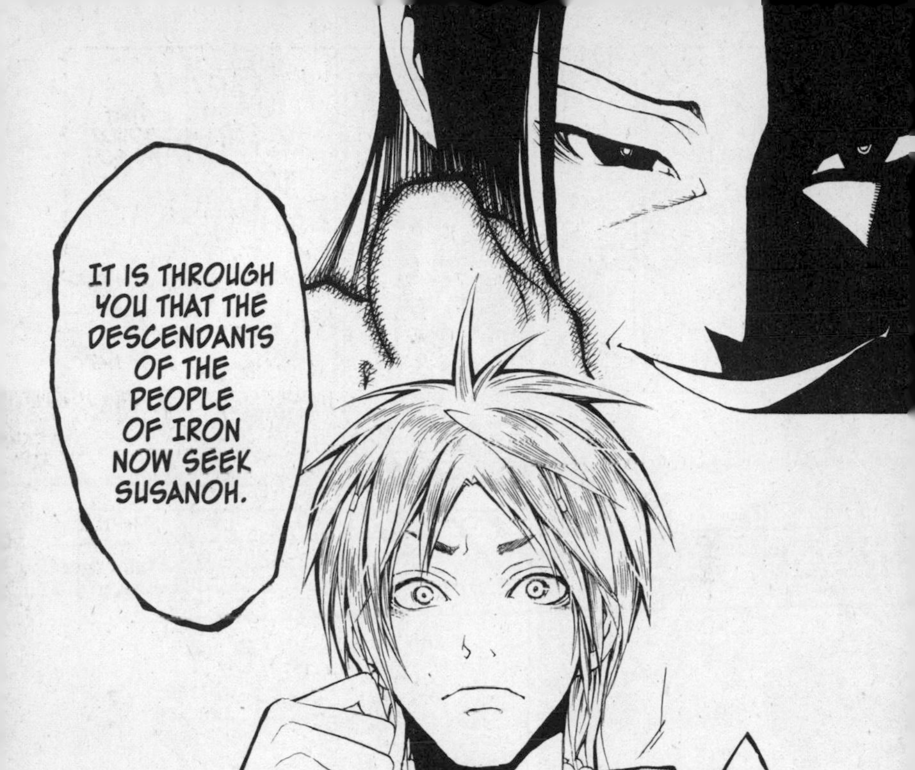
IT IS THROUGH YOU THAT THE DESCENDANTS OF THE PEOPLE OF IRON NOW SEEK SUSANOH.

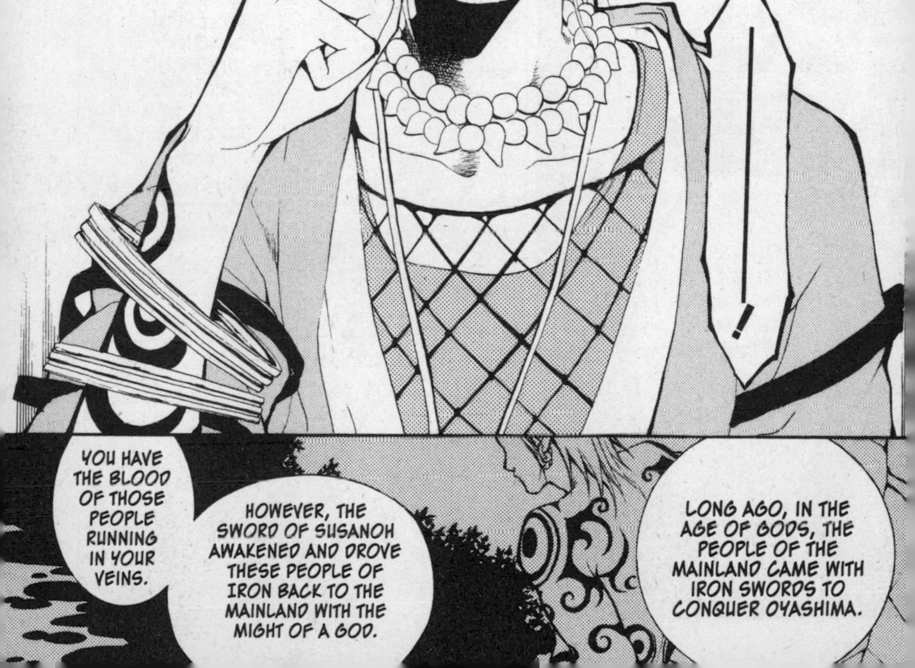
LONG AGO, IN THE AGE OF GODS, THE PEOPLE OF THE MAINLAND CAME WITH IRON SWORDS TO CONQUER OYASHIMA.
HOWEVER, THE SWORD OF SUSANOH AWAKENED AND DROVE THESE PEOPLE OF IRON BACK TO THE MAINLAND WITH THE MIGHT OF A GOD.
YOU HAVE THE BLOOD OF THOSE PEOPLE RUNNING IN YOUR VEINS.

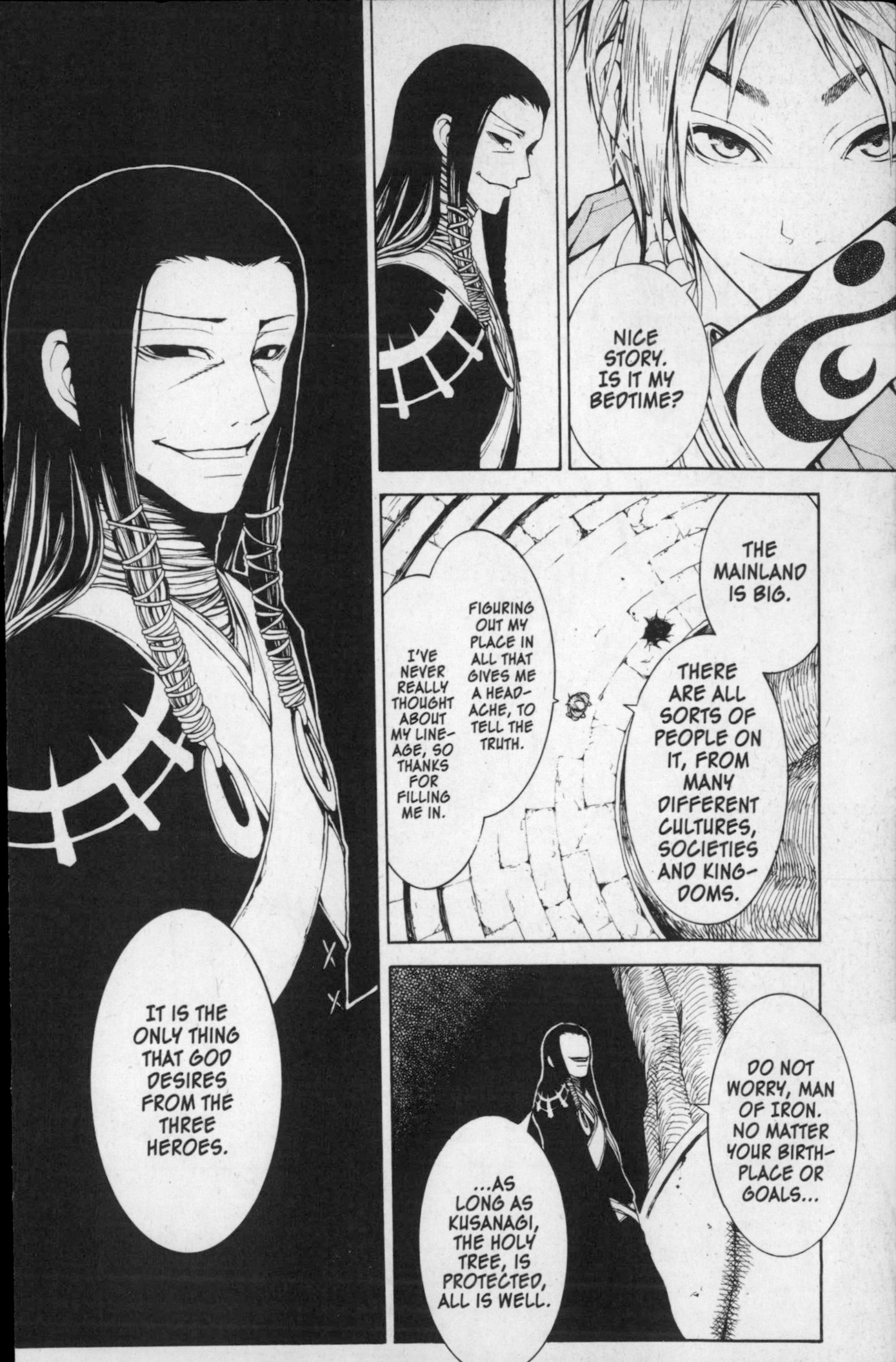
NICE STORY. IS IT MY BEDTIME?
THE MAINLAND IS BIG.
THERE ARE ALL SORTS OF PEOPLE ON IT, FROM MANY DIFFERENT CULTURES, SOCIETIES AND KING-DOMS.
I'VE NEVER REALLY THOUGHT ABOUT MY LINE-AGE, SO THANKS FOR FILLING ME IN.
FIGURING OUT MY PLACE IN ALL THAT GIVES ME A HEAD-ACHE, TO TELL THE TRUTH.
DO NOT WORRY, MAN OF IRON. NO MATTER YOUR BIRTH-PLACE OR GOALS...
...AS LONG AS KUSANAGI, THE HOLY TREE, IS PROTECTED, ALL IS WELL.
IT IS THE ONLY THING THAT GOD DESIRES FROM THE THREE HEROES.

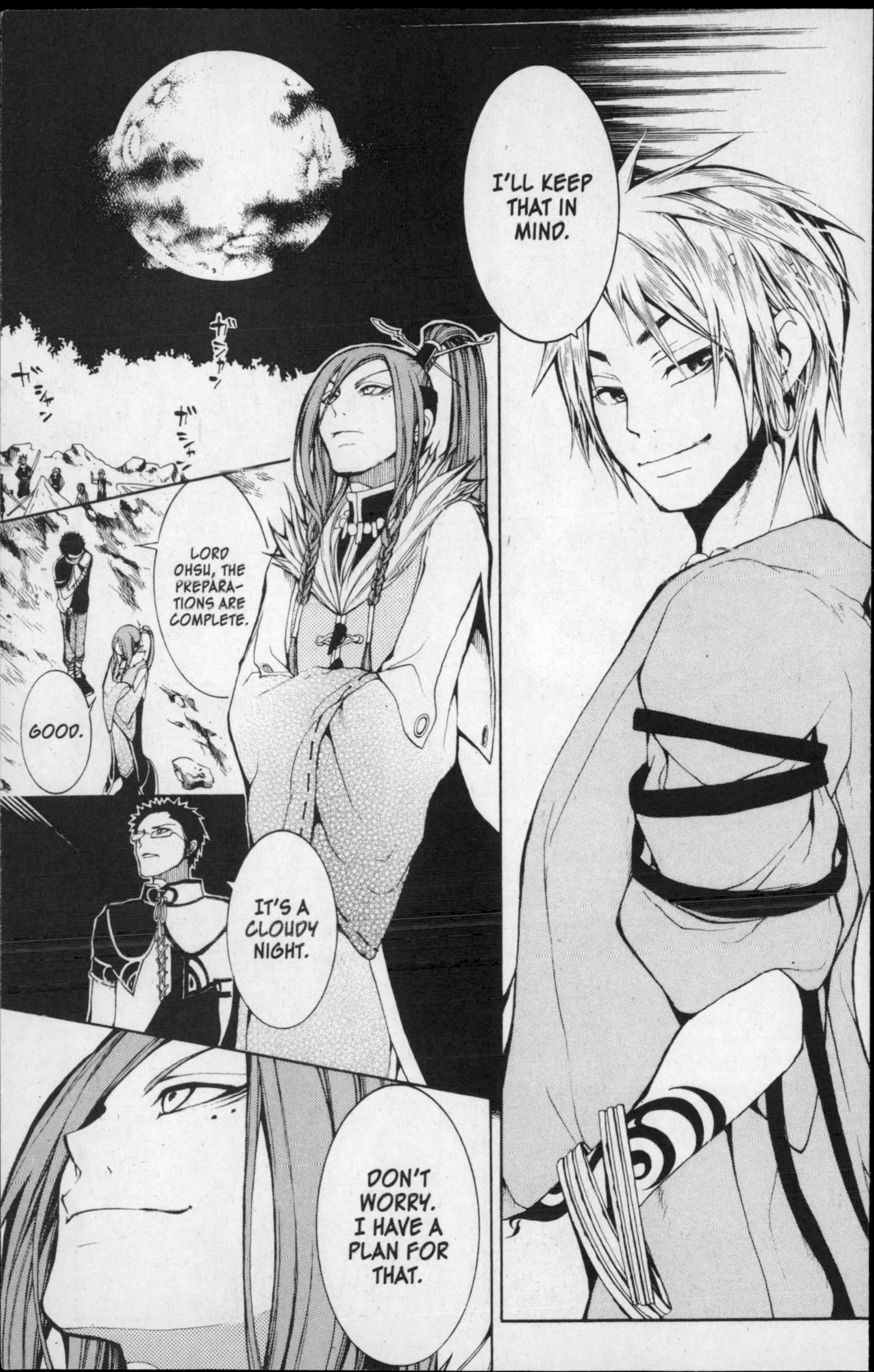
I'LL KEEP THAT IN MIND.
LORD OHSU, THE PREPARATIONS ARE COMPLETE.
GOOD.
IT'S A CLOUDY NIGHT.
DON'T WORRY. I HAVE A PLAN FOR THAT.

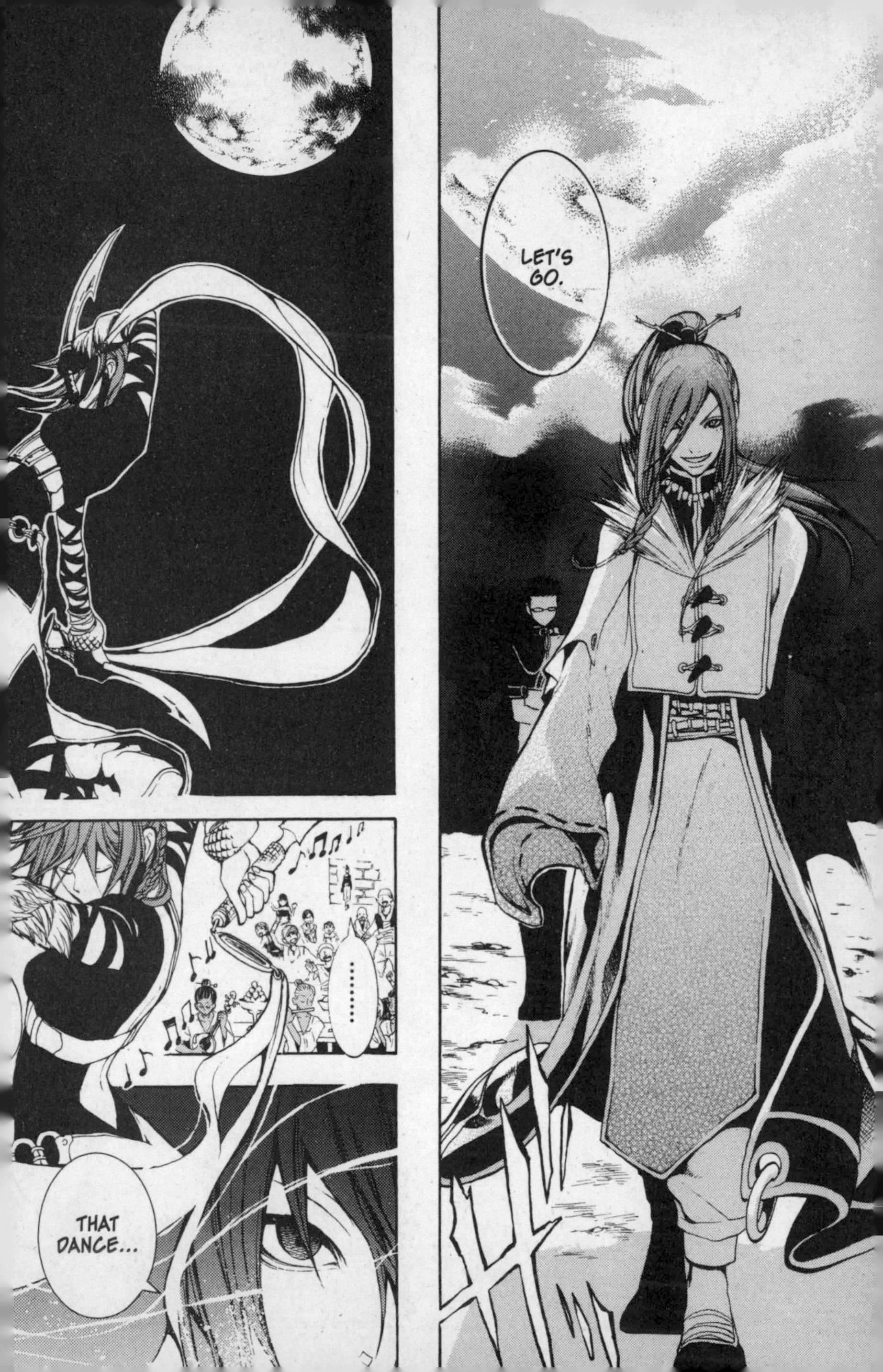
LET'S GO.
......
THAT DANCE...

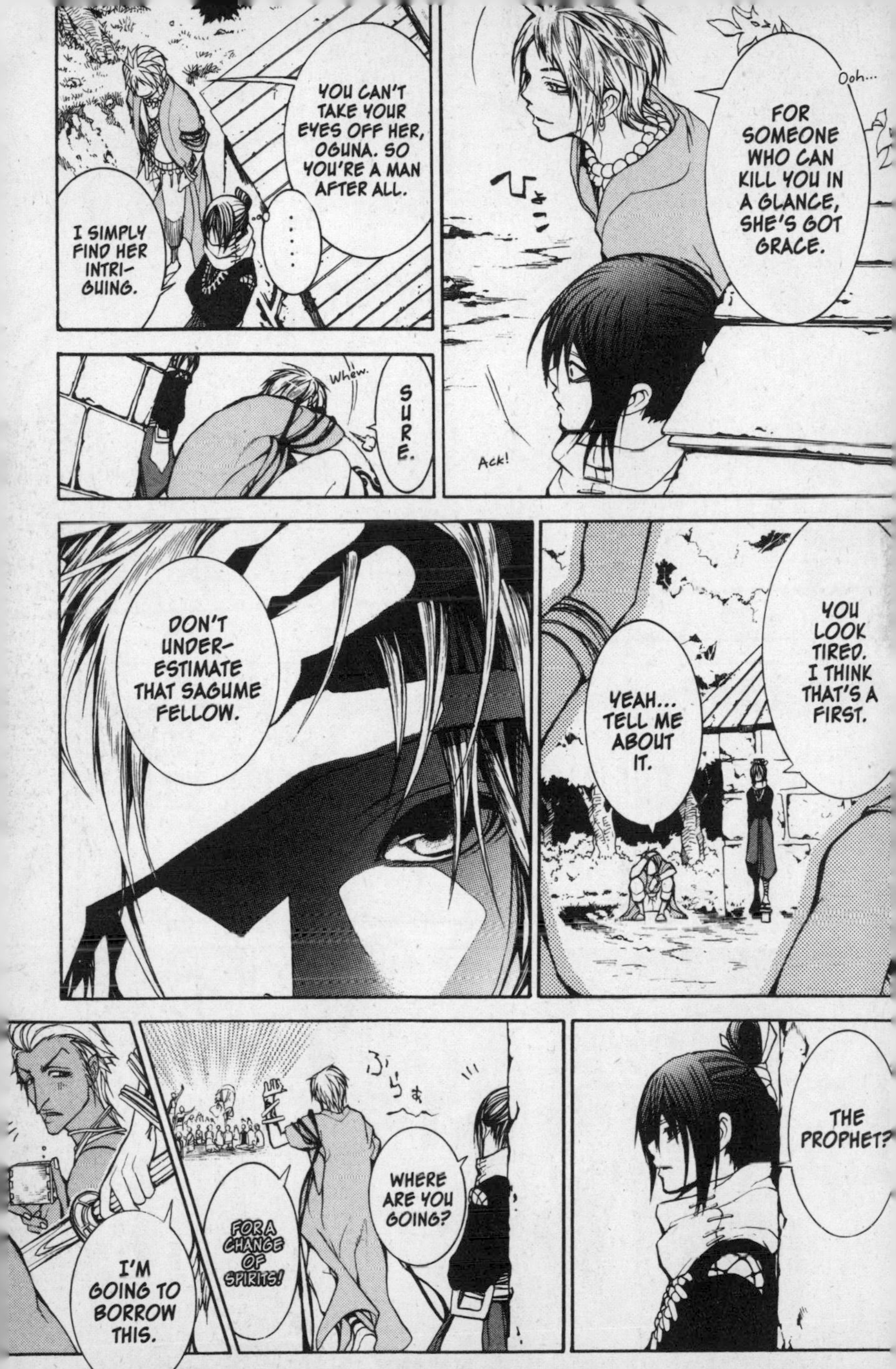
Ooh...
FOR SOMEONE WHO CAN KILL YOU IN A GLANCE, SHE'S GOT GRACE.
Ack!
YOU CAN'T TAKE YOUR EYES OFF HER, OGUNA. SO YOU'RE A MAN AFTER ALL.
......
I SIMPLY FIND HER INTRI-GUING.
Whew.
SURE.
YOU LOOK TIRED. I THINK THAT'S A FIRST.
YEAH... TELL ME ABOUT IT.
DON'T UNDER-ESTIMATE THAT SAGUME FELLOW.
THE PROPHET?
WHERE ARE YOU GOING?
FOR A CHANGE OF SPIRITS!
I'M GOING TO BORROW THIS.

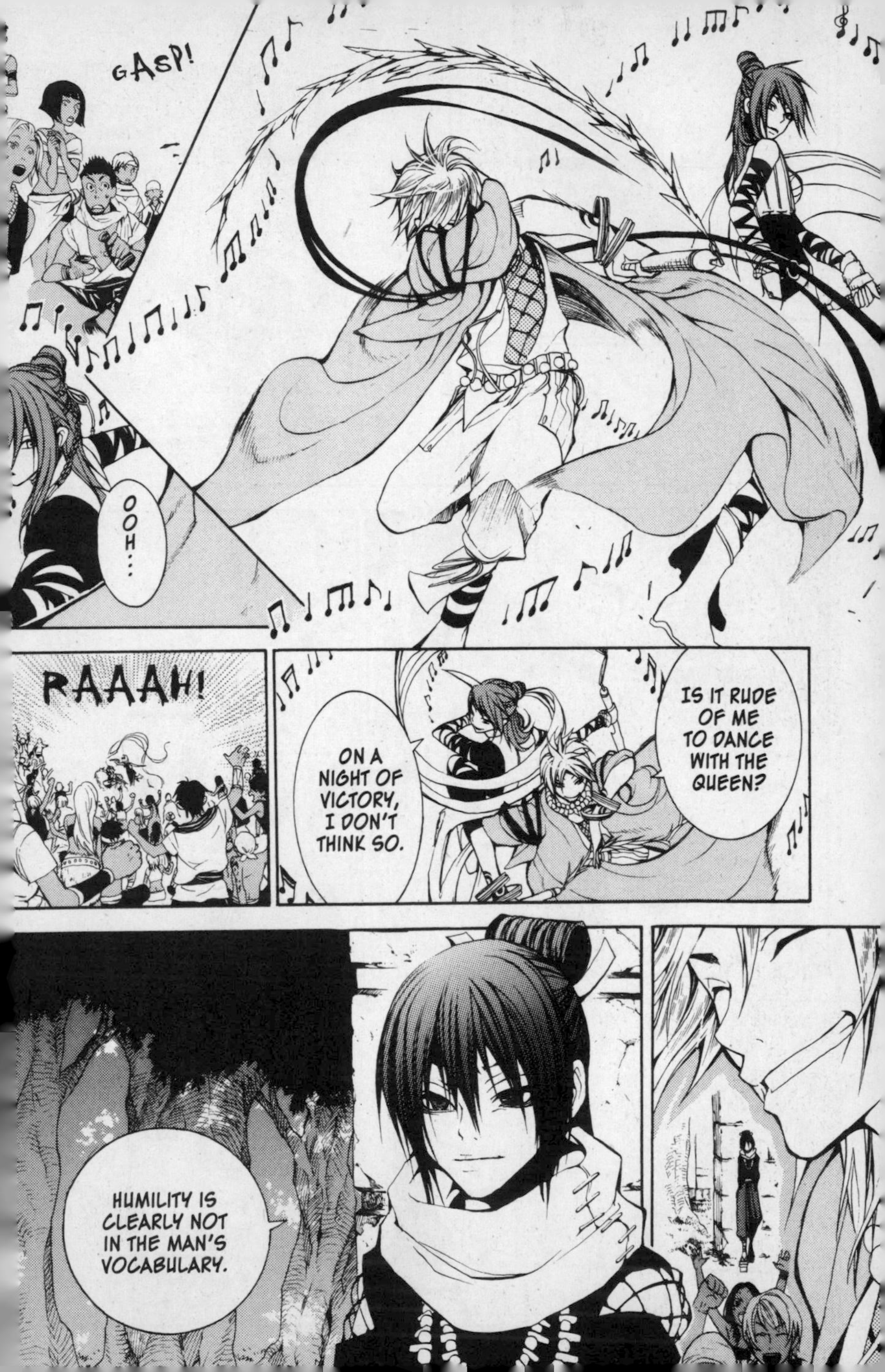
GASP!
OOH...
IS IT RUDE OF ME TO DANCE WITH THE QUEEN?
ON A NIGHT OF VICTORY, I DON'T THINK SO.
RAAAH!
HUMILITY IS CLEARLY NOT IN THE MAN'S VOCABULARY.

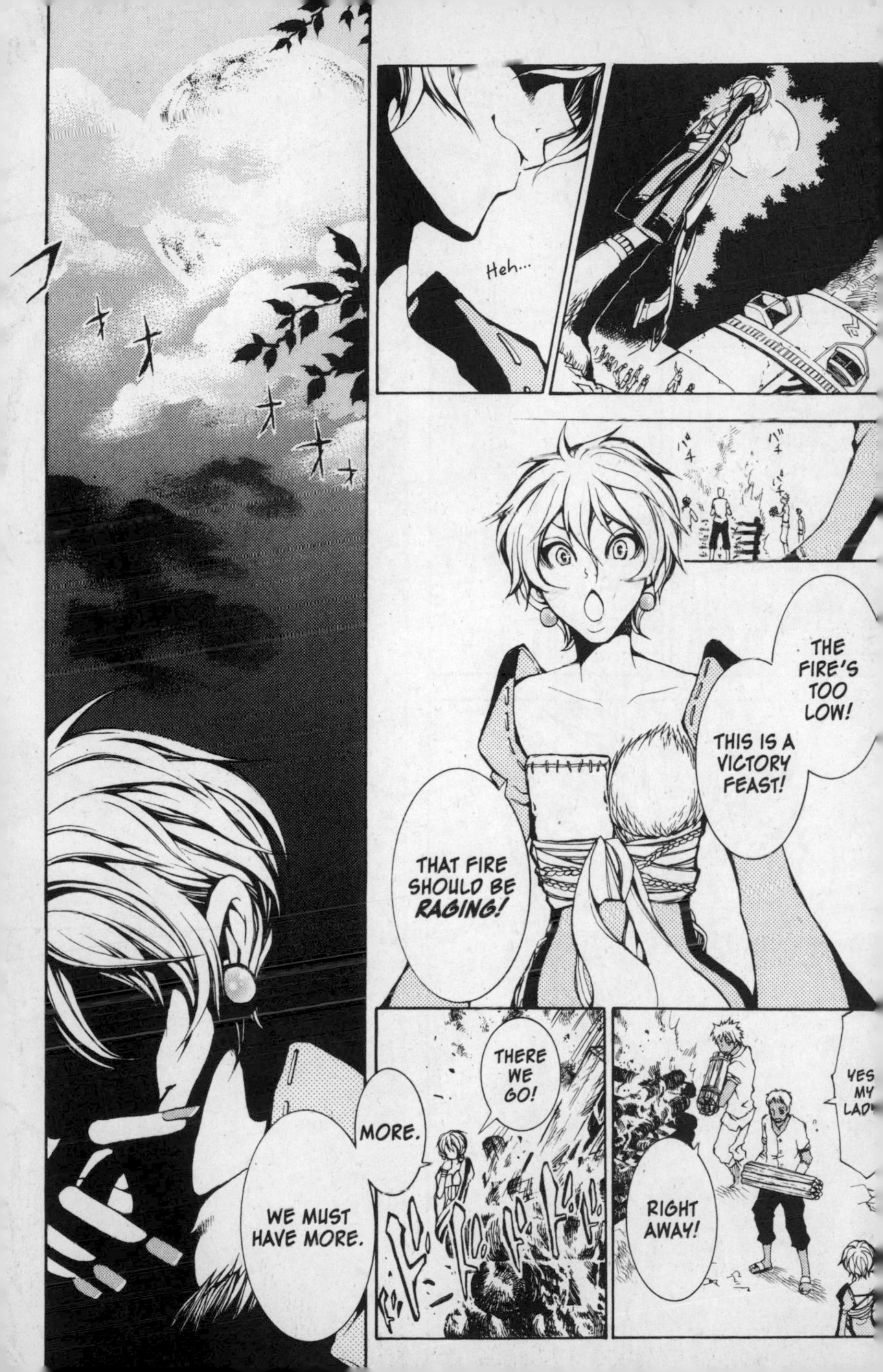
Heh...
THE FIRE'S TOO LOW!
THIS IS A VICTORY FEAST!
THAT FIRE SHOULD BE RAGING!
YES MY LAD
RIGHT AWAY!
THERE WE GO!
MORE.
WE MUST HAVE MORE.

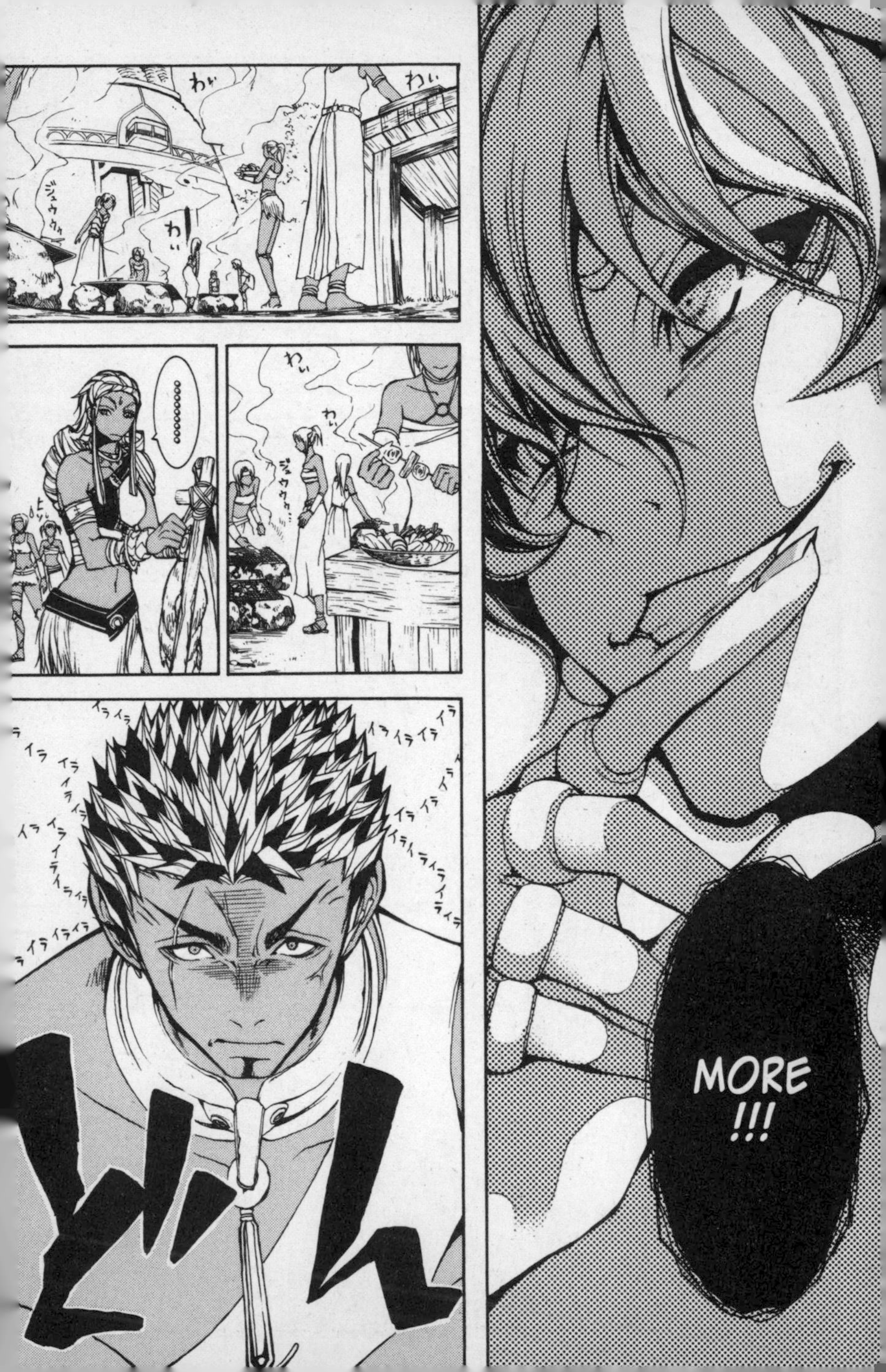
MORE !!!
わい
わい
わい
ジュウウゥ
わい
わい
ジュウウゥ
……………
イライラ

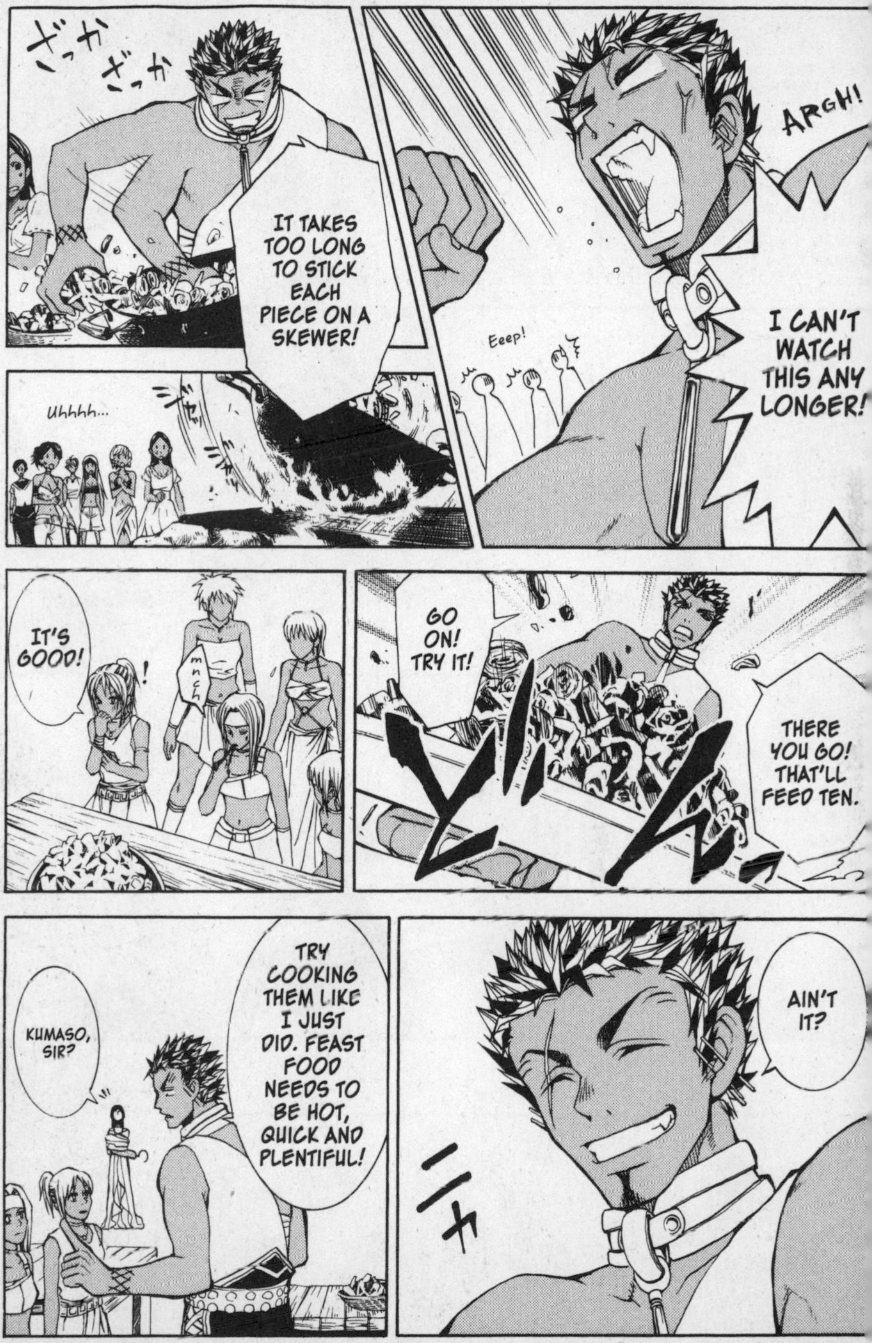
ARGH!
I CAN'T WATCH THIS ANY LONGER!
Eeep!
ざっか ざっか
IT TAKES TOO LONG TO STICK EACH PIECE ON A SKEWER!
Uhhhh...
THERE YOU GO! THAT'LL FEED TEN.
GO ON! TRY IT!
IT'S GOOD!
mnch
AIN'T IT?
TRY COOKING THEM LIKE I JUST DID. FEAST FOOD NEEDS TO BE HOT, QUICK AND PLENTIFUL!
KUMASO, SIR?

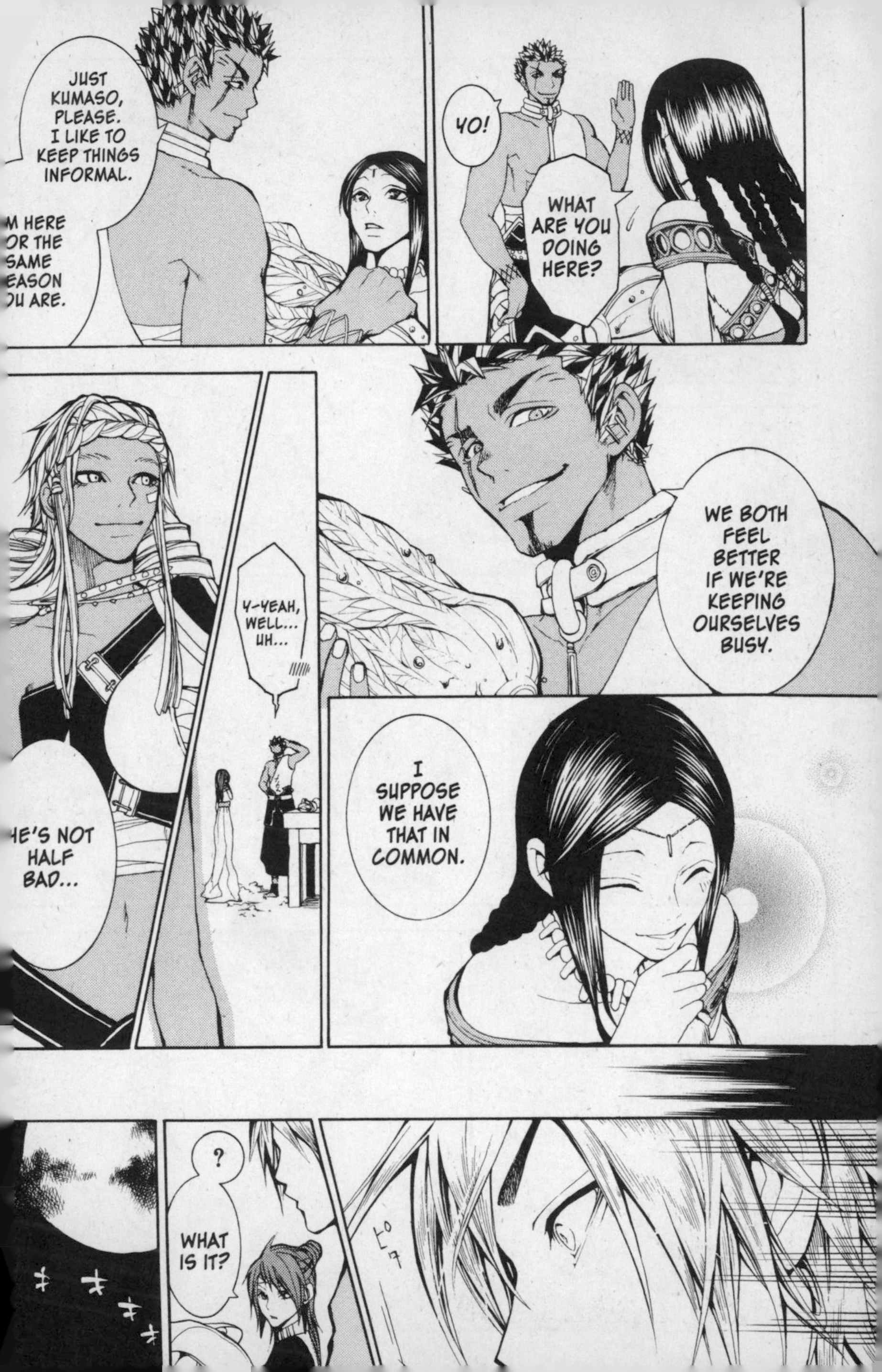
YO!
WHAT ARE YOU DOING HERE?
JUST KUMASO, PLEASE. I LIKE TO KEEP THINGS INFORMAL.
M HERE OR THE SAME EASON OU ARE.
WE BOTH FEEL BETTER IF WE'RE KEEPING OURSELVES BUSY.
I SUPPOSE WE HAVE THAT IN COMMON.
Y-YEAH, WELL... UH...
E'S NOT HALF BAD...
?
WHAT IS IT?

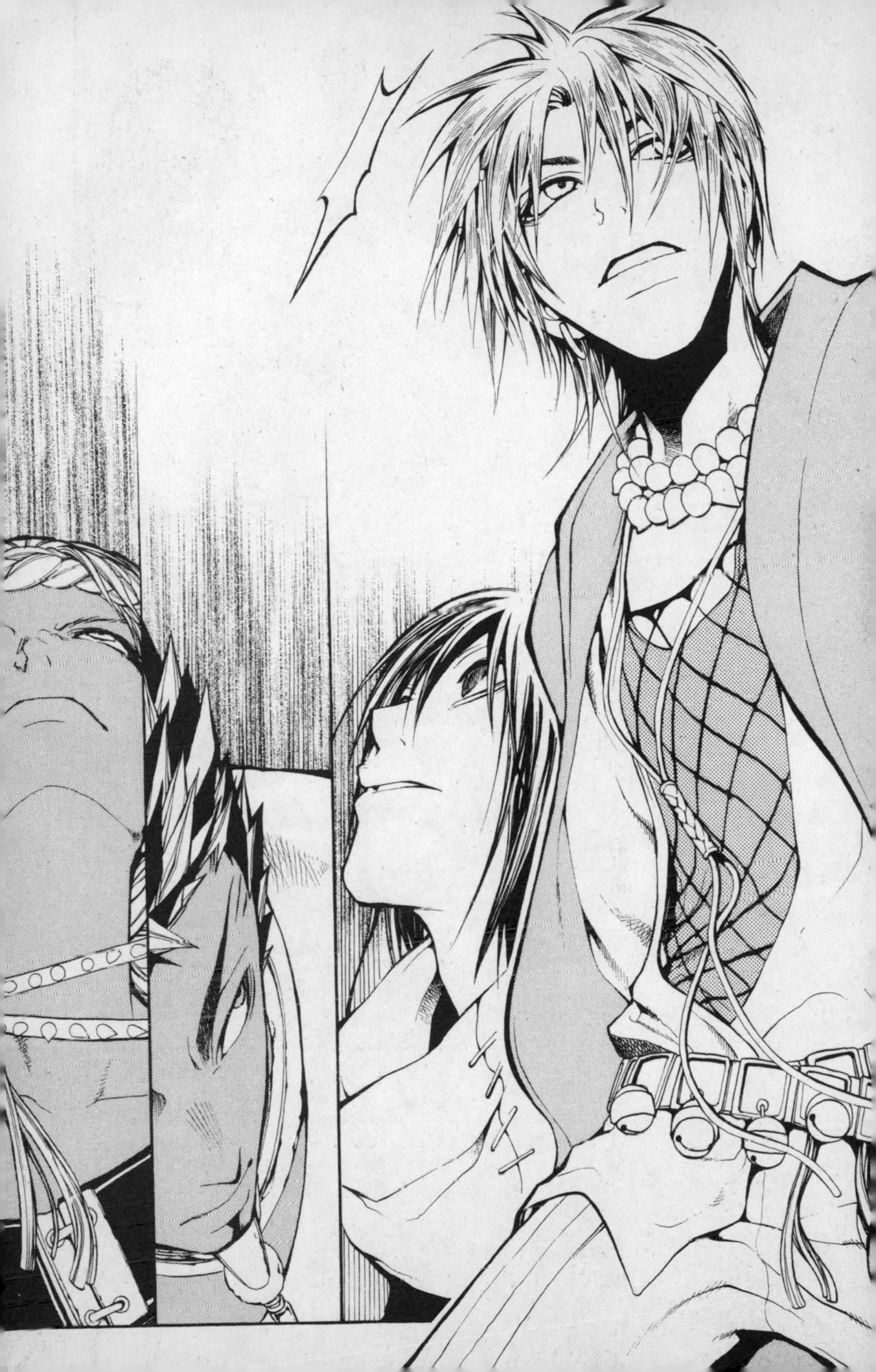

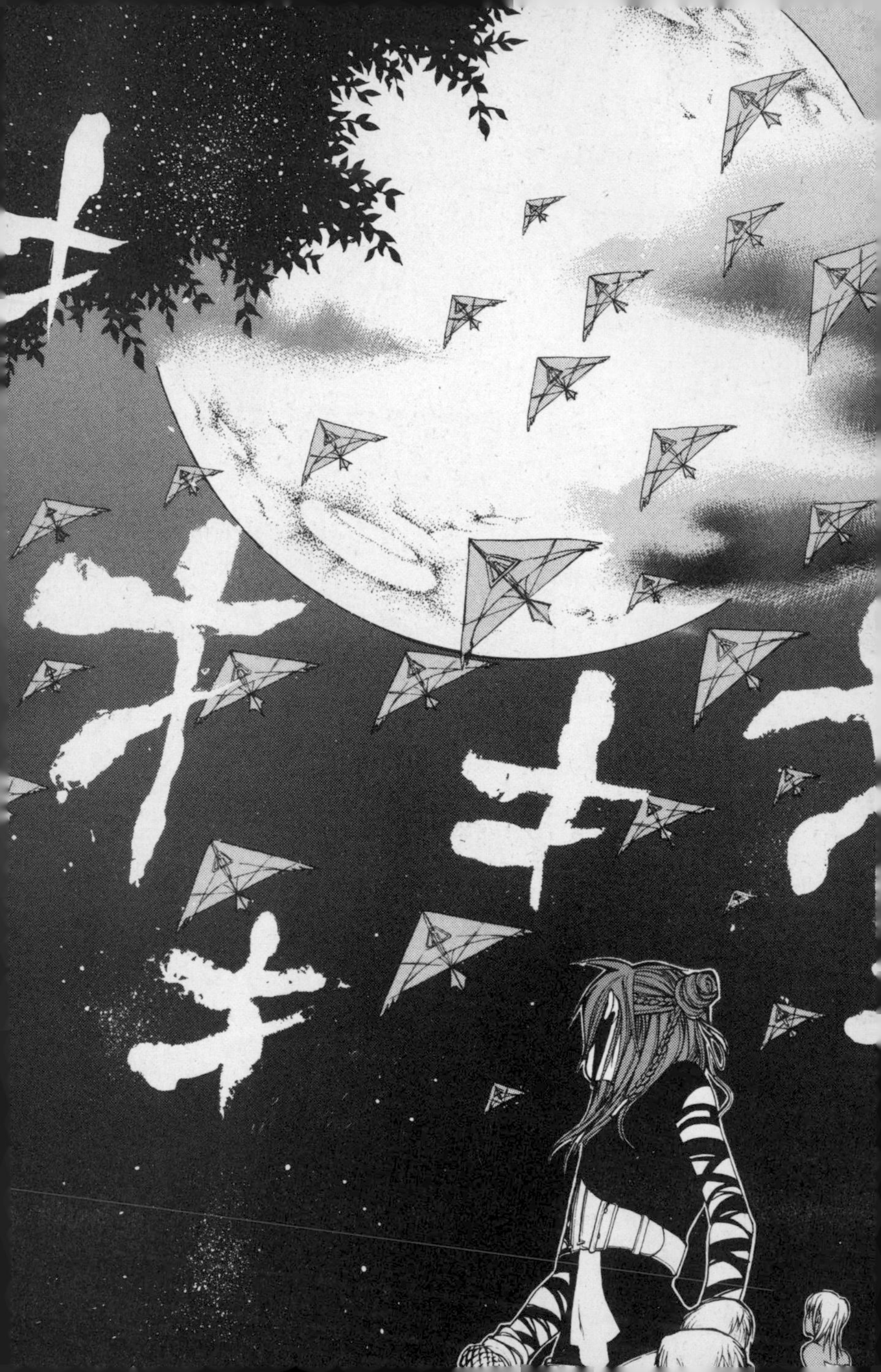

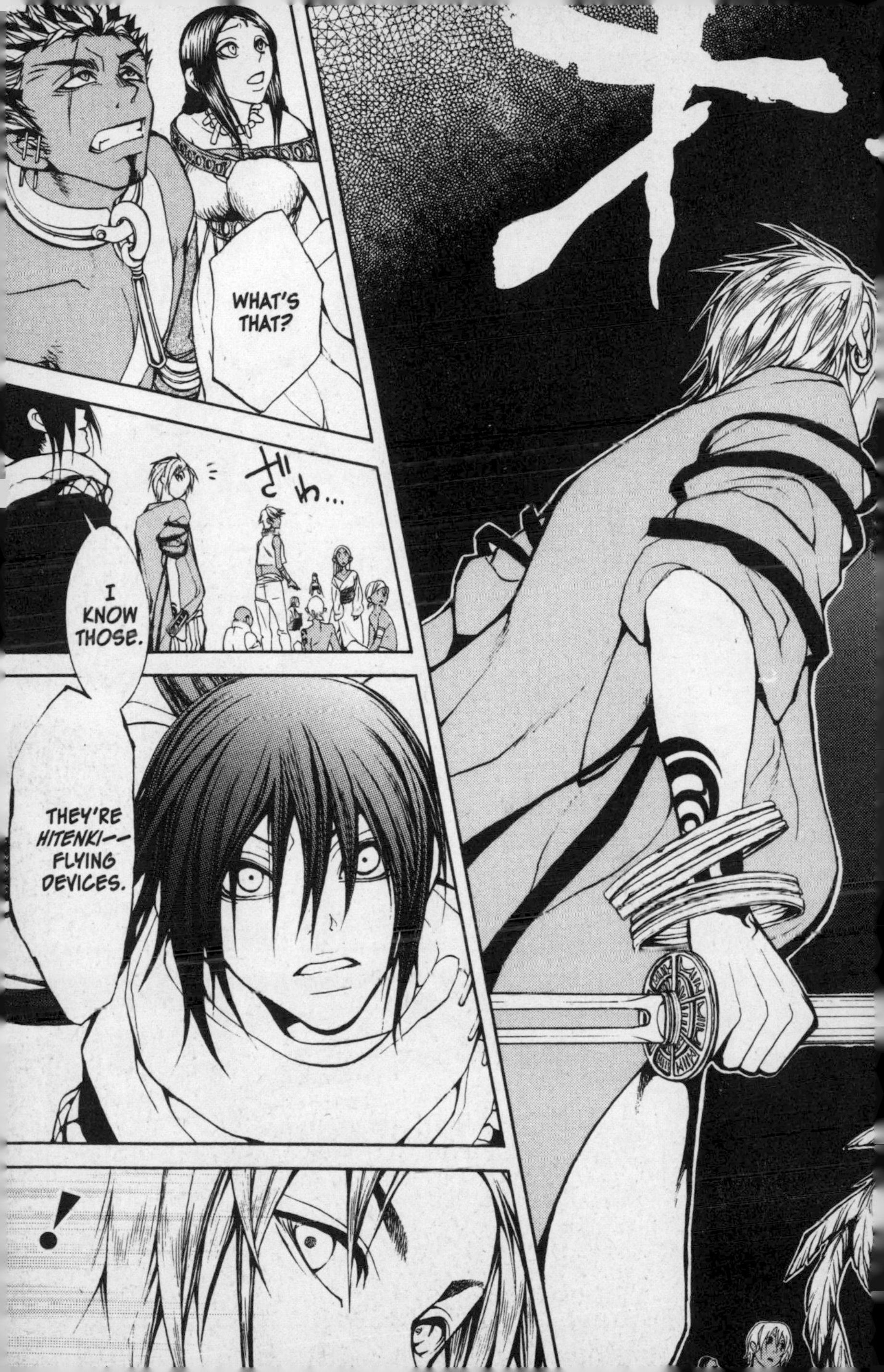
WHAT'S THAT?
ざわ...
I KNOW THOSE.
THEY'RE HITENKI--FLYING DEVICES.
!

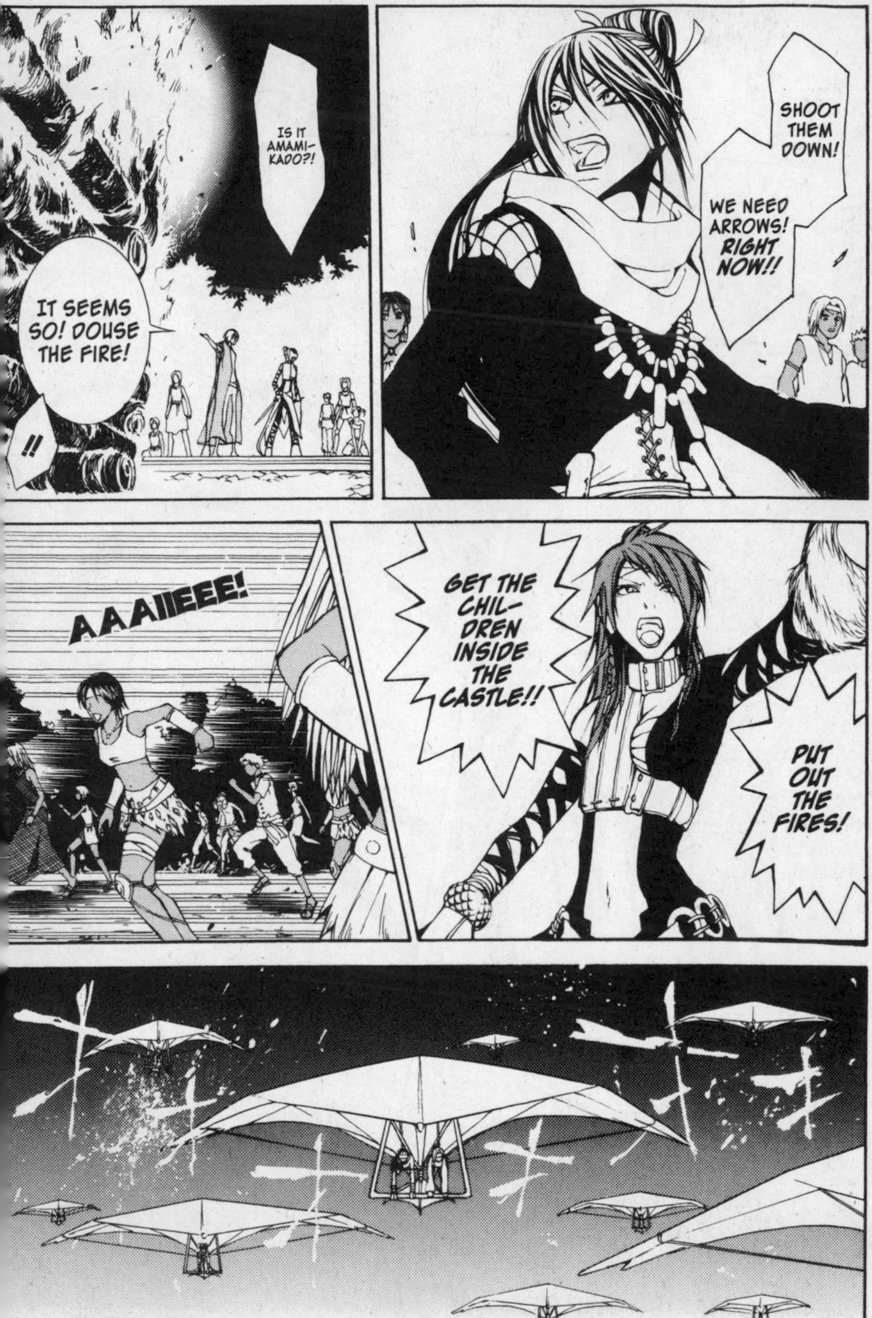
SHOOT THEM DOWN!
WE NEED ARROWS! RIGHT NOW!!
IS IT AMAMI-KADO?!
IT SEEMS SO! DOUSE THE FIRE!
!!
GET THE CHIL-DREN INSIDE THE CASTLE!!
PUT OUT THE FIRES!
AAAIIEEE!

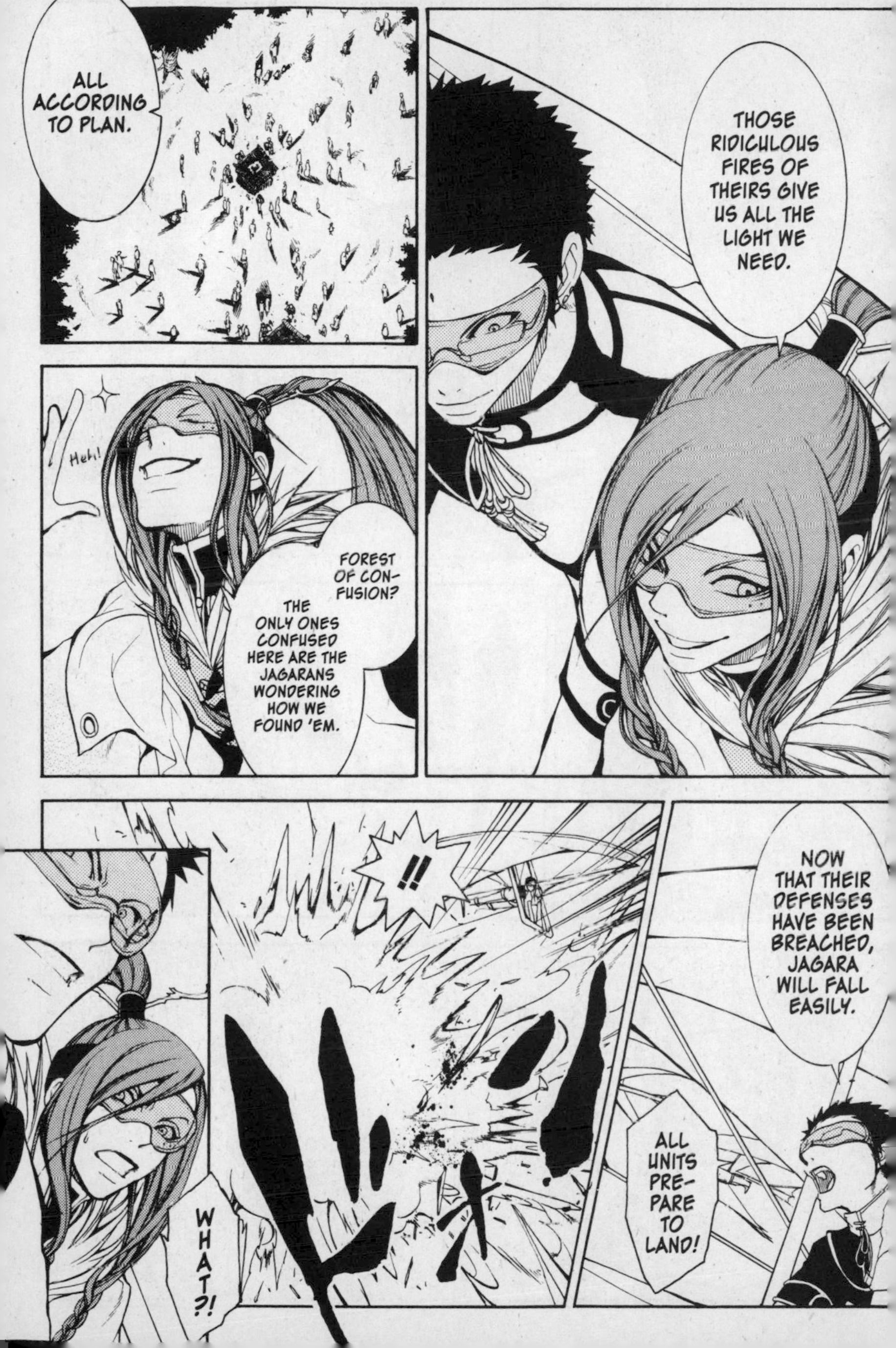
THOSE RIDICULOUS FIRES OF THEIRS GIVE US ALL THE LIGHT WE NEED.
ALL ACCORDING TO PLAN.
Heh!
FOREST OF CONFUSION?
THE ONLY ONES CONFUSED HERE ARE THE JAGARANS WONDERING HOW WE FOUND 'EM.
NOW THAT THEIR DEFENSES HAVE BEEN BREACHED, JAGARA WILL FALL EASILY.
ALL UNITS PREPARE TO LAND!
!!
WHAT?!

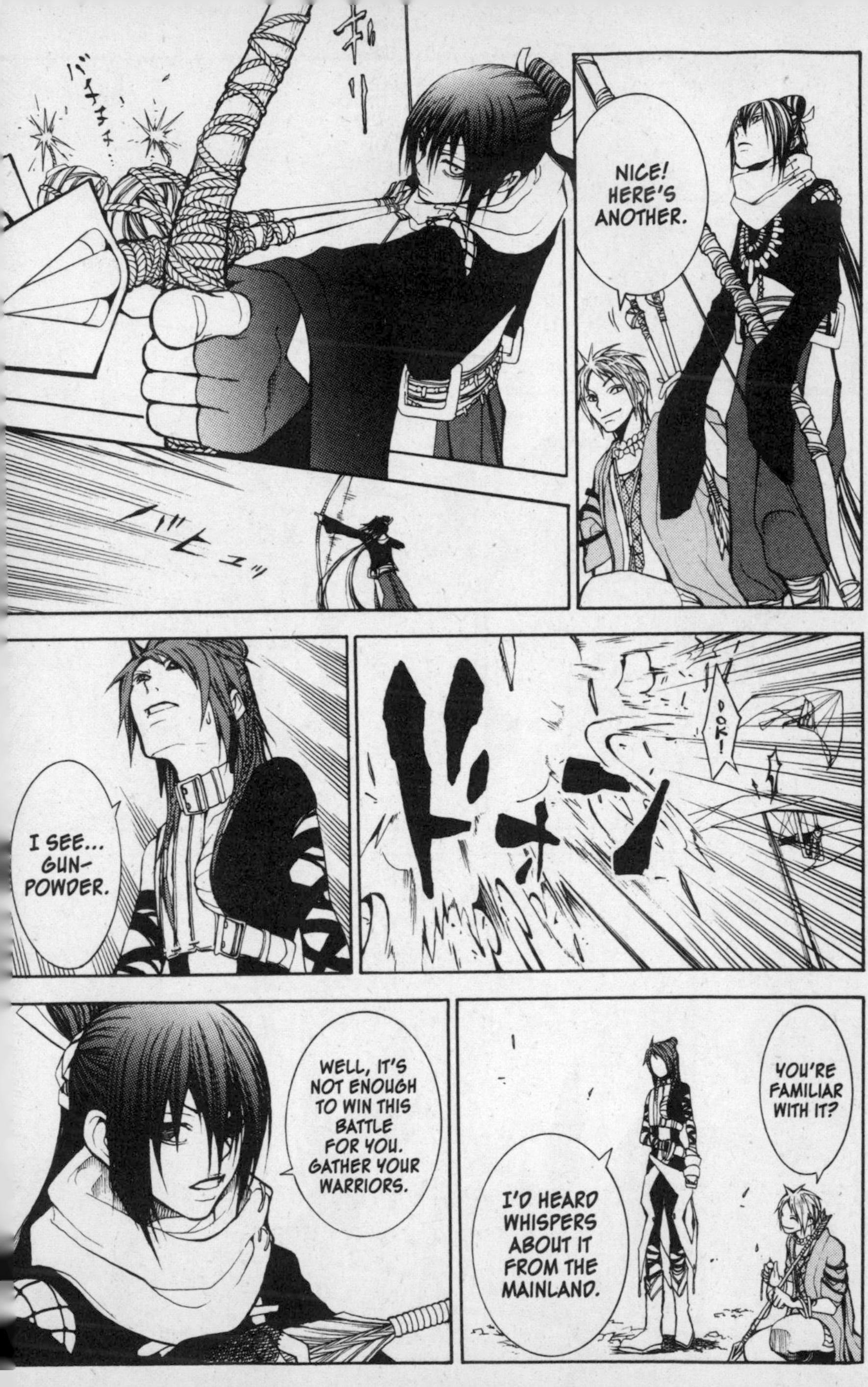
NICE! HERE'S ANOTHER.
DOK!
I SEE... GUN-POWDER.
YOU'RE FAMILIAR WITH IT?
I'D HEARD WHISPERS ABOUT IT FROM THE MAINLAND.
WELL, IT'S NOT ENOUGH TO WIN THIS BATTLE FOR YOU. GATHER YOUR WARRIORS.

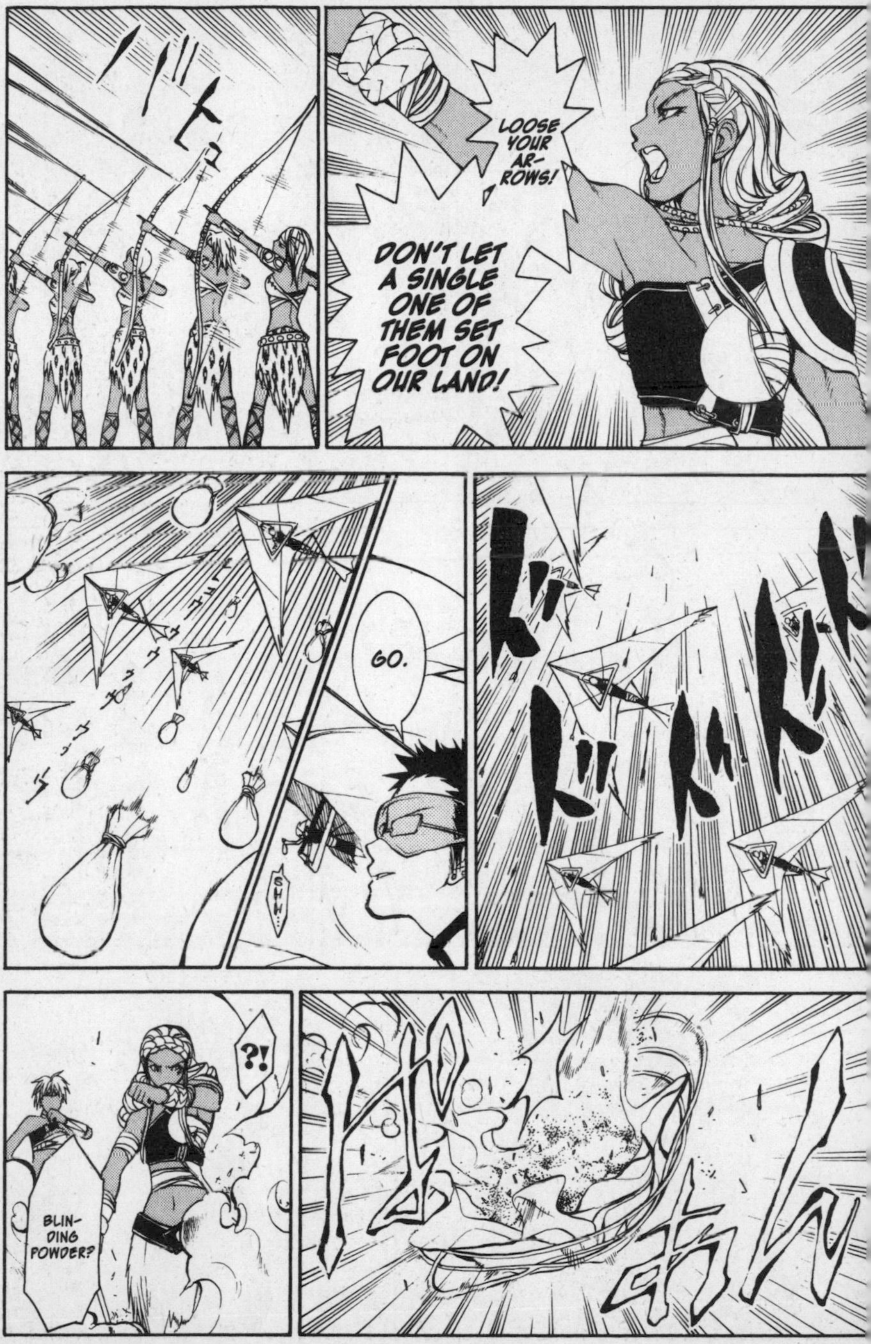
LOOSE YOUR AR-ROWS!
DON'T LET A SINGLE ONE OF THEM SET FOOT ON OUR LAND!
GO.
SHH...
?!
BLIN-DING POWDER?

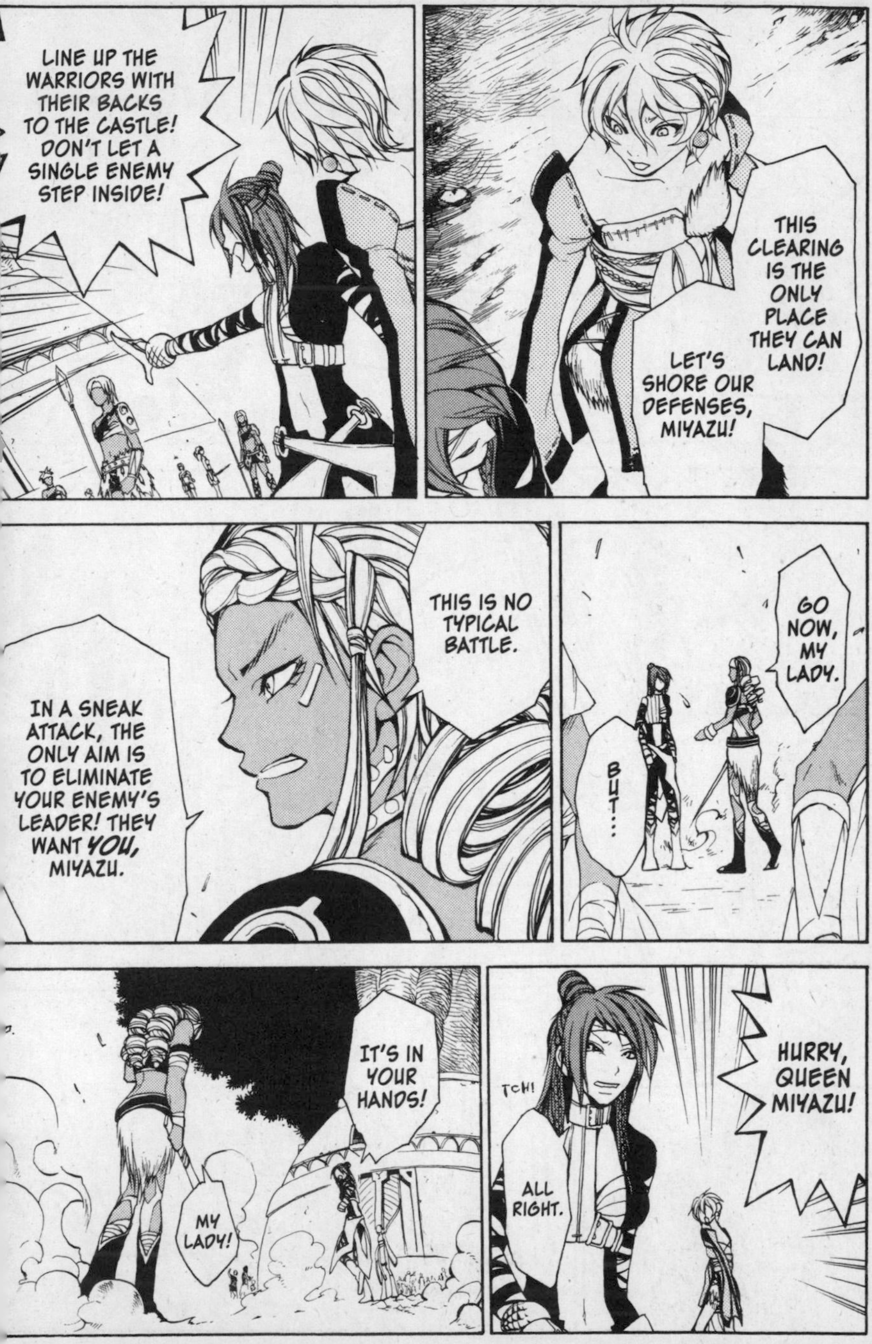
THIS CLEARING IS THE ONLY PLACE THEY CAN LAND!
LET'S SHORE OUR DEFENSES, MIYAZU!
LINE UP THE WARRIORS WITH THEIR BACKS TO THE CASTLE! DON'T LET A SINGLE ENEMY STEP INSIDE!
GO NOW, MY LADY.
BUT...
THIS IS NO TYPICAL BATTLE.
IN A SNEAK ATTACK, THE ONLY AIM IS TO ELIMINATE YOUR ENEMY'S LEADER! THEY WANT *YOU*, MIYAZU.
HURRY, QUEEN MIYAZU!
TCH!
ALL RIGHT.
IT'S IN YOUR HANDS!
MY LADY!

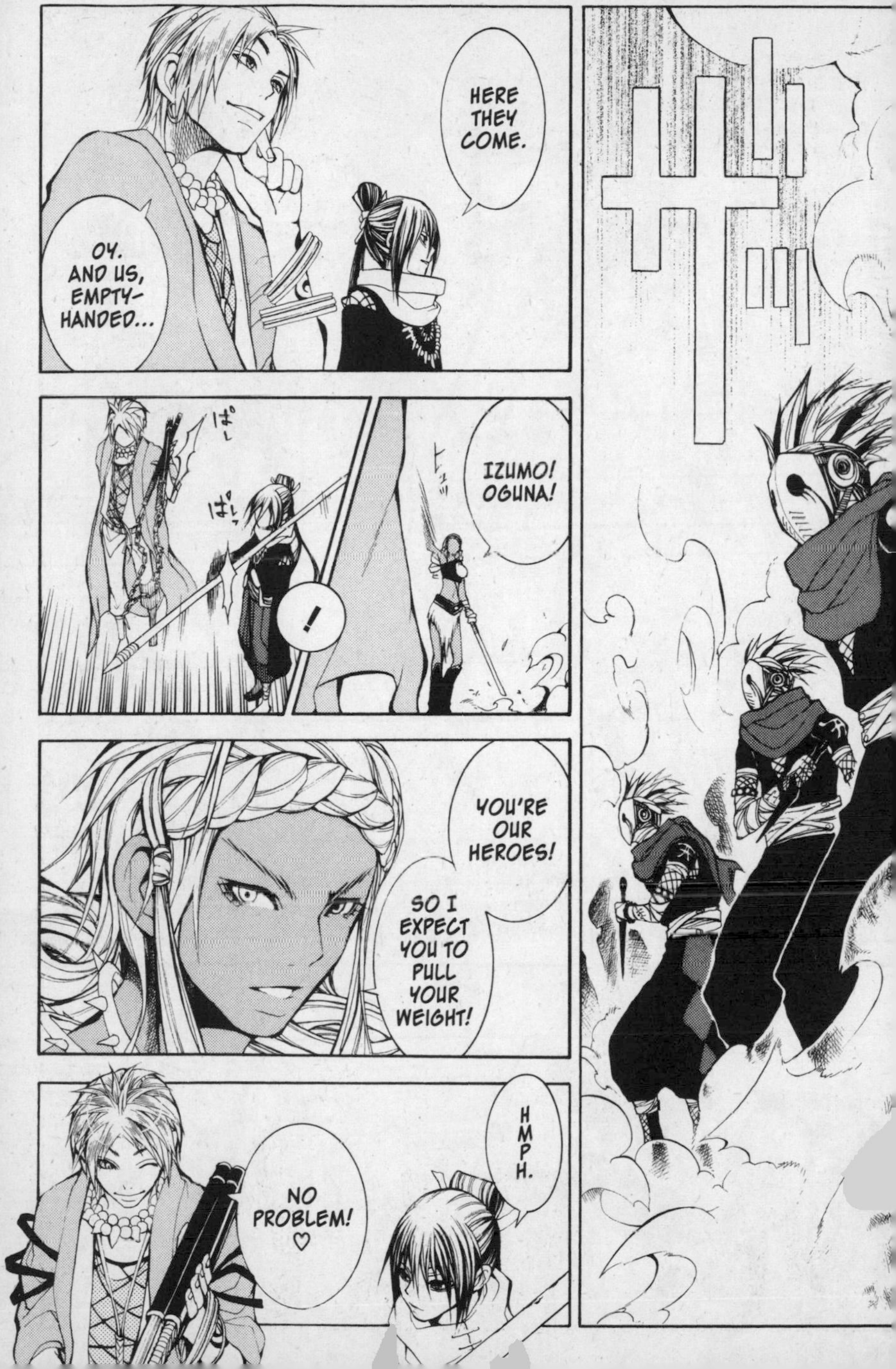
HERE THEY COME.
OY. AND US, EMPTY-HANDED...
IZUMO! OGUNA!
!
YOU'RE OUR HEROES!
SO I EXPECT YOU TO PULL YOUR WEIGHT!
HMPH.
NO PROBLEM! ♡

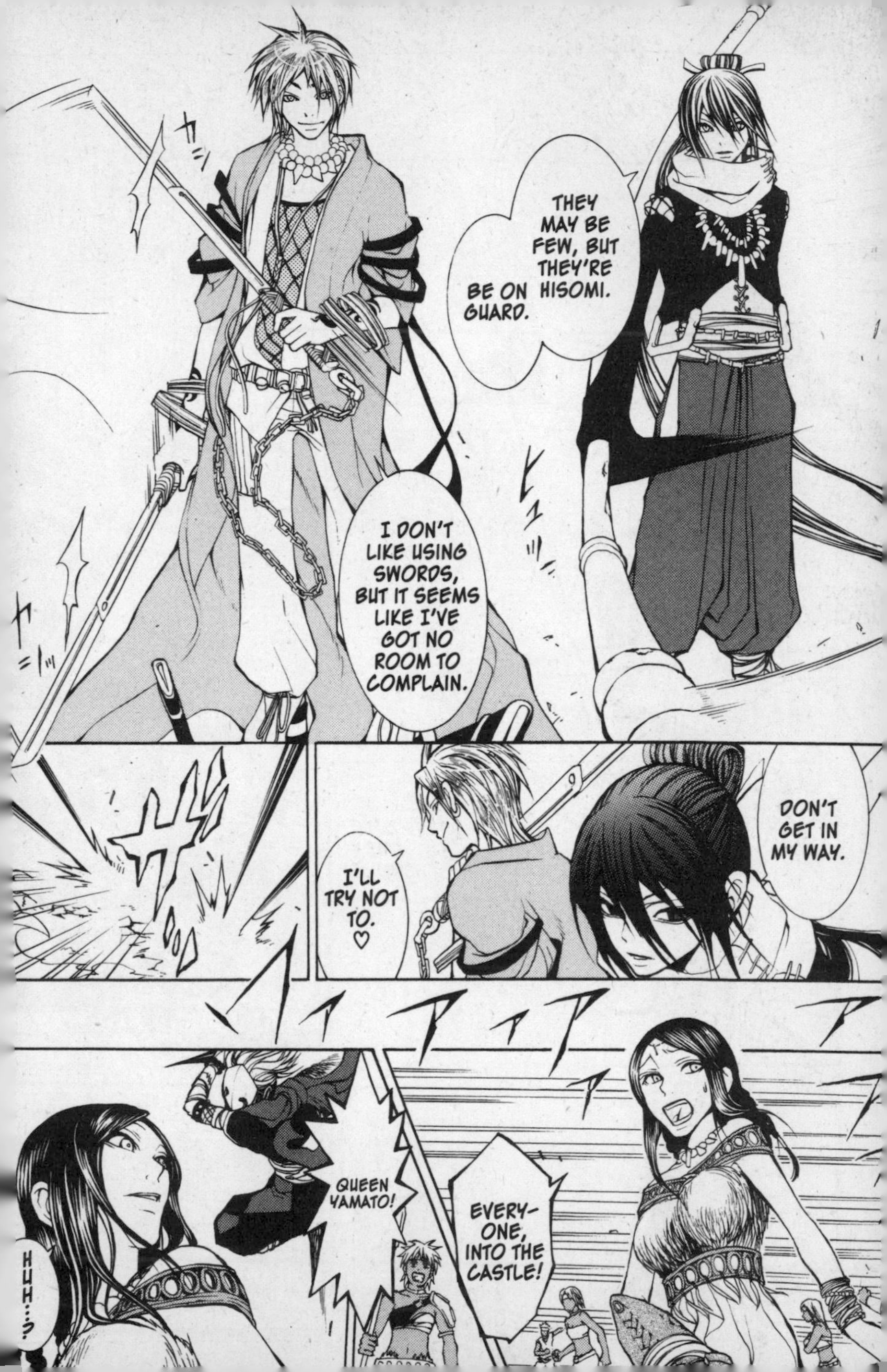
THEY MAY BE FEW, BUT THEY'RE HISOMI.
BE ON GUARD.
I DON'T LIKE USING SWORDS, BUT IT SEEMS LIKE I'VE GOT NO ROOM TO COMPLAIN.
DON'T GET IN MY WAY.
I'LL TRY NOT TO. ♡
EVERY-ONE, INTO THE CASTLE!
QUEEN YAMATO!
HUH...?

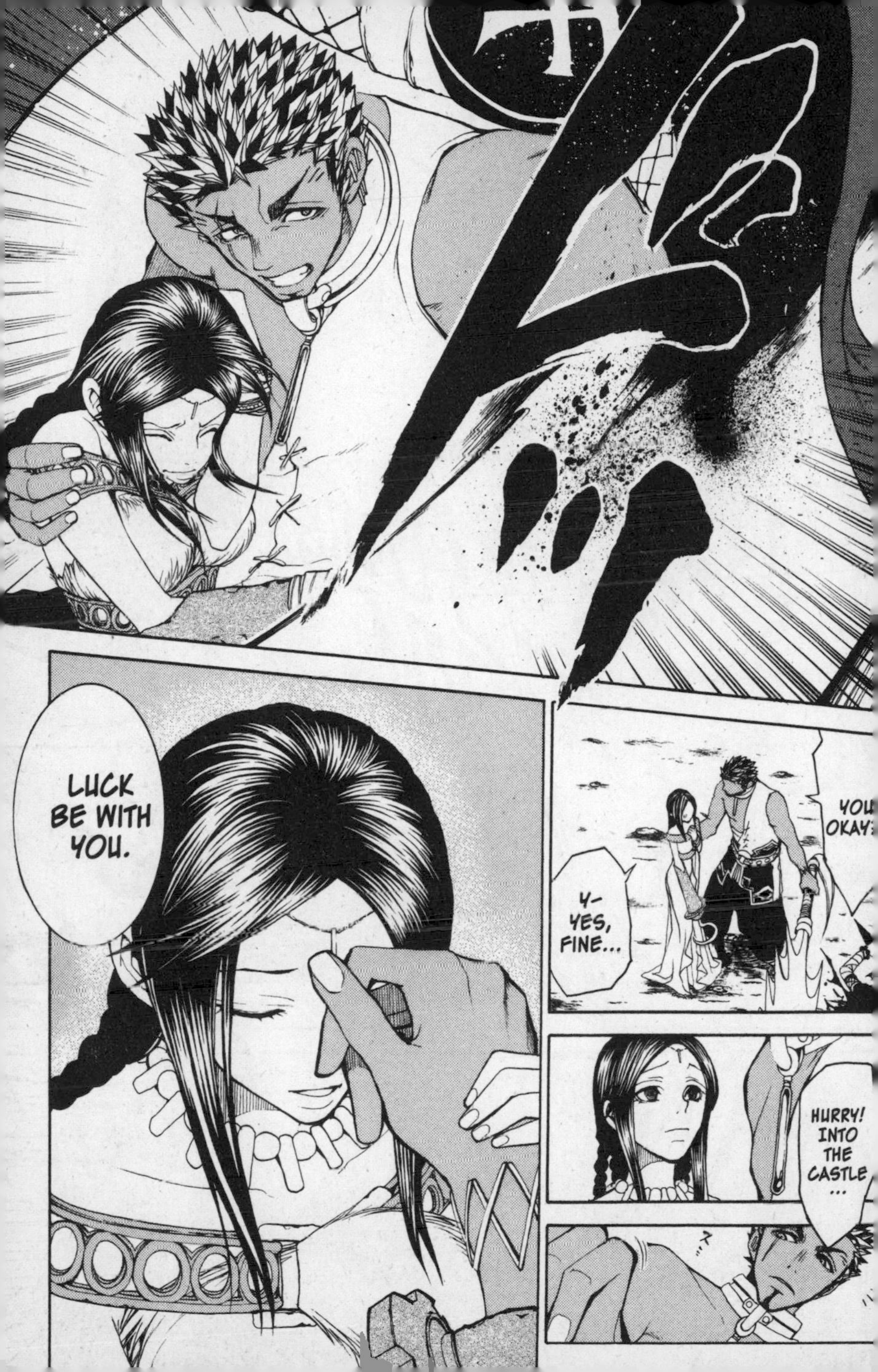
YOU OKAY?
Y-YES, FINE...
HURRY! INTO THE CASTLE...
LUCK BE WITH YOU.

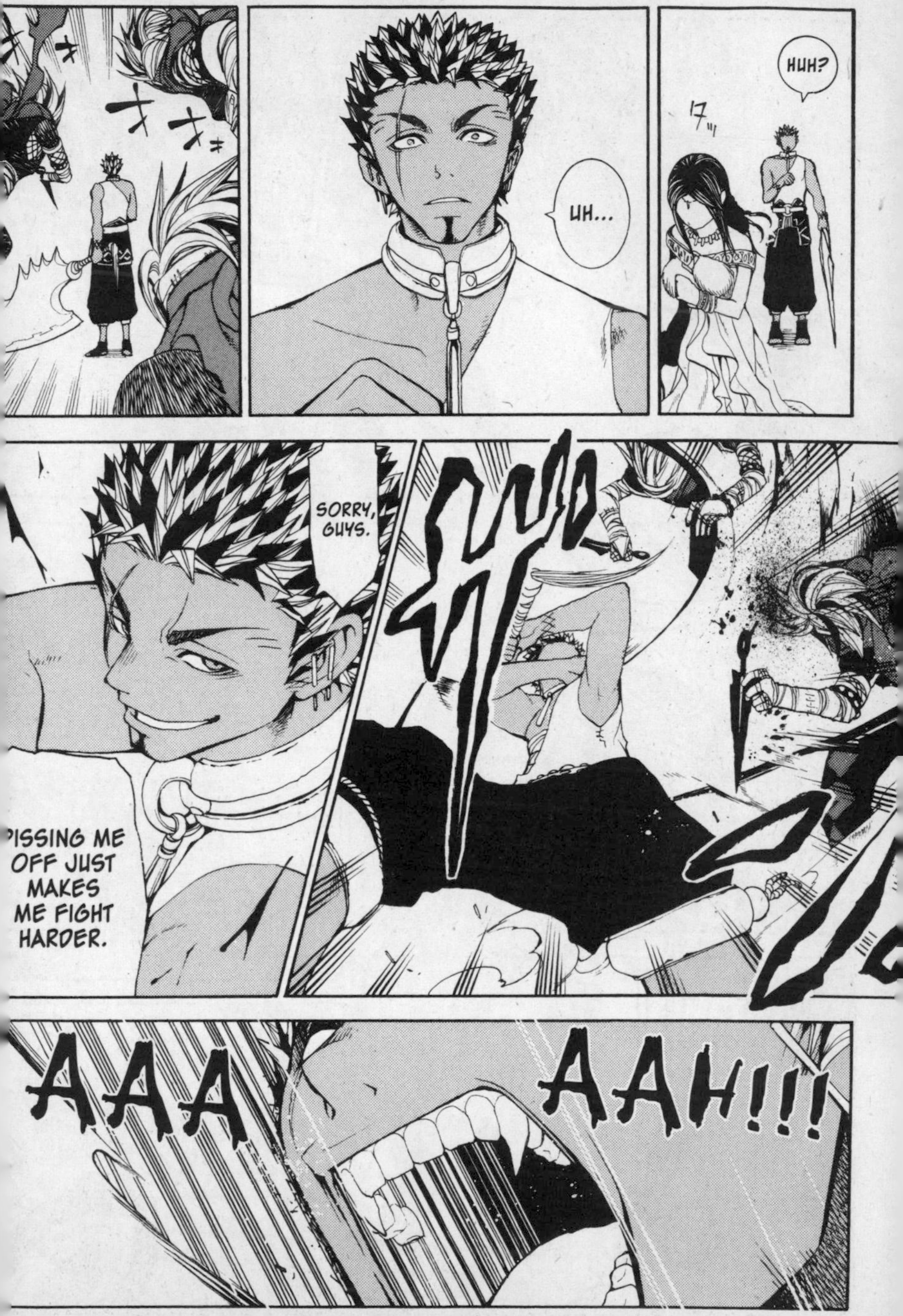
HUH?
UH...
SORRY, GUYS.
PISSING ME OFF JUST MAKES ME FIGHT HARDER.
AAA AAH!!!

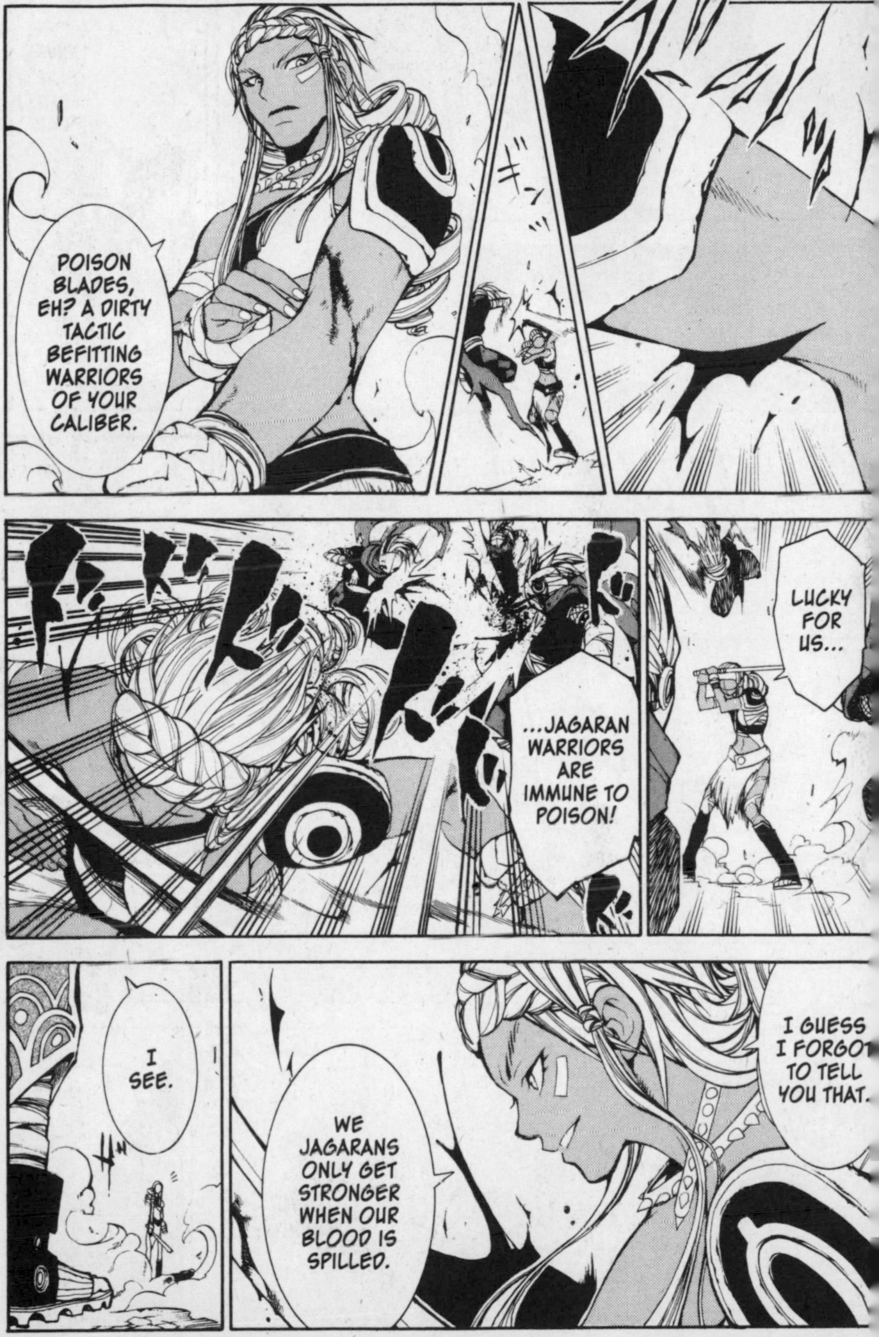
POISON BLADES, EH? A DIRTY TACTIC BEFITTING WARRIORS OF YOUR CALIBER.
LUCKY FOR US...
...JAGARAN WARRIORS ARE IMMUNE TO POISON!
I GUESS I FORGOT TO TELL YOU THAT.
WE JAGARANS ONLY GET STRONGER WHEN OUR BLOOD IS SPILLED.
I SEE.

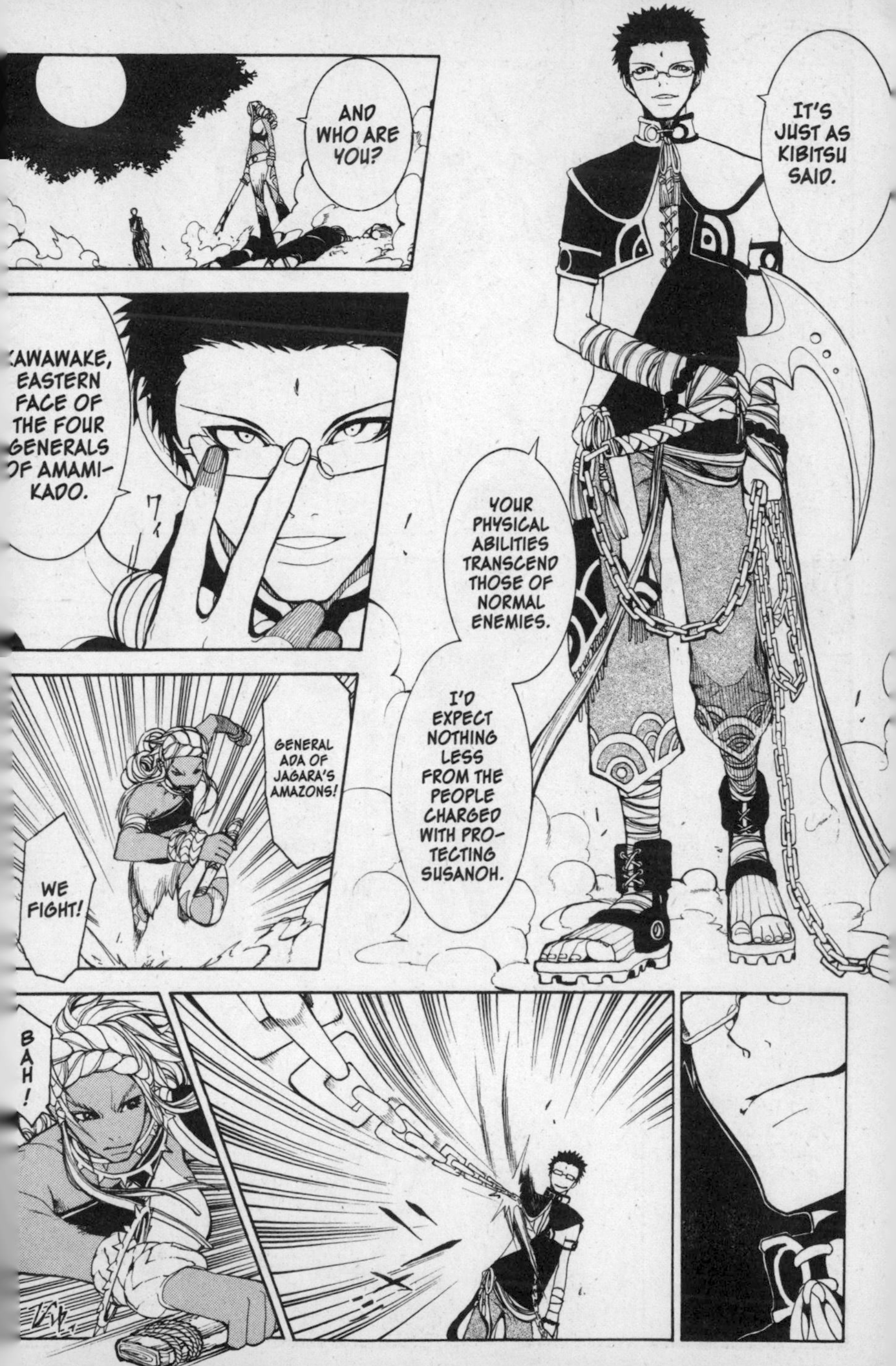
IT'S JUST AS KIBITSU SAID.
YOUR PHYSICAL ABILITIES TRANSCEND THOSE OF NORMAL ENEMIES.
I'D EXPECT NOTHING LESS FROM THE PEOPLE CHARGED WITH PRO-TECTING SUSANOH.
AND WHO ARE YOU?
KAWAWAKE, EASTERN FACE OF THE FOUR GENERALS OF AMAMI-KADO.
GENERAL ADA OF JAGARA'S AMAZONS!
WE FIGHT!
BAH!

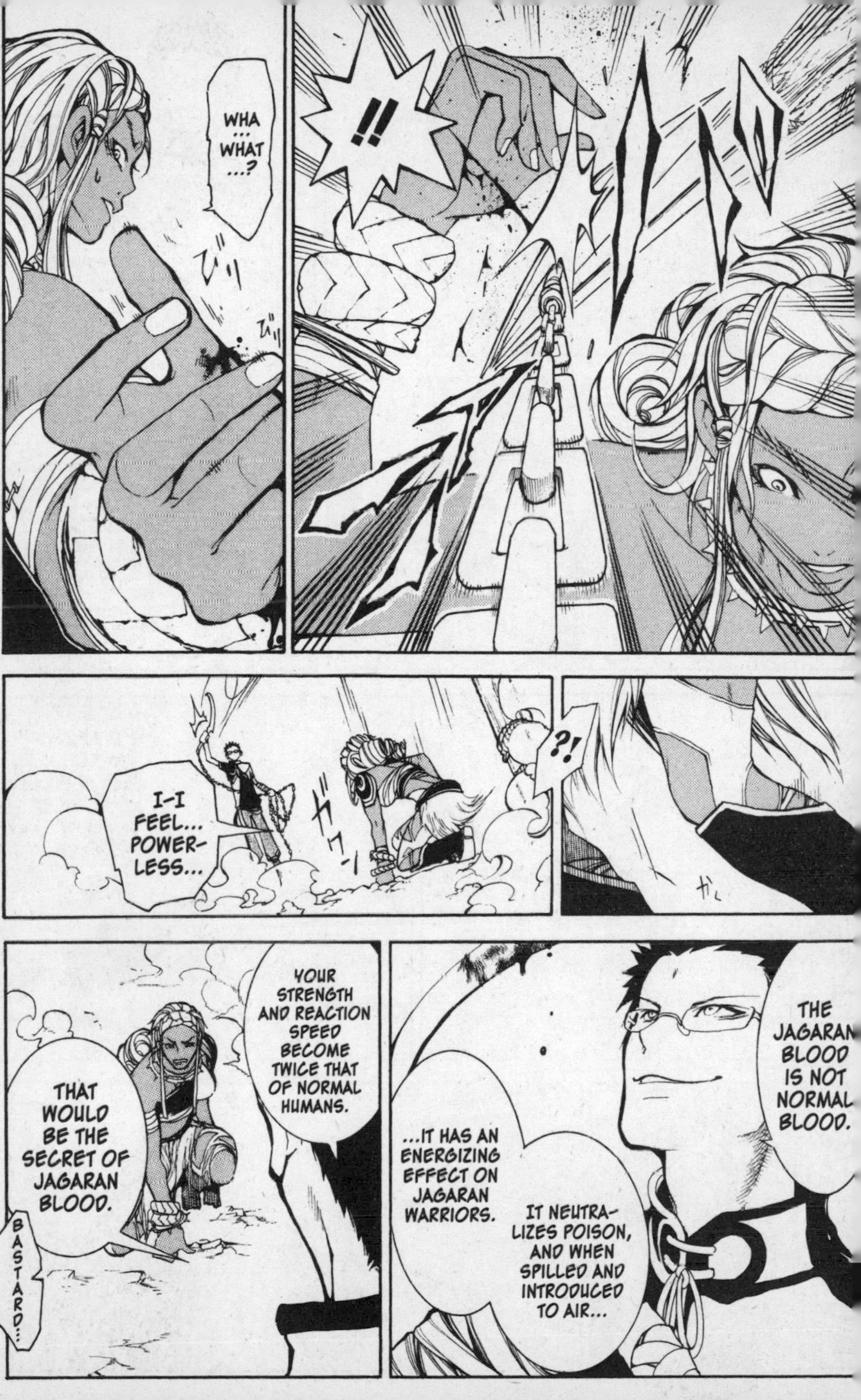
!!
WHA... WHAT...?
?!
I-I FEEL... POWER-LESS...
THE JAGARAN BLOOD IS NOT NORMAL BLOOD.
IT NEUTRA-LIZES POISON, AND WHEN SPILLED AND INTRODUCED TO AIR...
...IT HAS AN ENERGIZING EFFECT ON JAGARAN WARRIORS.
YOUR STRENGTH AND REACTION SPEED BECOME TWICE THAT OF NORMAL HUMANS.
THAT WOULD BE THE SECRET OF JAGARAN BLOOD.
BASTARD...

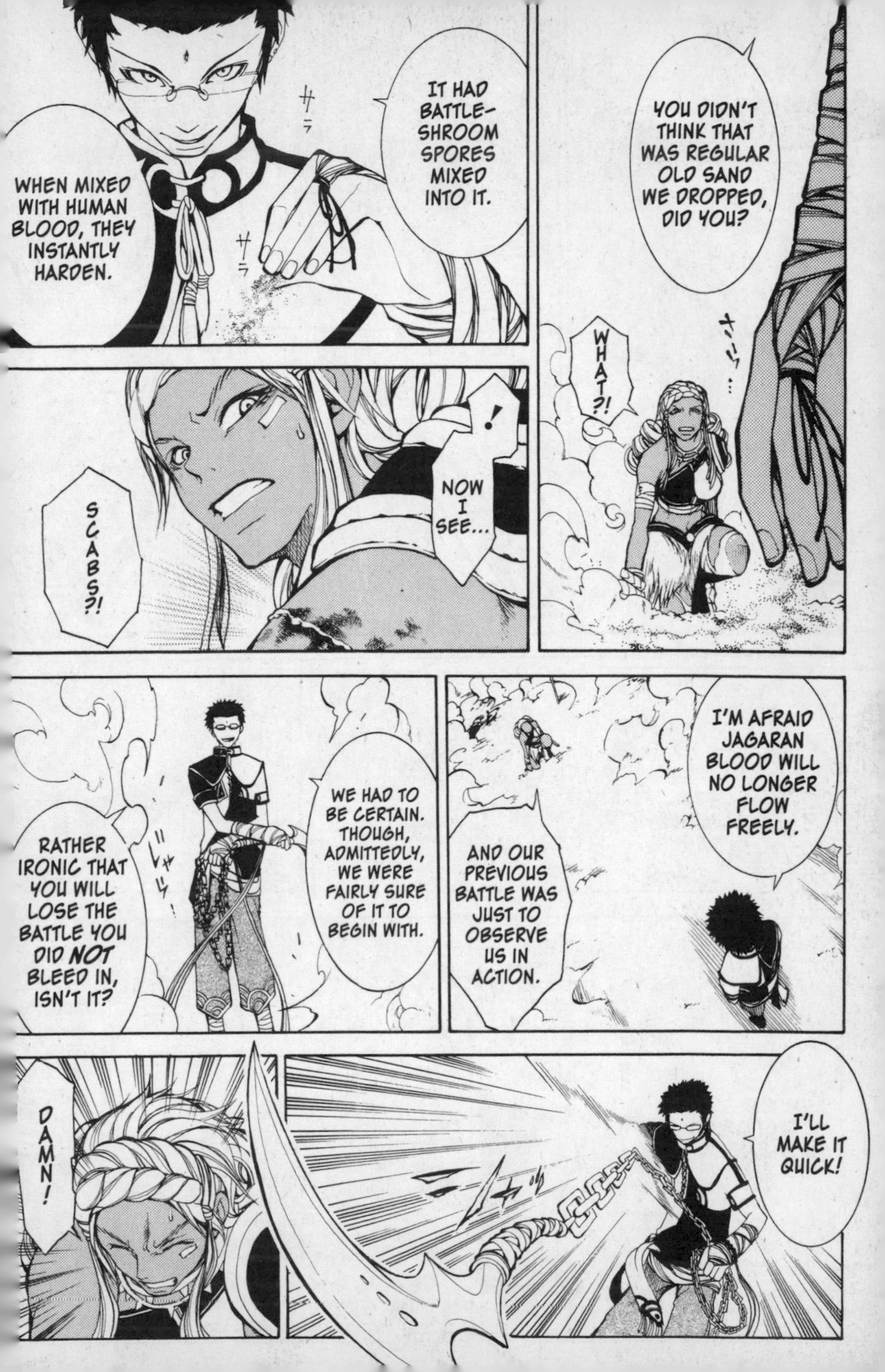

YOU DIDN'T THINK THAT WAS REGULAR OLD SAND WE DROPPED, DID YOU?
IT HAD BATTLE-SHROOM SPORES MIXED INTO IT.
WHEN MIXED WITH HUMAN BLOOD, THEY INSTANTLY HARDEN.
WHAT?!
!
NOW I SEE...
SCABS?!
I'M AFRAID JAGARAN BLOOD WILL NO LONGER FLOW FREELY.
AND OUR PREVIOUS BATTLE WAS JUST TO OBSERVE US IN ACTION.
WE HAD TO BE CERTAIN. THOUGH, ADMITTEDLY, WE WERE FAIRLY SURE OF IT TO BEGIN WITH.
RATHER IRONIC THAT YOU WILL LOSE THE BATTLE YOU DID NOT BLEED IN, ISN'T IT?
I'LL MAKE IT QUICK!
DAMN!

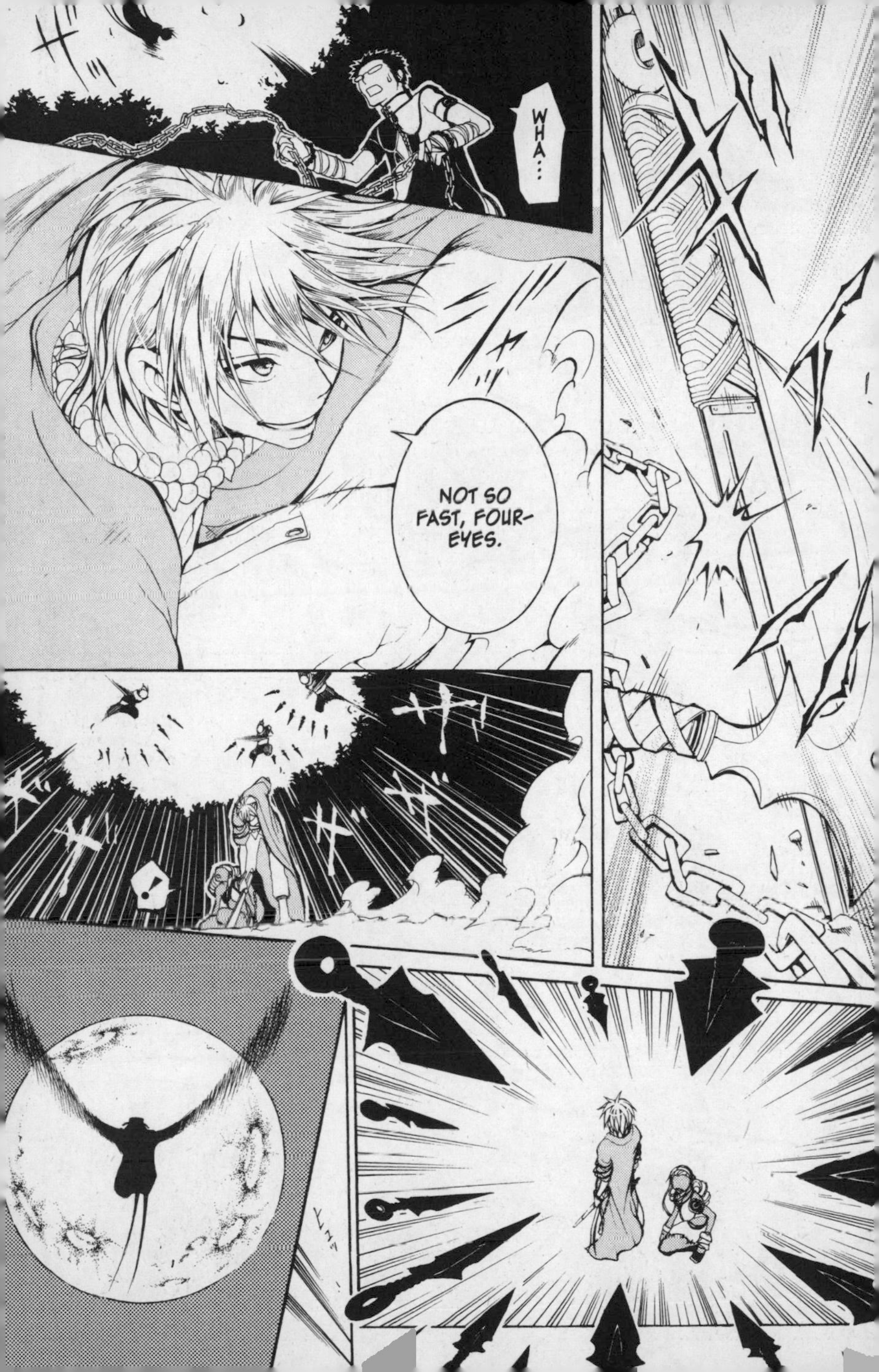
WHA...
NOT SO FAST, FOUR-EYES.
!

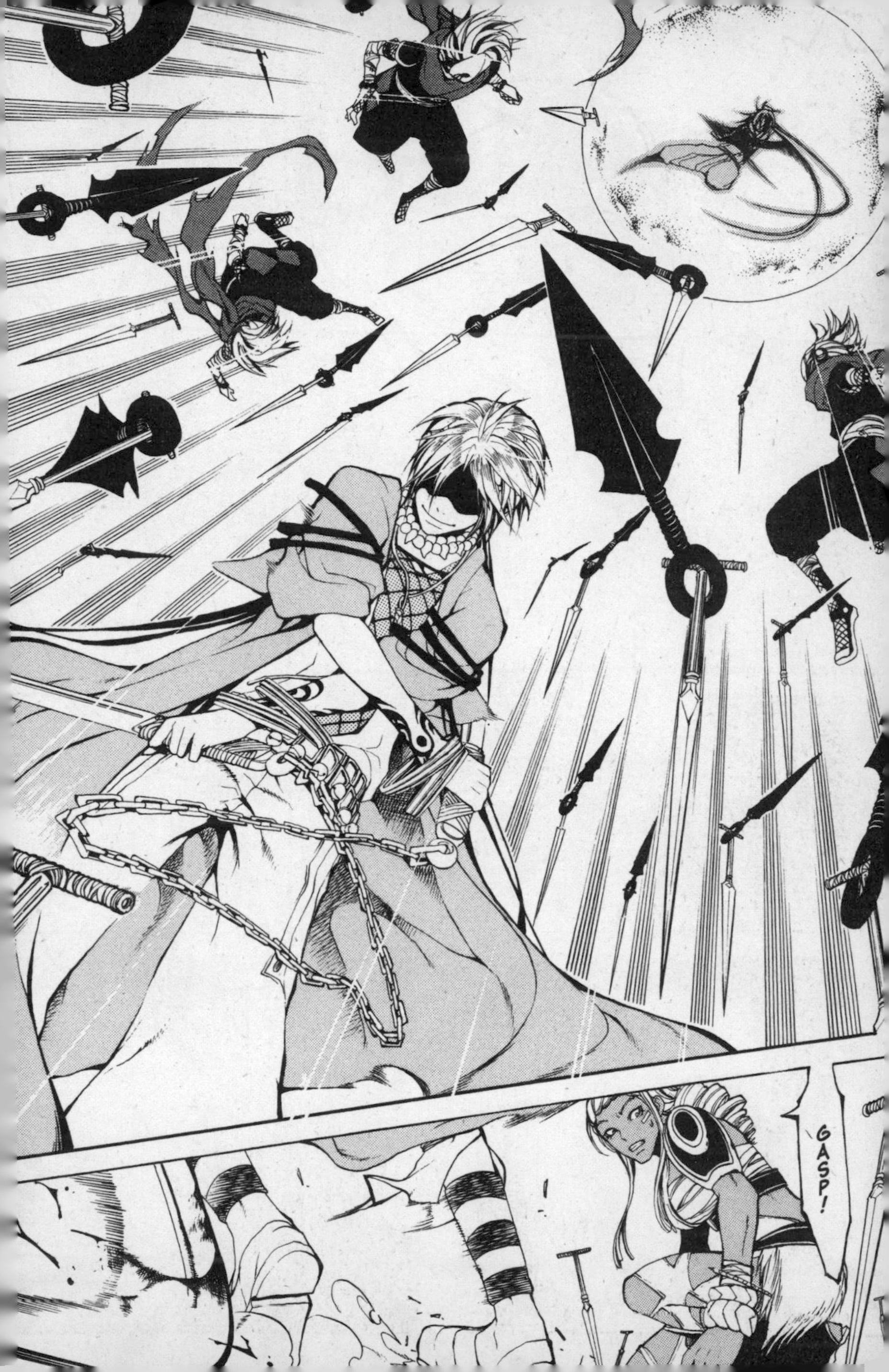
GASP!

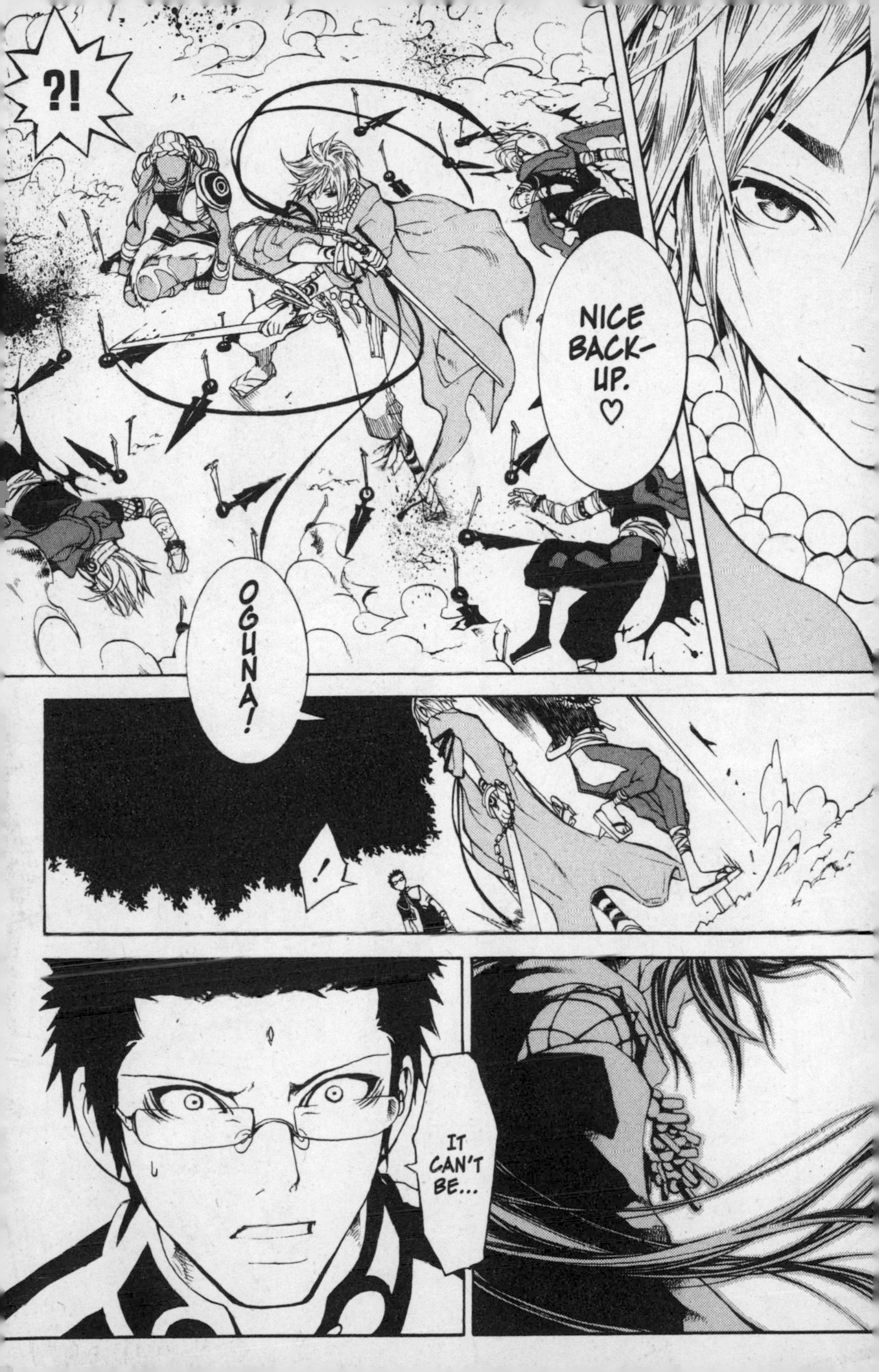
NICE BACK-UP. ♡
?!
OGUNA!
!
IT CAN'T BE...

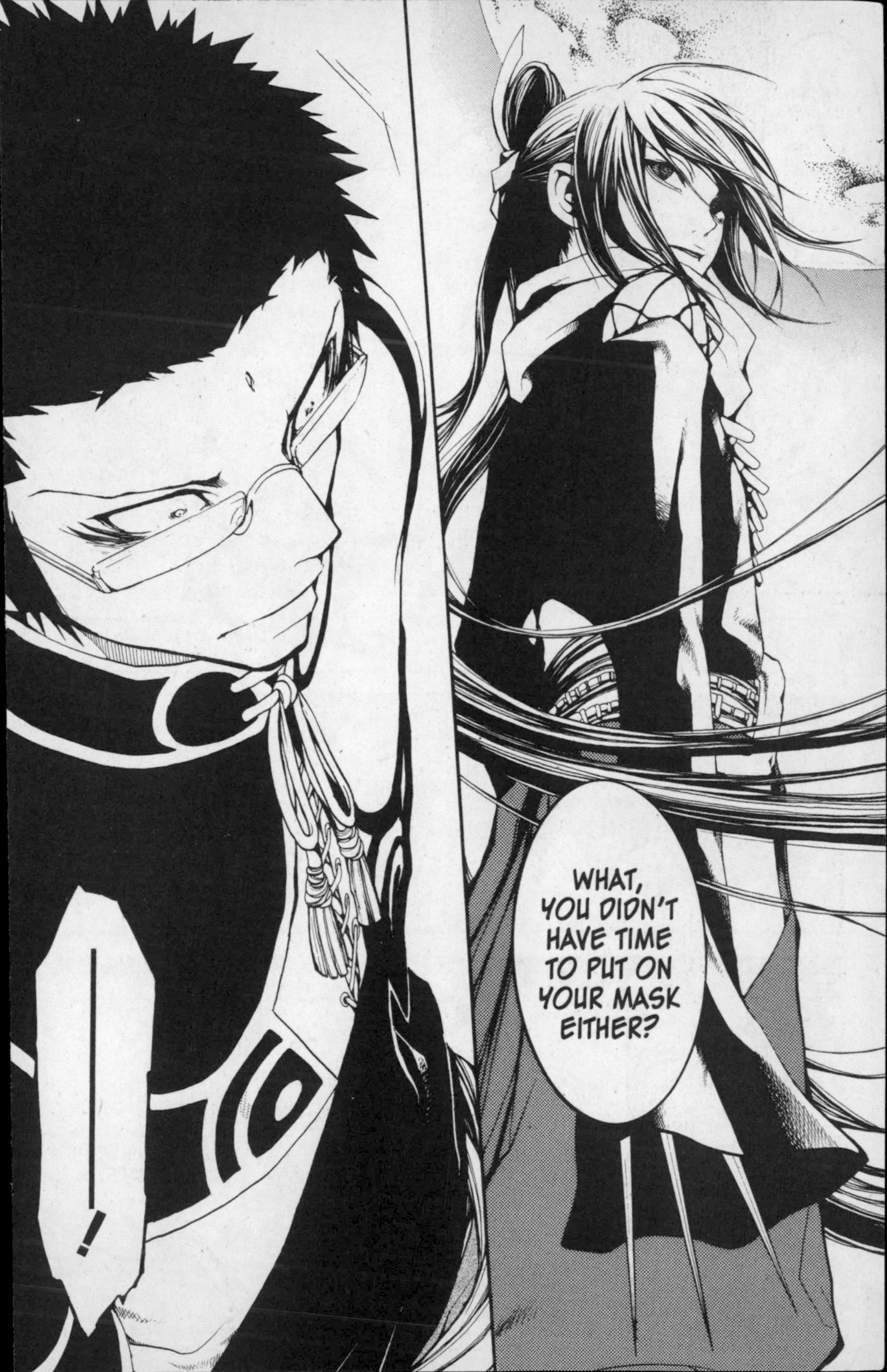
WHAT, YOU DIDN'T HAVE TIME TO PUT ON YOUR MASK EITHER?
—!

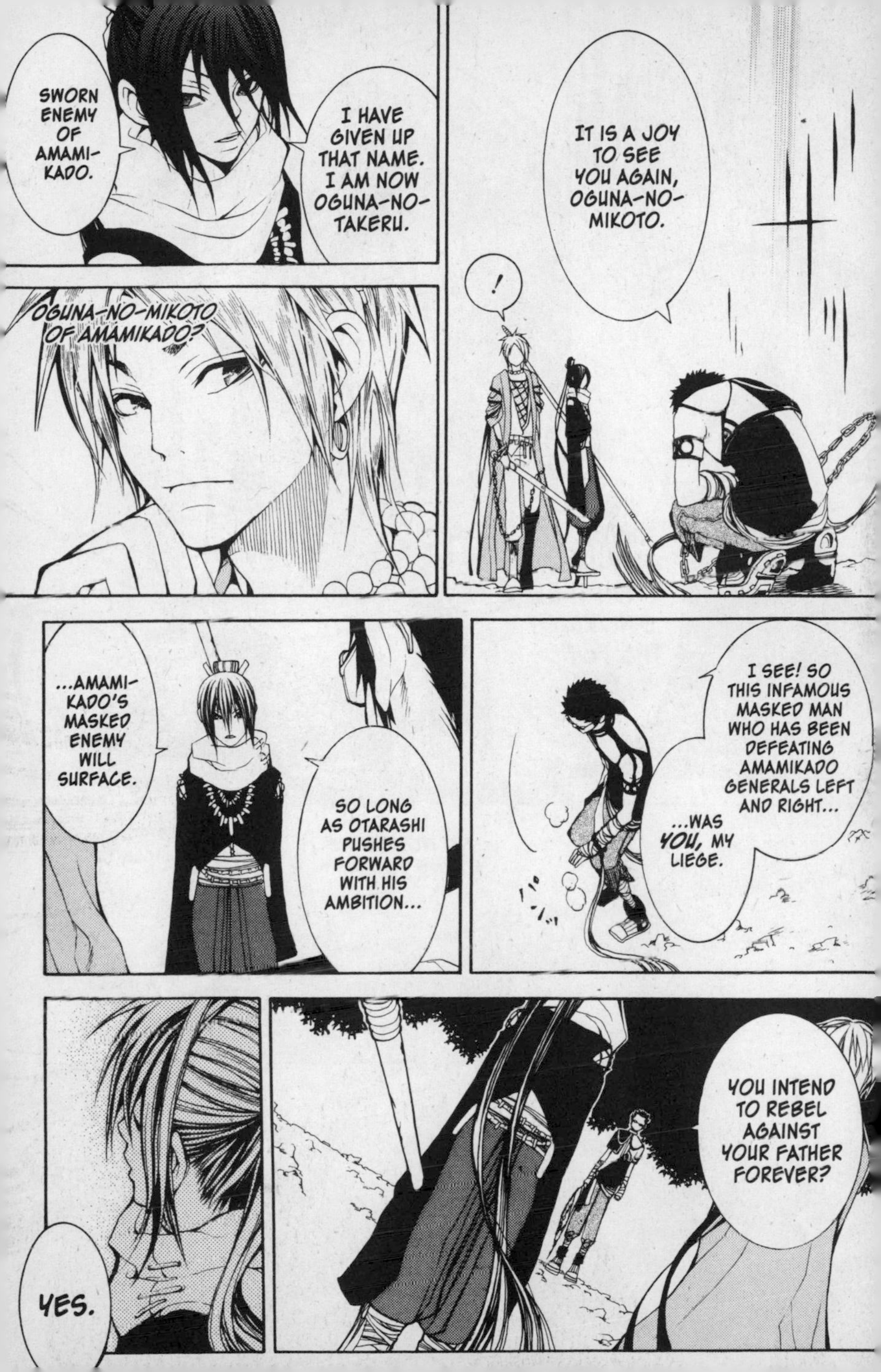
IT IS A JOY TO SEE YOU AGAIN, OGUNA-NO-MIKOTO.
!
I HAVE GIVEN UP THAT NAME. I AM NOW OGUNA-NO-TAKERU.
SWORN ENEMY OF AMAMI-KADO.
OGUNA-NO-MIKOTO OF AMAMIKADO?
I SEE! SO THIS INFAMOUS MASKED MAN WHO HAS BEEN DEFEATING AMAMIKADO GENERALS LEFT AND RIGHT...
...WAS YOU, MY LIEGE.
SO LONG AS OTARASHI PUSHES FORWARD WITH HIS AMBITION...
...AMAMI-KADO'S MASKED ENEMY WILL SURFACE.
YOU INTEND TO REBEL AGAINST YOUR FATHER FOREVER?
YES.

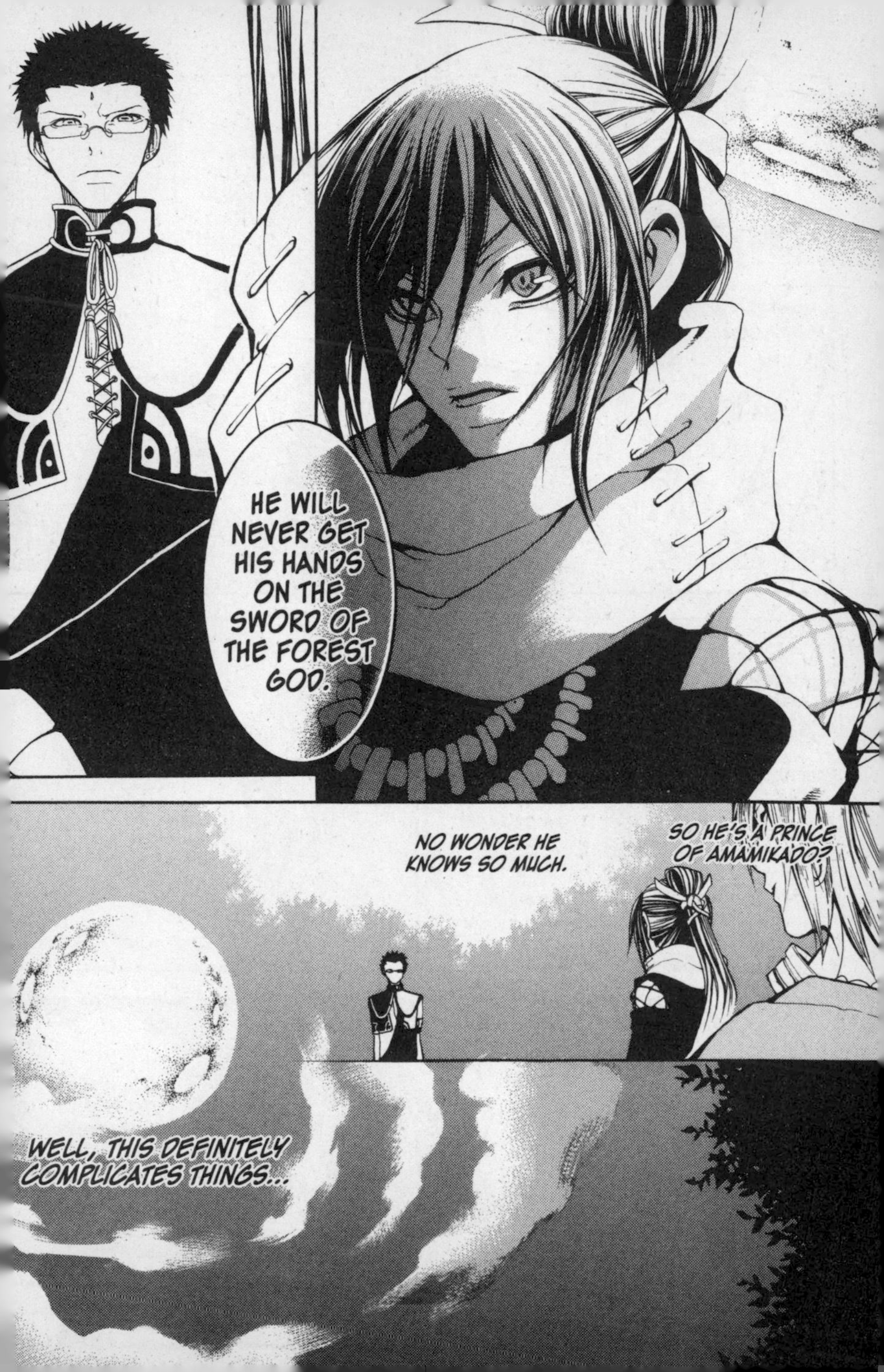
HE WILL NEVER GET HIS HANDS ON THE SWORD OF THE FOREST GOD.
SO HE'S A PRINCE OF AMAMIKADO?
NO WONDER HE KNOWS SO MUCH.
WELL, THIS DEFINITELY COMPLICATES THINGS...

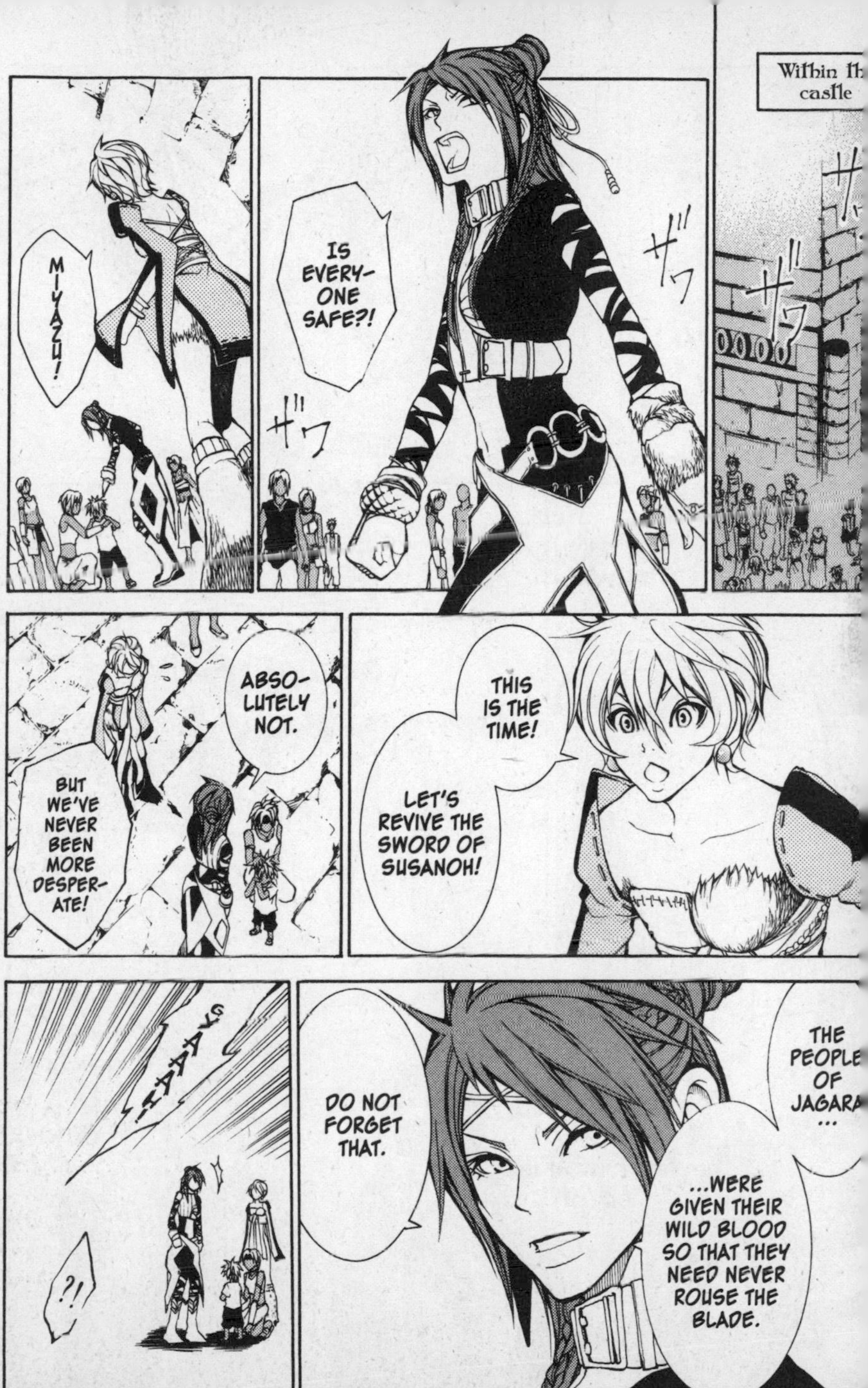
Within th
castle
ザワ
ザワ
ザワ
IS EVERY-ONE SAFE?!
ザワ
MIYAZU!
THIS IS THE TIME!
LET'S REVIVE THE SWORD OF SUSANOH!
ABSO-LUTELY NOT.
BUT WE'VE NEVER BEEN MORE DESPER-ATE!
THE PEOPLE OF JAGARA...
...WERE GIVEN THEIR WILD BLOOD SO THAT THEY NEED NEVER ROUSE THE BLADE.
DO NOT FORGET THAT.
GYAAAH!
?!

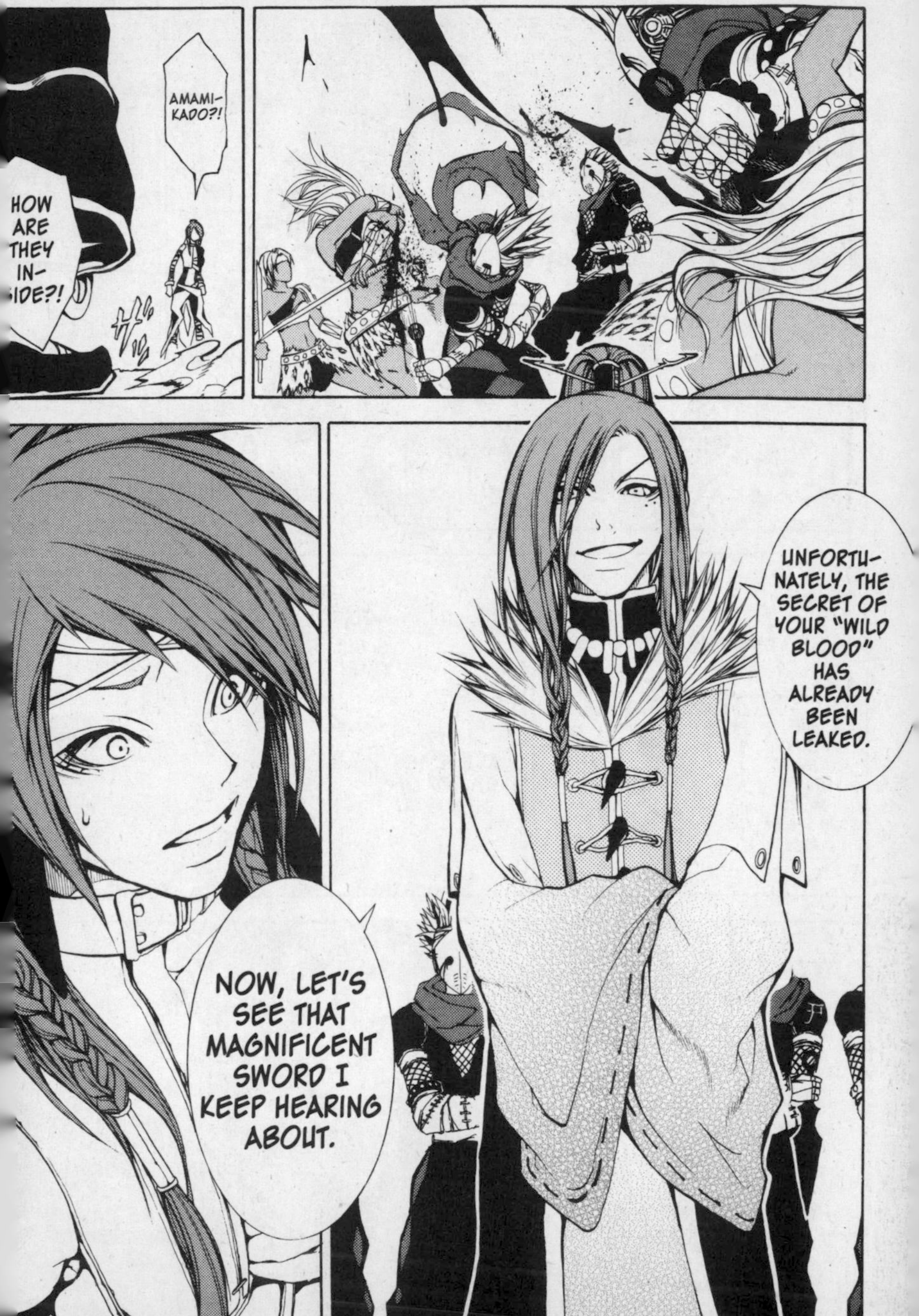
AMAMI-KADO?!
HOW ARE THEY IN-SIDE?!
UNFORTU-NATELY, THE SECRET OF YOUR "WILD BLOOD" HAS ALREADY BEEN LEAKED.
NOW, LET'S SEE THAT MAGNIFICENT SWORD I KEEP HEARING ABOUT.

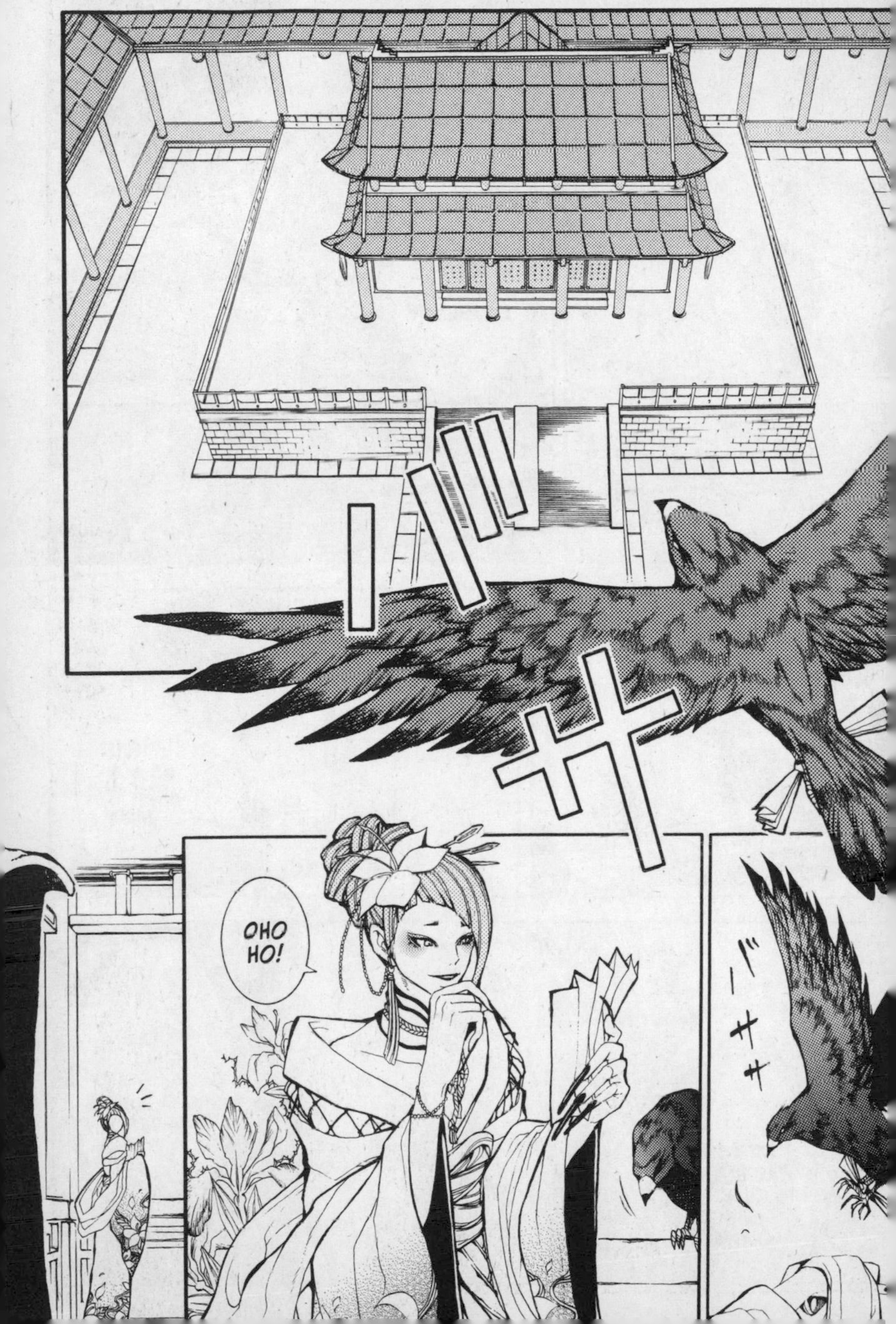
OHO
HO!

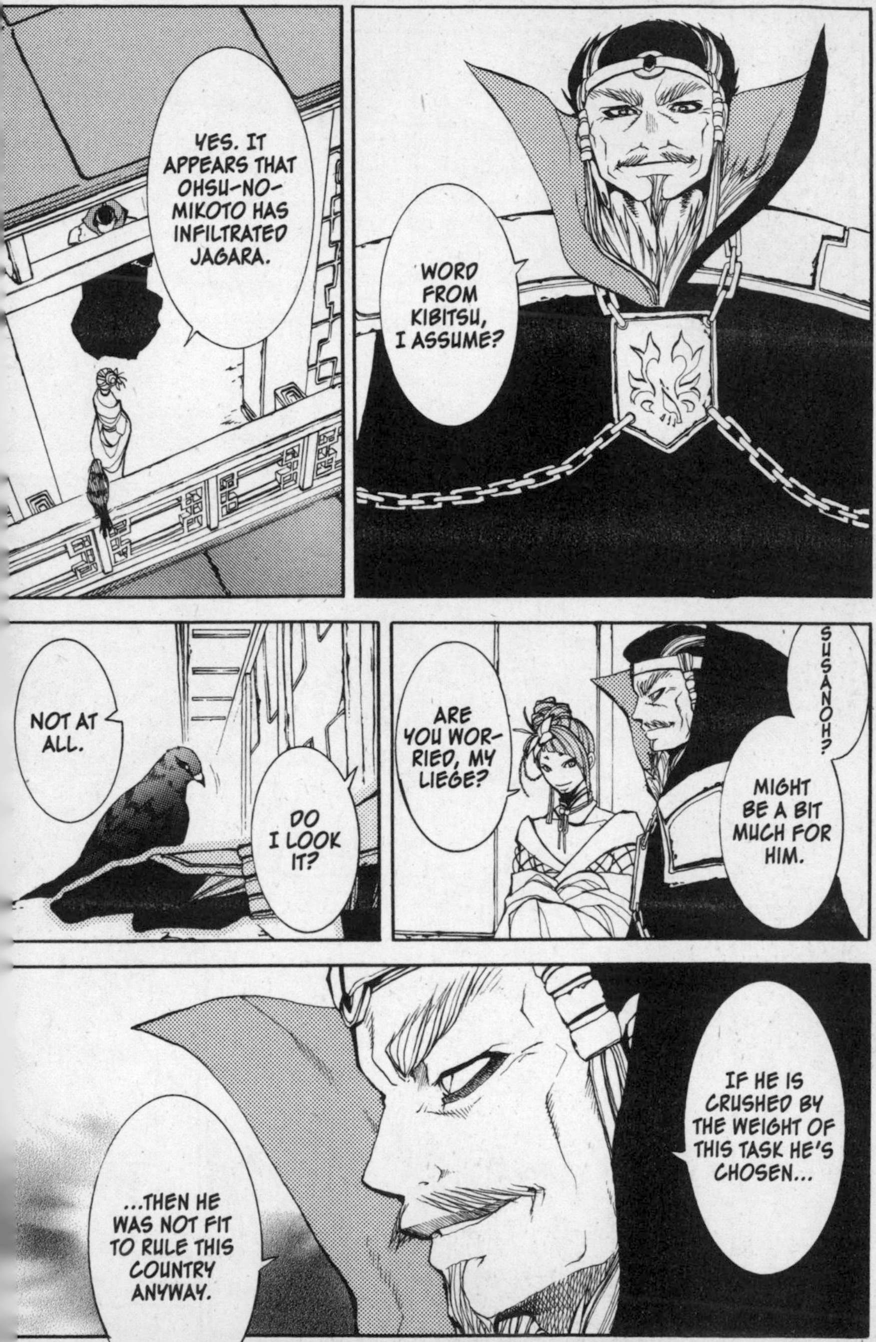
WORD FROM KIBITSU, I ASSUME?
YES. IT APPEARS THAT OHSU-NO-MIKOTO HAS INFILTRATED JAGARA.
SUSANOH?
MIGHT BE A BIT MUCH FOR HIM.
ARE YOU WORRIED, MY LIEGE?
DO I LOOK IT?
NOT AT ALL.
IF HE IS CRUSHED BY THE WEIGHT OF THIS TASK HE'S CHOSEN...
...THEN HE WAS NOT FIT TO RULE THIS COUNTRY ANYWAY.

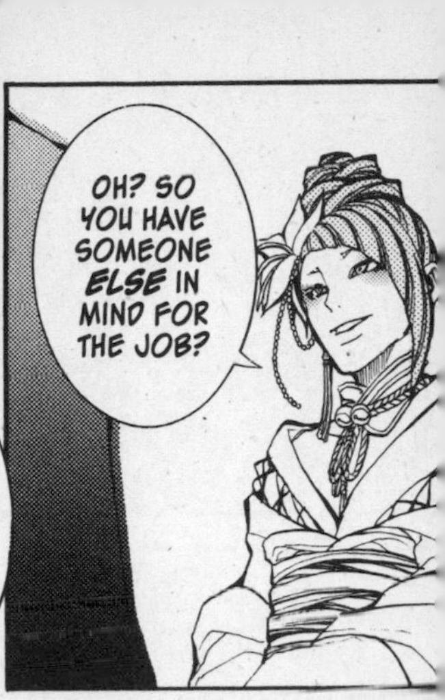
OH? SO YOU HAVE SOMEONE ELSE IN MIND FOR THE JOB?
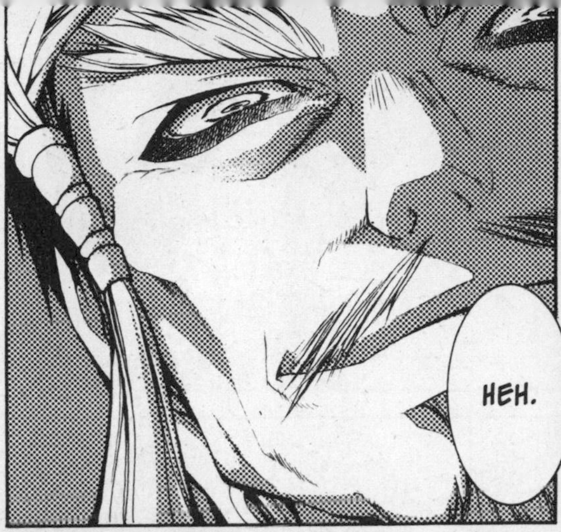
HEH.
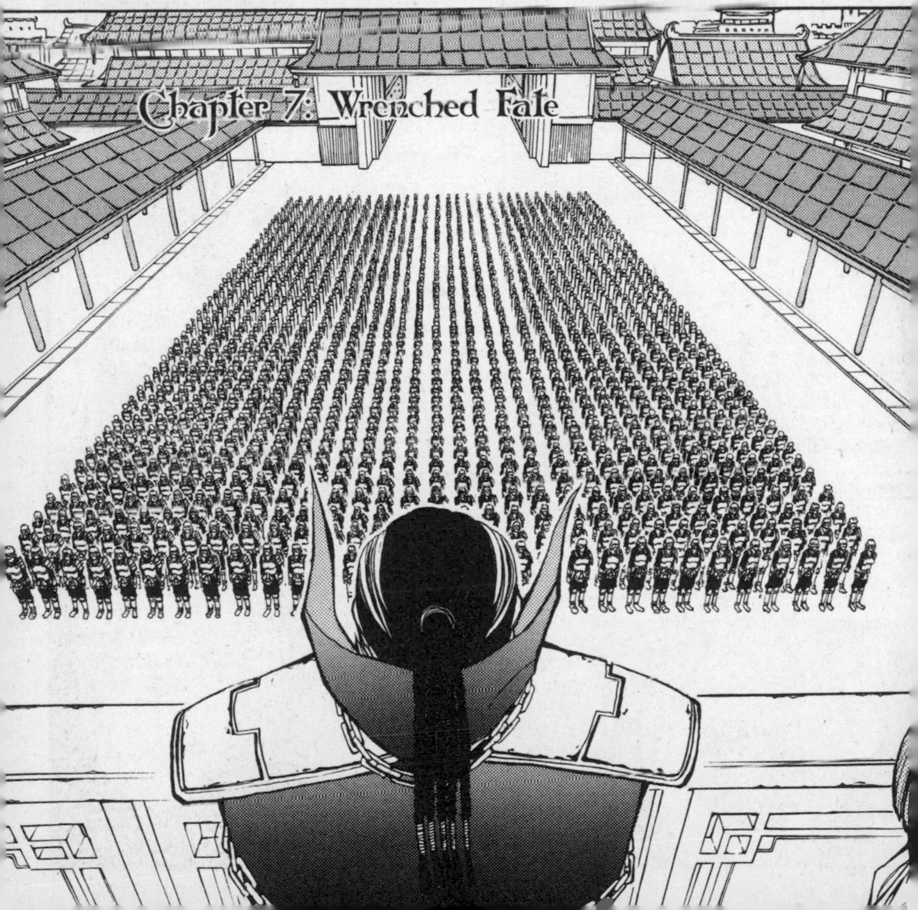
Chapter 7: Wrenched Fate

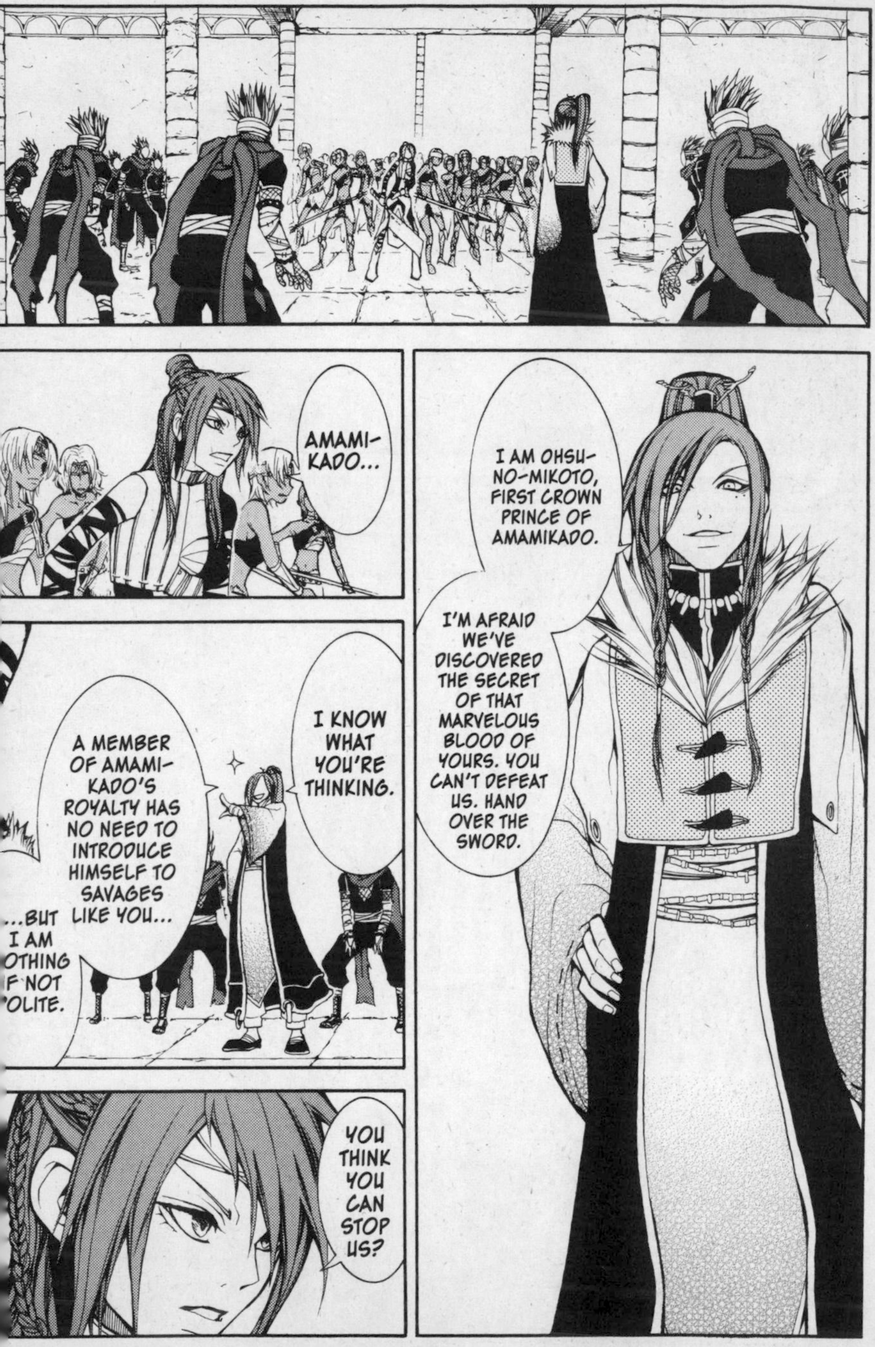

I AM OHSU-NO-MIKOTO, FIRST CROWN PRINCE OF AMAMIKADO.
I'M AFRAID WE'VE DISCOVERED THE SECRET OF THAT MARVELOUS BLOOD OF YOURS. YOU CAN'T DEFEAT US. HAND OVER THE SWORD.
AMAMI-KADO...
I KNOW WHAT YOU'RE THINKING.
A MEMBER OF AMAMI-KADO'S ROYALTY HAS NO NEED TO INTRODUCE HIMSELF TO SAVAGES LIKE YOU...
...BUT I AM OTHING F NOT OLITE.
YOU THINK YOU CAN STOP US?

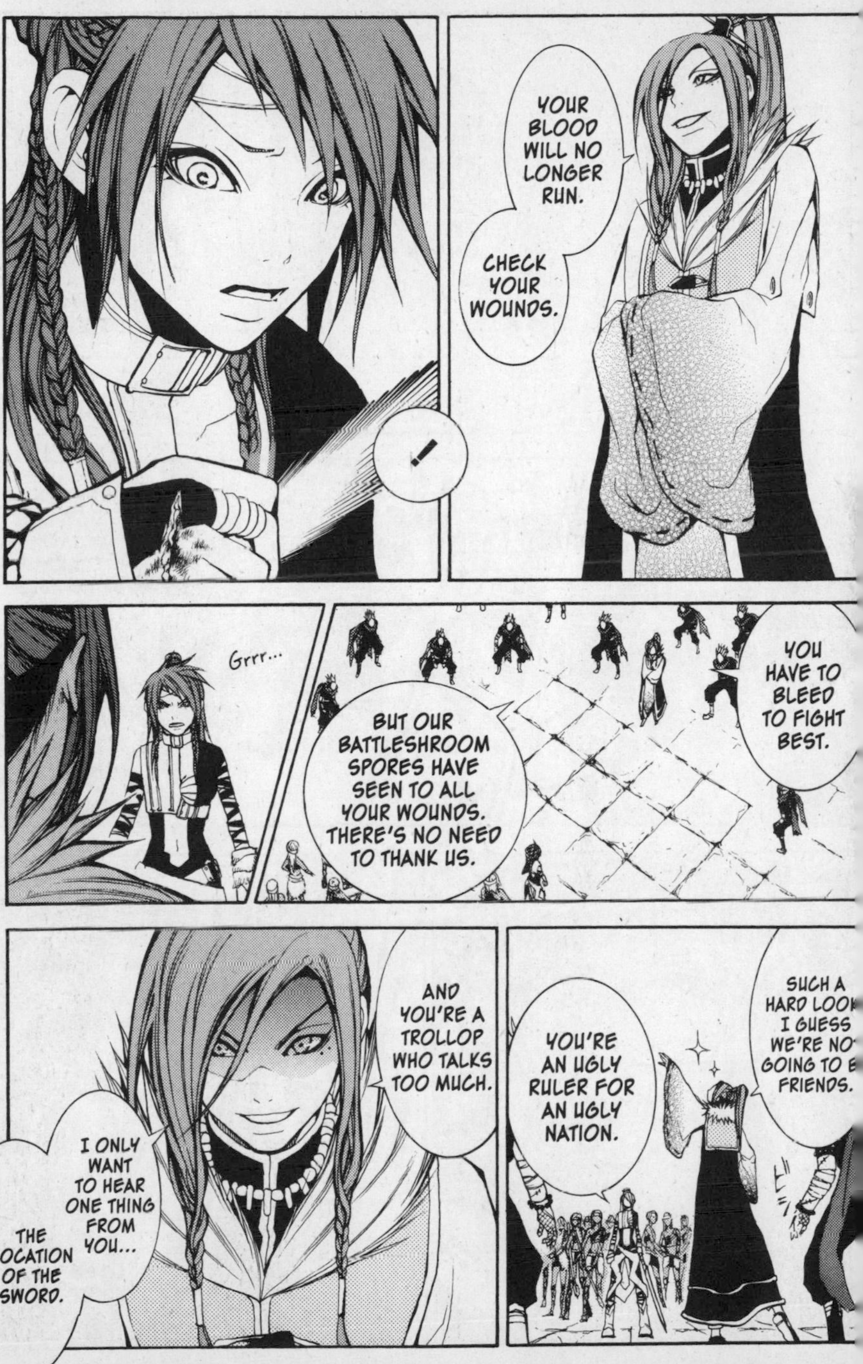
YOUR BLOOD WILL NO LONGER RUN.
CHECK YOUR WOUNDS.
!
YOU HAVE TO BLEED TO FIGHT BEST.
BUT OUR BATTLESHROOM SPORES HAVE SEEN TO ALL YOUR WOUNDS. THERE'S NO NEED TO THANK US.
Grrr...
SUCH A HARD LOOK I GUESS WE'RE NO GOING TO B FRIENDS.
YOU'RE AN UGLY RULER FOR AN UGLY NATION.
AND YOU'RE A TROLLOP WHO TALKS TOO MUCH.
I ONLY WANT TO HEAR ONE THING FROM YOU...
THE LOCATION OF THE SWORD.

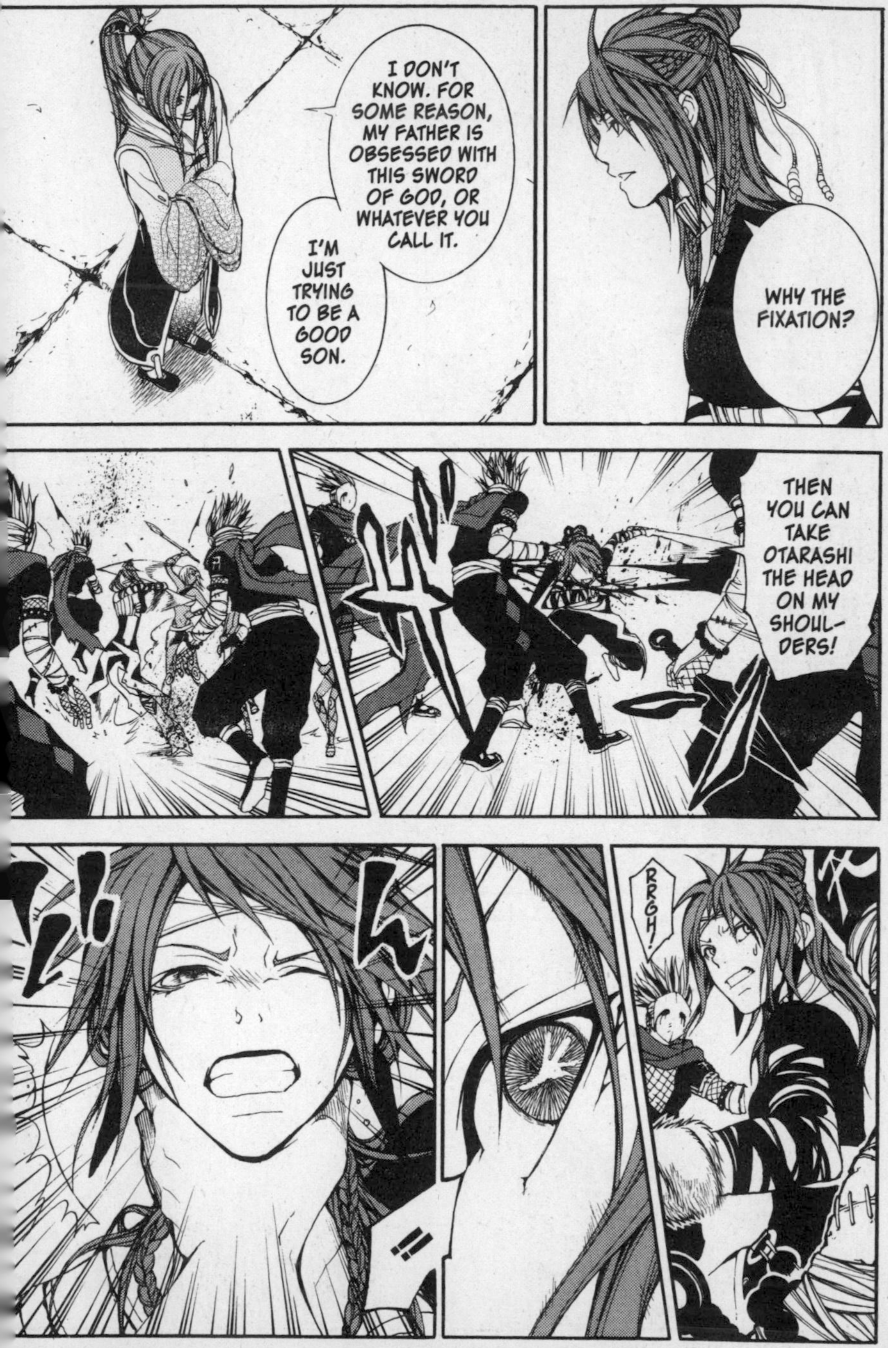
WHY THE FIXATION?
I DON'T KNOW. FOR SOME REASON, MY FATHER IS OBSESSED WITH THIS SWORD OF GOD, OR WHATEVER YOU CALL IT.
I'M JUST TRYING TO BE A GOOD SON.
THEN YOU CAN TAKE OTARASHI THE HEAD ON MY SHOULDERS!
RRGH!

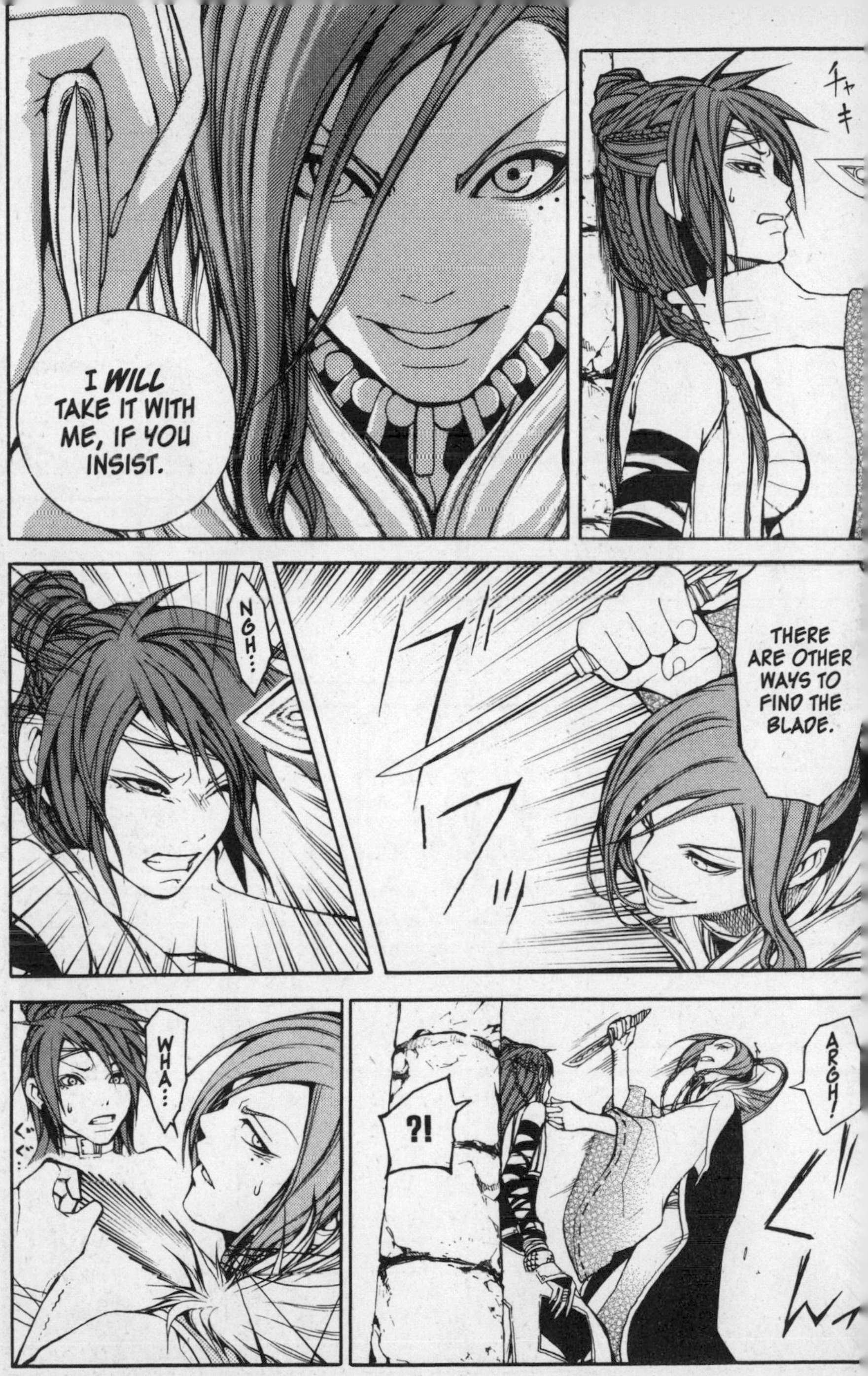

チャキ
I WILL TAKE IT WITH ME, IF YOU INSIST.
THERE ARE OTHER WAYS TO FIND THE BLADE.
NGH...
ARGH!
?!
WHA...

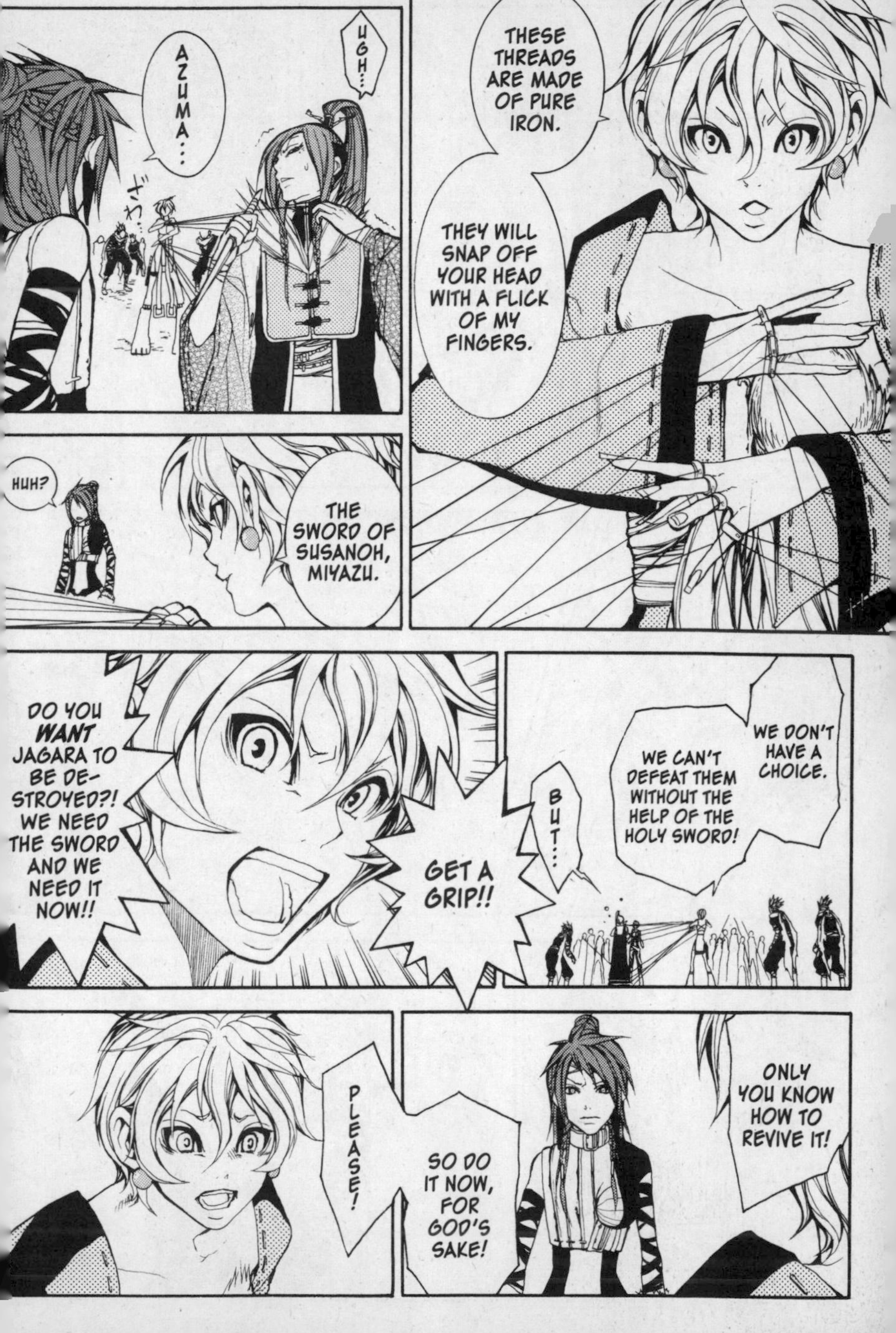
THESE THREADS ARE MADE OF PURE IRON.
THEY WILL SNAP OFF YOUR HEAD WITH A FLICK OF MY FINGERS.
UGH...
AZUMA...
ざわ…
THE SWORD OF SUSANOH, MIYAZU.
HUH?
WE DON'T HAVE A CHOICE.
WE CAN'T DEFEAT THEM WITHOUT THE HELP OF THE HOLY SWORD!
BUT...
GET A GRIP!!
DO YOU *WANT* JAGARA TO BE DE-STROYED?! WE NEED THE SWORD AND WE NEED IT NOW!!
ONLY YOU KNOW HOW TO REVIVE IT!
SO DO IT NOW, FOR GOD'S SAKE!
PLEASE!

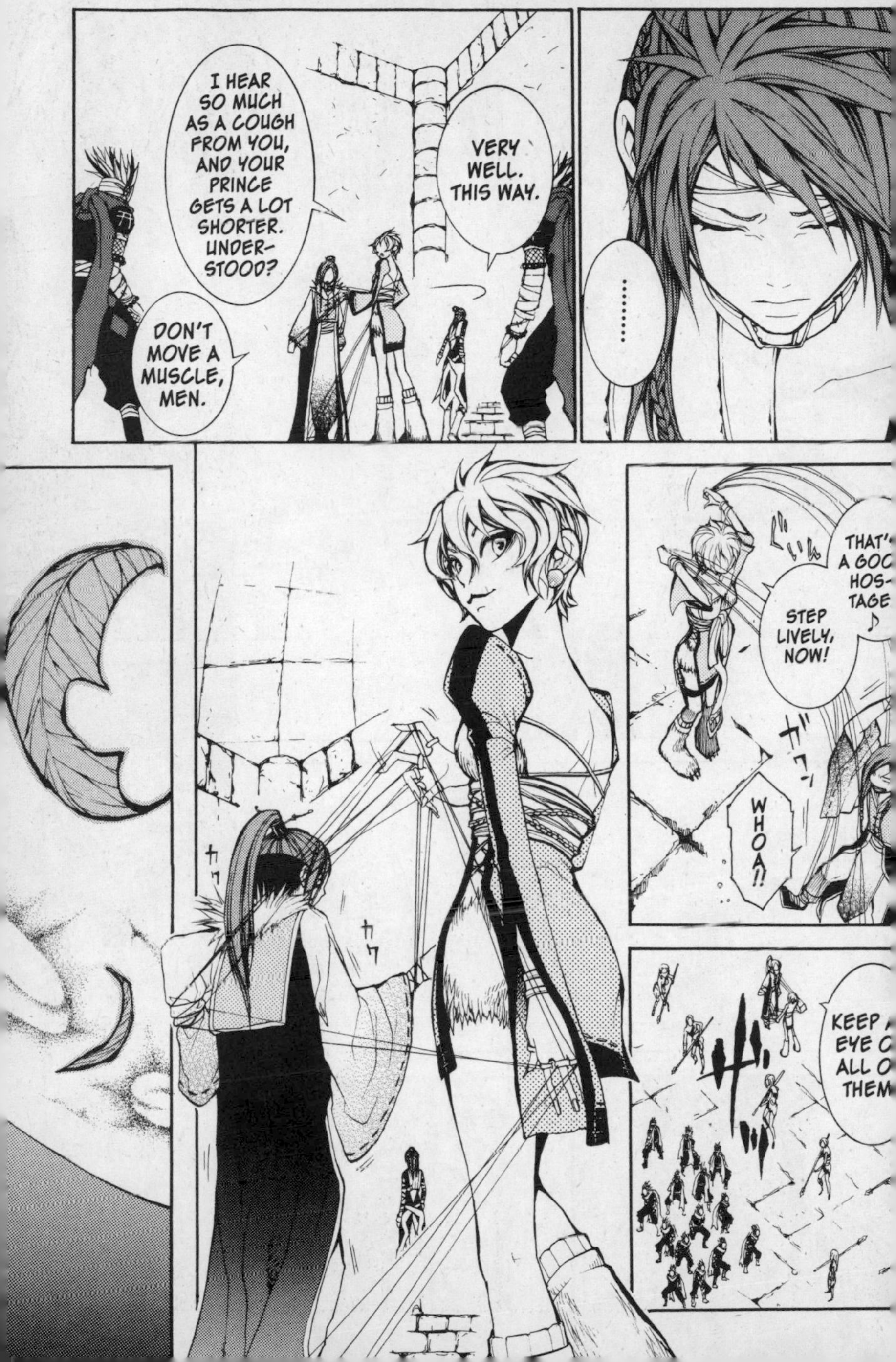
......
I HEAR SO MUCH AS A COUGH FROM YOU, AND YOUR PRINCE GETS A LOT SHORTER. UNDER-STOOD?
VERY WELL. THIS WAY.
DON'T MOVE A MUSCLE, MEN.
THAT' A GOO HOS-TAGE ♪
STEP LIVELY, NOW!
WHOA!!
KEEP A EYE O ALL O THEM

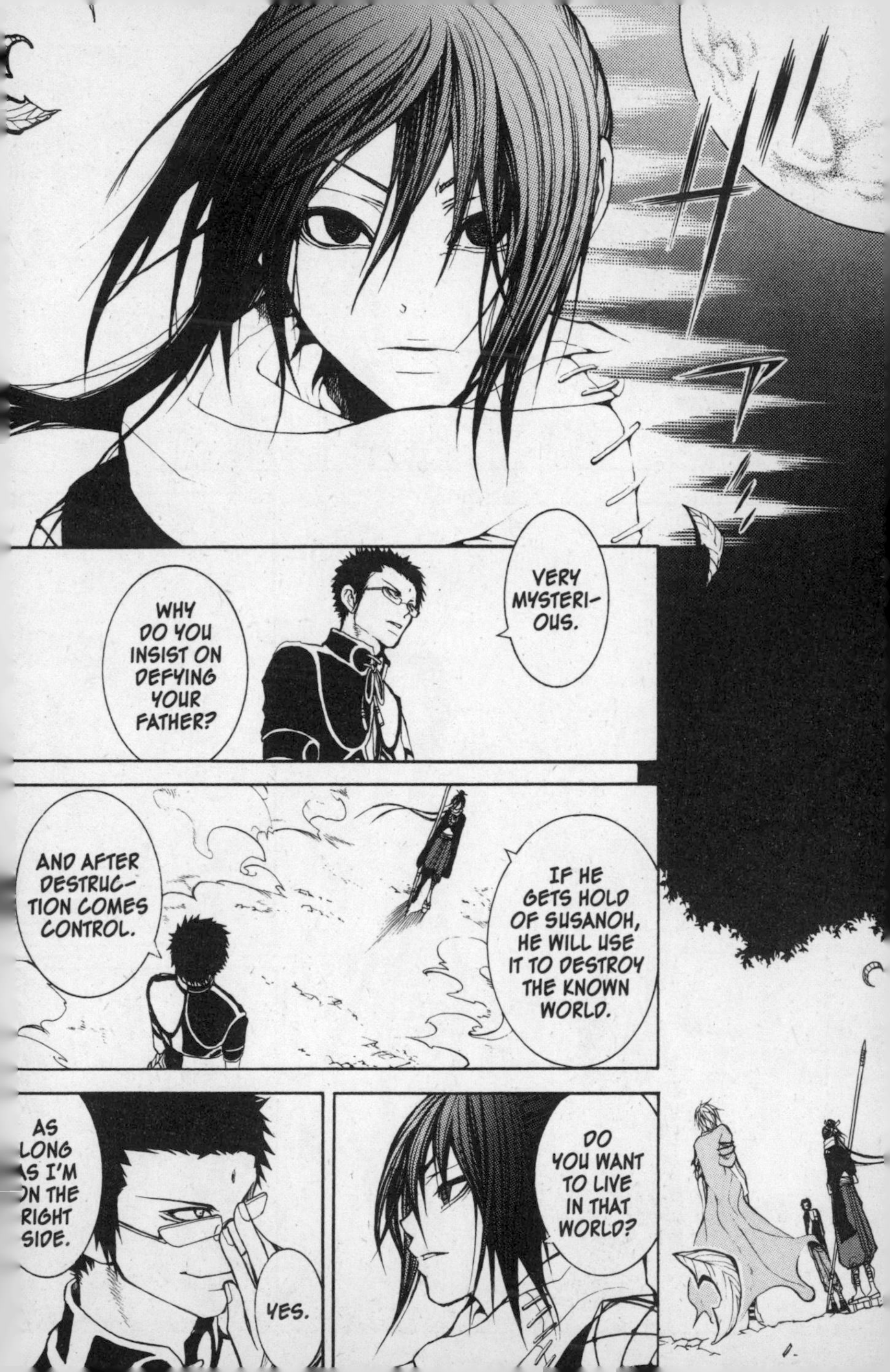
VERY MYSTERI-OUS.
WHY DO YOU INSIST ON DEFYING YOUR FATHER?
IF HE GETS HOLD OF SUSANOH, HE WILL USE IT TO DESTROY THE KNOWN WORLD.
AND AFTER DESTRUC-TION COMES CONTROL.
DO YOU WANT TO LIVE IN THAT WORLD?
YES.
AS LONG AS I'M ON THE RIGHT SIDE.

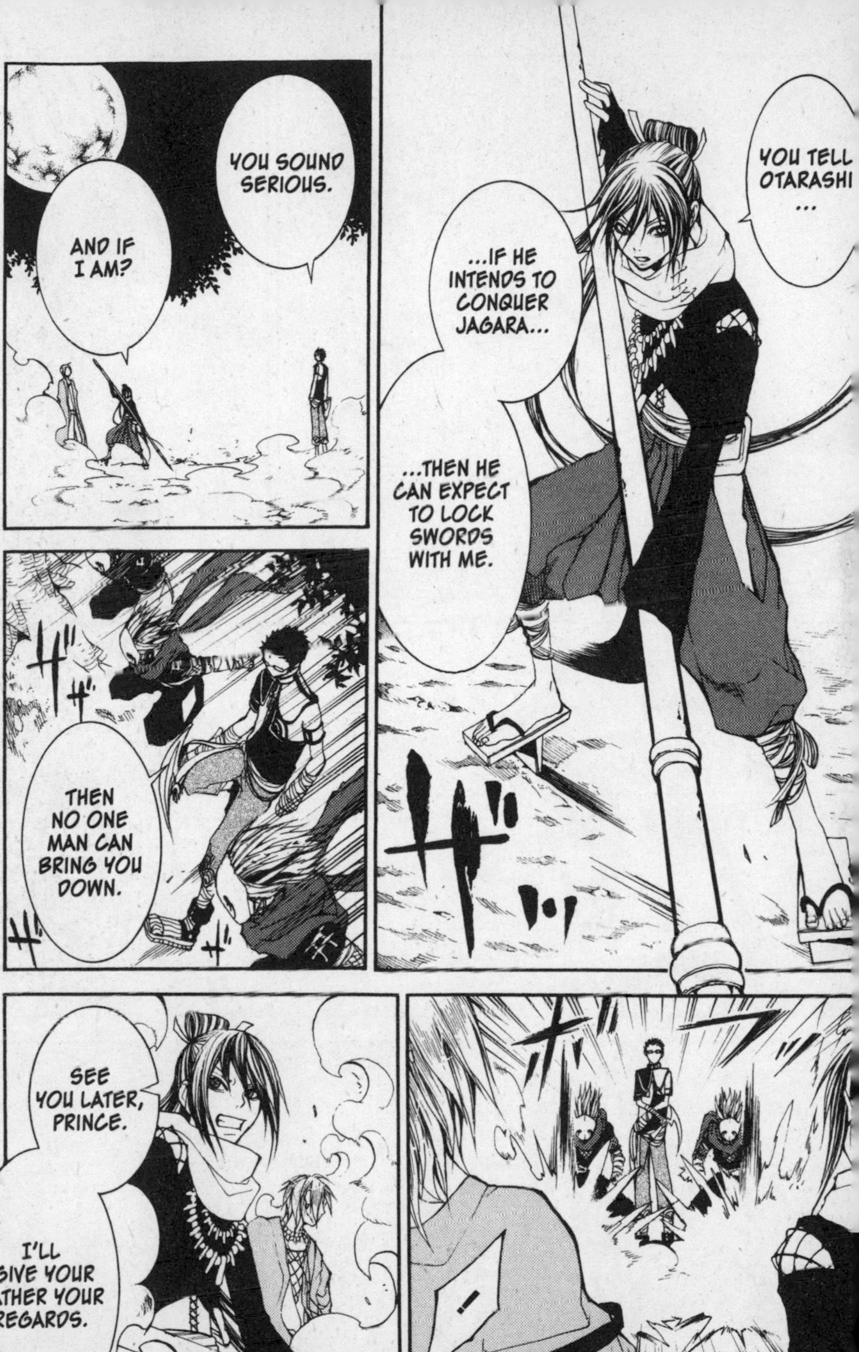
YOU TELL OTARASHI ...
...IF HE INTENDS TO CONQUER JAGARA...
...THEN HE CAN EXPECT TO LOCK SWORDS WITH ME.
YOU SOUND SERIOUS.
AND IF I AM?
THEN NO ONE MAN CAN BRING YOU DOWN.
!
SEE YOU LATER, PRINCE.
I'LL GIVE YOUR FATHER YOUR REGARDS.

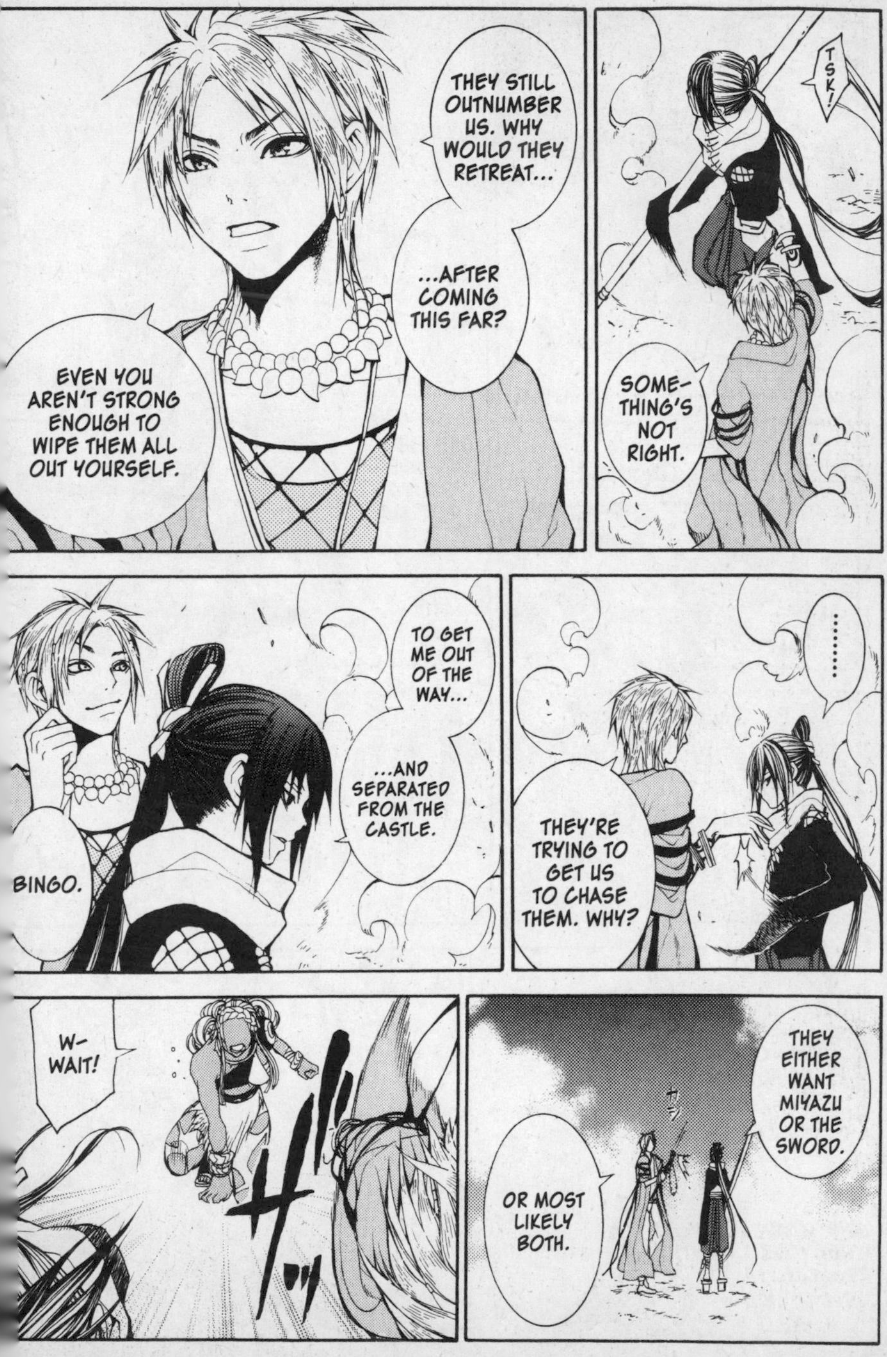
TSK!
SOME-THING'S NOT RIGHT.
THEY STILL OUTNUMBER US. WHY WOULD THEY RETREAT...
...AFTER COMING THIS FAR?
EVEN YOU AREN'T STRONG ENOUGH TO WIPE THEM ALL OUT YOURSELF.
......
THEY'RE TRYING TO GET US TO CHASE THEM. WHY?
TO GET ME OUT OF THE WAY...
...AND SEPARATED FROM THE CASTLE.
BINGO.
THEY EITHER WANT MIYAZU OR THE SWORD.
OR MOST LIKELY BOTH.
W-WAIT!

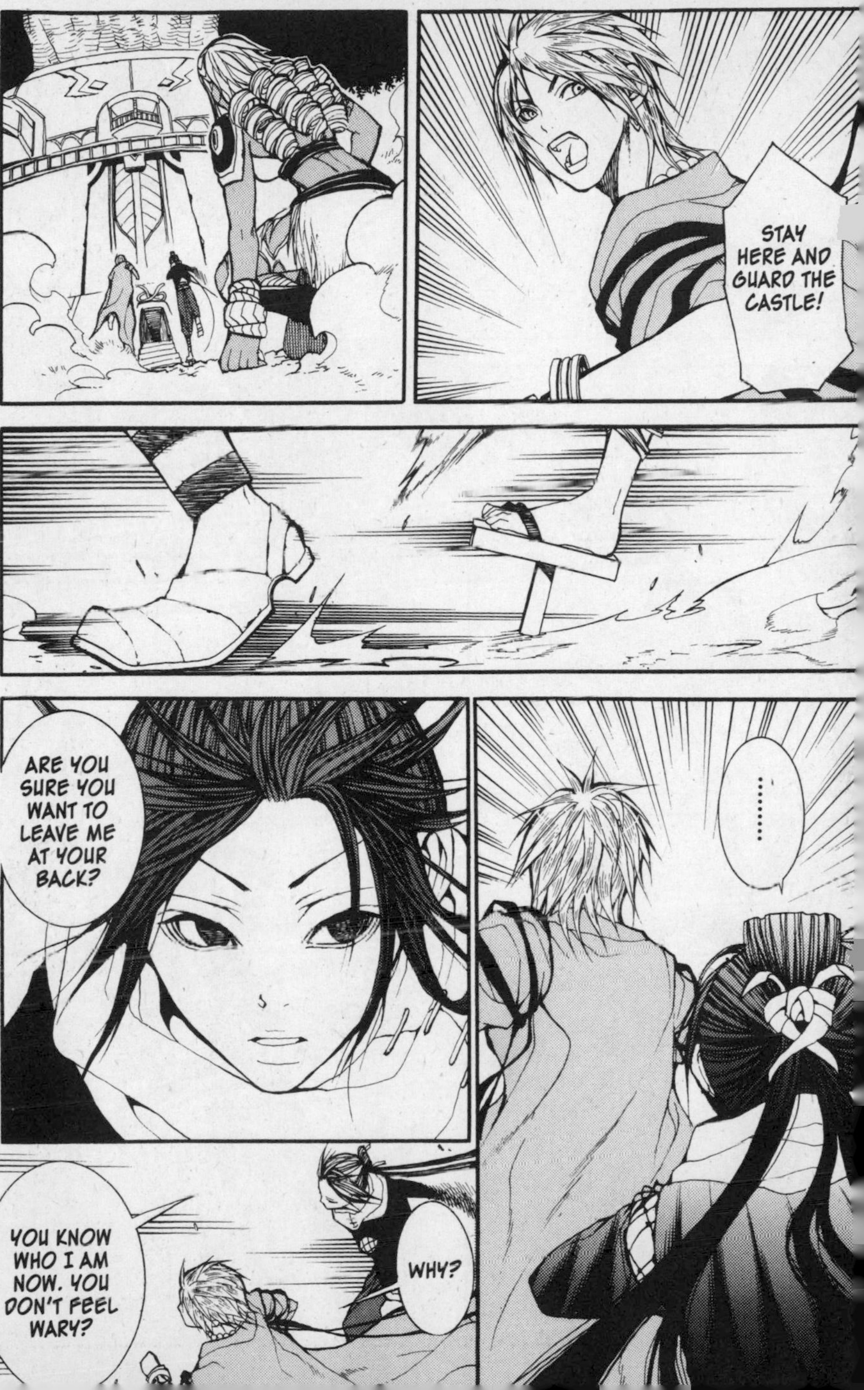
STAY HERE AND GUARD THE CASTLE!
......
ARE YOU SURE YOU WANT TO LEAVE ME AT YOUR BACK?
WHY?
YOU KNOW WHO I AM NOW. YOU DON'T FEEL WARY?

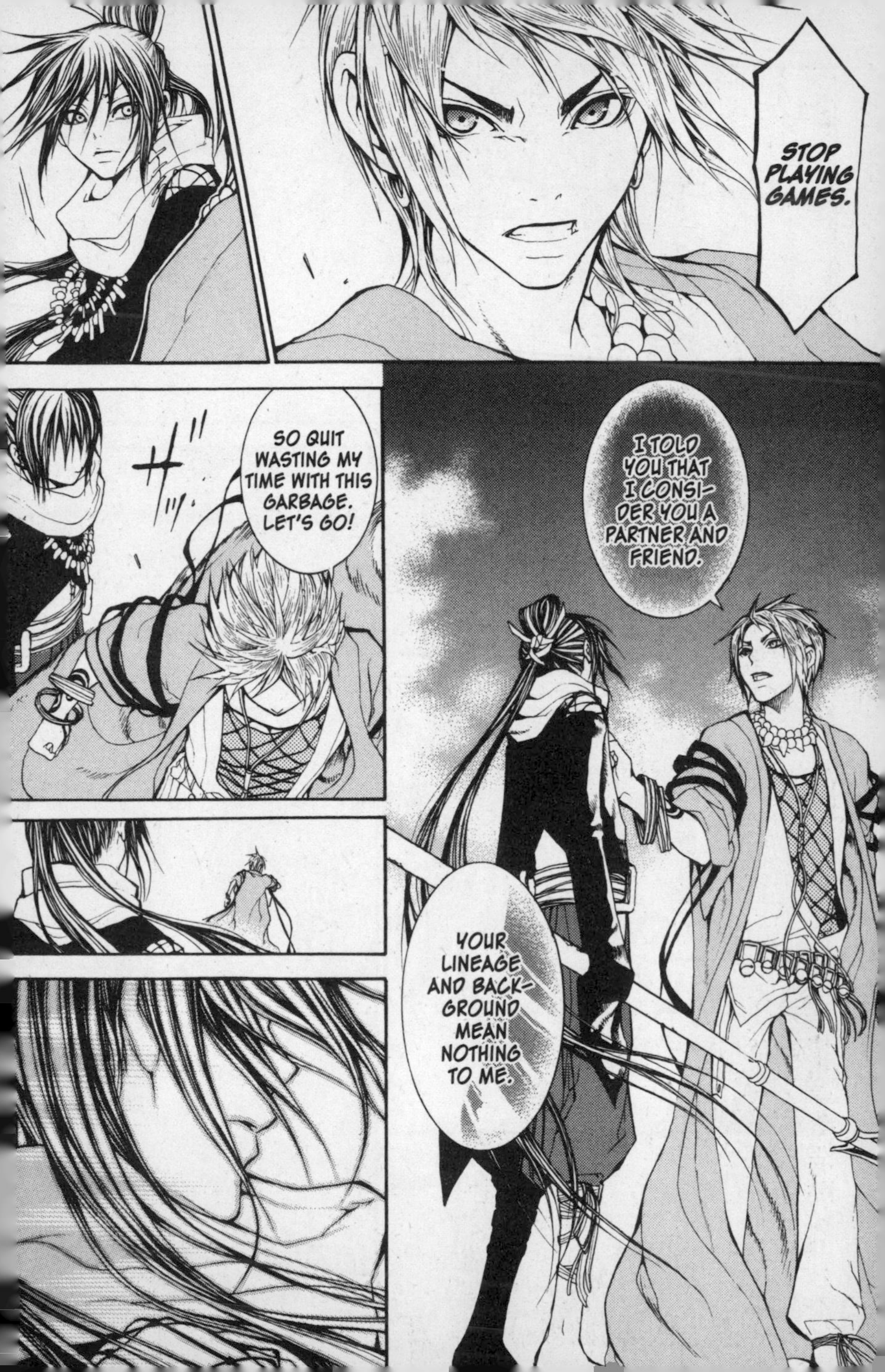
STOP PLAYING GAMES.
I TOLD YOU THAT I CONSI-DER YOU A PARTNER AND FRIEND.
YOUR LINEAGE AND BACK-GROUND MEAN NOTHING TO ME.
SO QUIT WASTING MY TIME WITH THIS GARBAGE. LET'S GO!

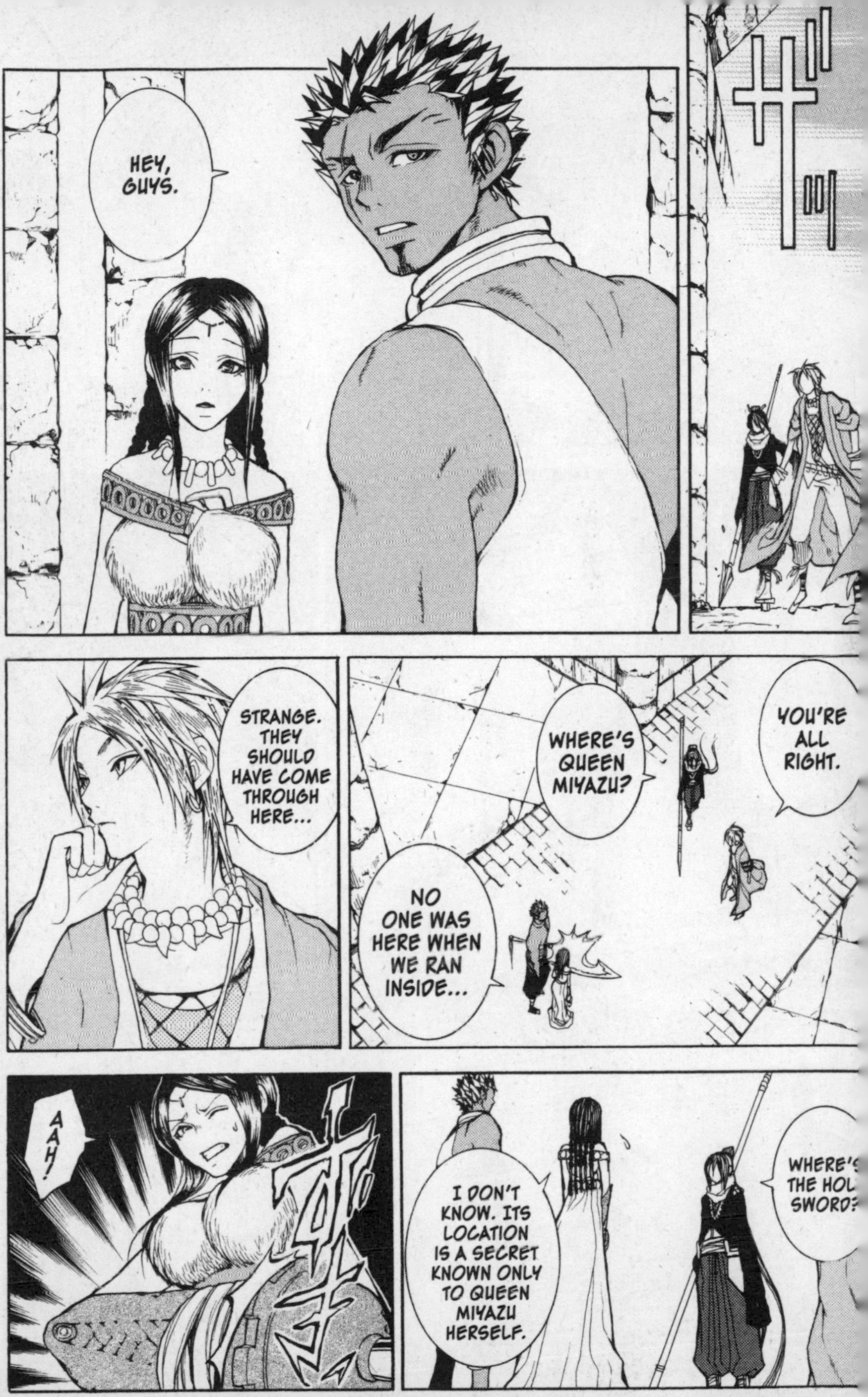
HEY, GUYS.
YOU'RE ALL RIGHT.
WHERE'S QUEEN MIYAZU?
NO ONE WAS HERE WHEN WE RAN INSIDE...
STRANGE. THEY SHOULD HAVE COME THROUGH HERE...
WHERE'S THE HOL SWORD?
I DON'T KNOW. ITS LOCATION IS A SECRET KNOWN ONLY TO QUEEN MIYAZU HERSELF.
AAH!

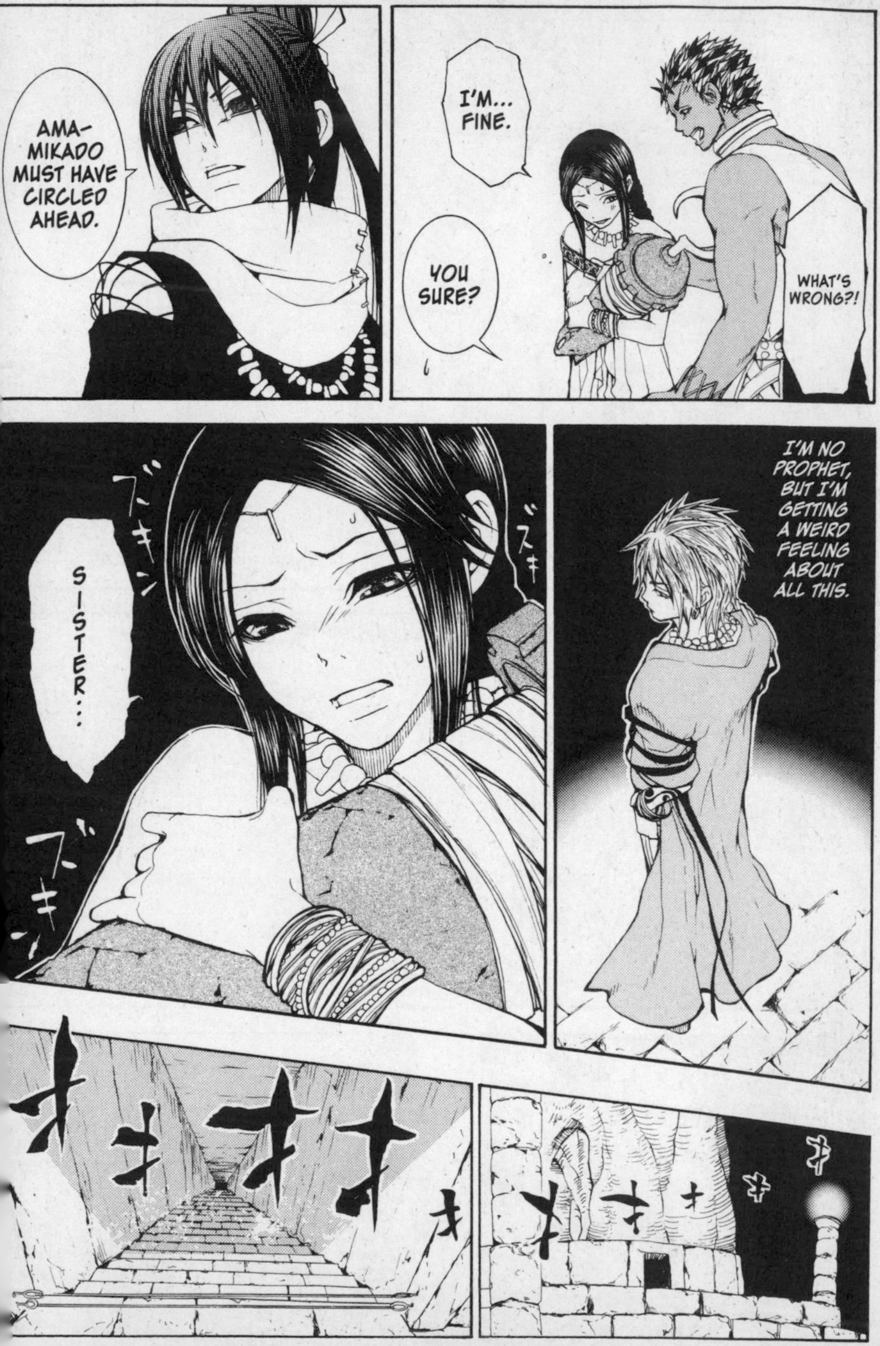
I'M... FINE.
WHAT'S WRONG?!
YOU SURE?
AMA-MIKADO MUST HAVE CIRCLED AHEAD.
I'M NO PROPHET, BUT I'M GETTING A WEIRD FEELING ABOUT ALL THIS.
ズキ
ズキン
SISTER...
ズキ

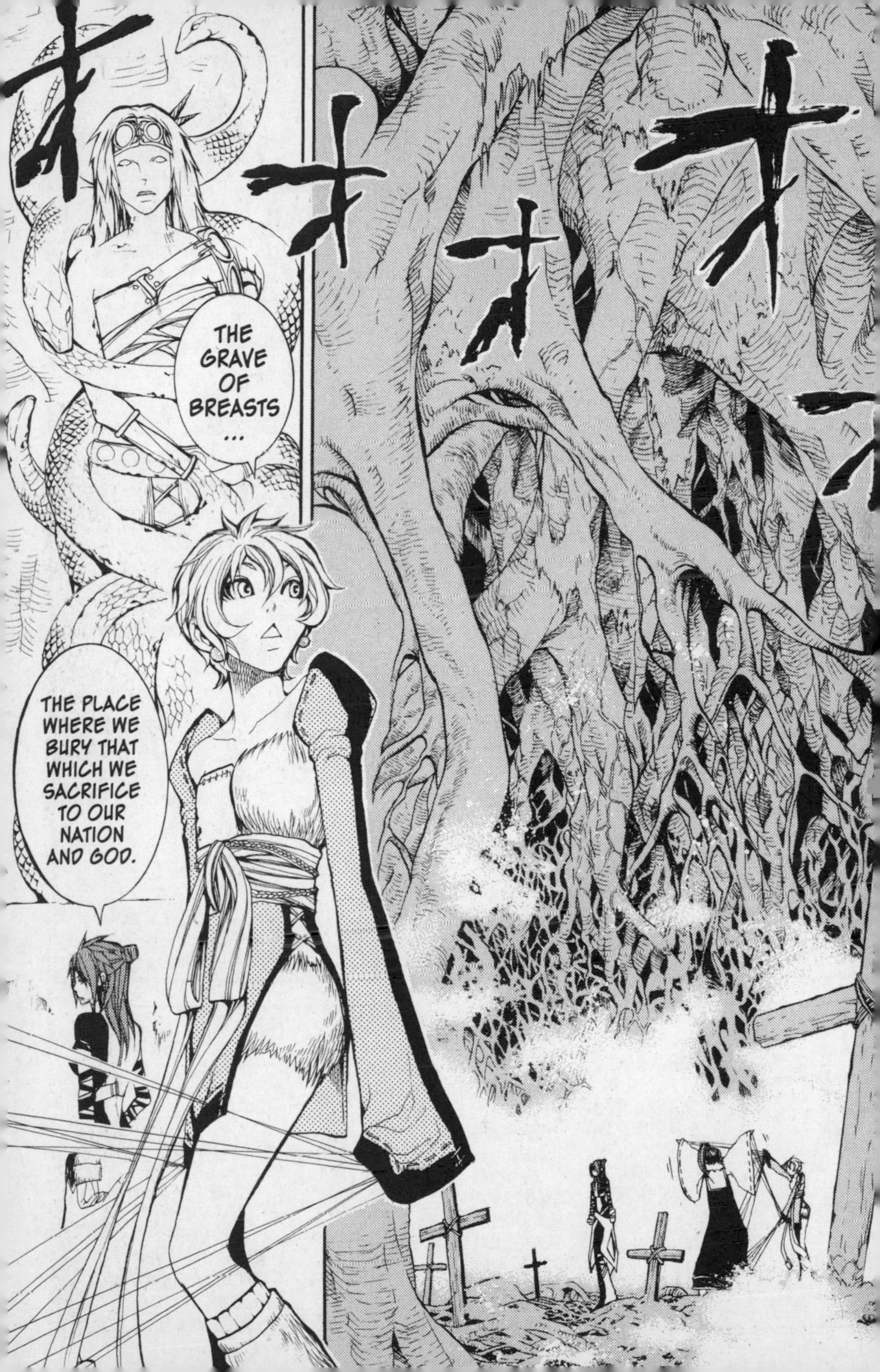
THE GRAVE OF BREASTS ...
THE PLACE WHERE WE BURY THAT WHICH WE SACRIFICE TO OUR NATION AND GOD.

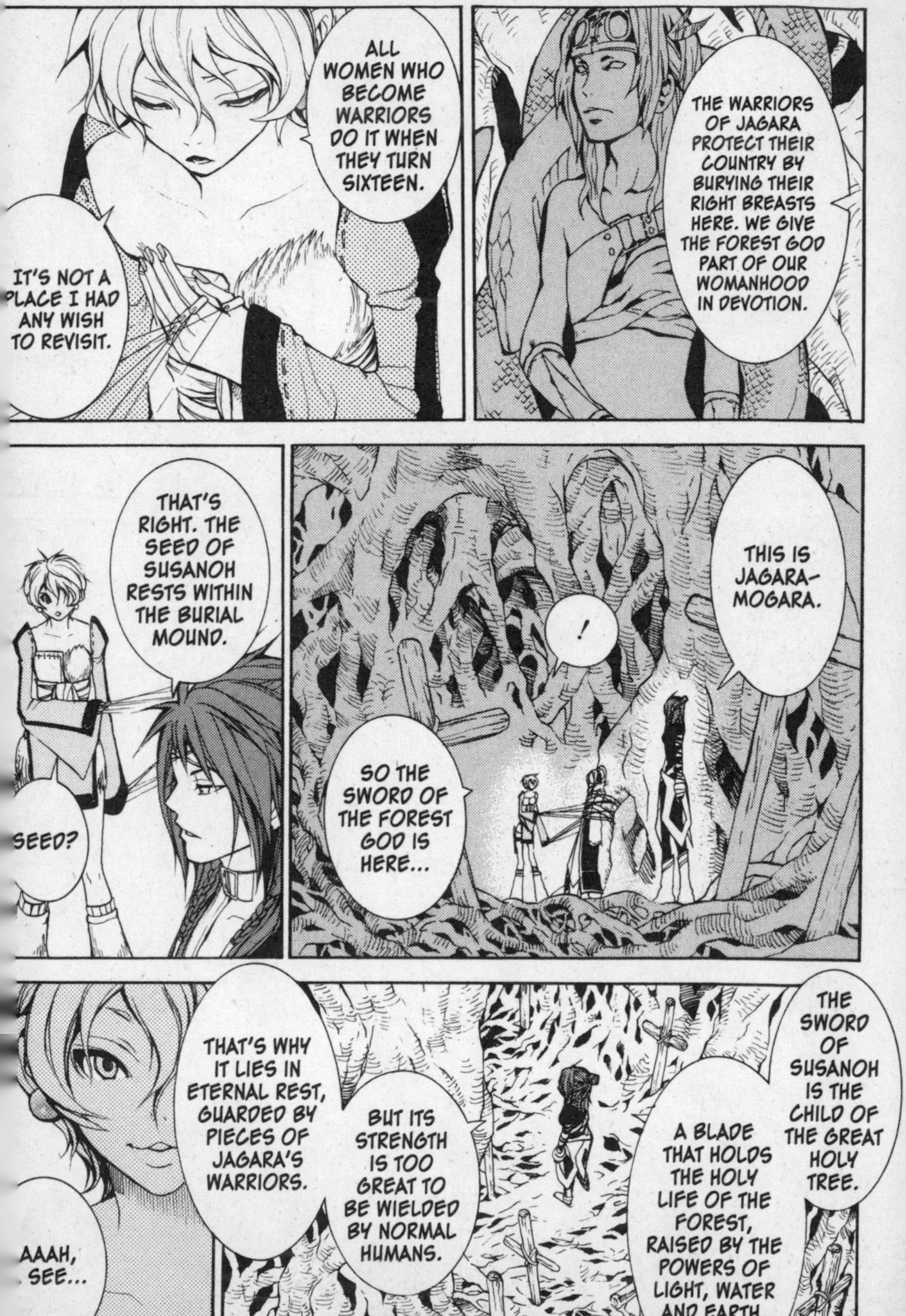
THE WARRIORS OF JAGARA PROTECT THEIR COUNTRY BY BURYING THEIR RIGHT BREASTS HERE. WE GIVE THE FOREST GOD PART OF OUR WOMANHOOD IN DEVOTION.
ALL WOMEN WHO BECOME WARRIORS DO IT WHEN THEY TURN SIXTEEN.
IT'S NOT A PLACE I HAD ANY WISH TO REVISIT.
THIS IS JAGARA-MOGARA.
!
SO THE SWORD OF THE FOREST GOD IS HERE...
THAT'S RIGHT. THE SEED OF SUSANOH RESTS WITHIN THE BURIAL MOUND.
SEED?
THE SWORD OF SUSANOH IS THE CHILD OF THE GREAT HOLY TREE.
A BLADE THAT HOLDS THE HOLY LIFE OF THE FOREST, RAISED BY THE POWERS OF LIGHT, WATER AND EARTH.
BUT ITS STRENGTH IS TOO GREAT TO BE WIELDED BY NORMAL HUMANS.
THAT'S WHY IT LIES IN ETERNAL REST, GUARDED BY PIECES OF JAGARA'S WARRIORS.
AAAH, SEE...

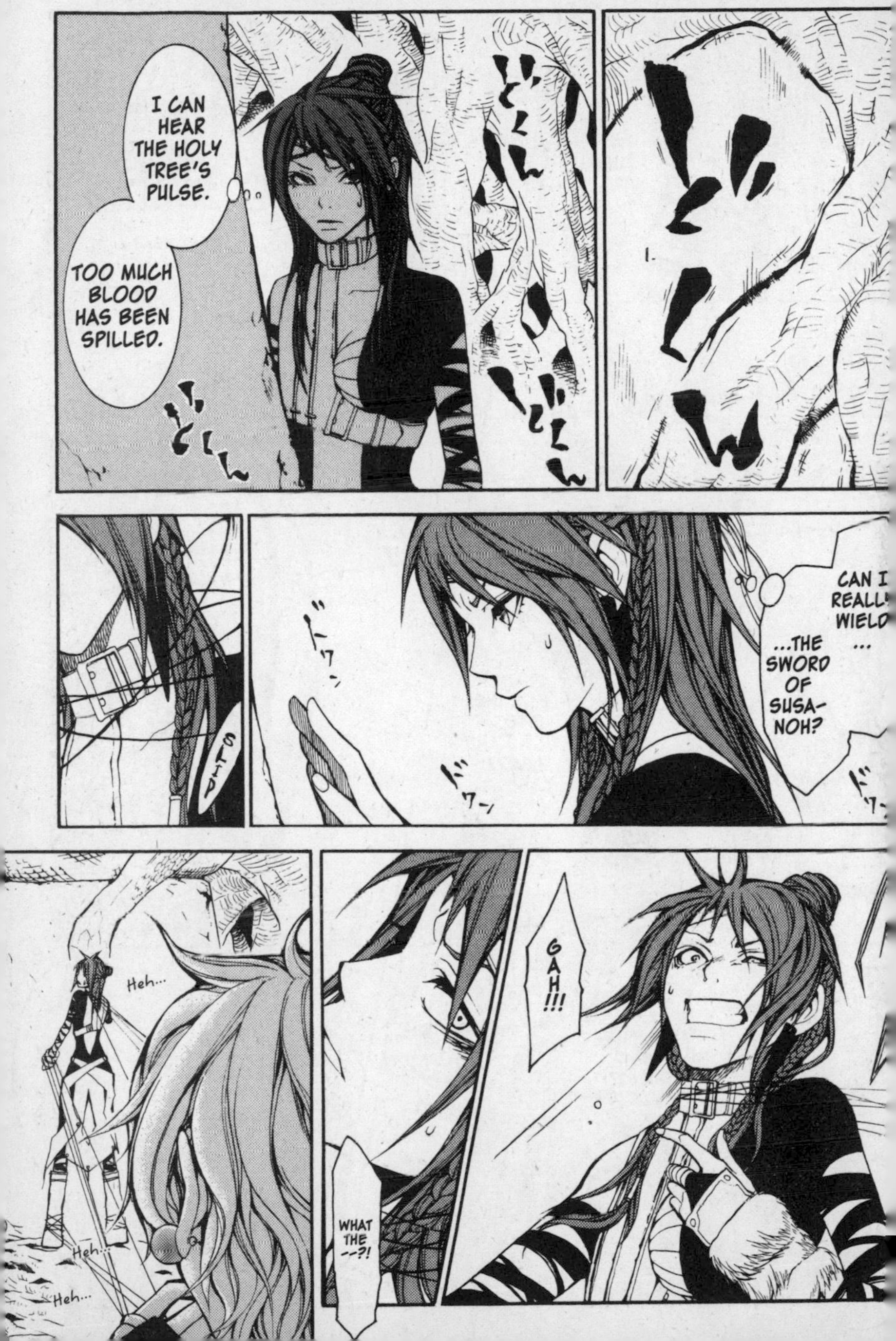
I CAN HEAR THE HOLY TREE'S PULSE.
TOO MUCH BLOOD HAS BEEN SPILLED.
CAN I REALL WIELD ...
...THE SWORD OF SUSA-NOH?
SLIP
GAH!!!
WHAT THE --?!
Heh...
Heh...
Heh...

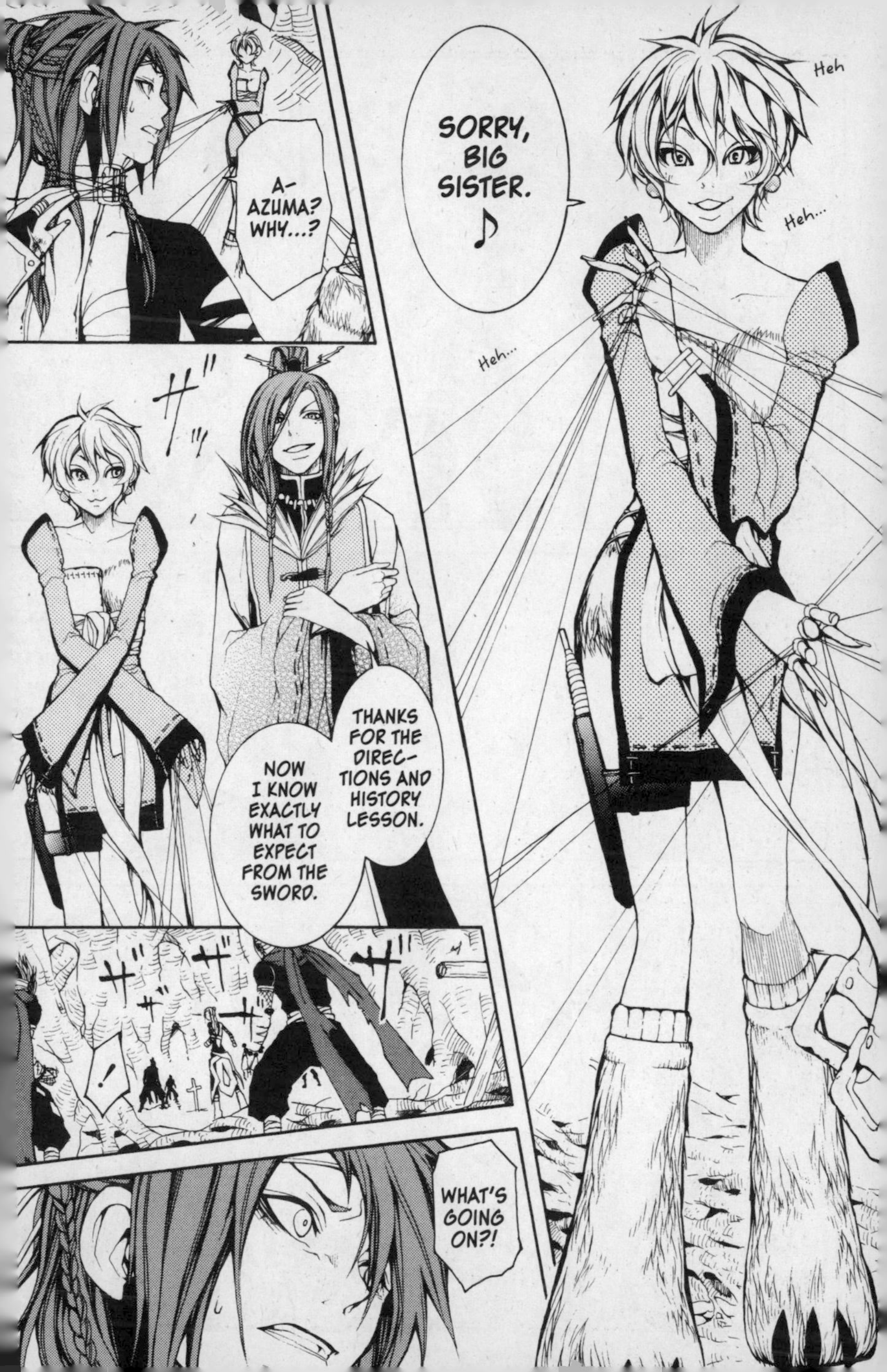
SORRY, BIG SISTER. ♪
Heh
Heh...
Heh...
A- AZUMA? WHY...?
THANKS FOR THE DIREC- TIONS AND HISTORY LESSON.
NOW I KNOW EXACTLY WHAT TO EXPECT FROM THE SWORD.
!
WHAT'S GOING ON?!

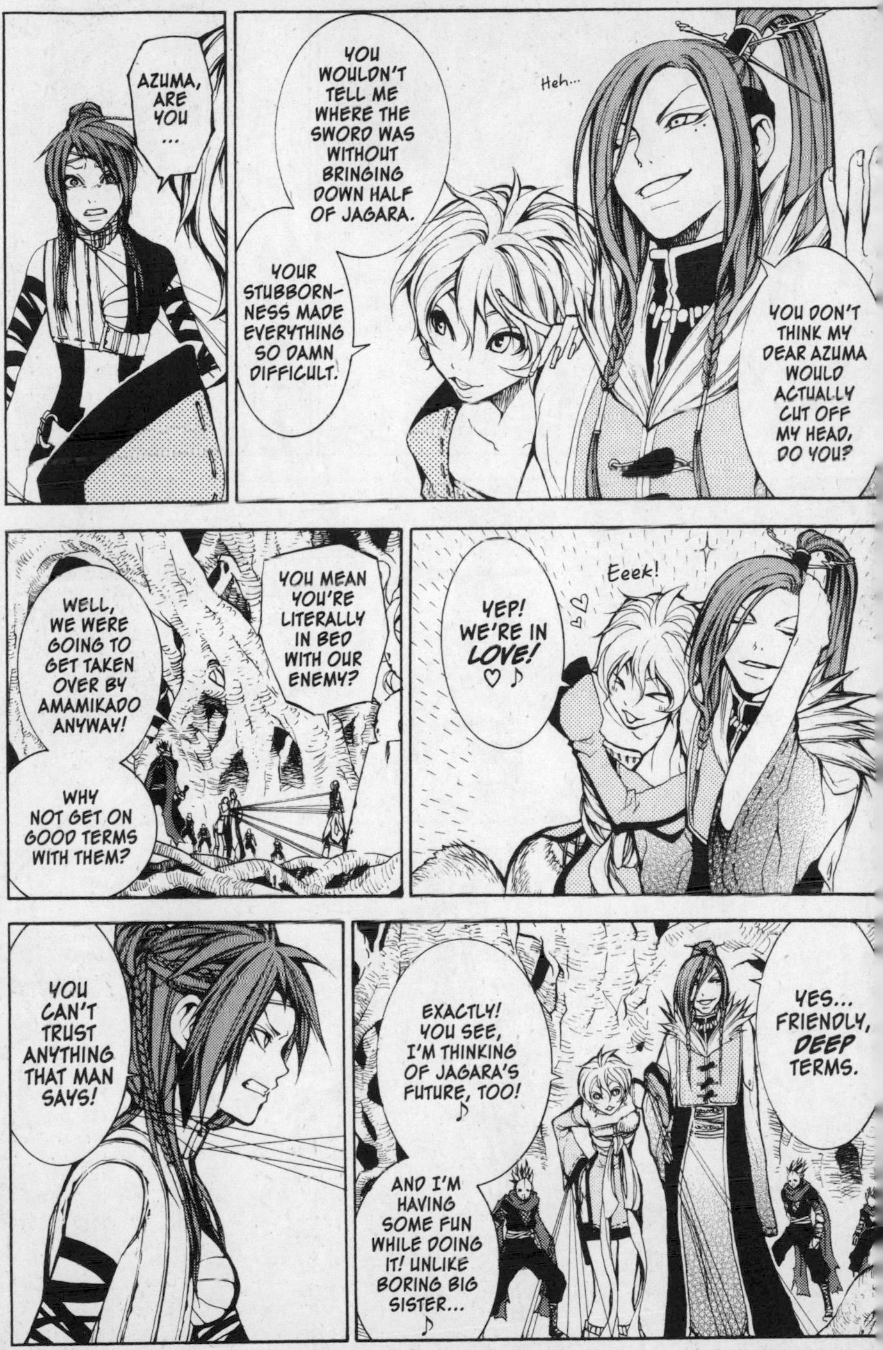
Heh...
YOU DON'T THINK MY DEAR AZUMA WOULD ACTUALLY CUT OFF MY HEAD, DO YOU?
YOU WOULDN'T TELL ME WHERE THE SWORD WAS WITHOUT BRINGING DOWN HALF OF JAGARA.
YOUR STUBBORNNESS MADE EVERYTHING SO DAMN DIFFICULT.
AZUMA, ARE YOU ...
Eeek!
YEP! WE'RE IN LOVE! ♡ ♪
YOU MEAN YOU'RE LITERALLY IN BED WITH OUR ENEMY?
WELL, WE WERE GOING TO GET TAKEN OVER BY AMAMIKADO ANYWAY!
WHY NOT GET ON GOOD TERMS WITH THEM?
YES... FRIENDLY, DEEP TERMS.
EXACTLY! YOU SEE, I'M THINKING OF JAGARA'S FUTURE, TOO! ♪
AND I'M HAVING SOME FUN WHILE DOING IT! UNLIKE BORING BIG SISTER... ♪
YOU CAN'T TRUST ANYTHING THAT MAN SAYS!

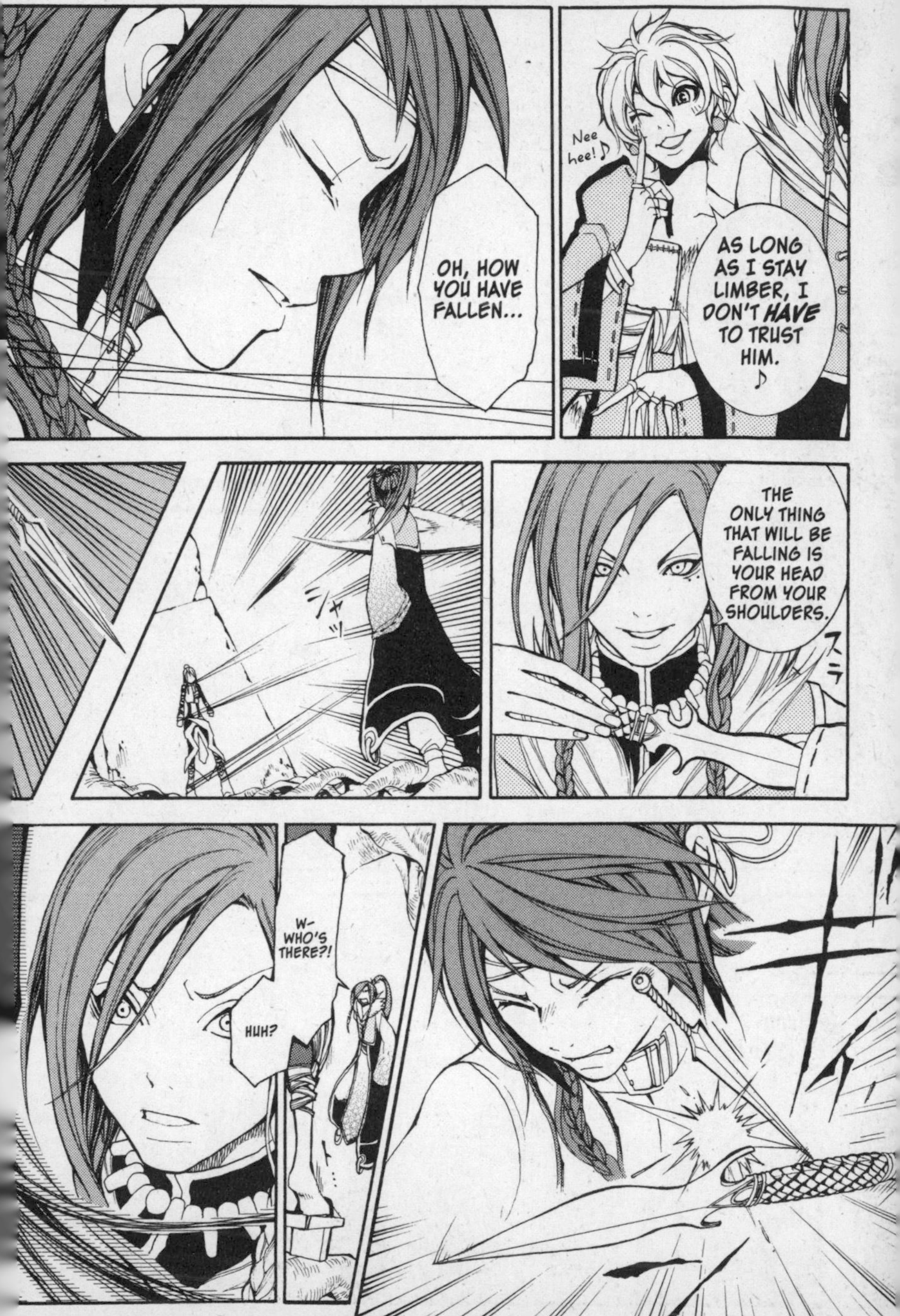
Nee hee! ♪
AS LONG AS I STAY LIMBER, I DON'T ***HAVE*** TO TRUST HIM. ♪
OH, HOW YOU HAVE FALLEN...
THE ONLY THING THAT WILL BE FALLING IS YOUR HEAD FROM YOUR SHOULDERS.
W-WHO'S THERE?!
HUH?

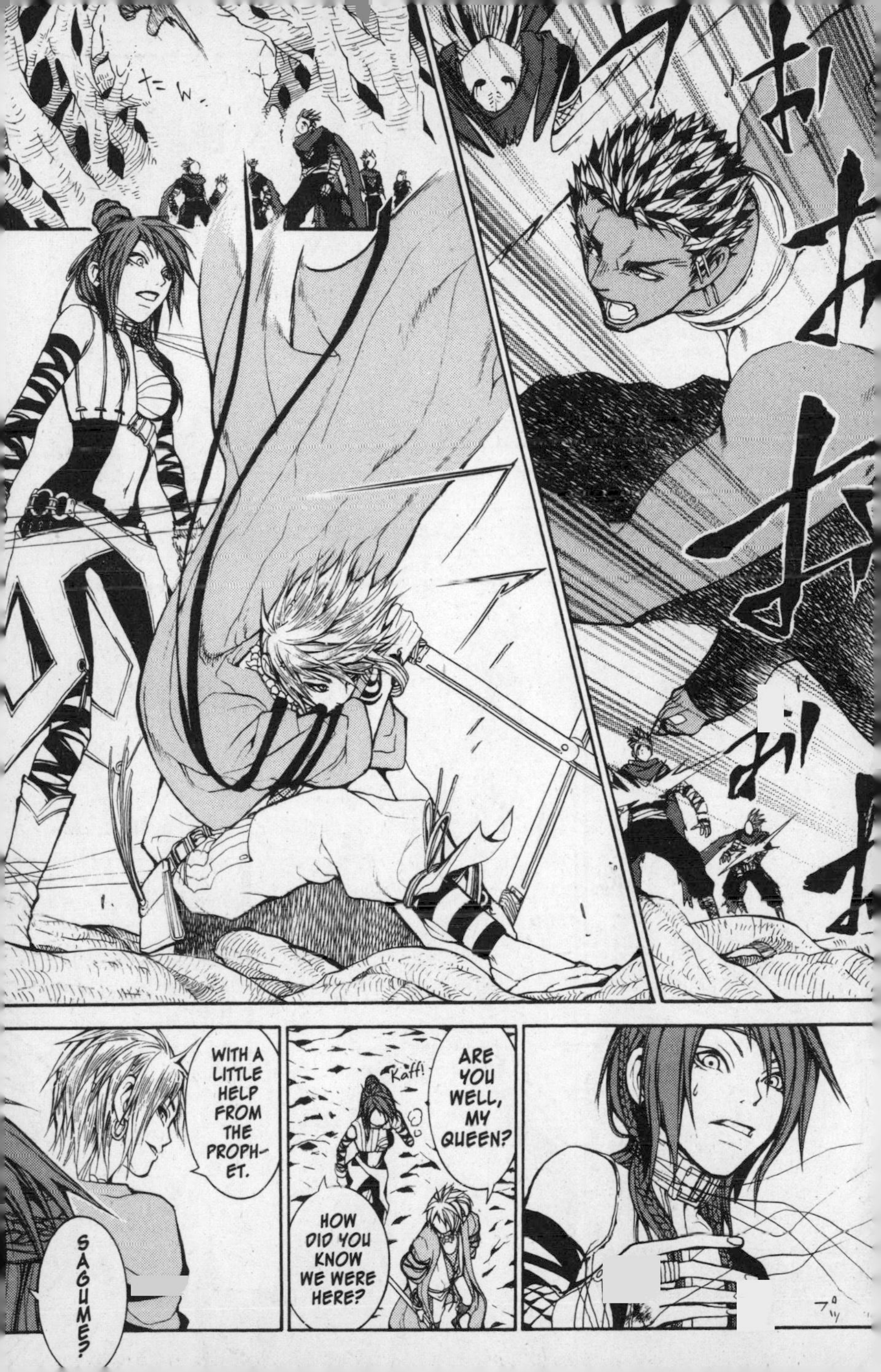
ARE YOU WELL, MY QUEEN?
Kaff!
HOW DID YOU KNOW WE WERE HERE?
WITH A LITTLE HELP FROM THE PROPHET.
SAGUME?

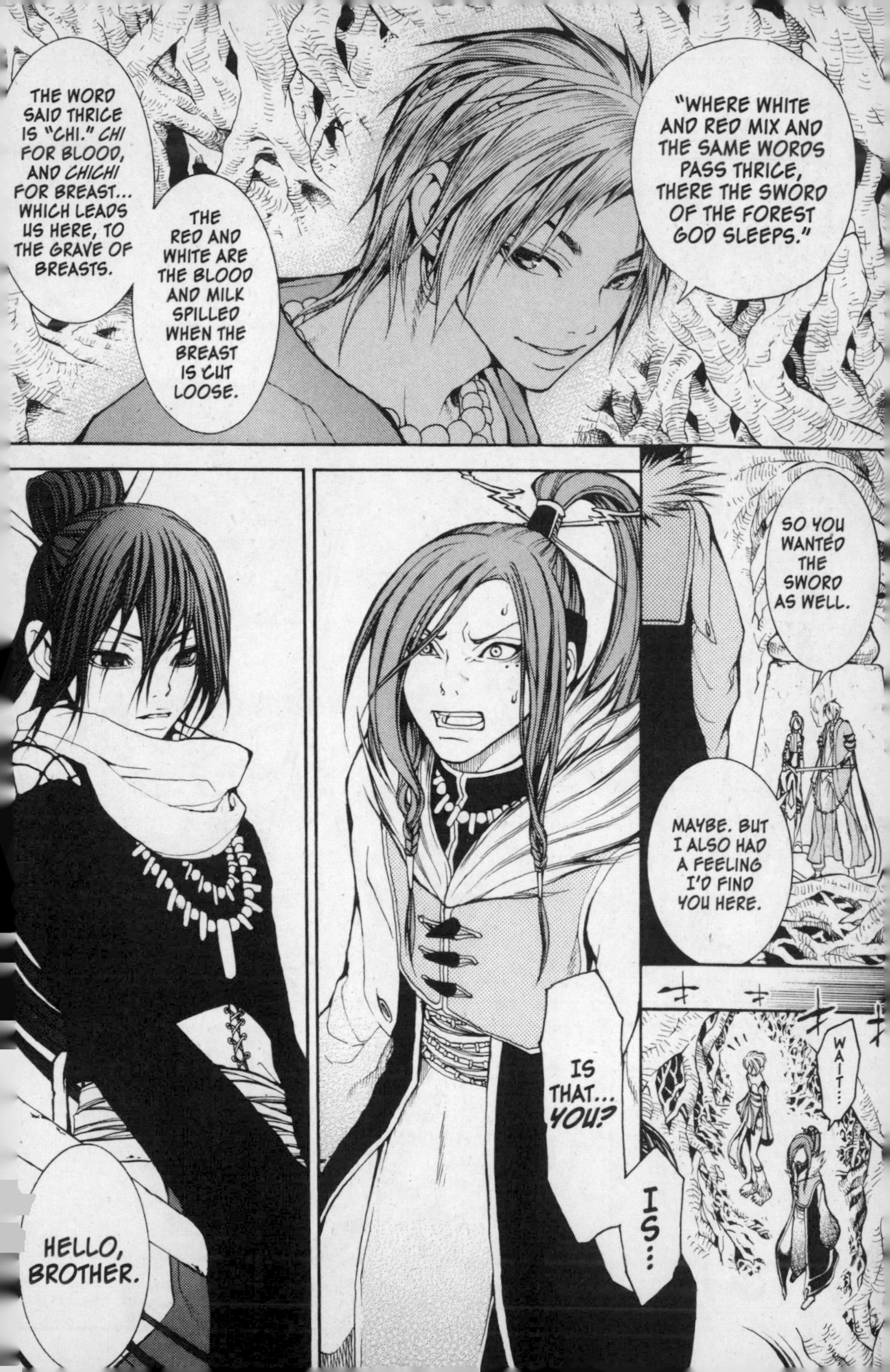
"WHERE WHITE AND RED MIX AND THE SAME WORDS PASS THRICE, THERE THE SWORD OF THE FOREST GOD SLEEPS."
THE RED AND WHITE ARE THE BLOOD AND MILK SPILLED WHEN THE BREAST IS CUT LOOSE.
THE WORD SAID THRICE IS "CHI." CHI FOR BLOOD, AND CHICHI FOR BREAST... WHICH LEADS US HERE, TO THE GRAVE OF BREASTS.
SO YOU WANTED THE SWORD AS WELL.
MAYBE. BUT I ALSO HAD A FEELING I'D FIND YOU HERE.
WAIT...
IS...
IS THAT... YOU?
HELLO, BROTHER.

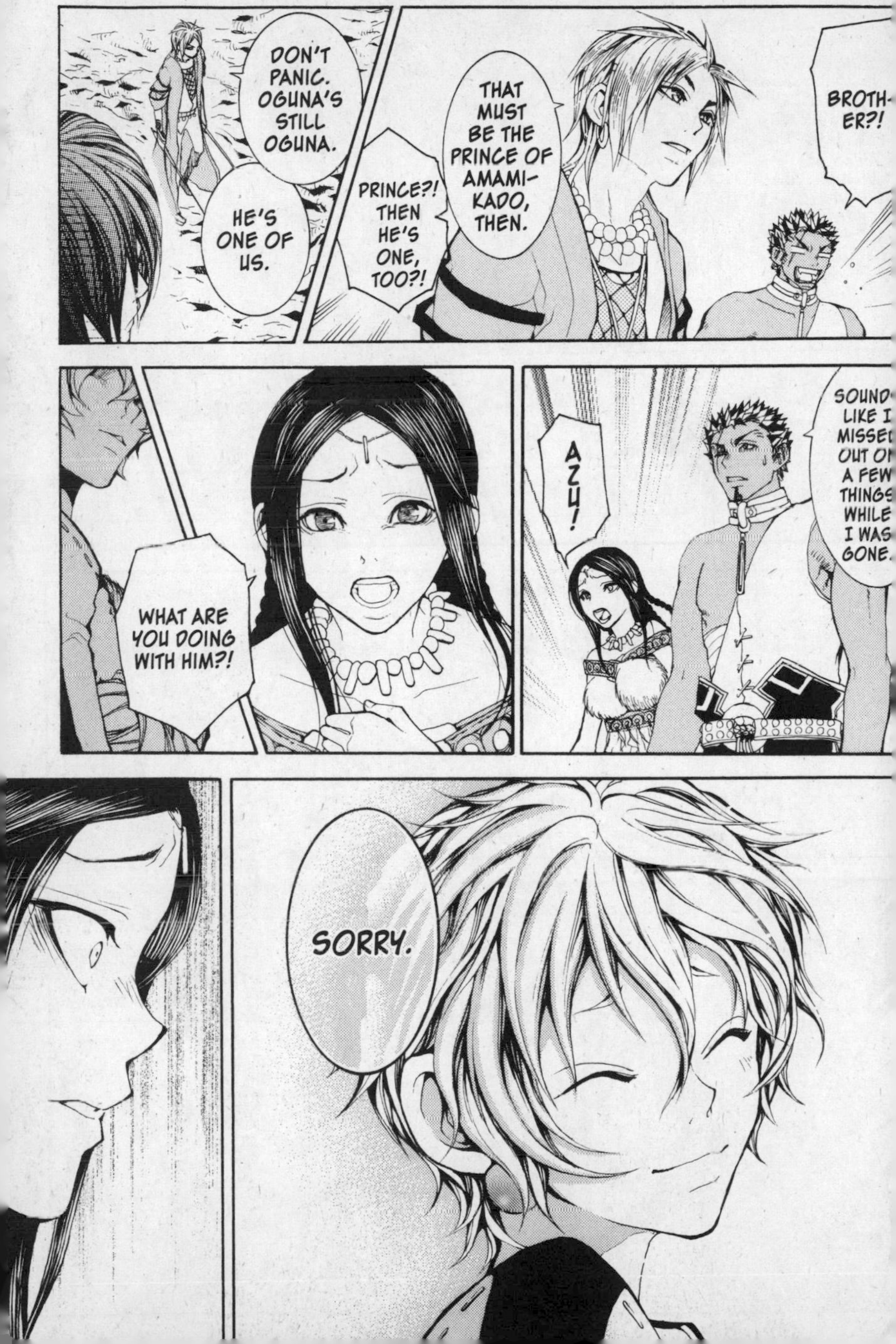
BROTHER?!
THAT MUST BE THE PRINCE OF AMAMI-KADO, THEN.
PRINCE?! THEN HE'S ONE, TOO?!
DON'T PANIC. OGUNA'S STILL OGUNA.
HE'S ONE OF US.
SOUND LIKE I MISSE OUT O A FEW THINGS WHILE I WAS GONE.
AZU!
WHAT ARE YOU DOING WITH HIM?!
SORRY.

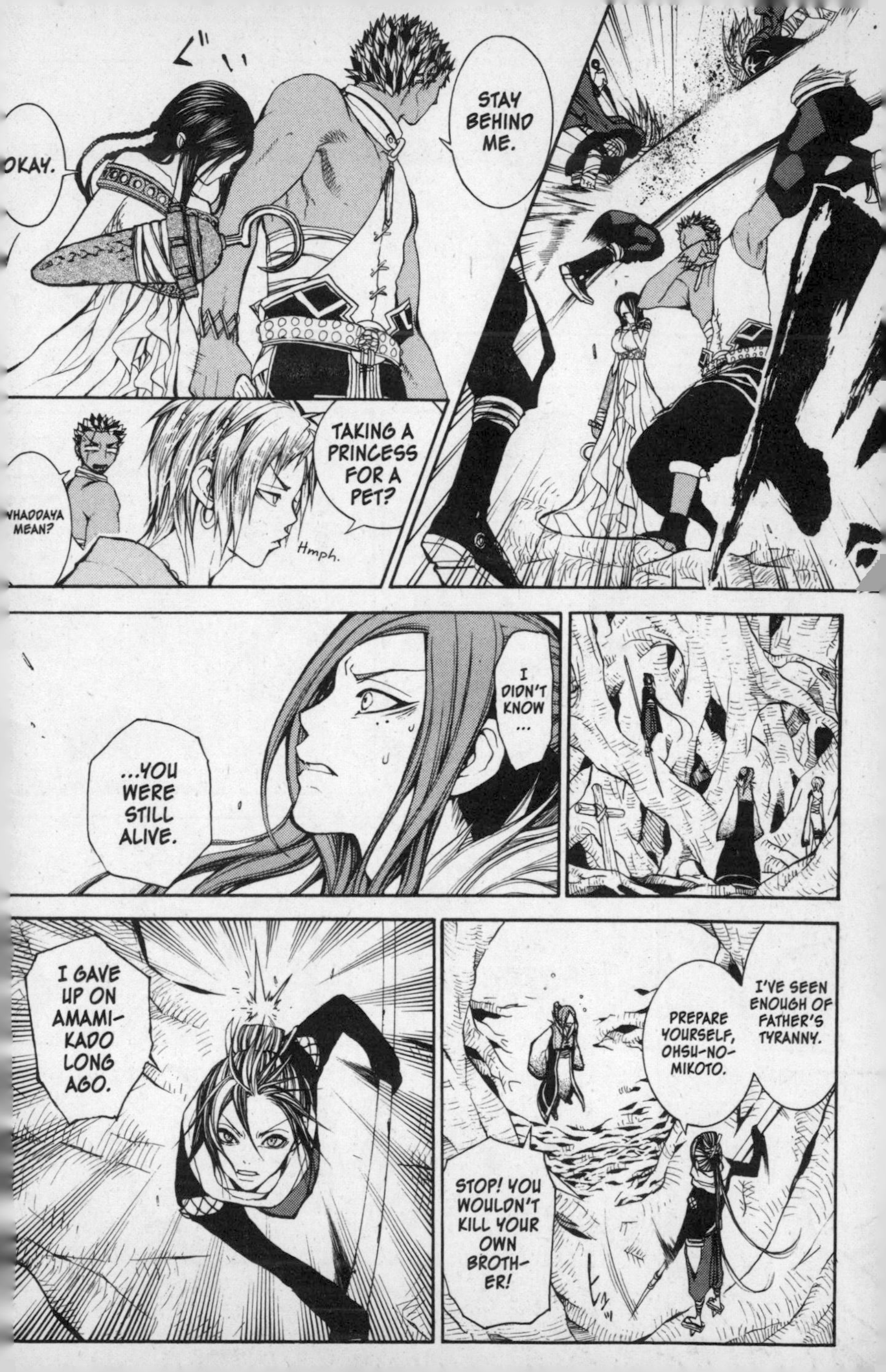
STAY BEHIND ME.
OKAY.
TAKING A PRINCESS FOR A PET?
WHADDAYA MEAN?
Hmph.
I DIDN'T KNOW ...
...YOU WERE STILL ALIVE.
I'VE SEEN ENOUGH OF FATHER'S TYRANNY.
PREPARE YOURSELF, OHSU-NO-MIKOTO.
STOP! YOU WOULDN'T KILL YOUR OWN BROTHER!
I GAVE UP ON AMAMI-KADO LONG AGO.

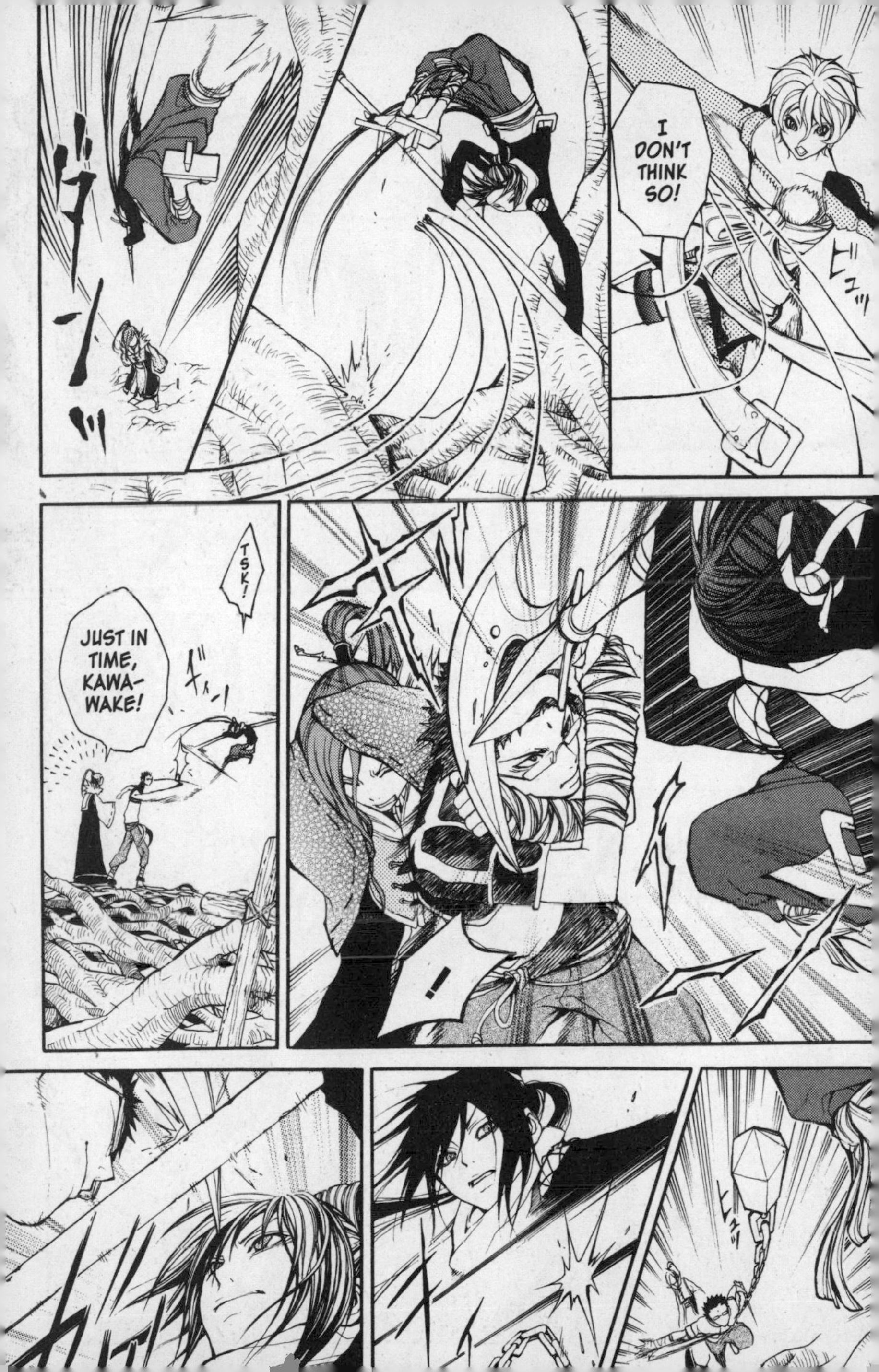
I DON'T THINK SO!
TSK!
JUST IN TIME, KAWA-WAKE!
!

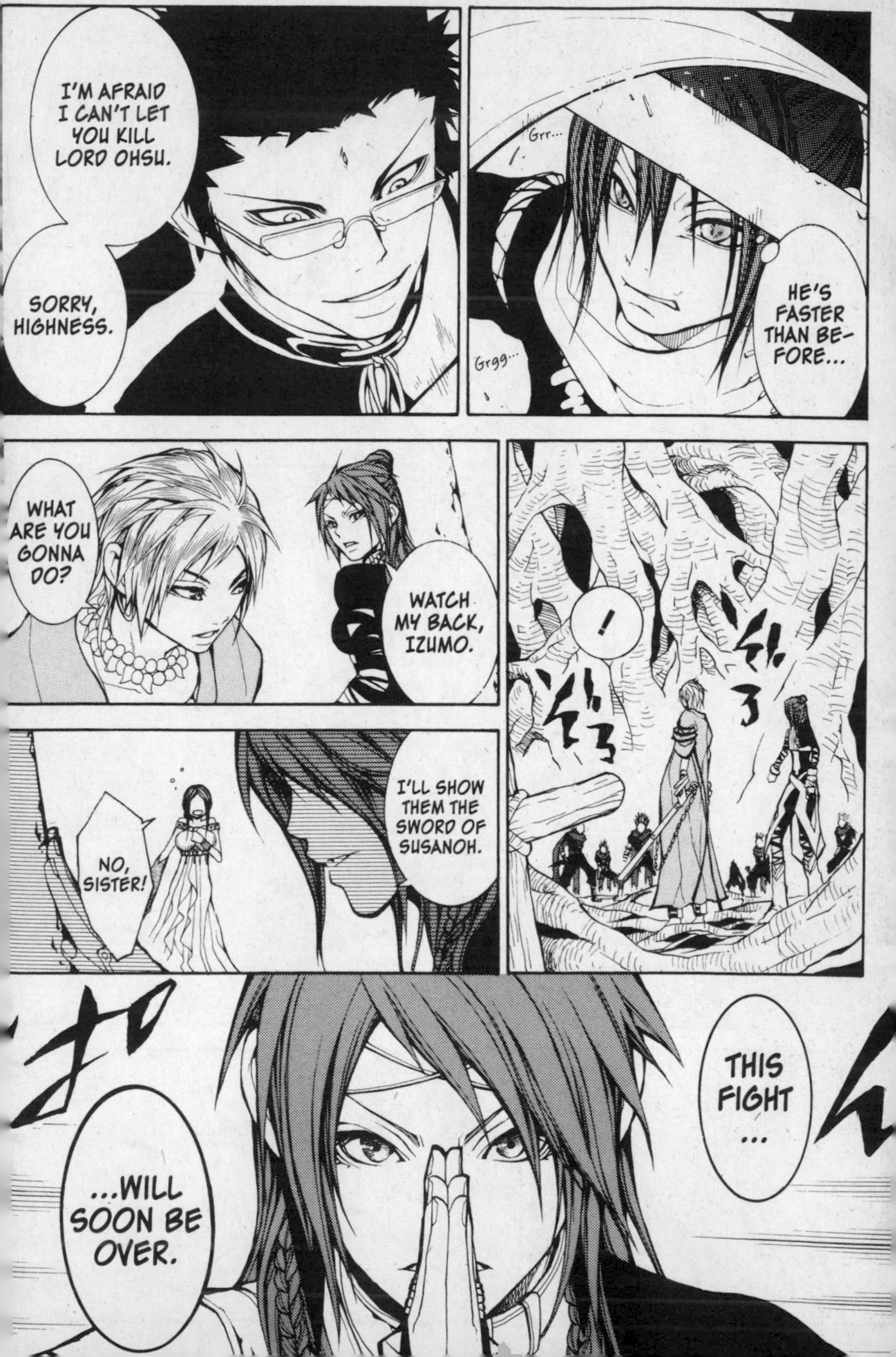
Grr...
HE'S FASTER THAN BE-FORE...
Grgg...
I'M AFRAID I CAN'T LET YOU KILL LORD OHSU.
SORRY, HIGHNESS.
!
WHAT ARE YOU GONNA DO?
WATCH MY BACK, IZUMO.
I'LL SHOW THEM THE SWORD OF SUSANOH.
NO, SISTER!
THIS FIGHT ...
...WILL SOON BE OVER.

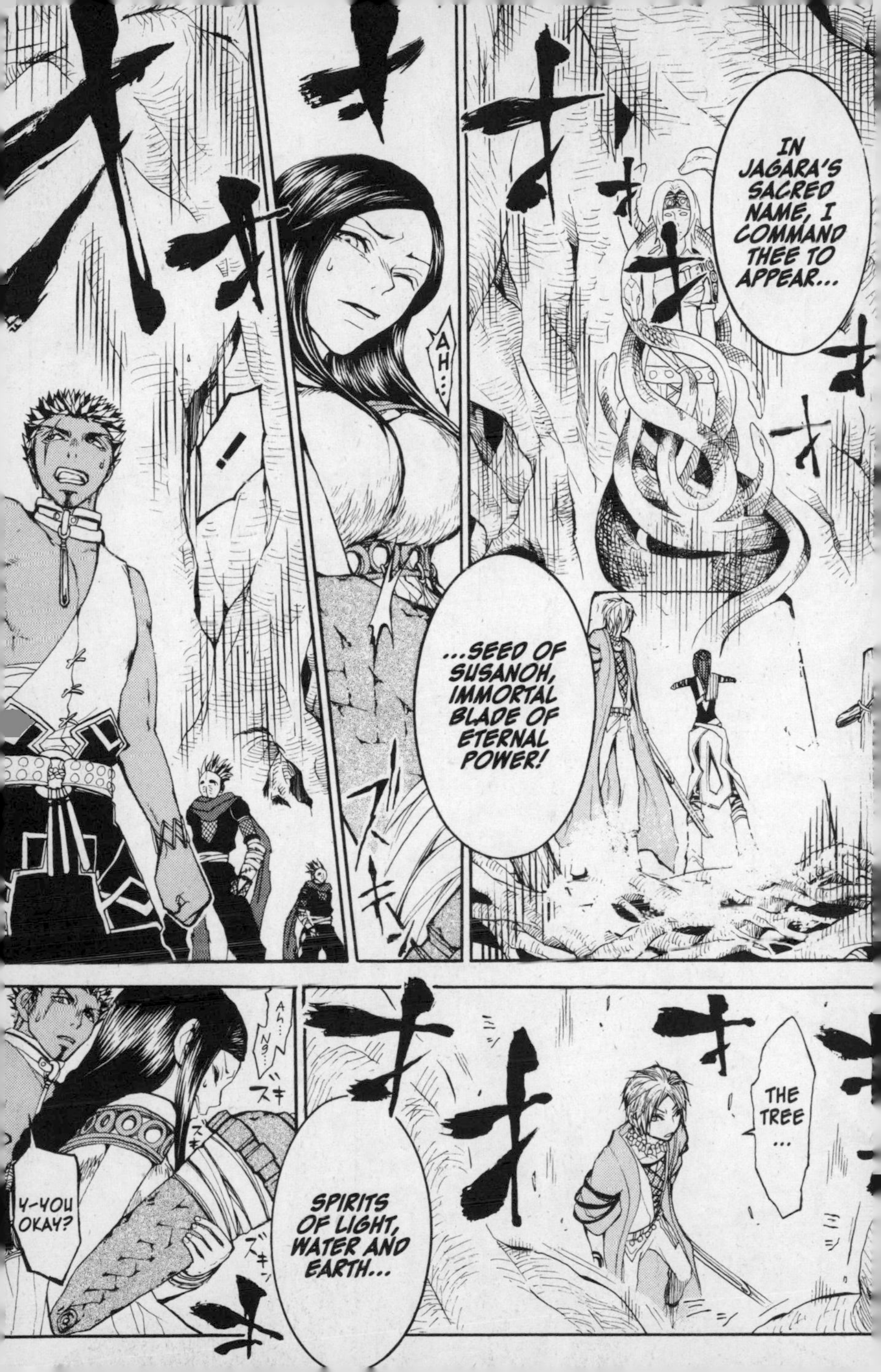
IN JAGARA'S SACRED NAME, I COMMAND THEE TO APPEAR...
...SEED OF SUSANOH, IMMORTAL BLADE OF ETERNAL POWER!
AH...
!
THE TREE ...
SPIRITS OF LIGHT, WATER AND EARTH...
Ah... Ng...
Y-YOU OKAY?

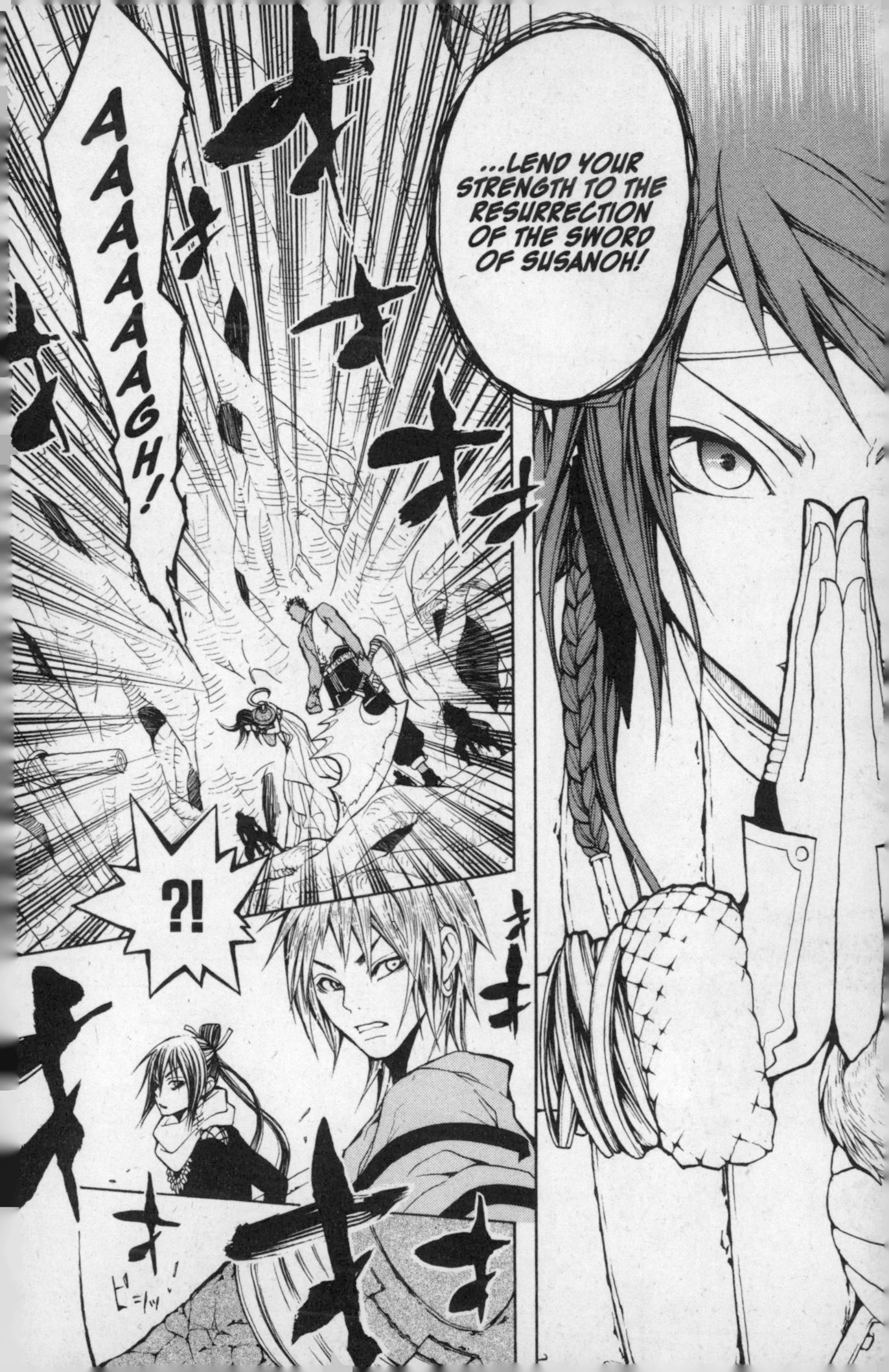
...LEND YOUR STRENGTH TO THE RESURRECTION OF THE SWORD OF SUSANOH!
AAAAAAGH!
?!

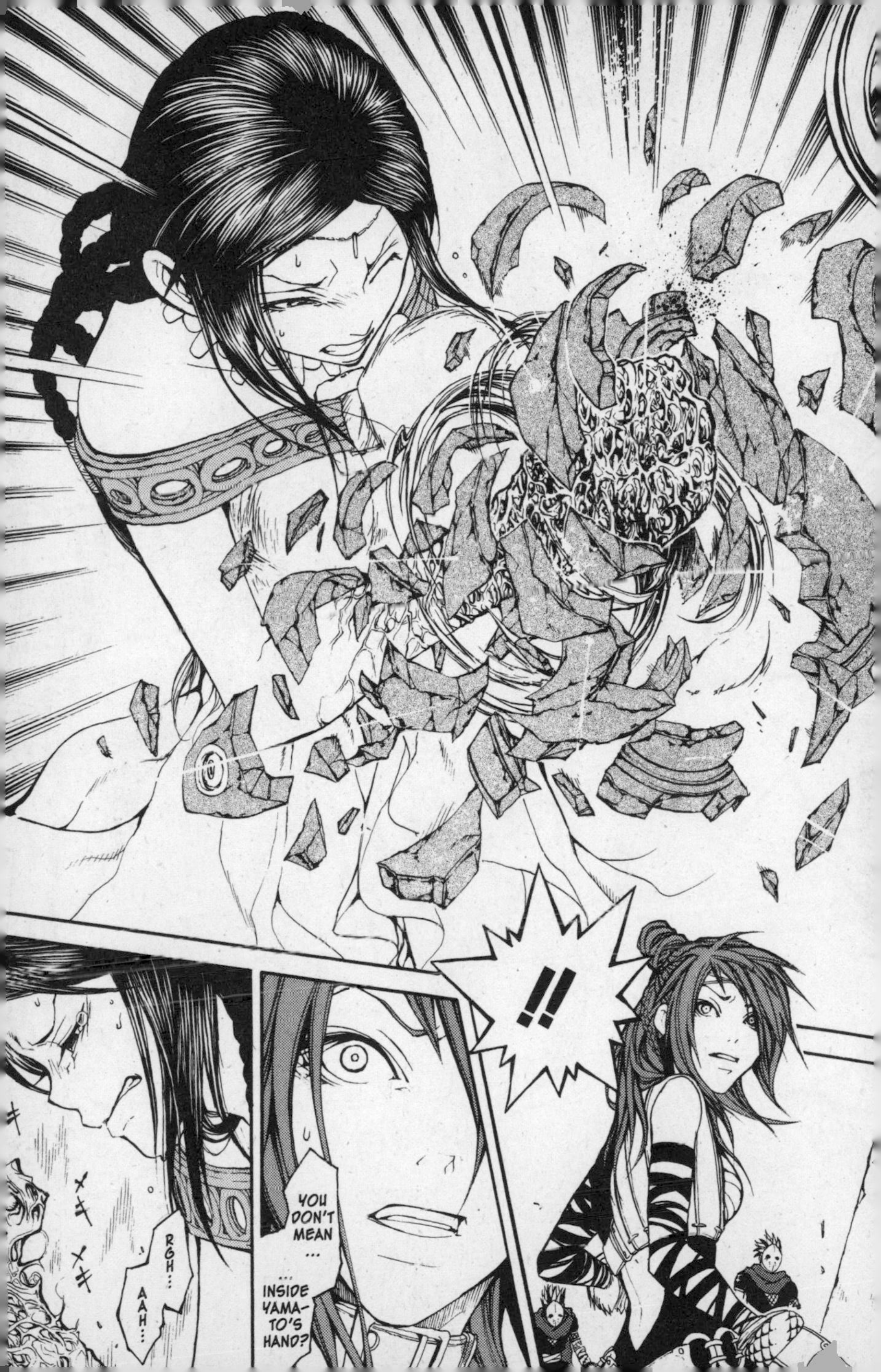
!!
YOU DON'T MEAN ...
... INSIDE YAMATO'S HAND?
RGH...
AAH...

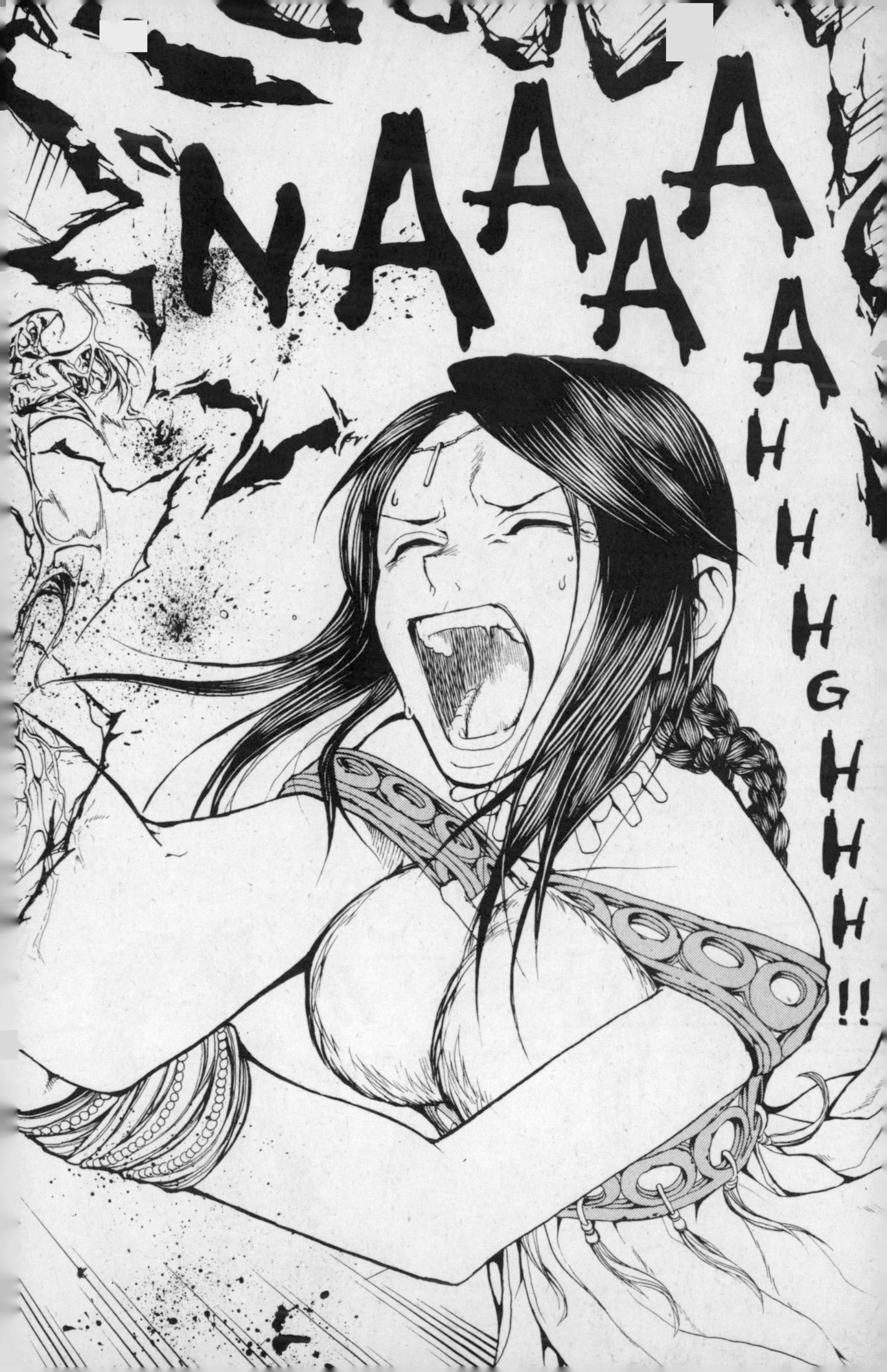
NAAAAAHHHGHHH!!

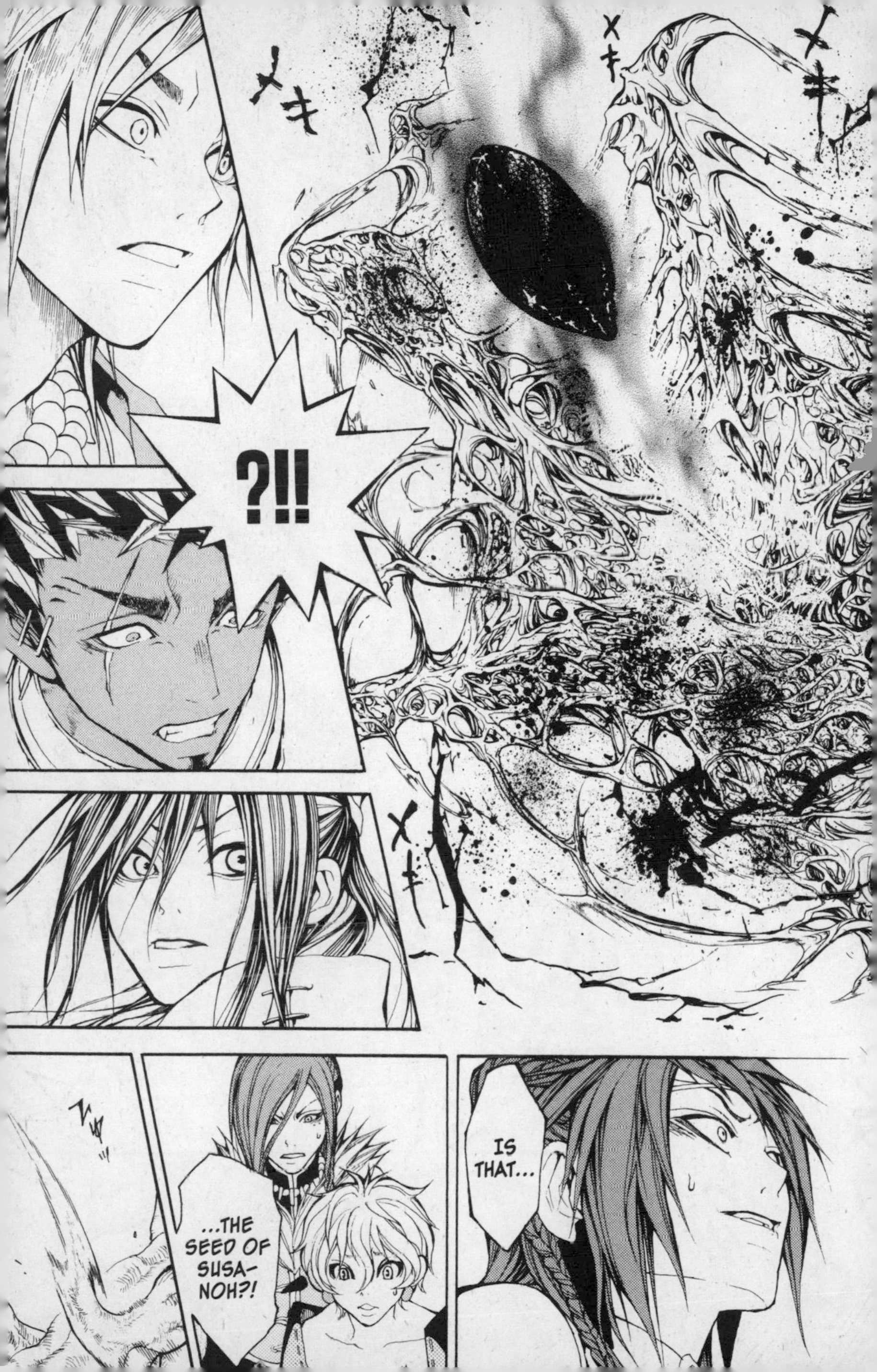
?!!
IS THAT...
...THE SEED OF SUSA-NOH?!

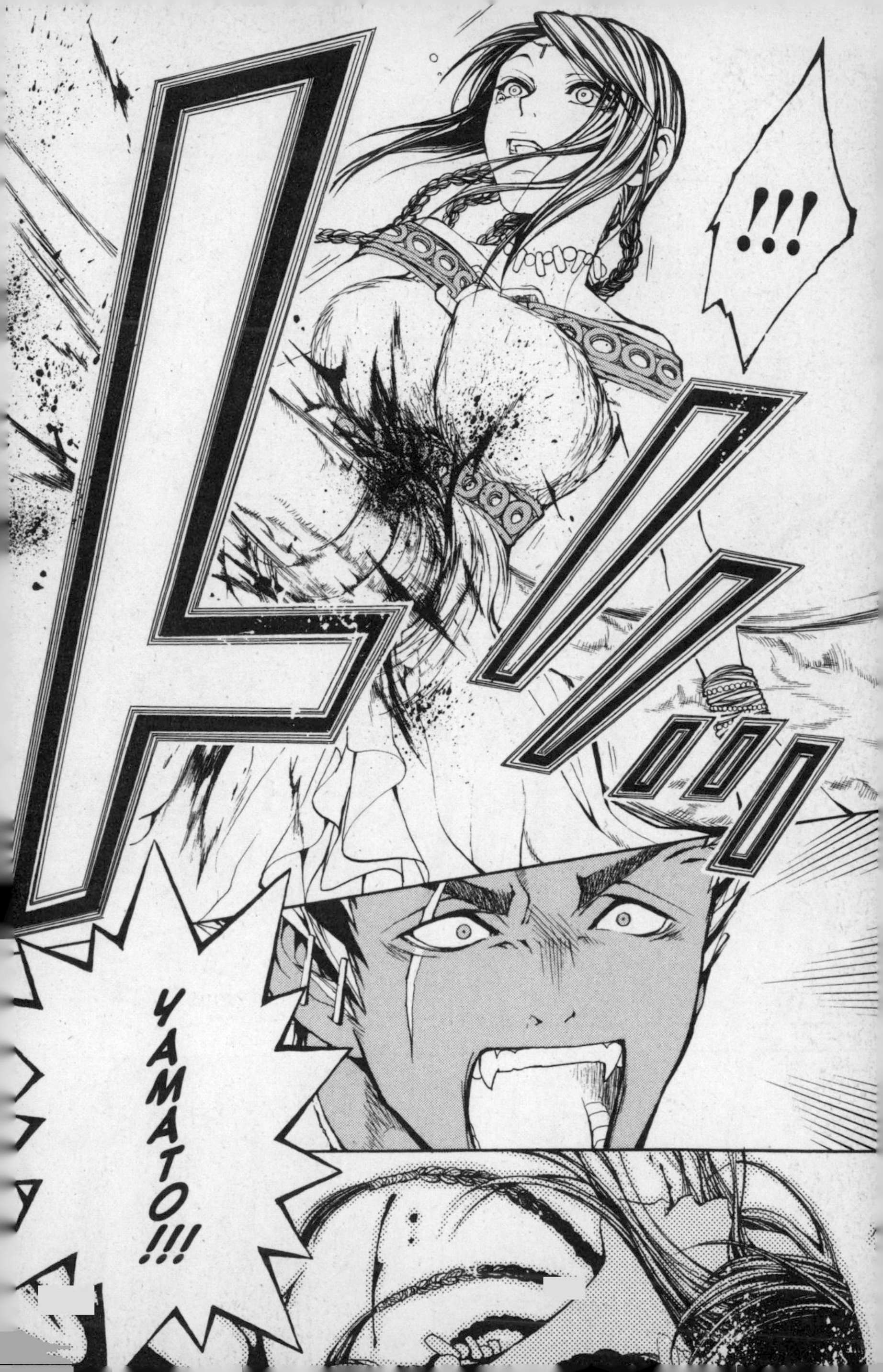
!!!
YAMATO!!!

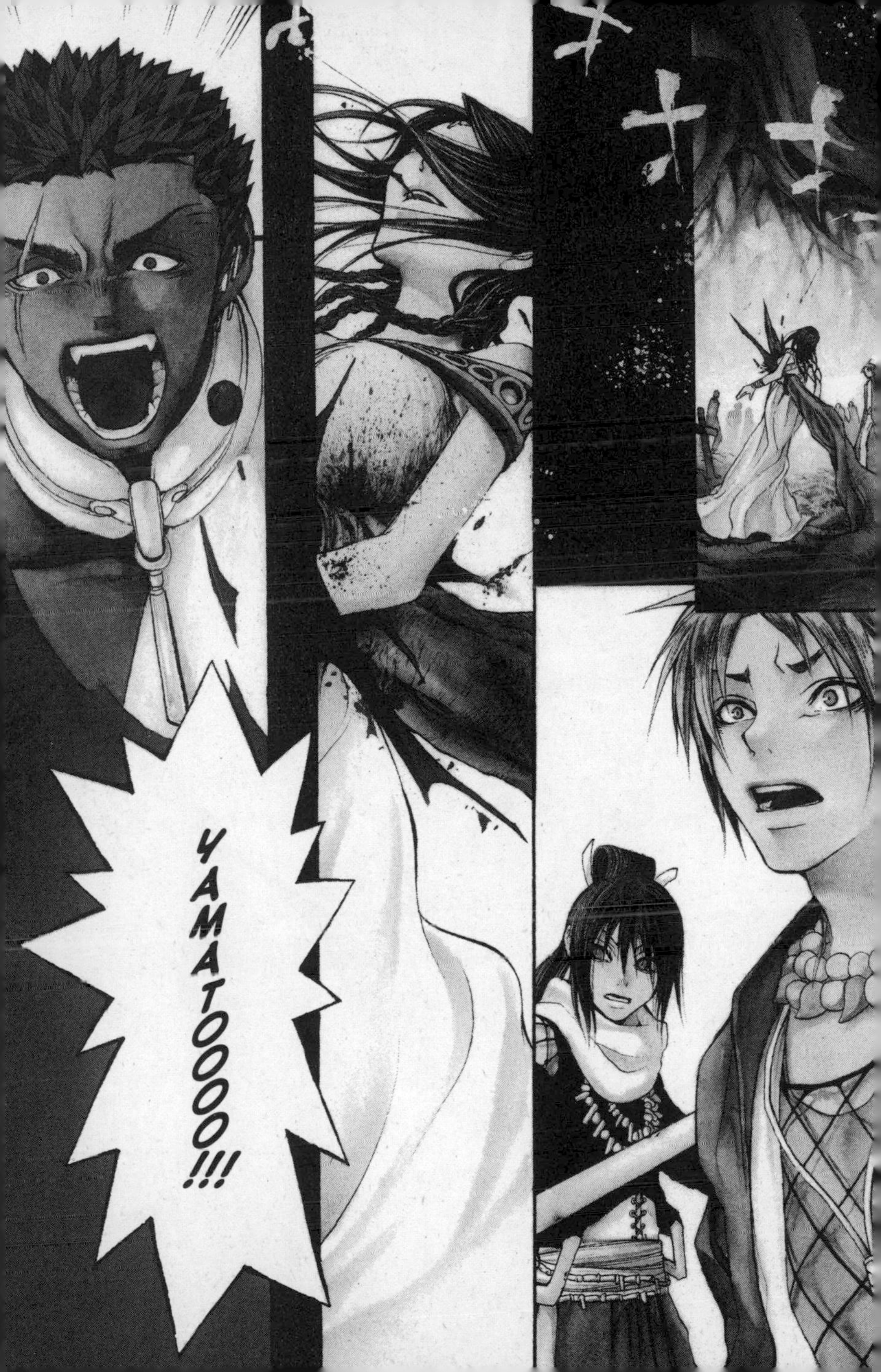
YAMATOOOOO!!!

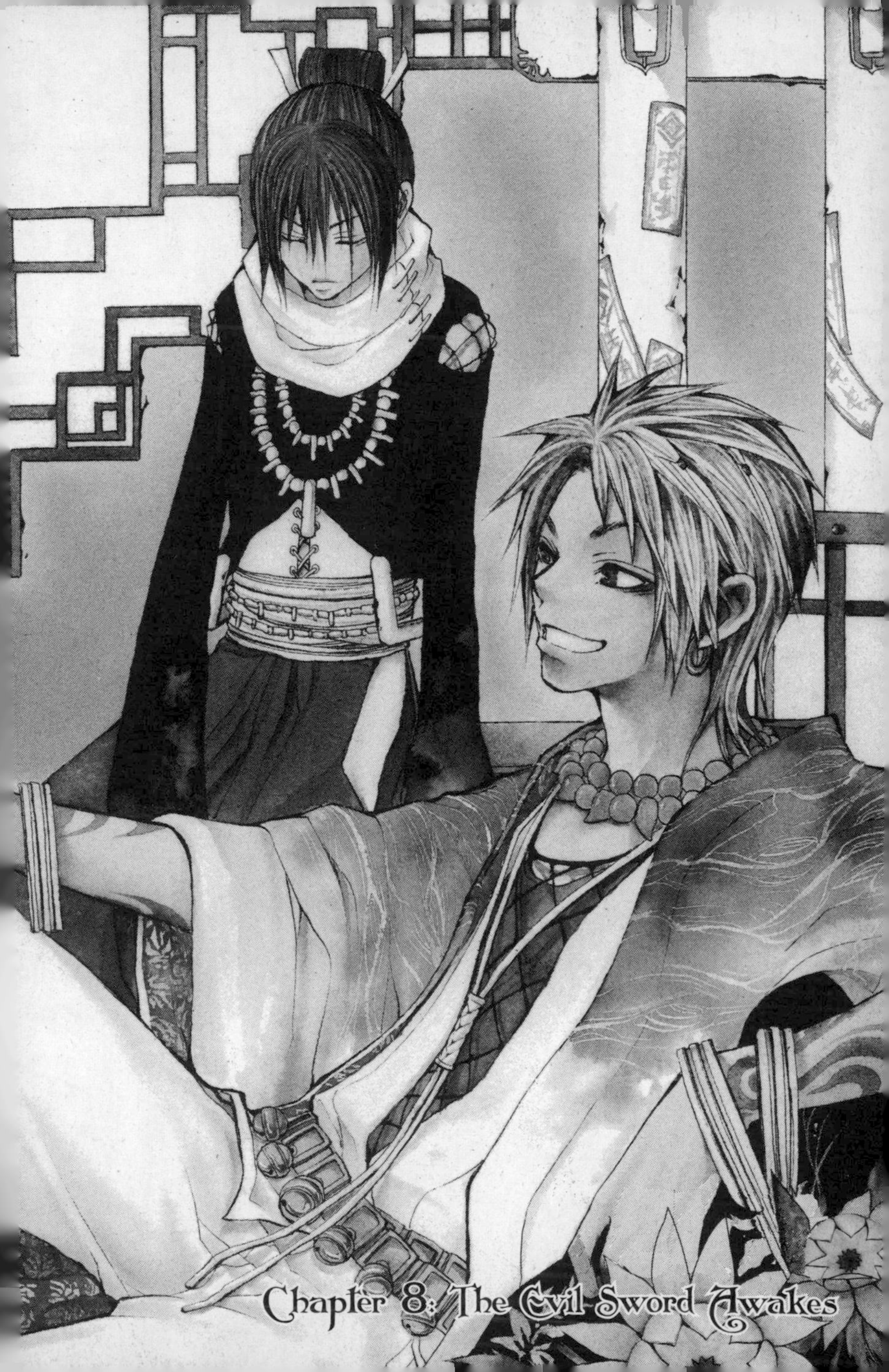

Chapter 8: The Evil Sword Awakes

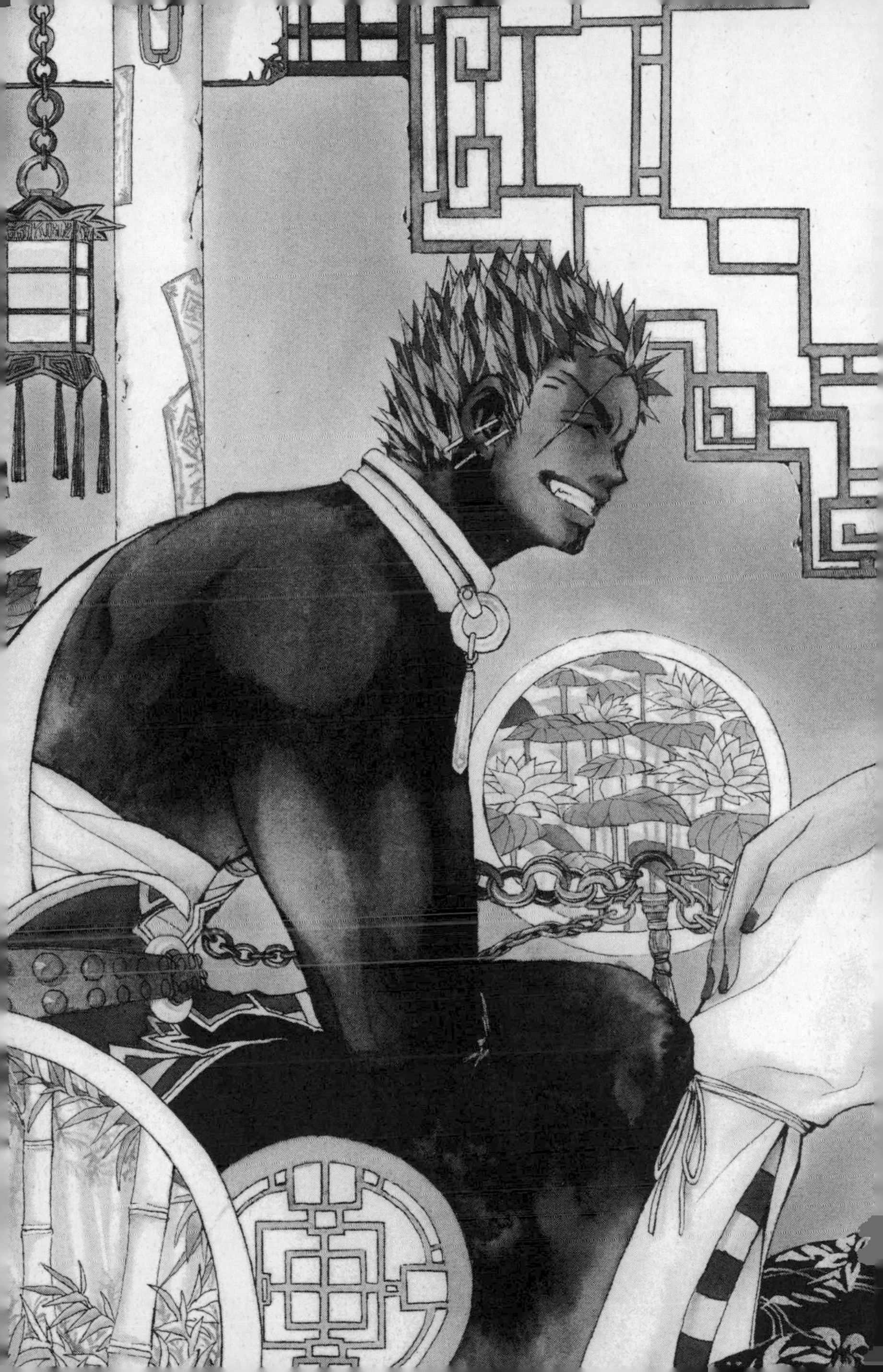

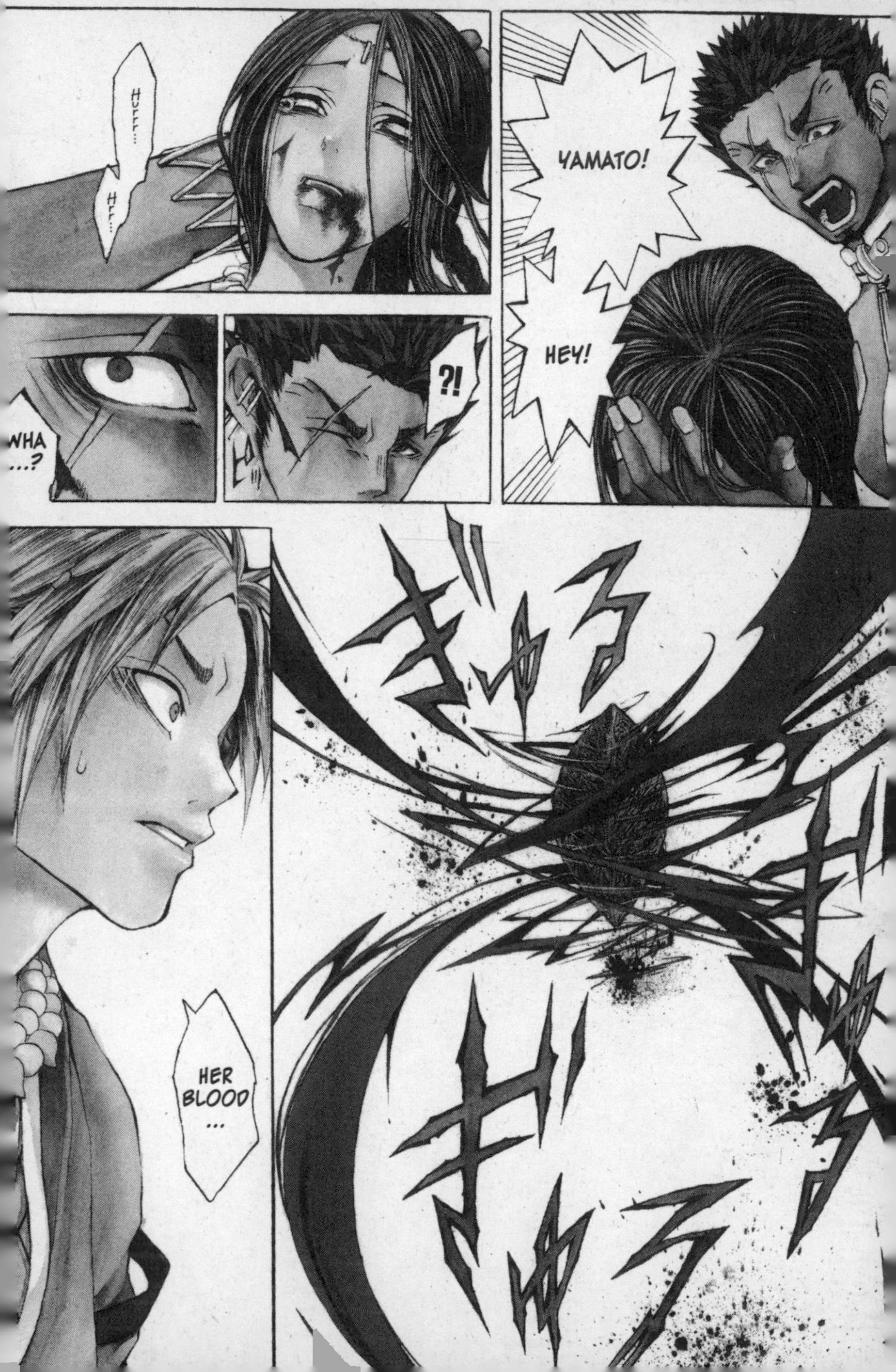
YAMATO!
HEY!
Hurrr...
Hrr...
?!
WHA ...?
HER BLOOD ...

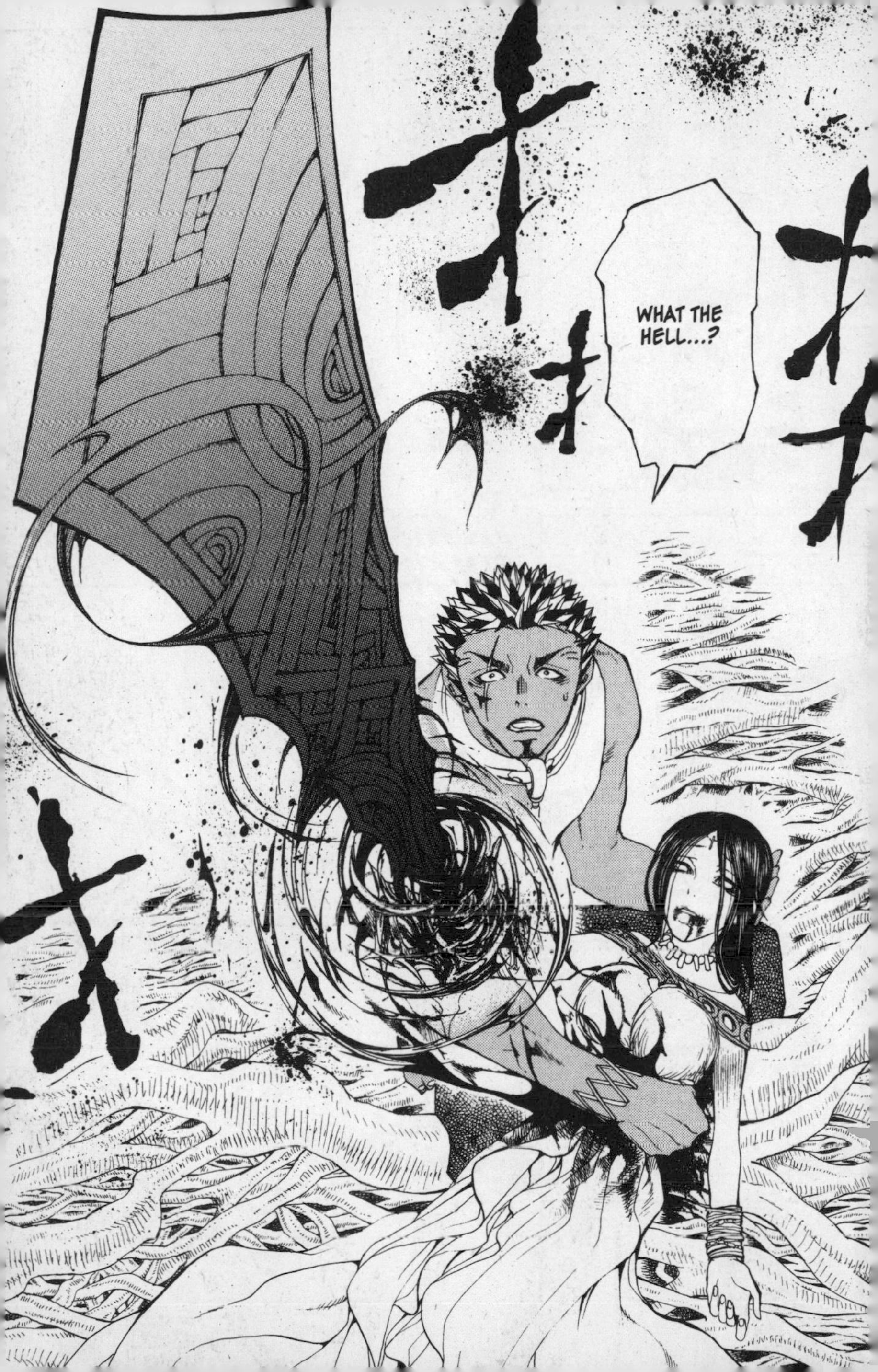
WHAT THE HELL...?

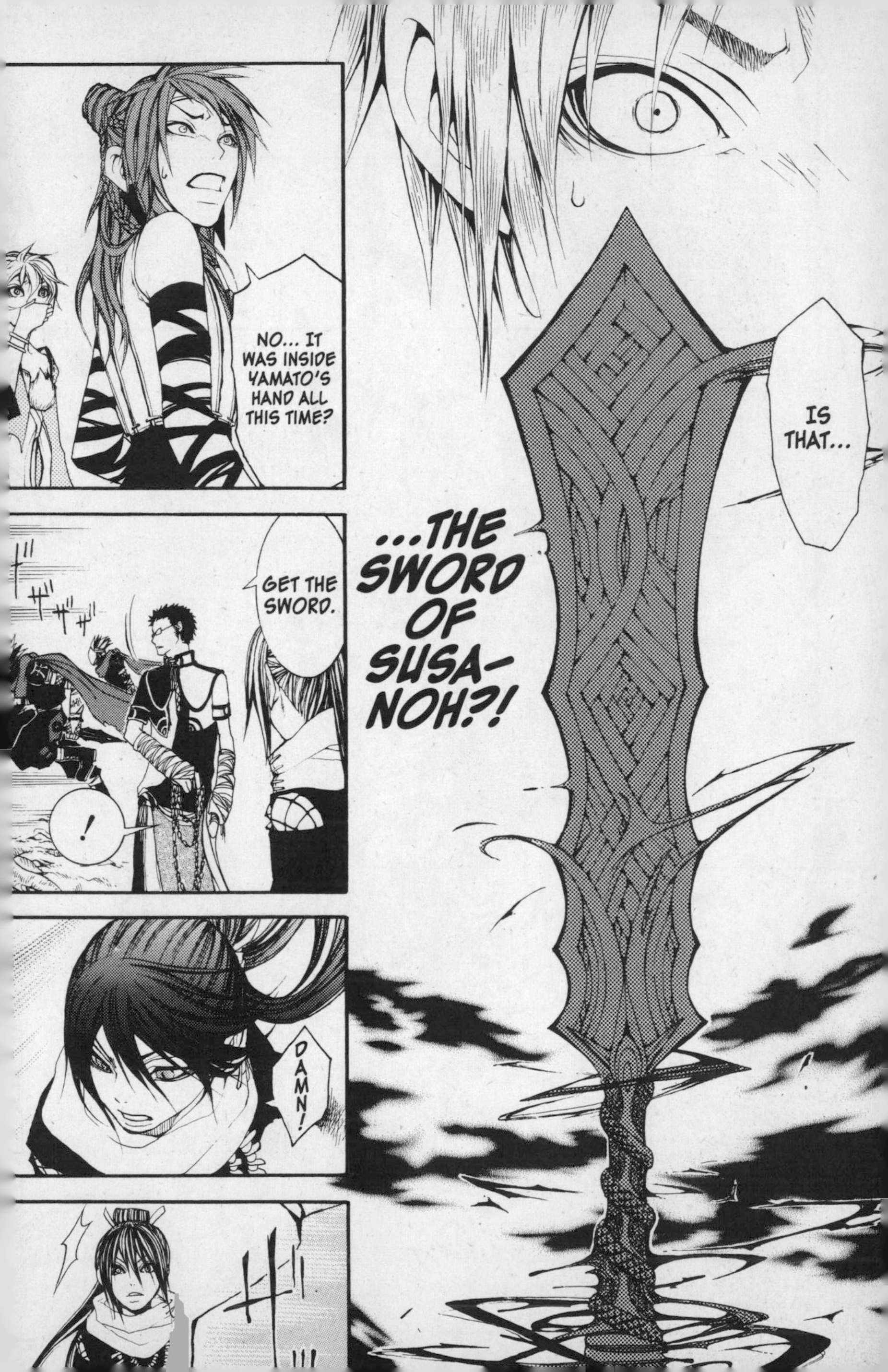

IS THAT...
...THE SWORD OF SUSA-NOH?!
NO... IT WAS INSIDE YAMATO'S HAND ALL THIS TIME?
GET THE SWORD.
!
DAMN!

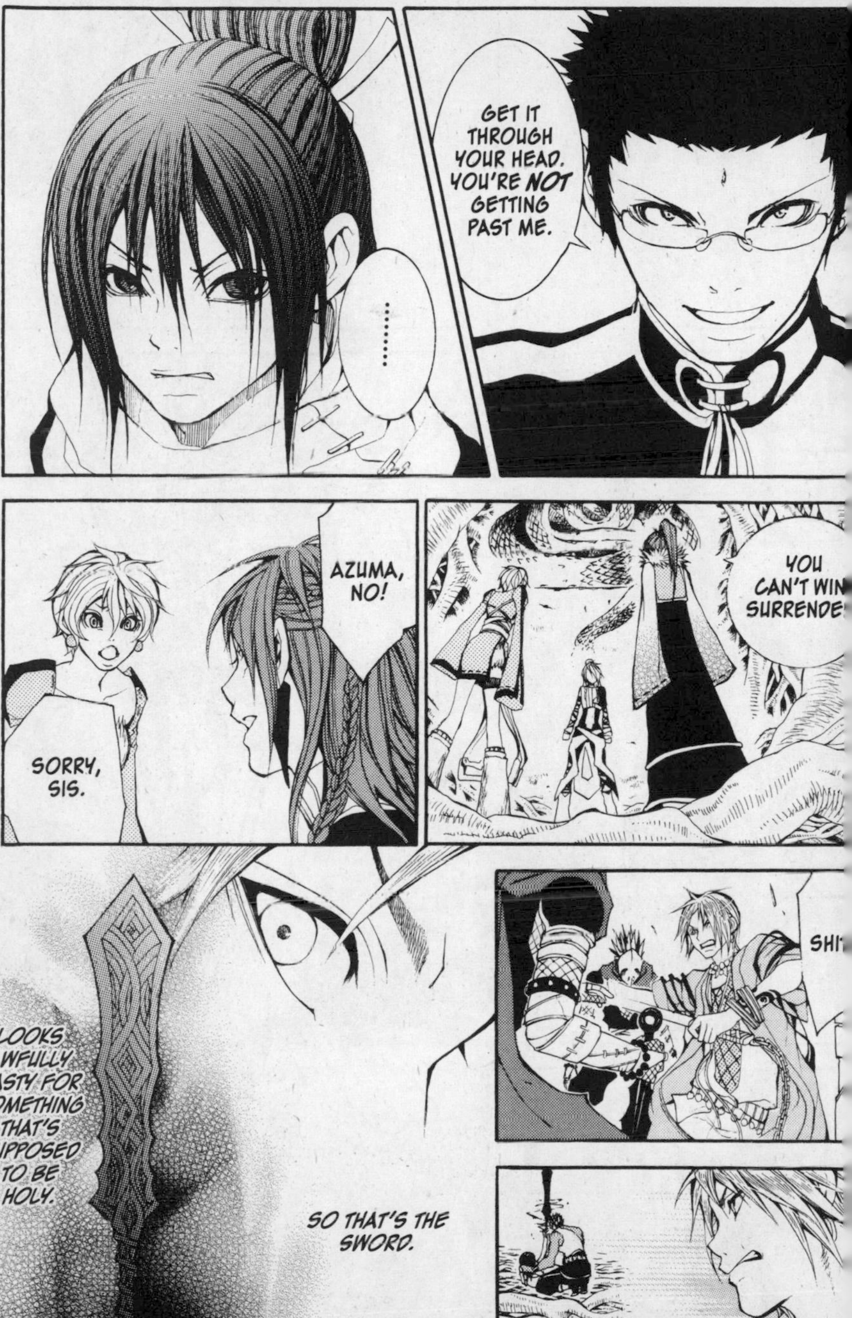
GET IT THROUGH YOUR HEAD. YOU'RE **NOT** GETTING PAST ME.
......
YOU CAN'T WIN SURRENDE
AZUMA, NO!
SORRY, SIS.
SHI
SO THAT'S THE SWORD.
LOOKS AWFULLY NASTY FOR SOMETHING THAT'S SUPPOSED TO BE HOLY.

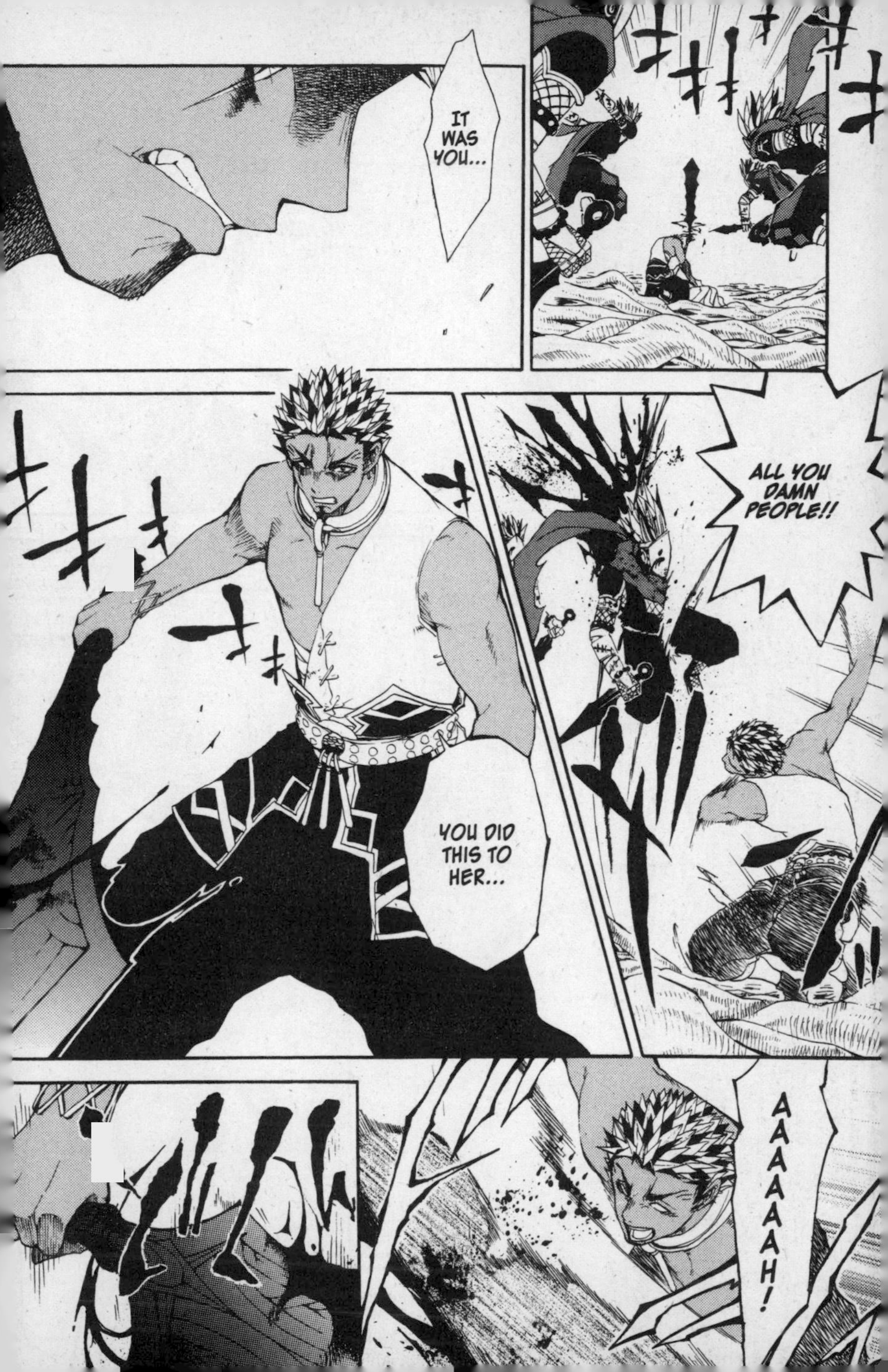
IT WAS YOU...
ALL YOU DAMN PEOPLE!!
YOU DID THIS TO HER...
AAAAAAH!

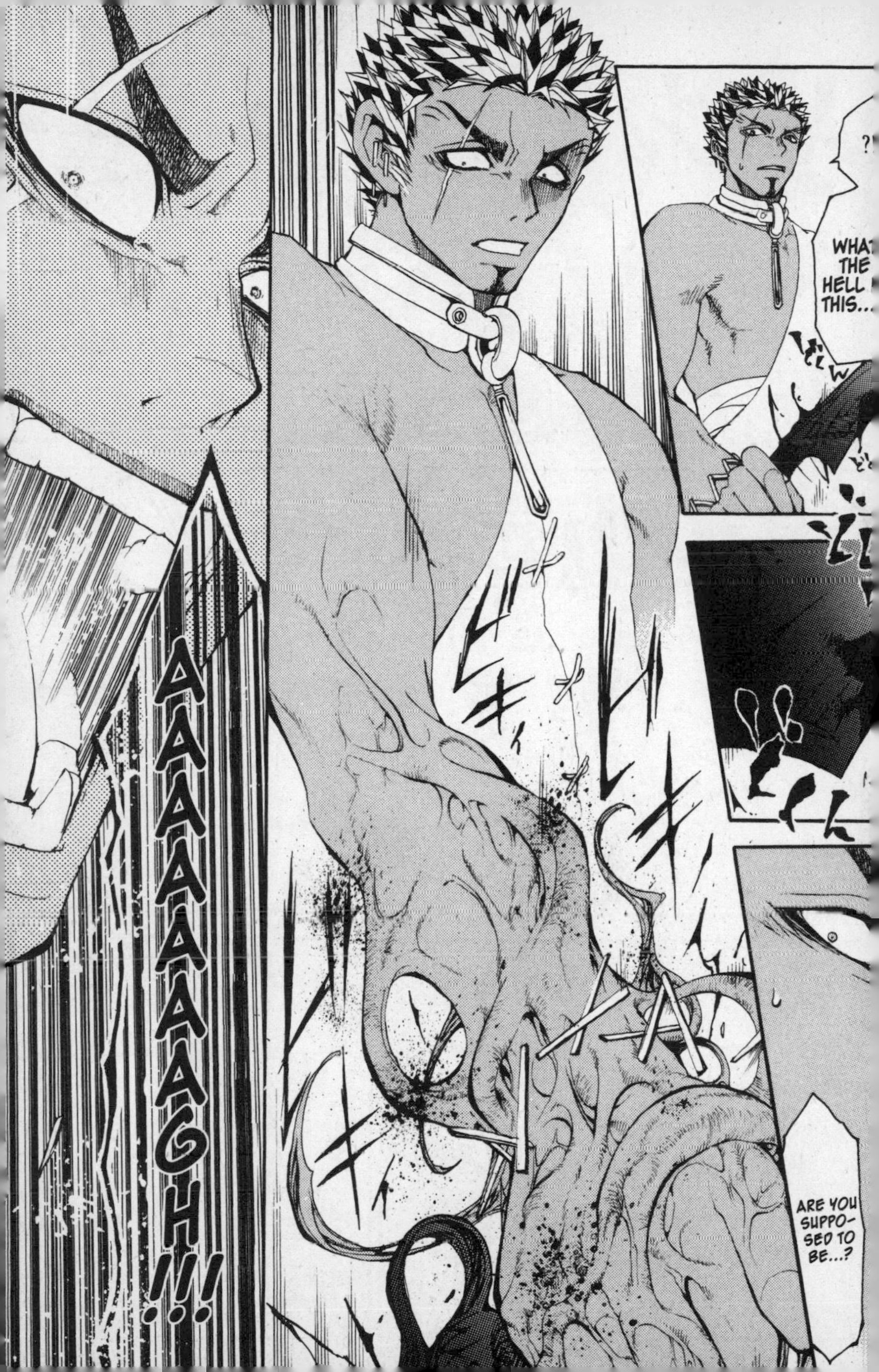
?!
WHAT THE HELL THIS...
ARE YOU SUPPO-SED TO BE...?
AAAAAAAAAGH!!!

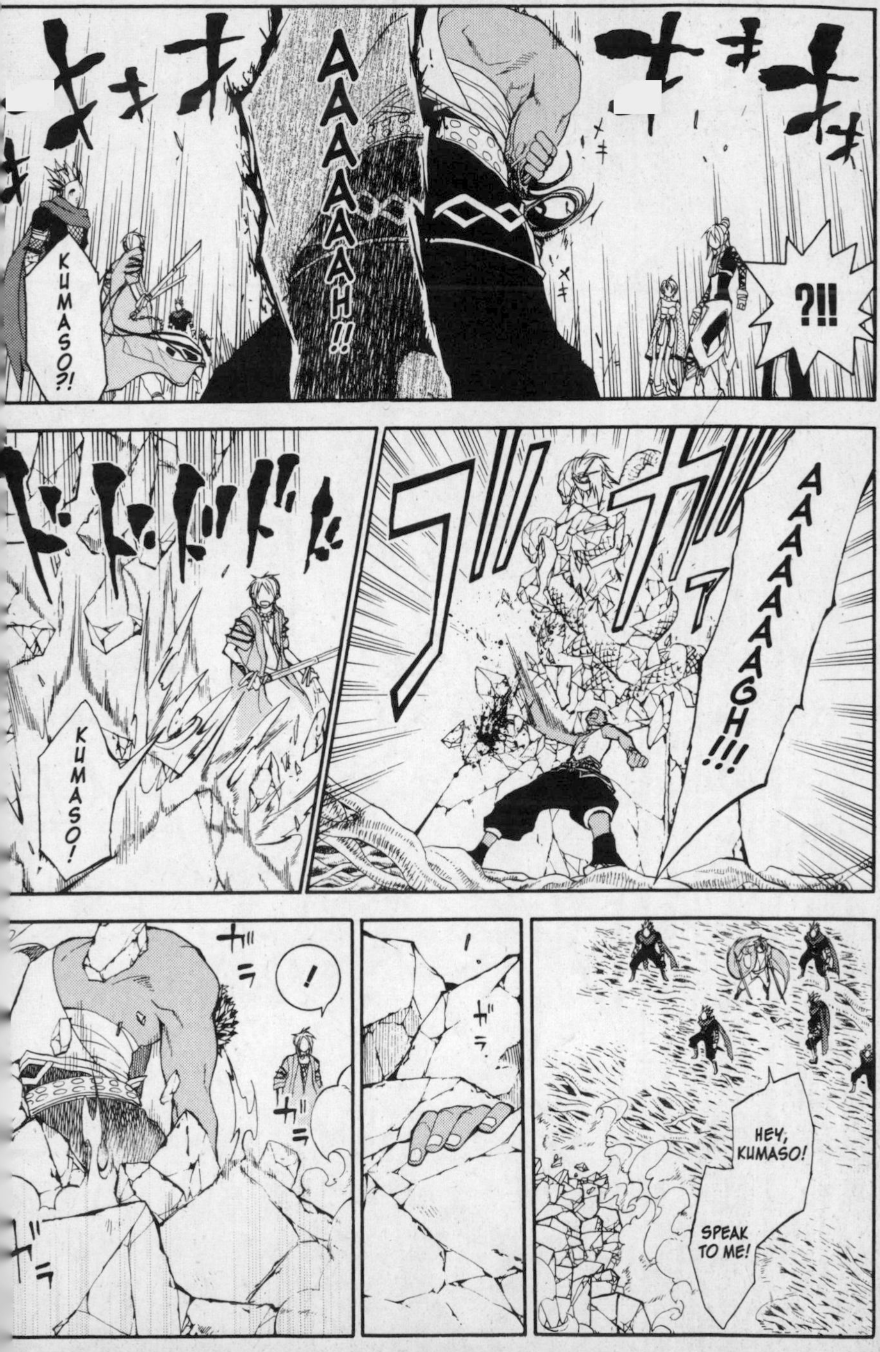
?!!
AAAAAAAH!!
KUMASO?!
AAAAAAAGH!!!
KUMASO!
HEY, KUMASO!
SPEAK TO ME!
!

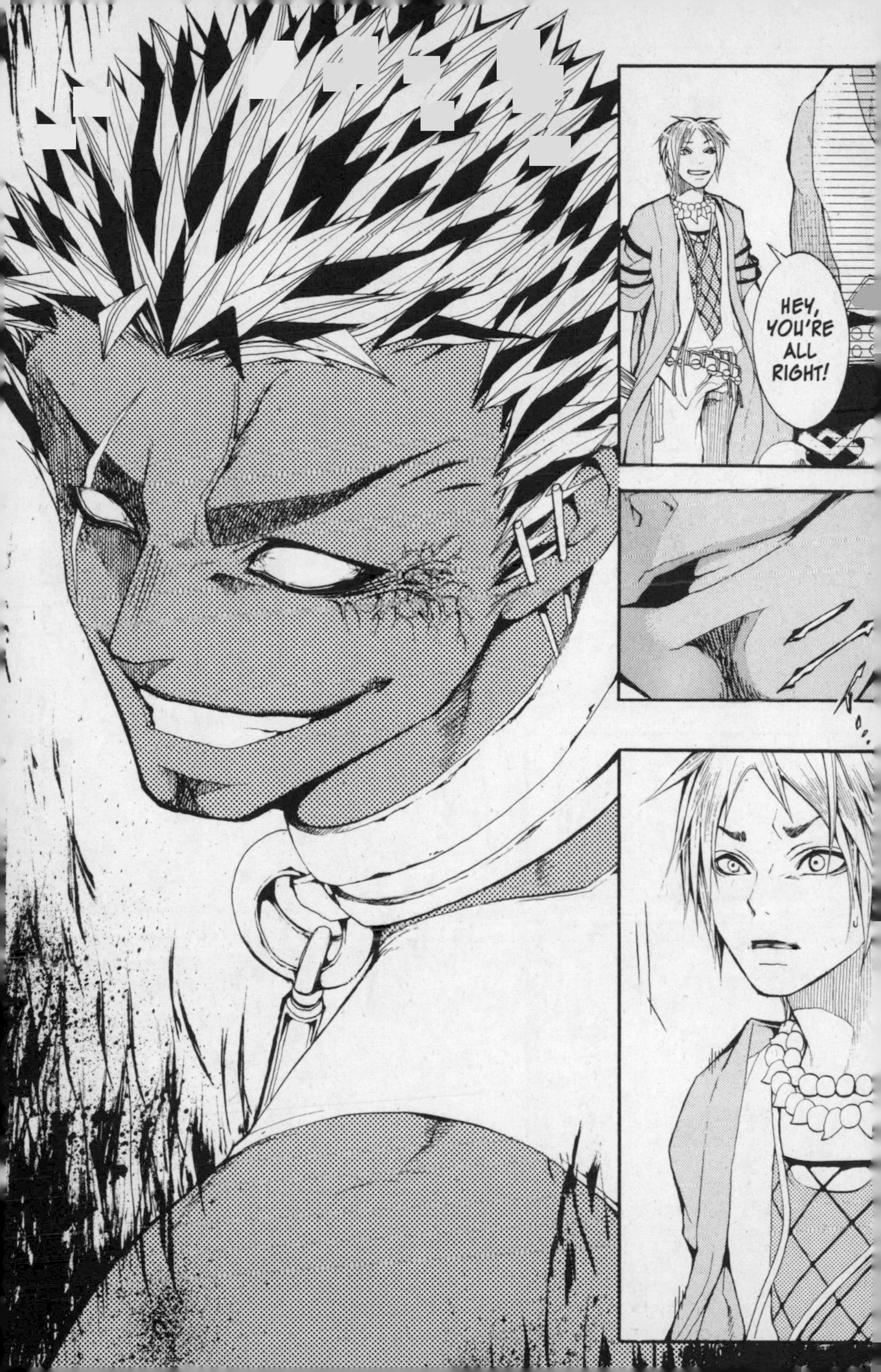
HEY, YOU'RE ALL RIGHT!

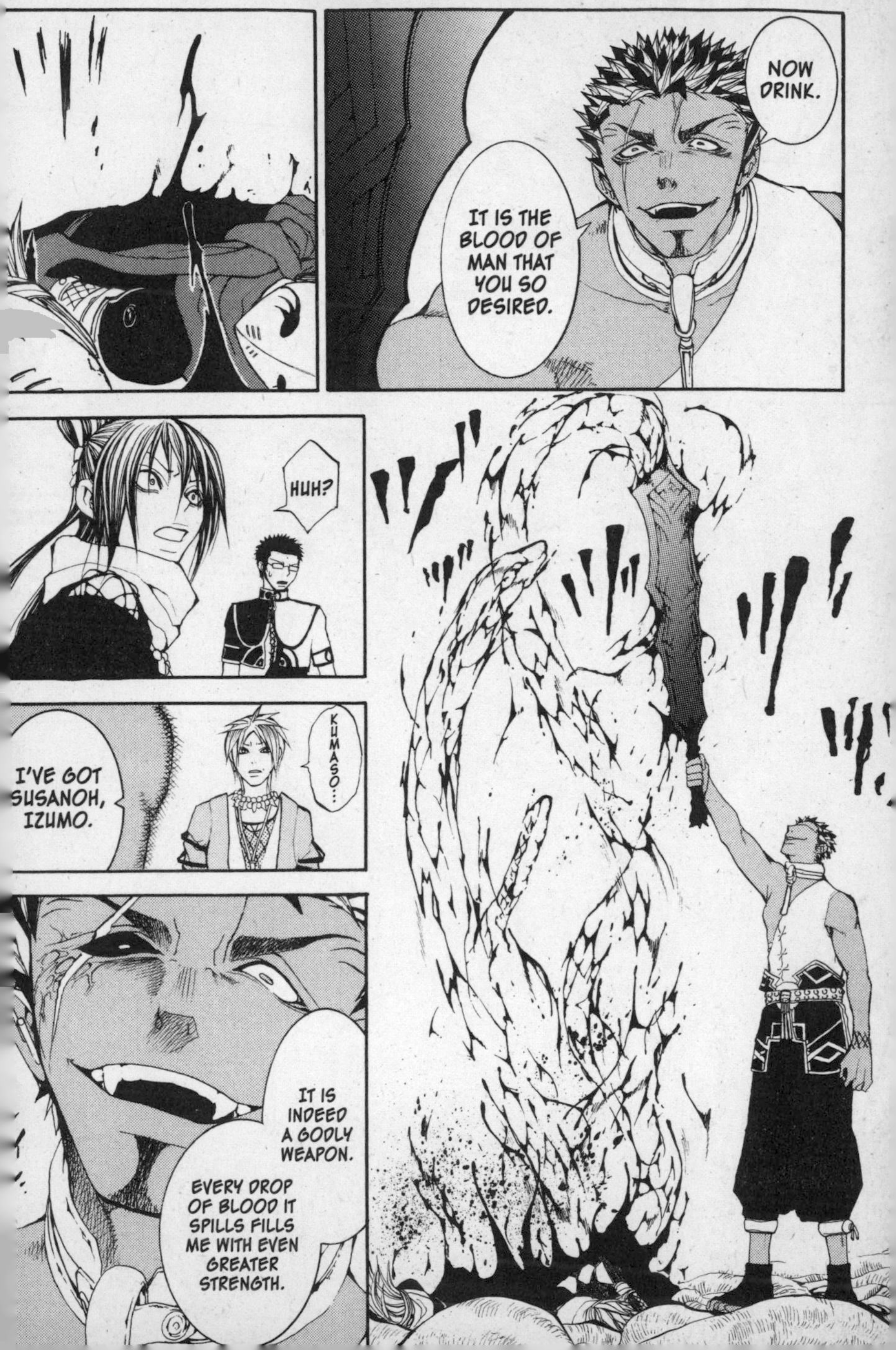
NOW DRINK.
IT IS THE BLOOD OF MAN THAT YOU SO DESIRED.
HUH?
KUMASO...
I'VE GOT SUSANOH, IZUMO.
IT IS INDEED A GODLY WEAPON.
EVERY DROP OF BLOOD IT SPILLS FILLS ME WITH EVEN GREATER STRENGTH.

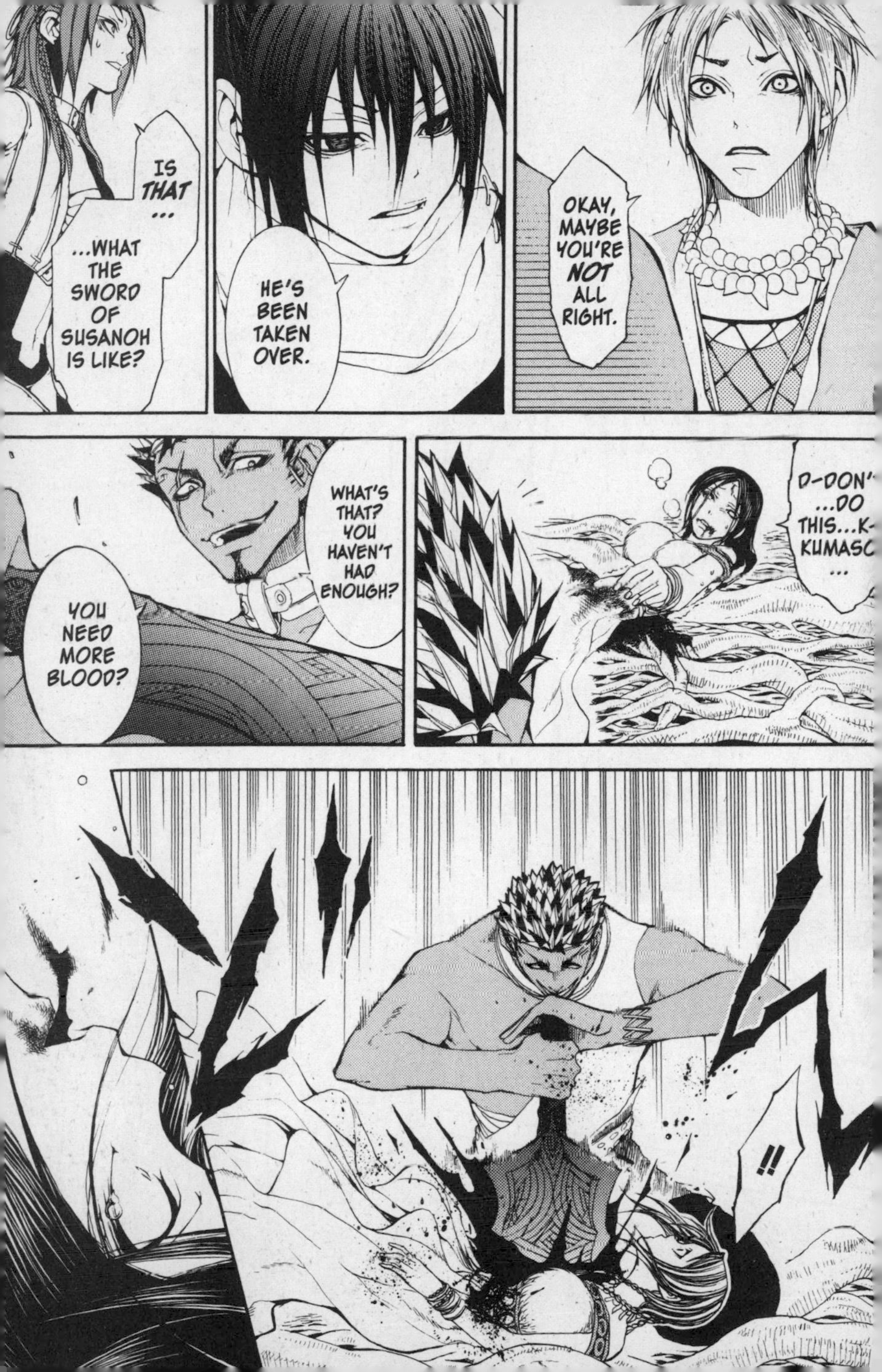
OKAY, MAYBE YOU'RE NOT ALL RIGHT.
HE'S BEEN TAKEN OVER.
IS THAT ...
...WHAT THE SWORD OF SUSANOH IS LIKE?
D-DON' ...DO THIS...K-KUMASC ...
WHAT'S THAT? YOU HAVEN'T HAD ENOUGH?
YOU NEED MORE BLOOD?
!!

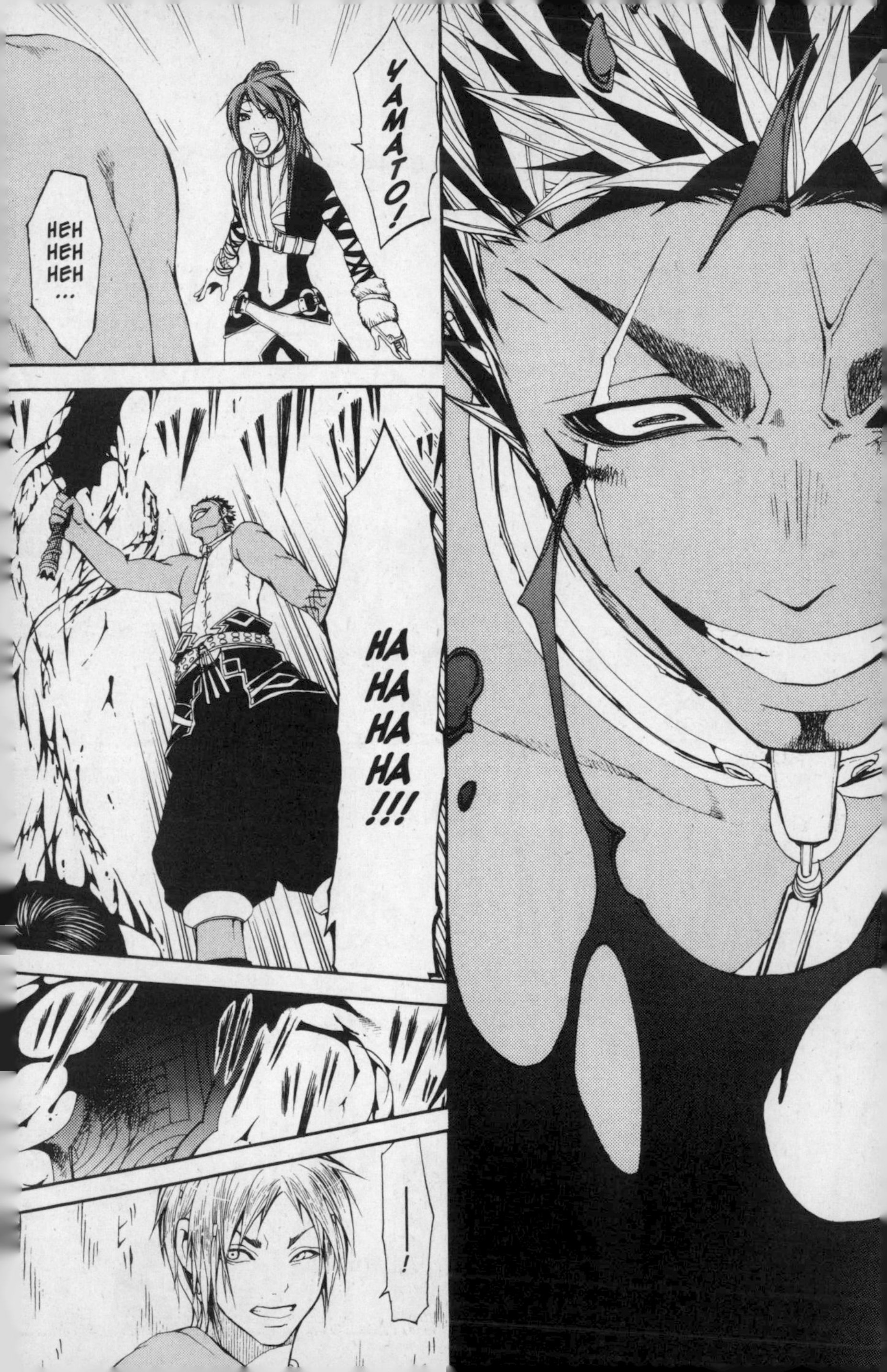
YAMATO!
HEH HEH HEH ...
HA HA HA HA!!!
—!

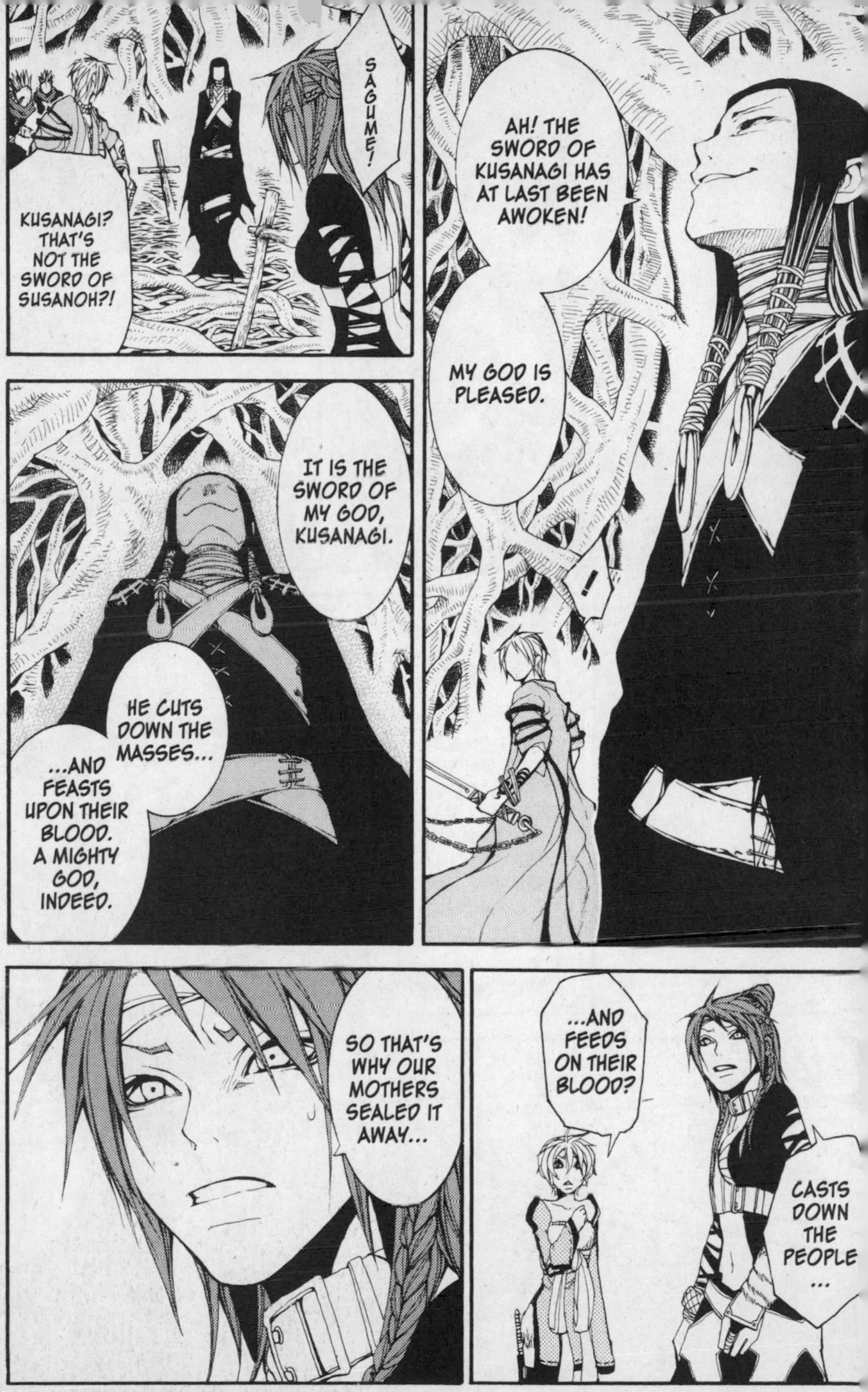
AH! THE SWORD OF KUSANAGI HAS AT LAST BEEN AWOKEN!
MY GOD IS PLEASED.
!
SAGUME!
KUSANAGI? THAT'S NOT THE SWORD OF SUSANOH?!
IT IS THE SWORD OF MY GOD, KUSANAGI.
HE CUTS DOWN THE MASSES...
...AND FEASTS UPON THEIR BLOOD. A MIGHTY GOD, INDEED.
CASTS DOWN THE PEOPLE ...
...AND FEEDS ON THEIR BLOOD?
SO THAT'S WHY OUR MOTHERS SEALED IT AWAY...

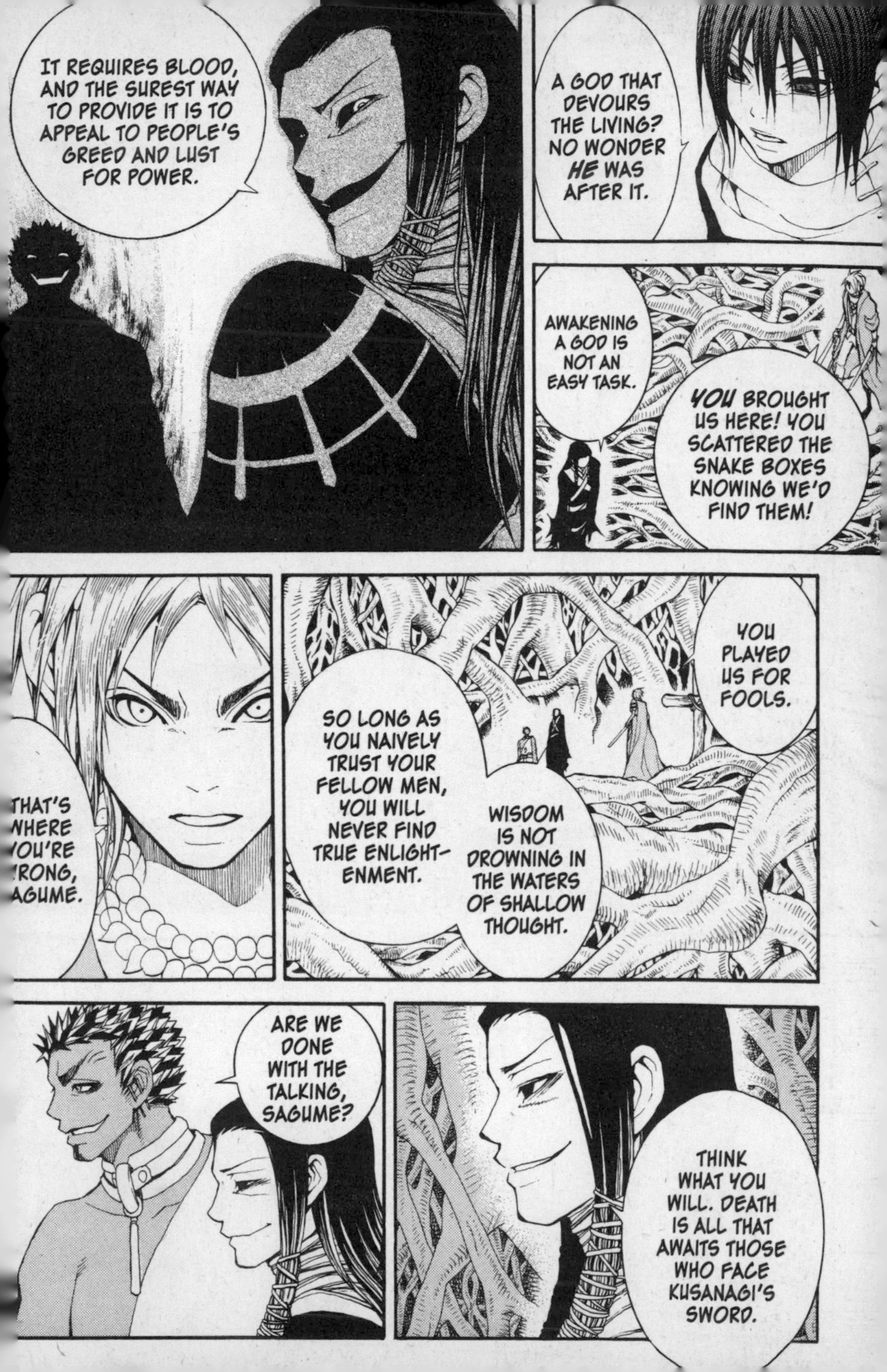
A GOD THAT DEVOURS THE LIVING? NO WONDER HE WAS AFTER IT.
YOU BROUGHT US HERE! YOU SCATTERED THE SNAKE BOXES KNOWING WE'D FIND THEM!
AWAKENING A GOD IS NOT AN EASY TASK.
IT REQUIRES BLOOD, AND THE SUREST WAY TO PROVIDE IT IS TO APPEAL TO PEOPLE'S GREED AND LUST FOR POWER.
YOU PLAYED US FOR FOOLS.
WISDOM IS NOT DROWNING IN THE WATERS OF SHALLOW THOUGHT.
SO LONG AS YOU NAIVELY TRUST YOUR FELLOW MEN, YOU WILL NEVER FIND TRUE ENLIGHT-ENMENT.
THAT'S WHERE YOU'RE WRONG, SAGUME.
THINK WHAT YOU WILL. DEATH IS ALL THAT AWAITS THOSE WHO FACE KUSANAGI'S SWORD.
ARE WE DONE WITH THE TALKING, SAGUME?

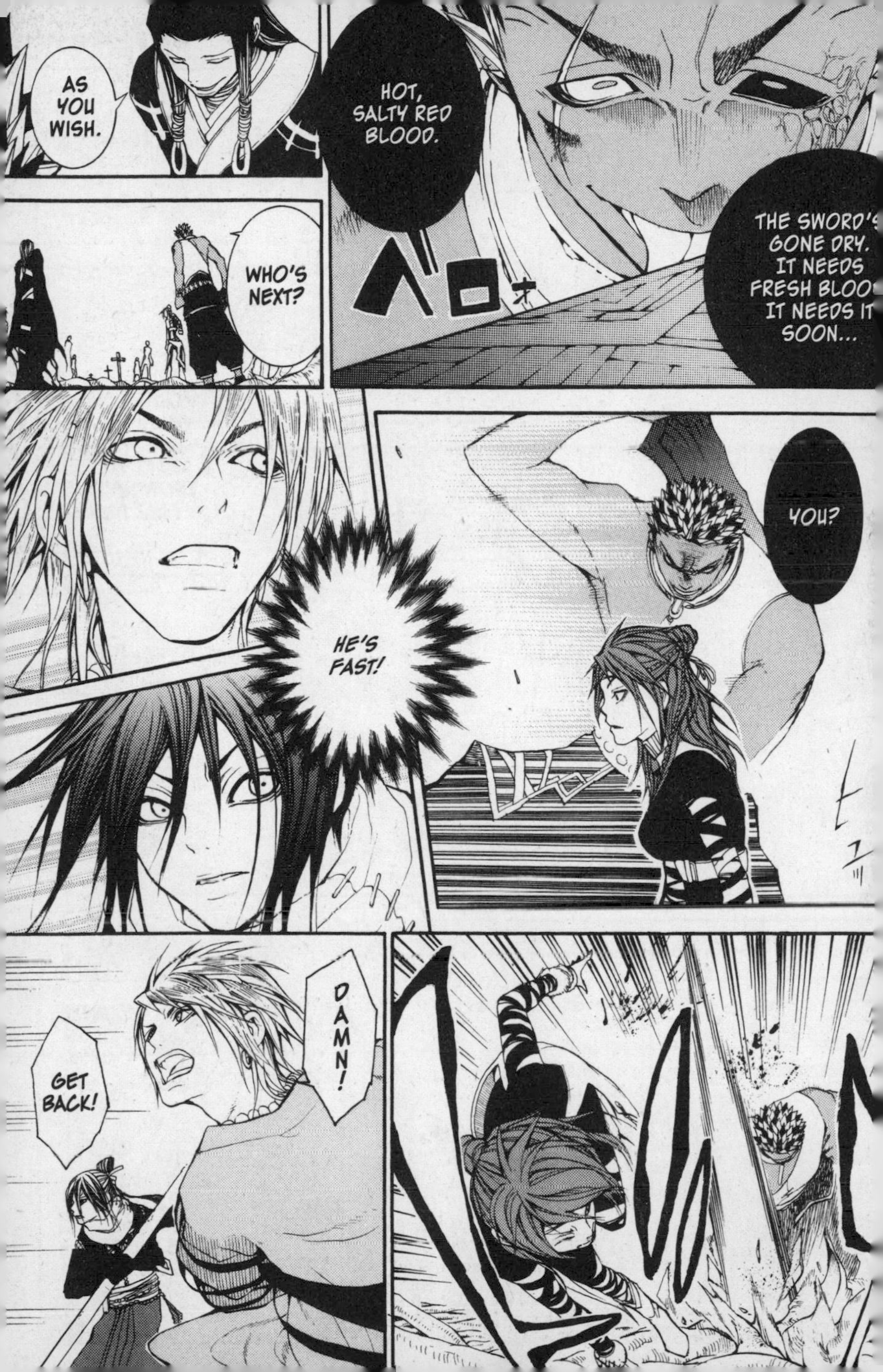
HOT, SALTY RED BLOOD.
ペロォ
THE SWORD'S GONE DRY. IT NEEDS FRESH BLOO IT NEEDS IT SOON...
AS YOU WISH.
WHO'S NEXT?
YOU?
HE'S FAST!
ヒュッ
DAMN!
GET BACK!

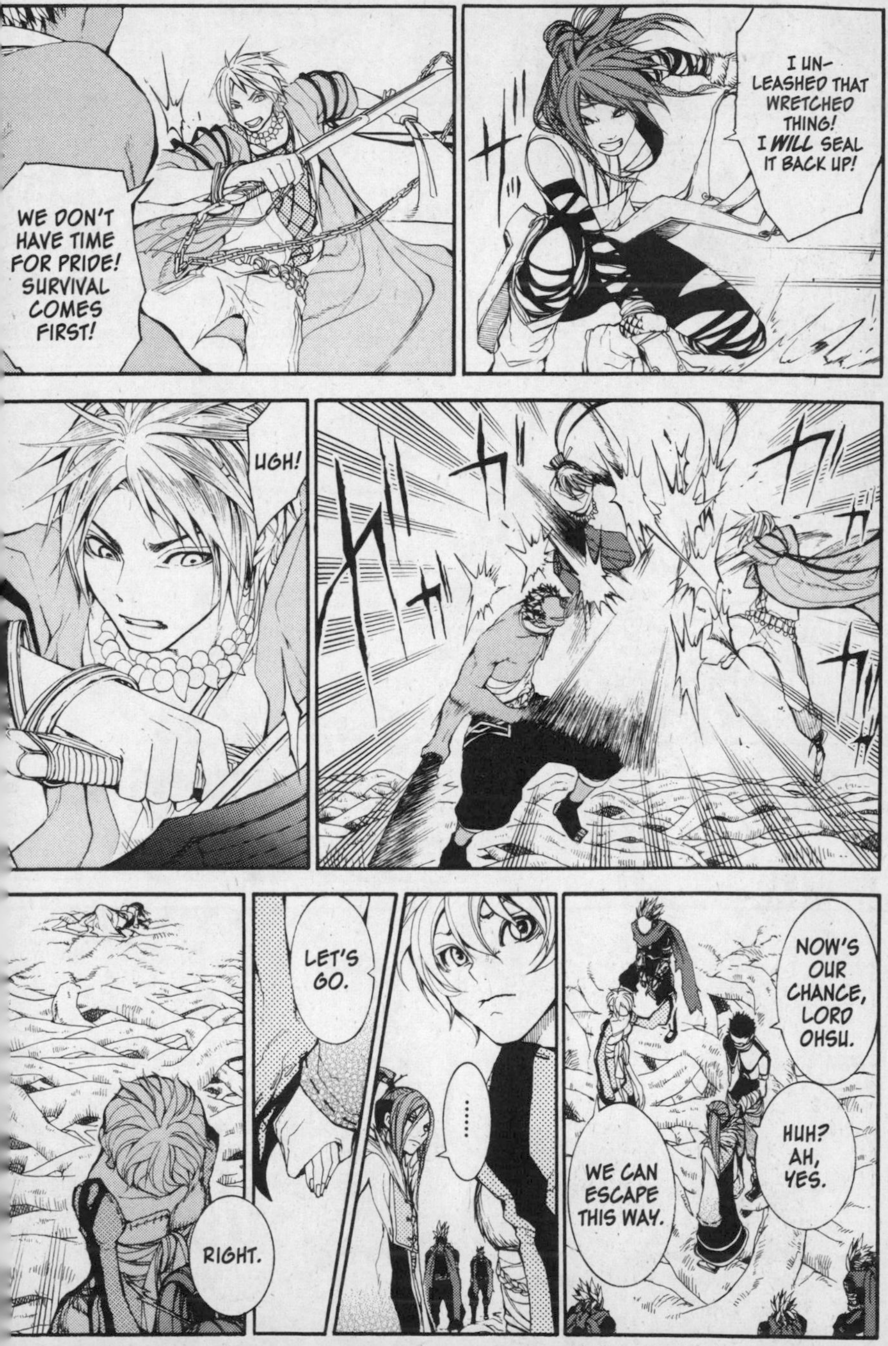
I UN-LEASHED THAT WRETCHED THING! I WILL SEAL IT BACK UP!
WE DON'T HAVE TIME FOR PRIDE! SURVIVAL COMES FIRST!
UGH!
NOW'S OUR CHANCE, LORD OHSU.
HUH? AH, YES.
WE CAN ESCAPE THIS WAY.
......
LET'S GO.
RIGHT.

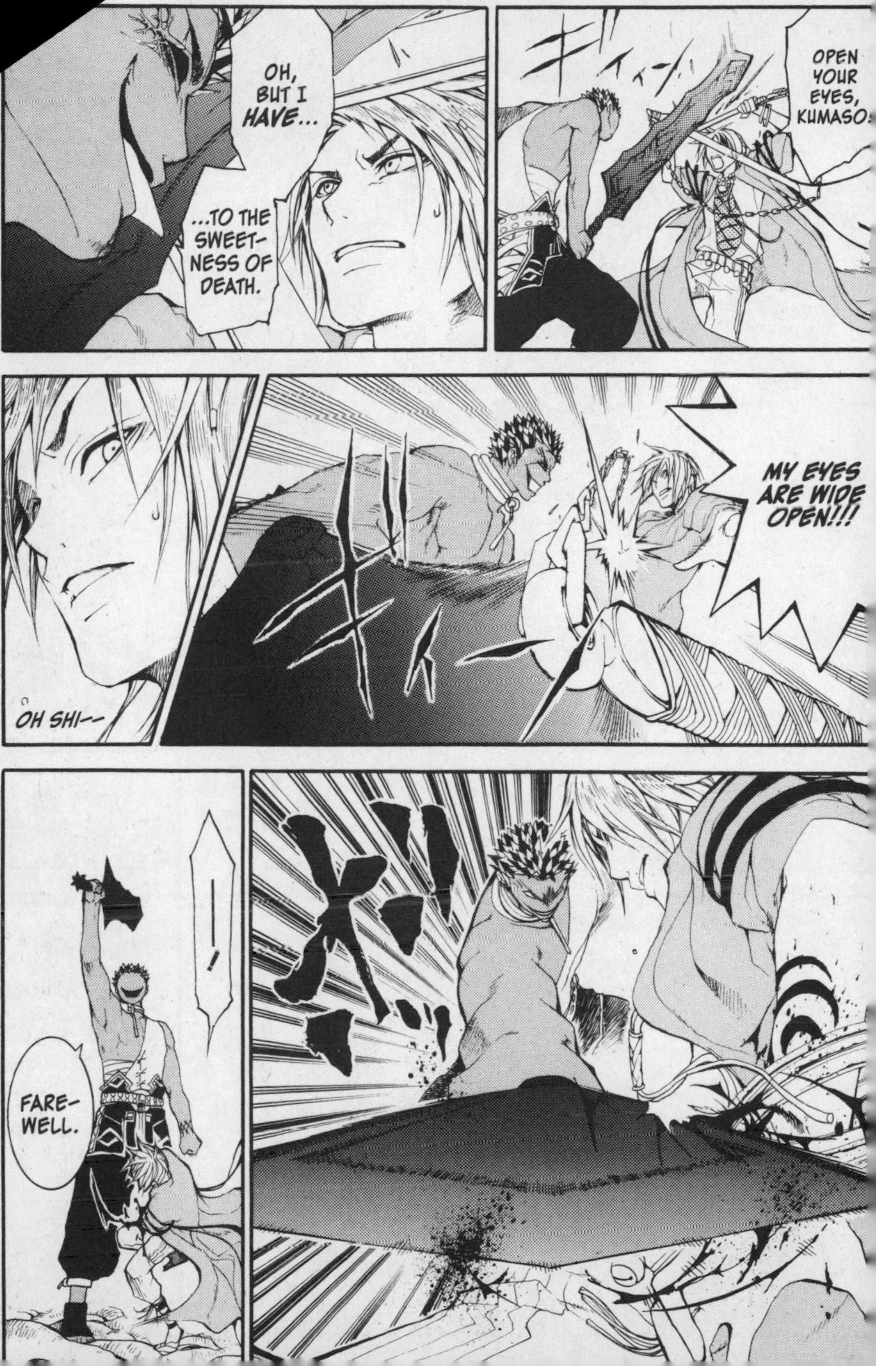
OPEN YOUR EYES, KUMASO!
OH, BUT I HAVE...
...TO THE SWEET-NESS OF DEATH.
MY EYES ARE WIDE OPEN!!!
OH SHI--
!
FARE-WELL.

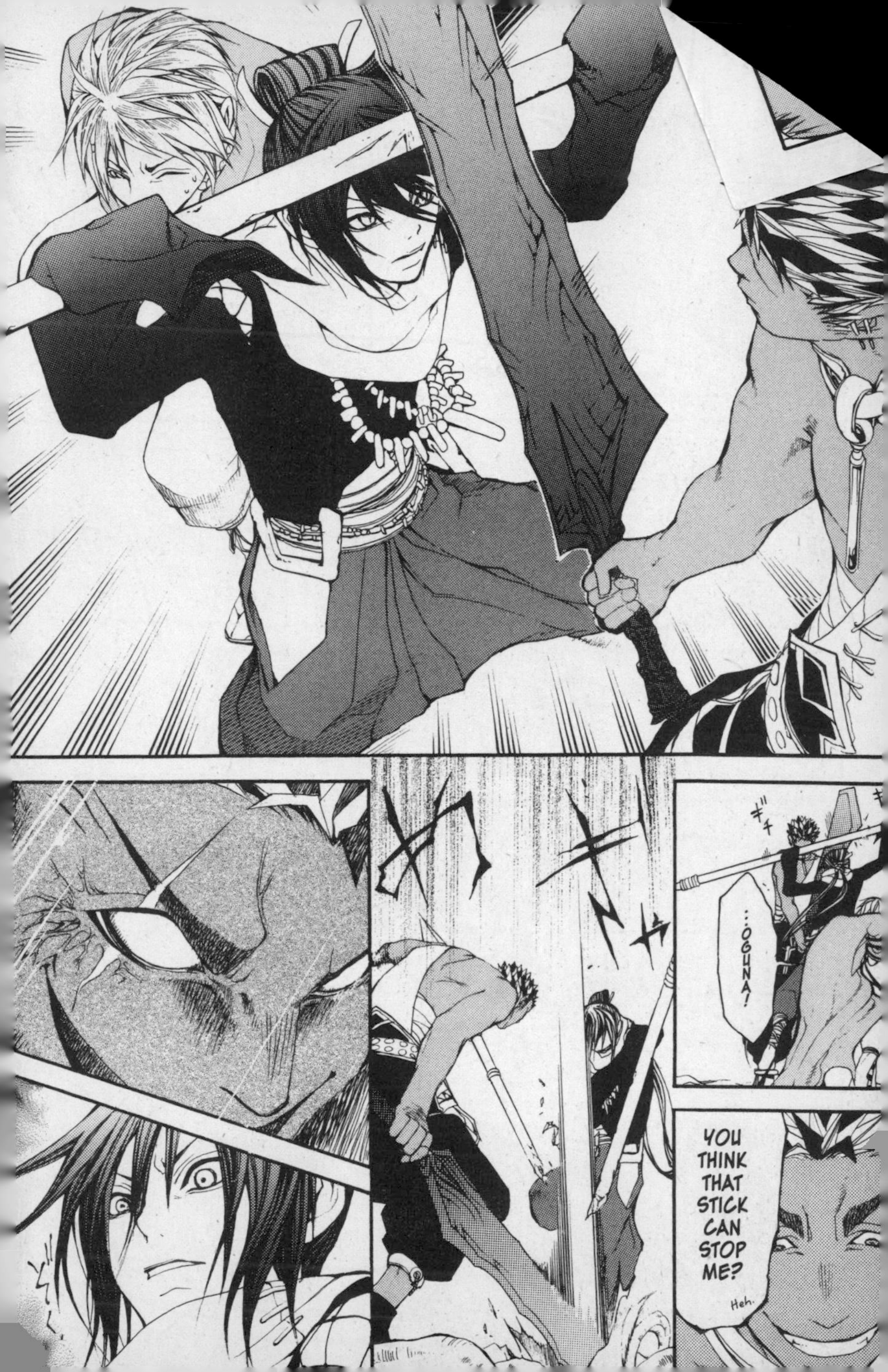
...OGUNA!
YOU THINK THAT STICK CAN STOP ME?
Heh.

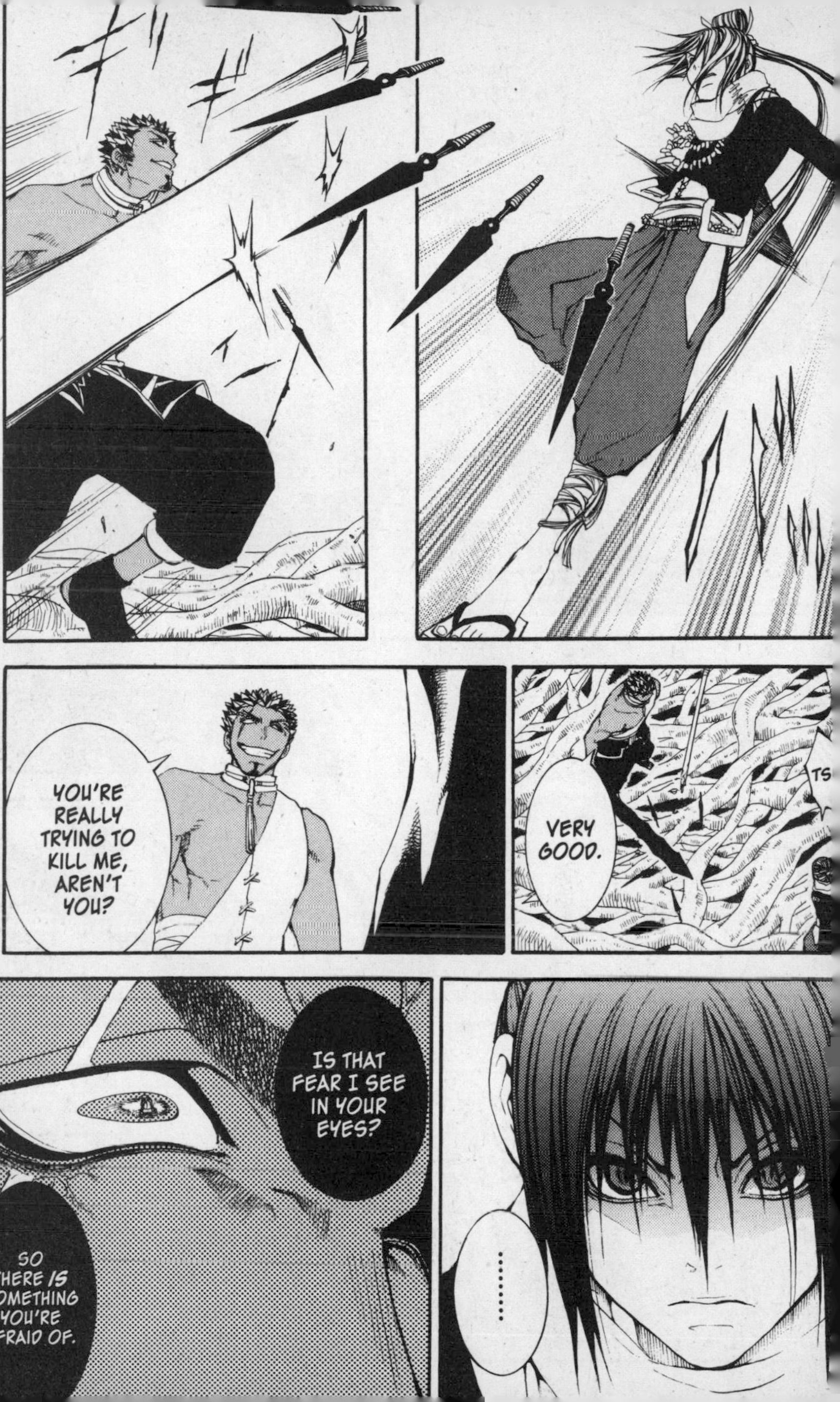
TS
VERY GOOD.
YOU'RE REALLY TRYING TO KILL ME, AREN'T YOU?
......
IS THAT FEAR I SEE IN YOUR EYES?
SO THERE *IS* SOMETHING YOU'RE AFRAID OF.

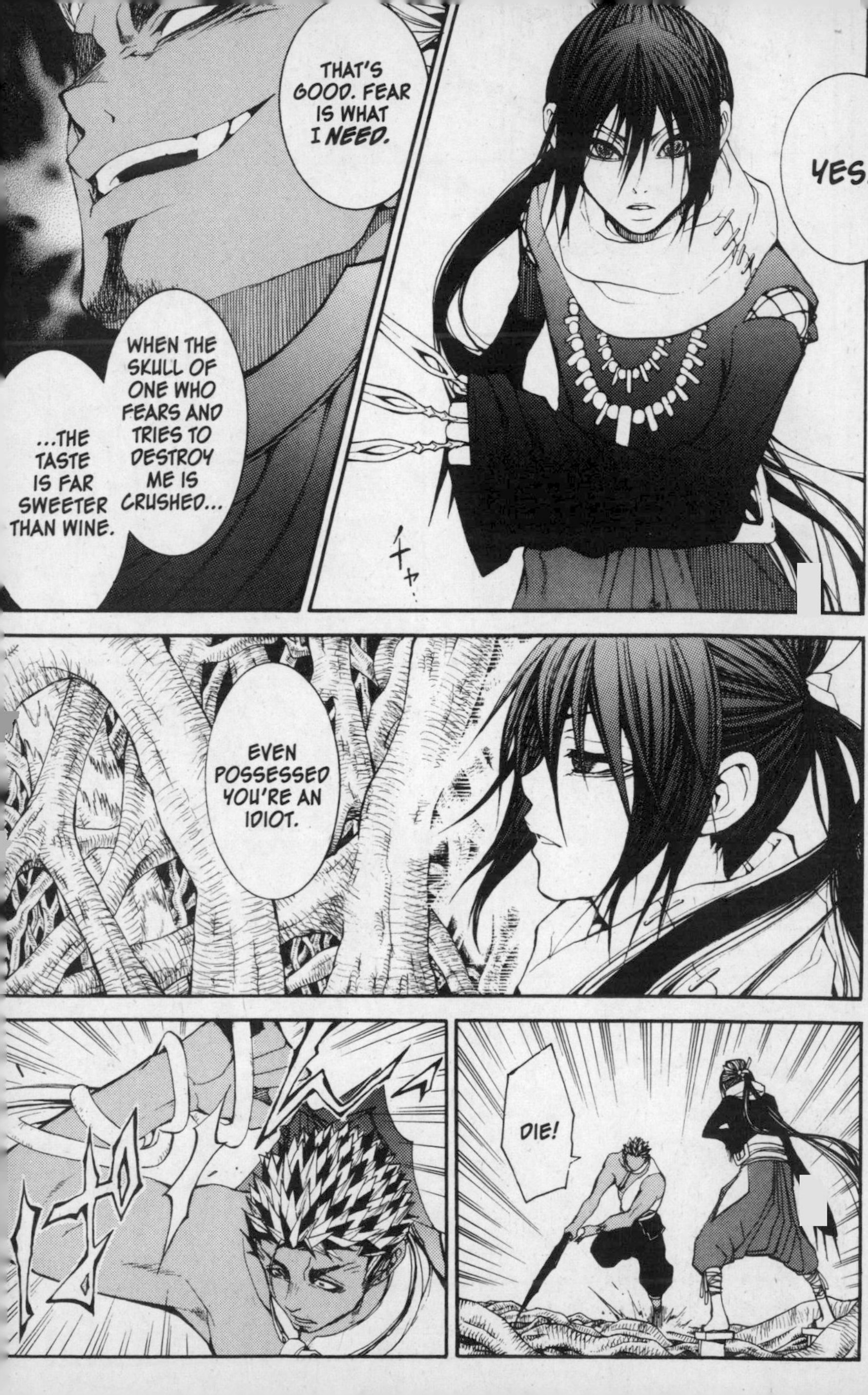
YES.
THAT'S GOOD. FEAR IS WHAT I NEED.
WHEN THE SKULL OF ONE WHO FEARS AND TRIES TO DESTROY ME IS CRUSHED...
...THE TASTE IS FAR SWEETER THAN WINE.
EVEN POSSESSED YOU'RE AN IDIOT.
DIE!

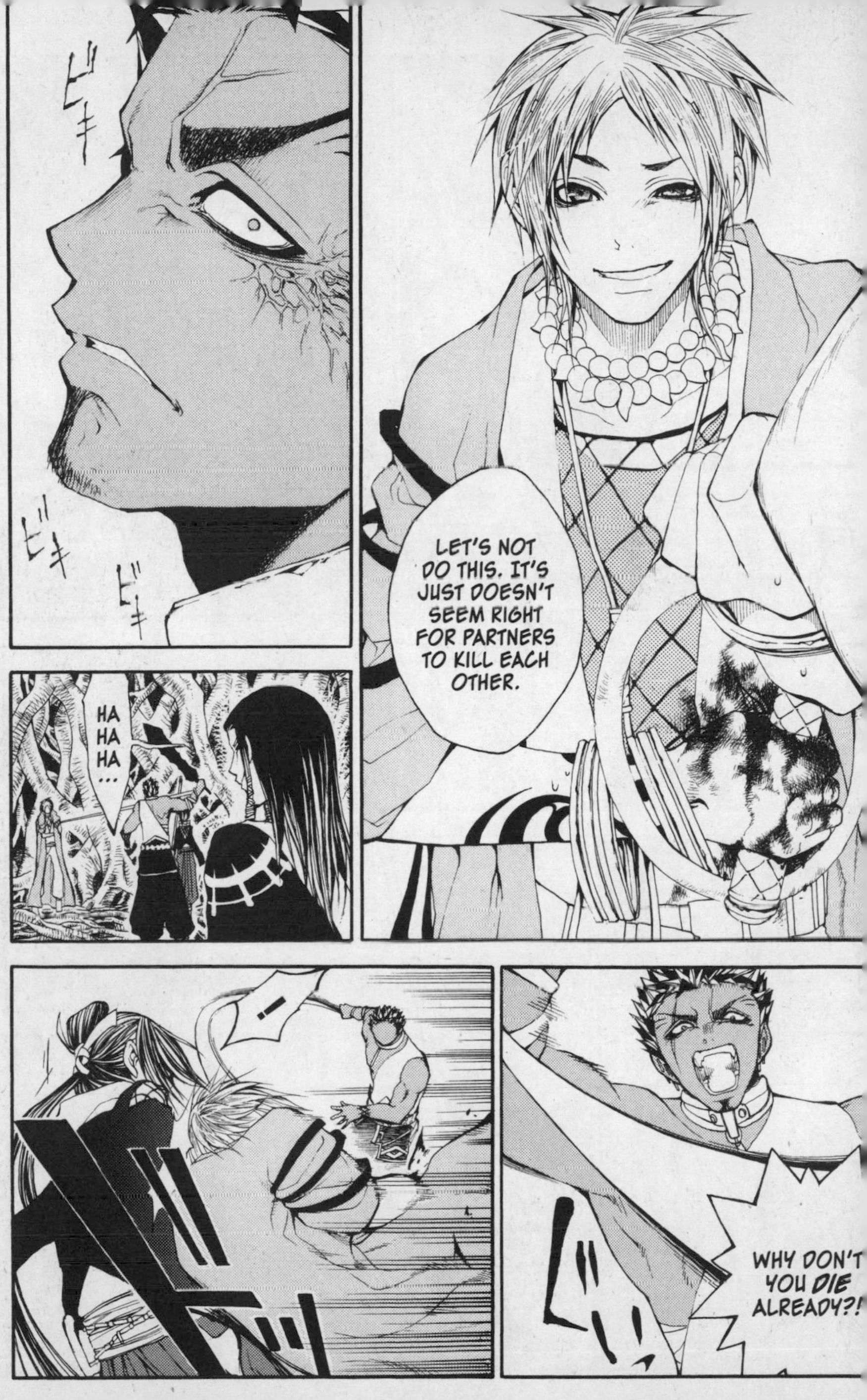
LET'S NOT DO THIS. IT'S JUST DOESN'T SEEM RIGHT FOR PARTNERS TO KILL EACH OTHER.
ビキ
ビキ
ビキ
HA HA HA ...
WHY DON'T YOU *DIE* ALREADY?!
!

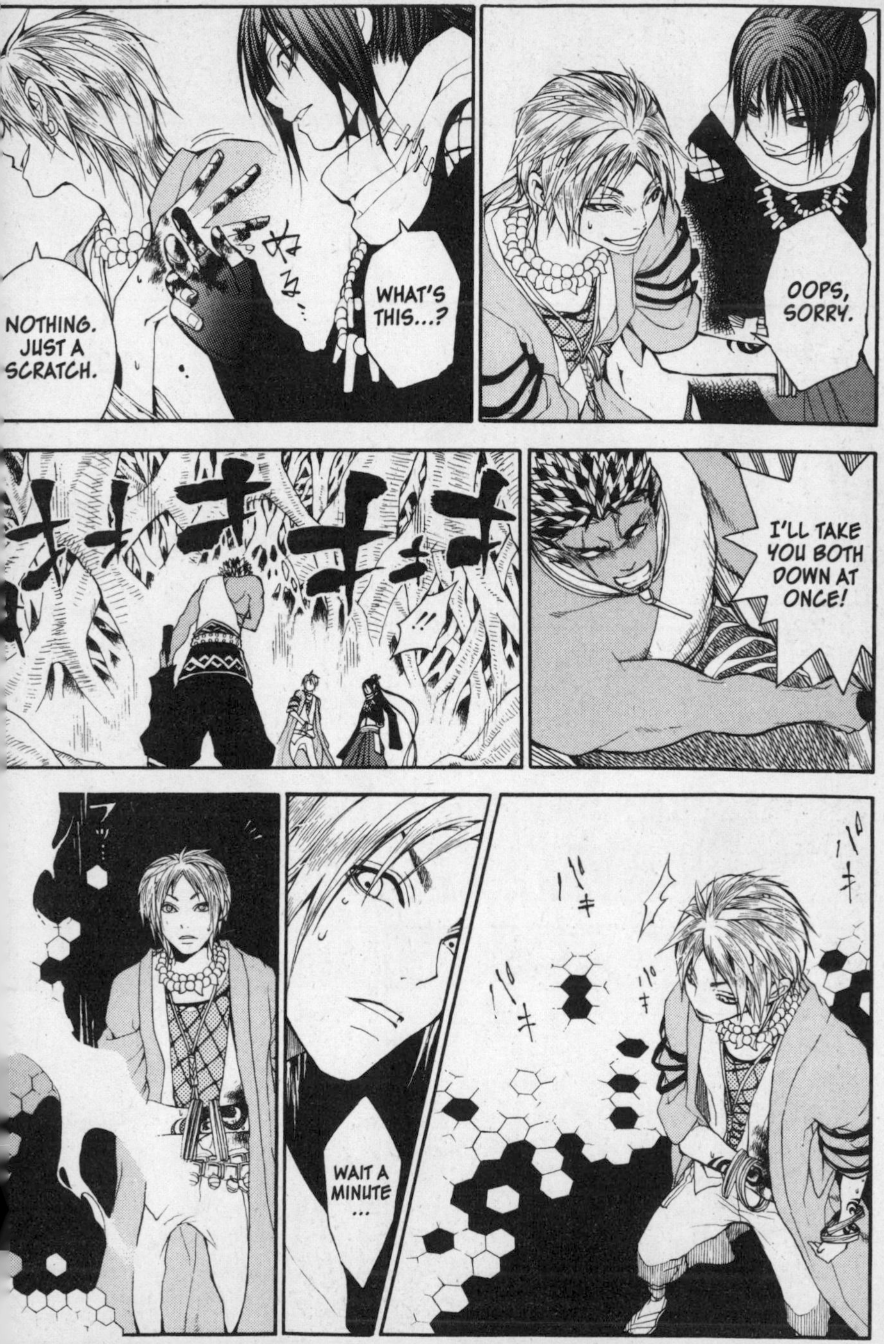
OOPS, SORRY.
WHAT'S THIS...?
NOTHING. JUST A SCRATCH.
I'LL TAKE YOU BOTH DOWN AT ONCE!
!!
WAIT A MINUTE ...

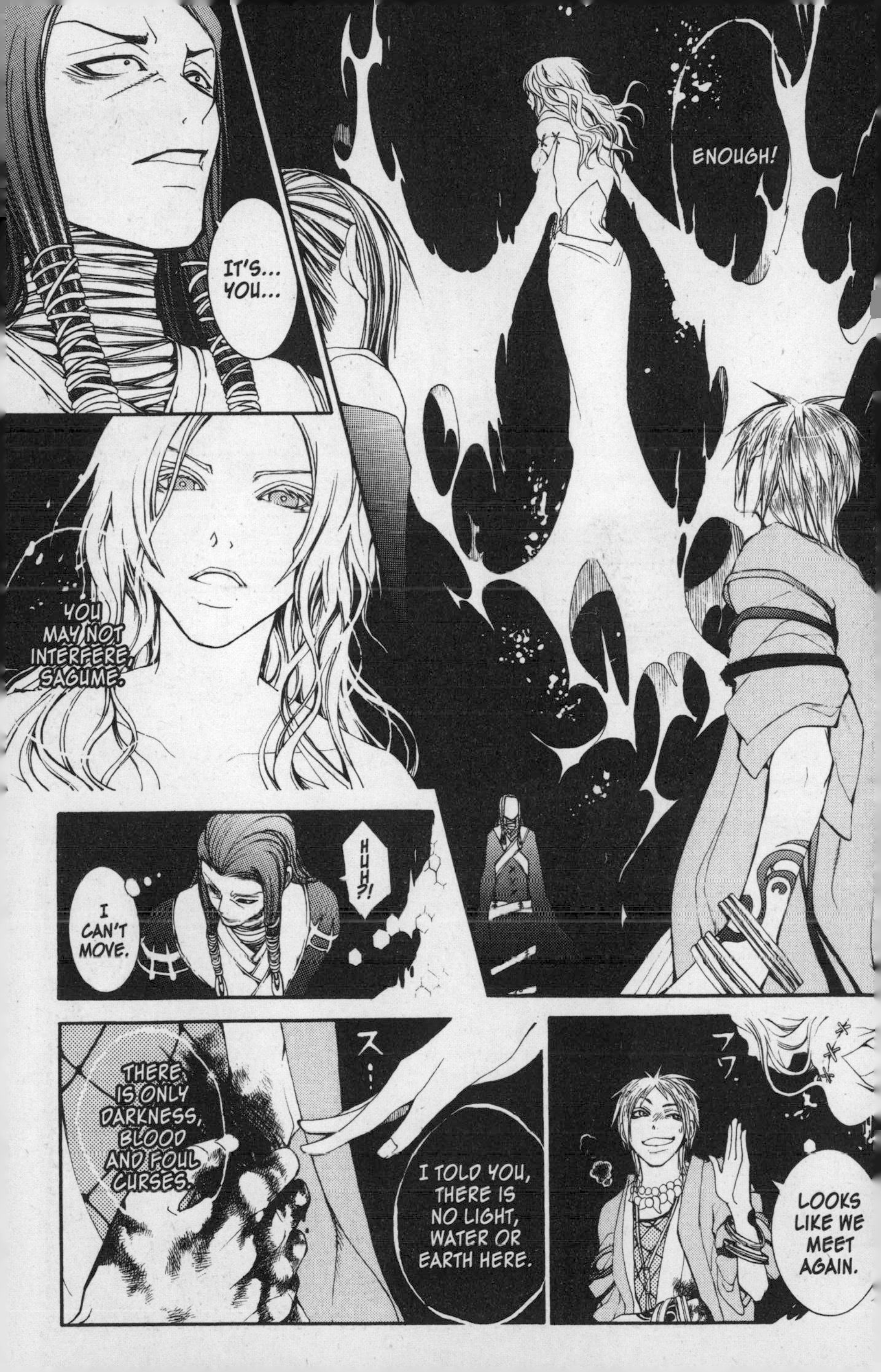

ENOUGH!
IT'S... YOU...
YOU MAY NOT INTERFERE, SAGUME.
HUH?!
I CAN'T MOVE.
フワ
LOOKS LIKE WE MEET AGAIN.
ス…
I TOLD YOU, THERE IS NO LIGHT, WATER OR EARTH HERE.
THERE IS ONLY DARKNESS, BLOOD AND FOUL CURSES.

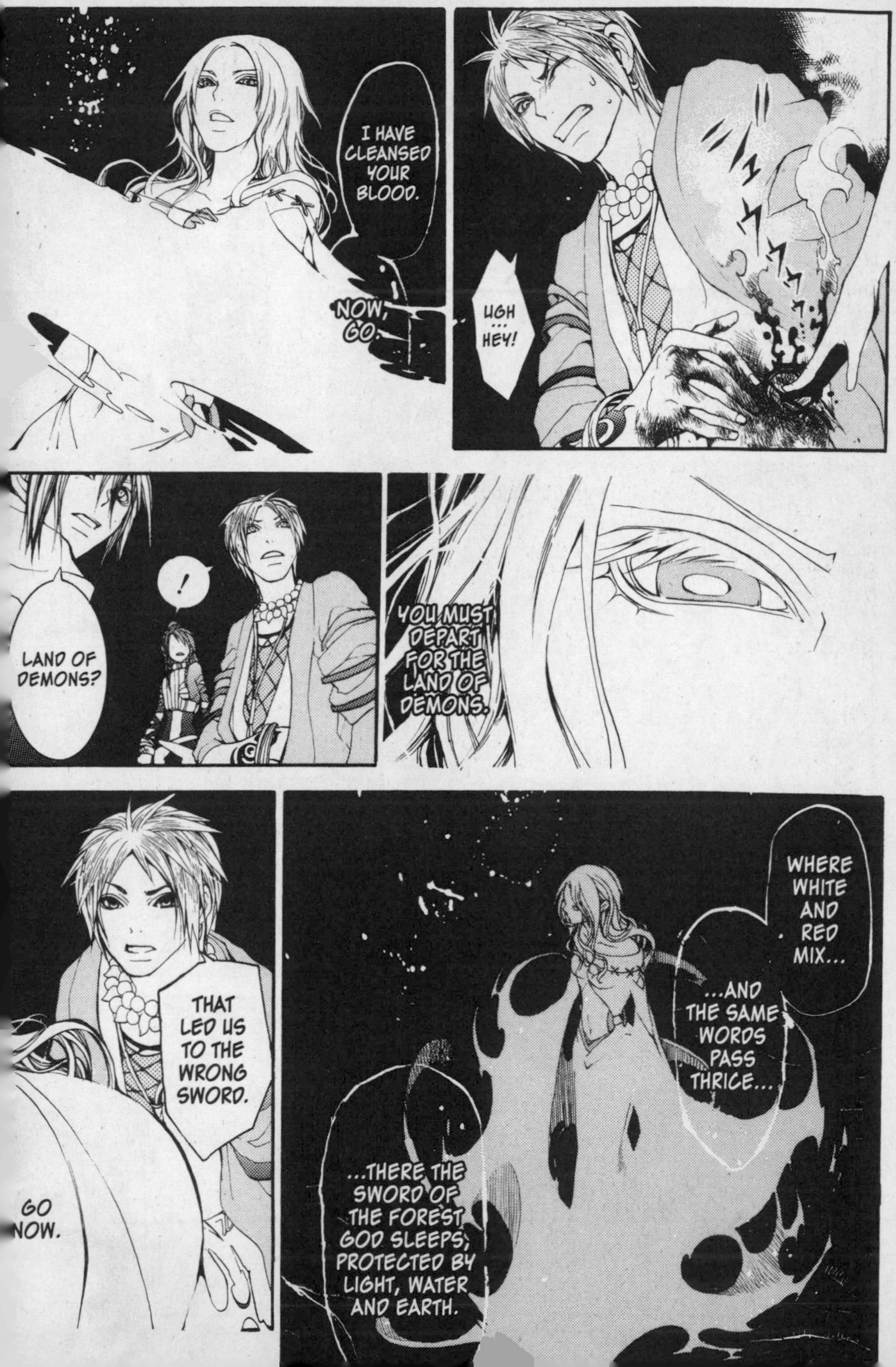
UGH... HEY!
I HAVE CLEANSED YOUR BLOOD.
NOW, GO.
YOU MUST DEPART FOR THE LAND OF DEMONS.
!
LAND OF DEMONS?
WHERE WHITE AND RED MIX...
...AND THE SAME WORDS PASS THRICE...
...THERE THE SWORD OF THE FOREST GOD SLEEPS, PROTECTED BY LIGHT, WATER AND EARTH.
THAT LED US TO THE WRONG SWORD.
GO NOW.

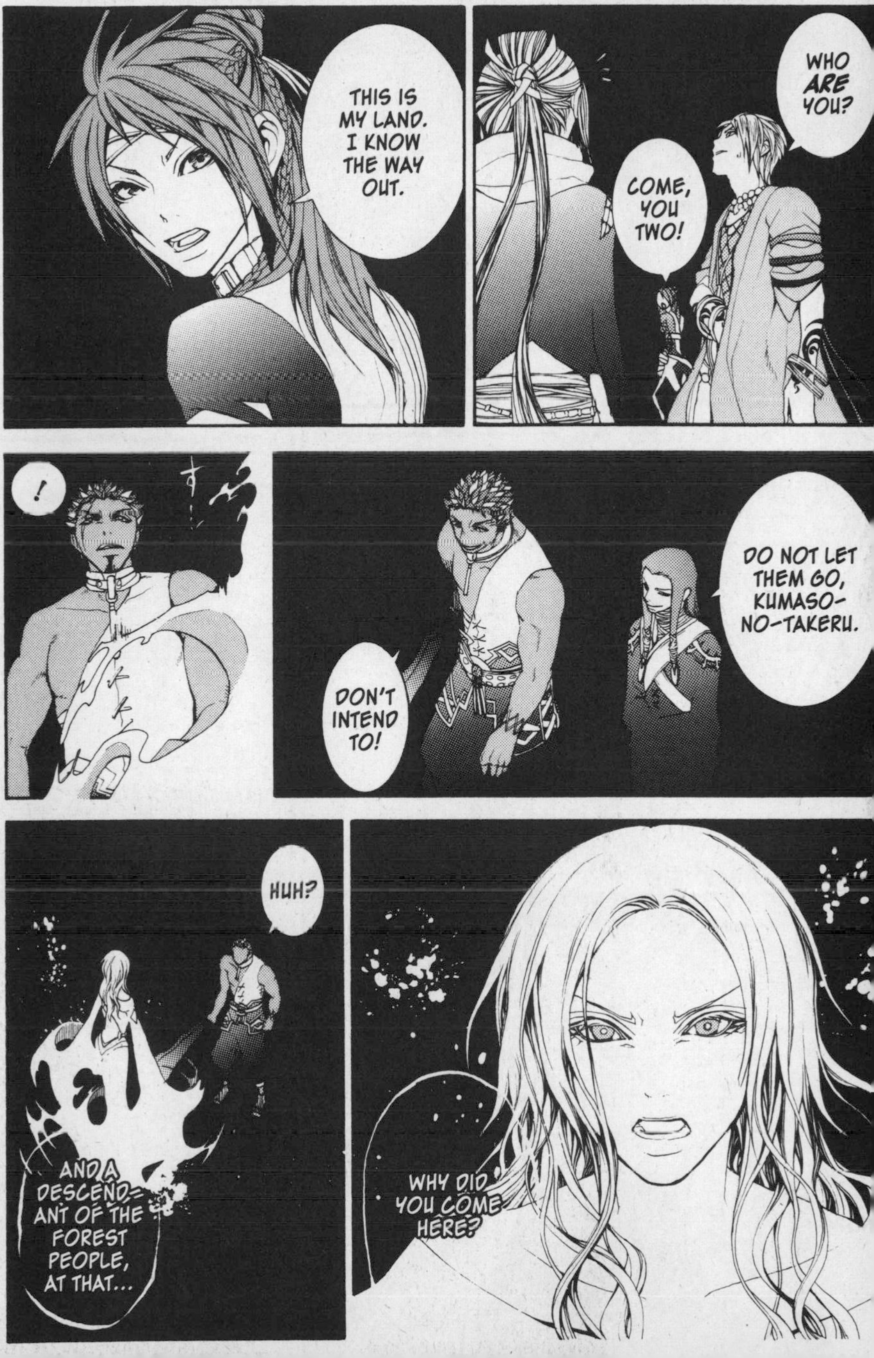
WHO ARE YOU?
COME, YOU TWO!
THIS IS MY LAND. I KNOW THE WAY OUT.
DO NOT LET THEM GO, KUMASO-NO-TAKERU.
DON'T INTEND TO!
!
WHY DID YOU COME HERE?
HUH?
AND A DESCEND-ANT OF THE FOREST PEOPLE, AT THAT...

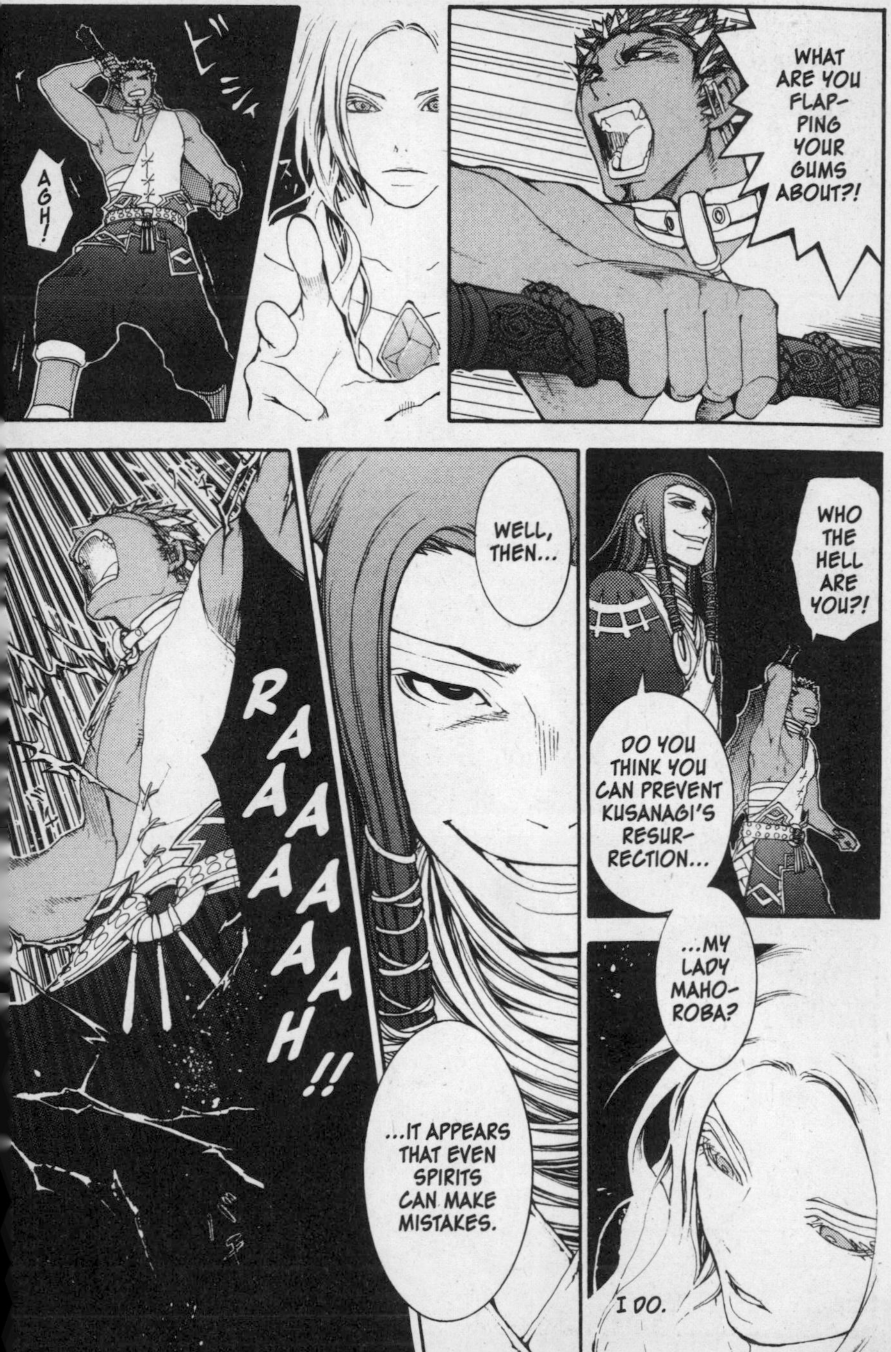
WHAT ARE YOU FLAPPING YOUR GUMS ABOUT?!
AGH!
WHO THE HELL ARE YOU?!
DO YOU THINK YOU CAN PREVENT KUSANAGI'S RESURRECTION...
...MY LADY MAHOROBA?
I DO.
WELL, THEN...
...IT APPEARS THAT EVEN SPIRITS CAN MAKE MISTAKES.
RAAAAAAAAH!!

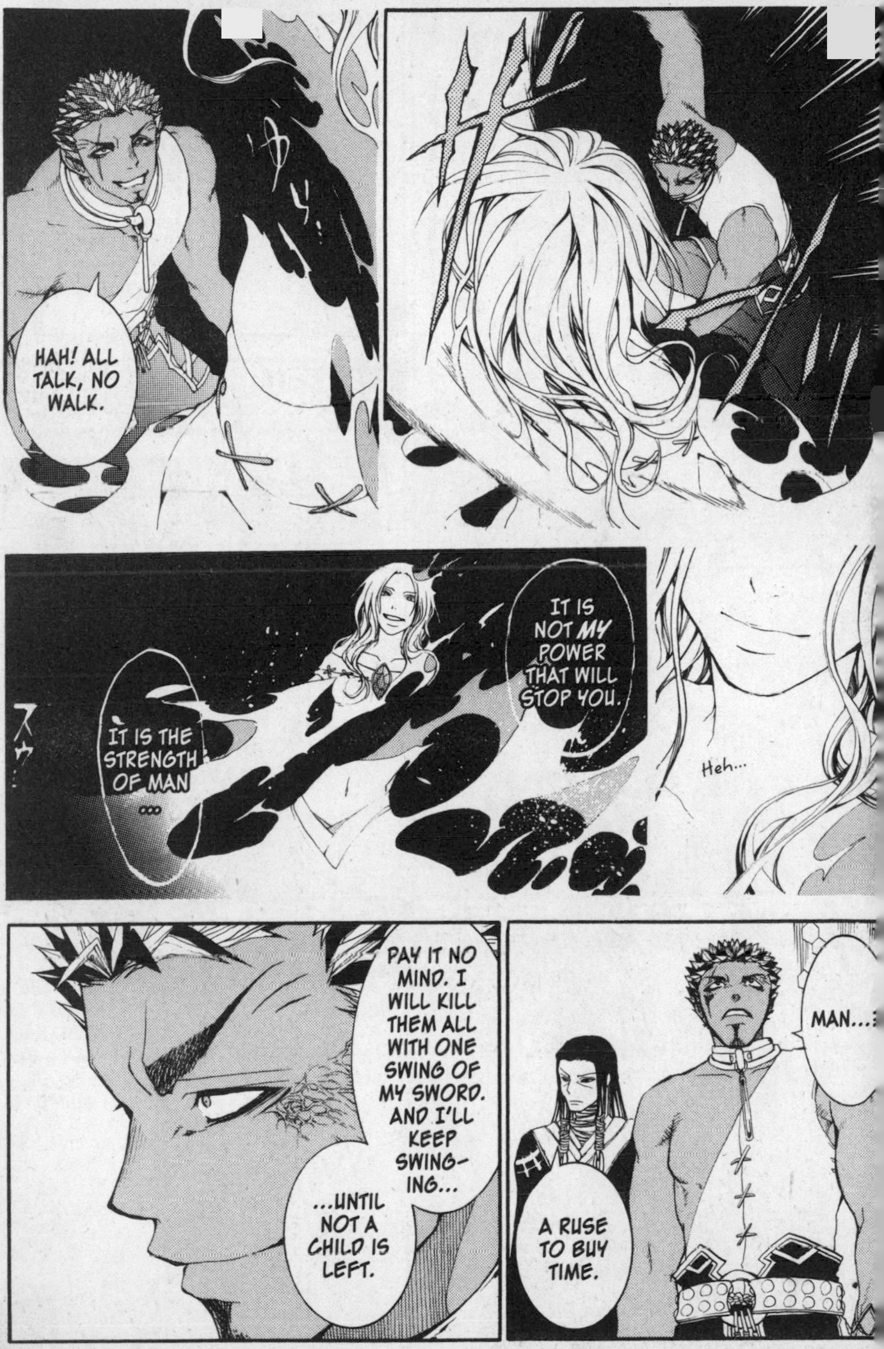
HAH! ALL TALK, NO WALK.
Heh...
IT IS NOT MY POWER THAT WILL STOP YOU.
IT IS THE STRENGTH OF MAN ...
スゥ…
MAN...?
A RUSE TO BUY TIME.
PAY IT NO MIND. I WILL KILL THEM ALL WITH ONE SWING OF MY SWORD. AND I'LL KEEP SWING-ING...
...UNTIL NOT A CHILD IS LEFT.

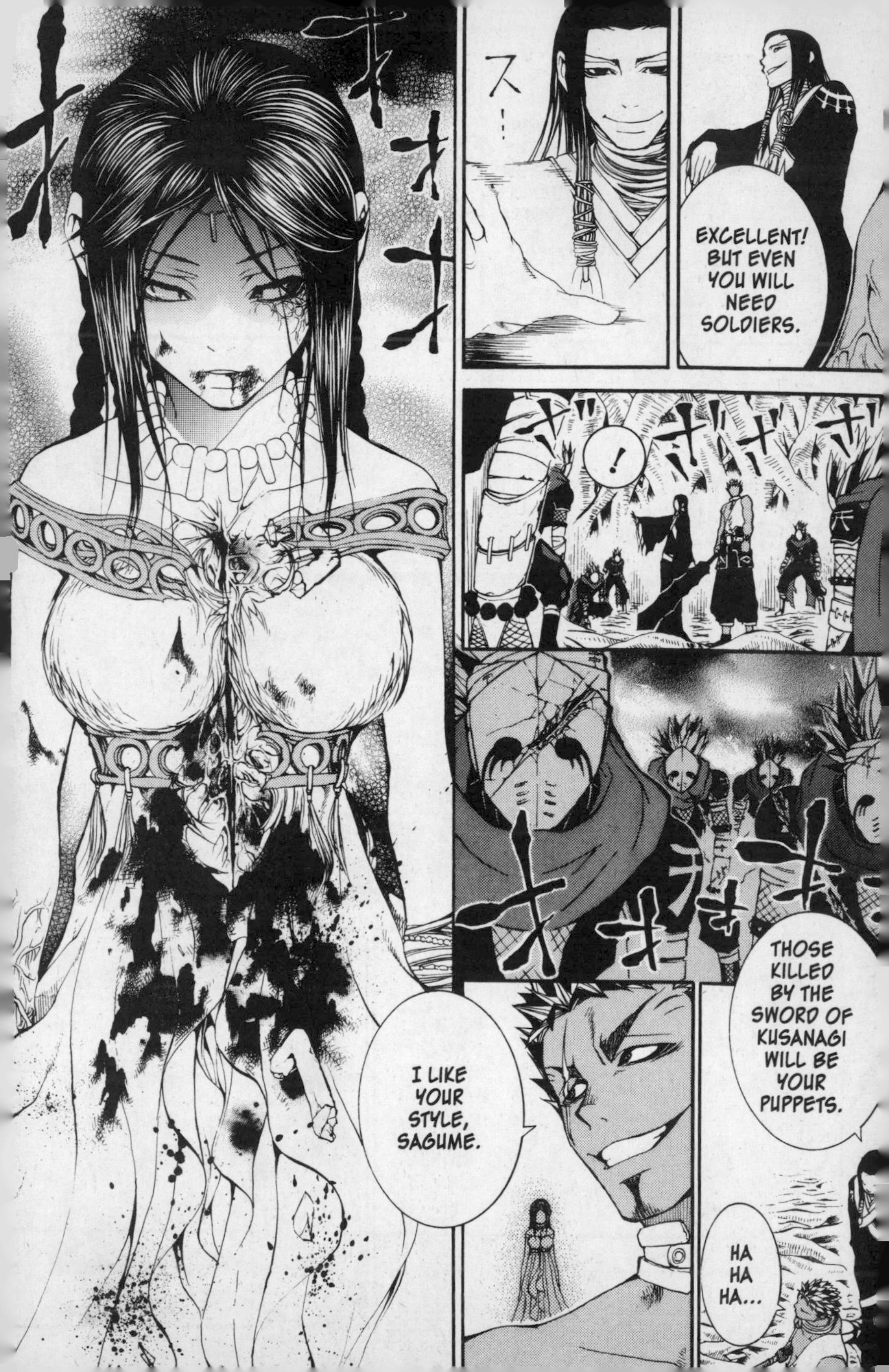

EXCELLENT! BUT EVEN YOU WILL NEED SOLDIERS.
ス！
!
THOSE KILLED BY THE SWORD OF KUSANAGI WILL BE YOUR PUPPETS.
I LIKE YOUR STYLE, SAGUME.
HA HA HA...

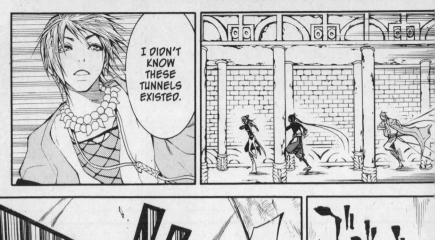

I DIDN'T KNOW THESE TUNNELS EXISTED.

?!!

WHAT'S THIS?

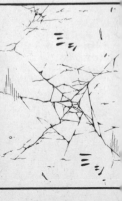

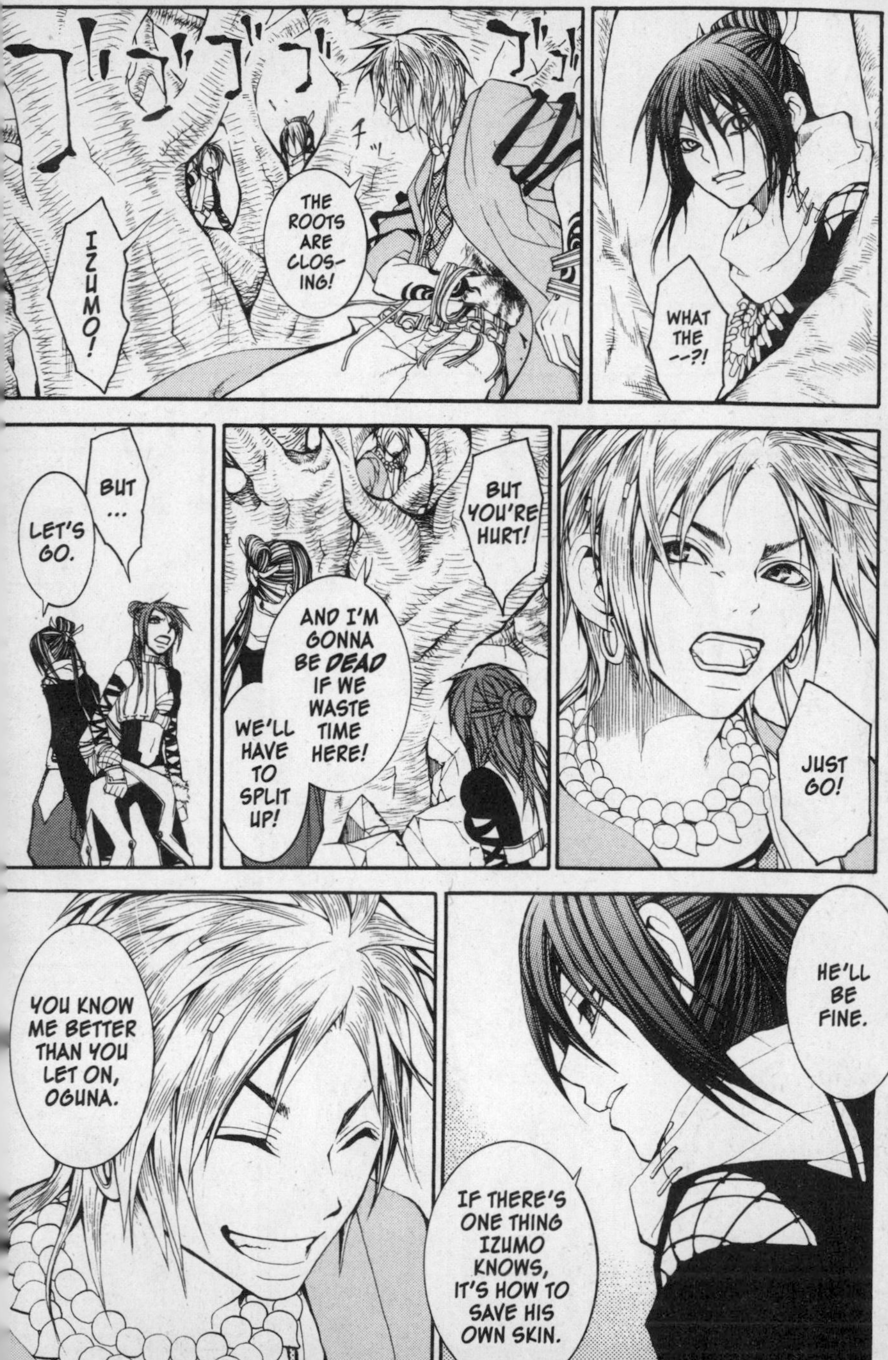
WHAT THE --?!
THE ROOTS ARE CLOSING!
IZUMO!
JUST GO!
BUT YOU'RE HURT!
AND I'M GONNA BE *DEAD* IF WE WASTE TIME HERE!
WE'LL HAVE TO SPLIT UP!
BUT ...
LET'S GO.
HE'LL BE FINE.
IF THERE'S ONE THING IZUMO KNOWS, IT'S HOW TO SAVE HIS OWN SKIN.
YOU KNOW ME BETTER THAN YOU LET ON, OGUNA.

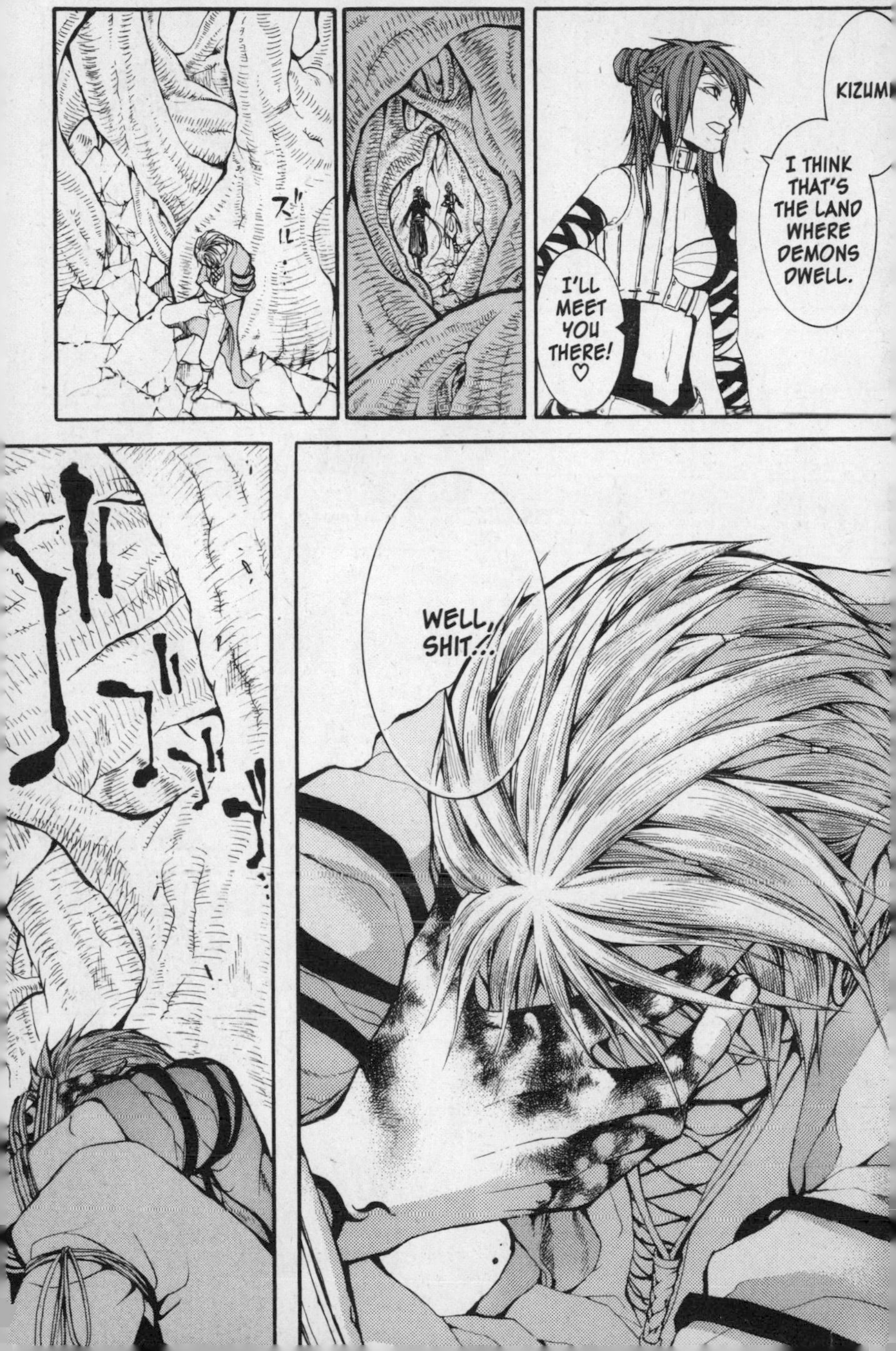
KIZUMI
I THINK THAT'S THE LAND WHERE DEMONS DWELL.
I'LL MEET YOU THERE! ♡
ズル…
WELL, SHIT...

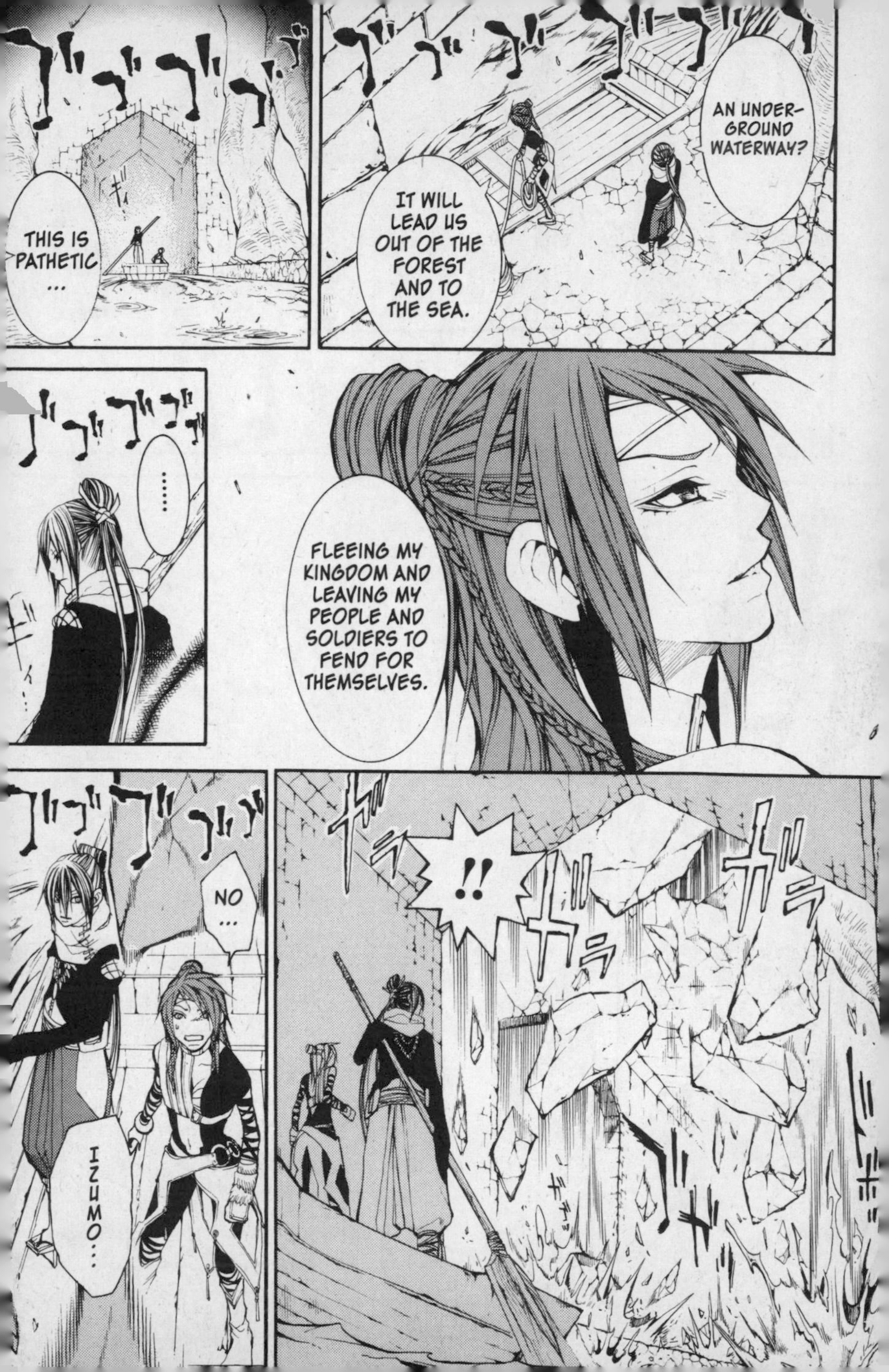
AN UNDER-GROUND WATERWAY?
IT WILL LEAD US OUT OF THE FOREST AND TO THE SEA.
THIS IS PATHETIC ...
FLEEING MY KINGDOM AND LEAVING MY PEOPLE AND SOLDIERS TO FEND FOR THEMSELVES.
......
!!
NO ...
IZUMO...

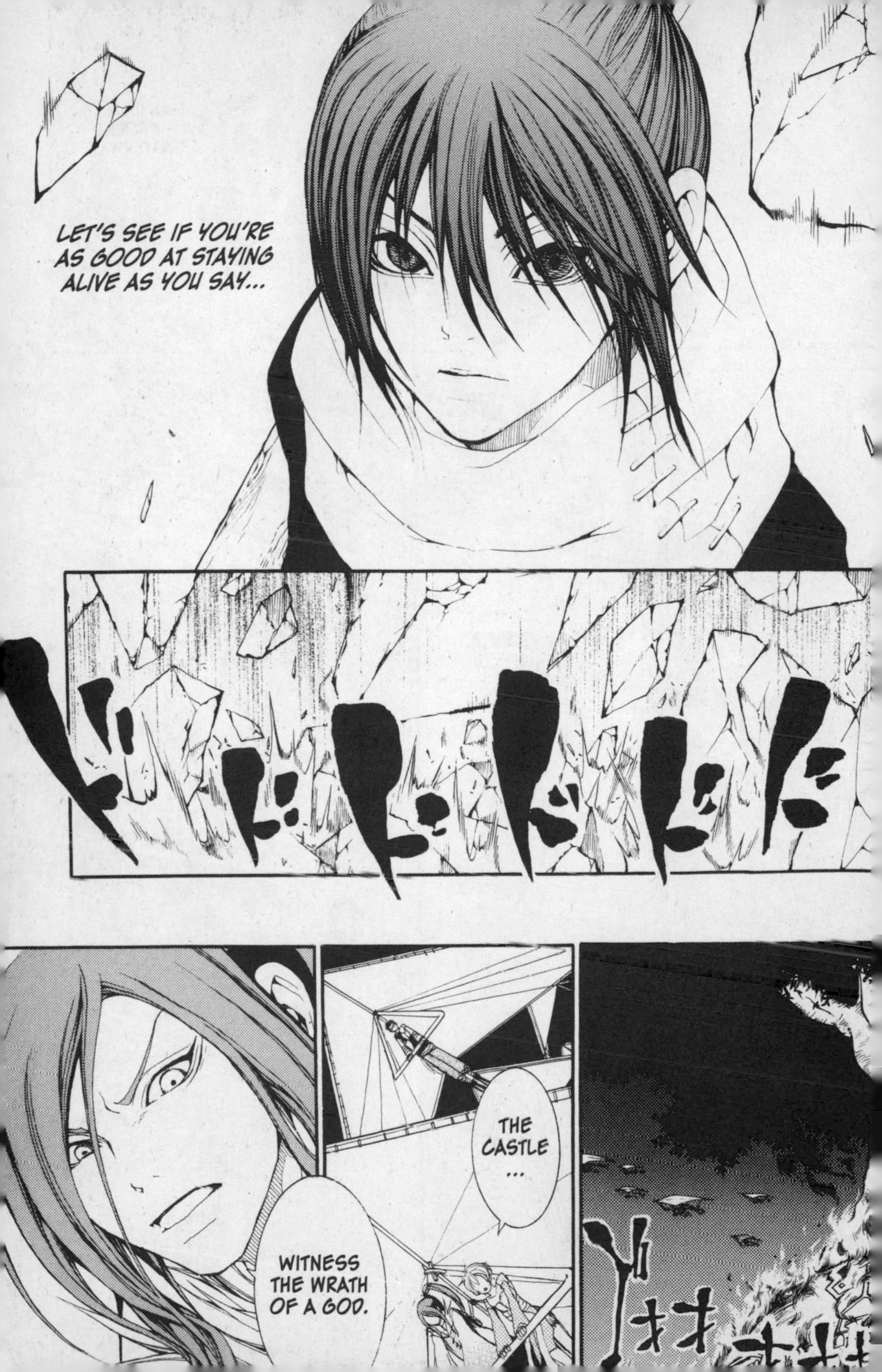
LET'S SEE IF YOU'RE AS GOOD AT STAYING ALIVE AS YOU SAY...
THE CASTLE ...
WITNESS THE WRATH OF A GOD.

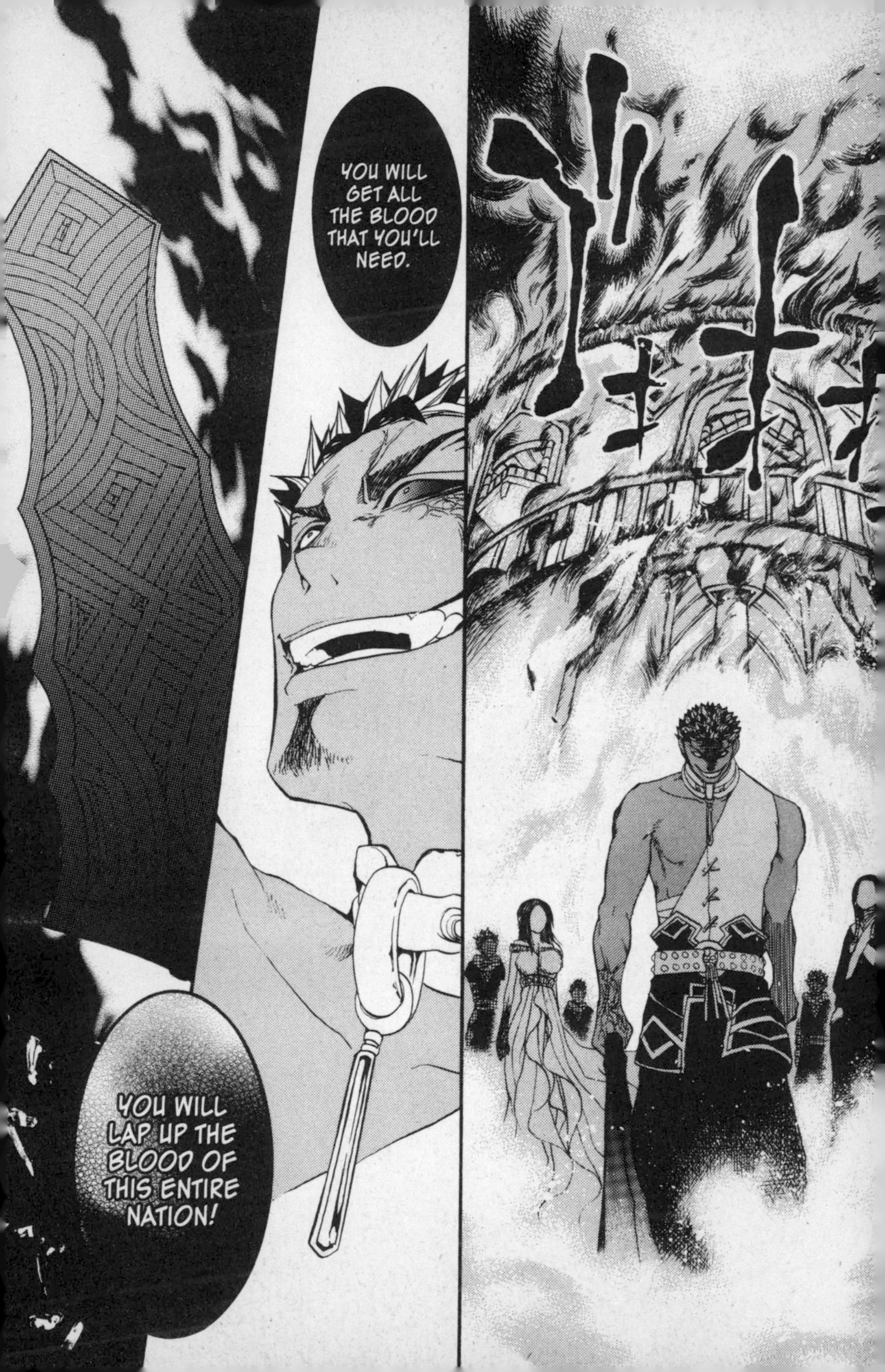
YOU WILL GET ALL THE BLOOD THAT YOU'LL NEED.
YOU WILL LAP UP THE BLOOD OF THIS ENTIRE NATION!

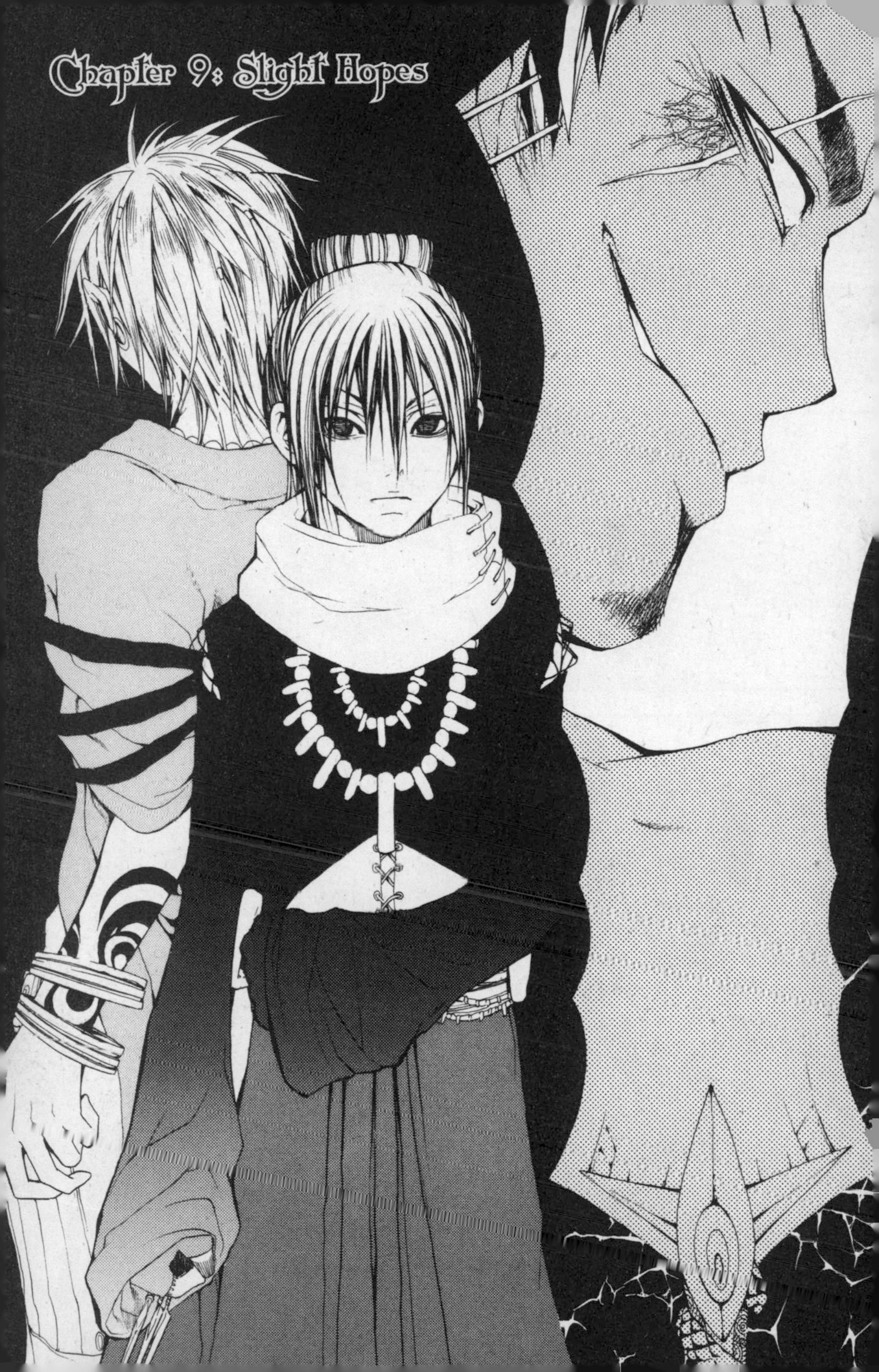
Chapter 9: Slight Hopes

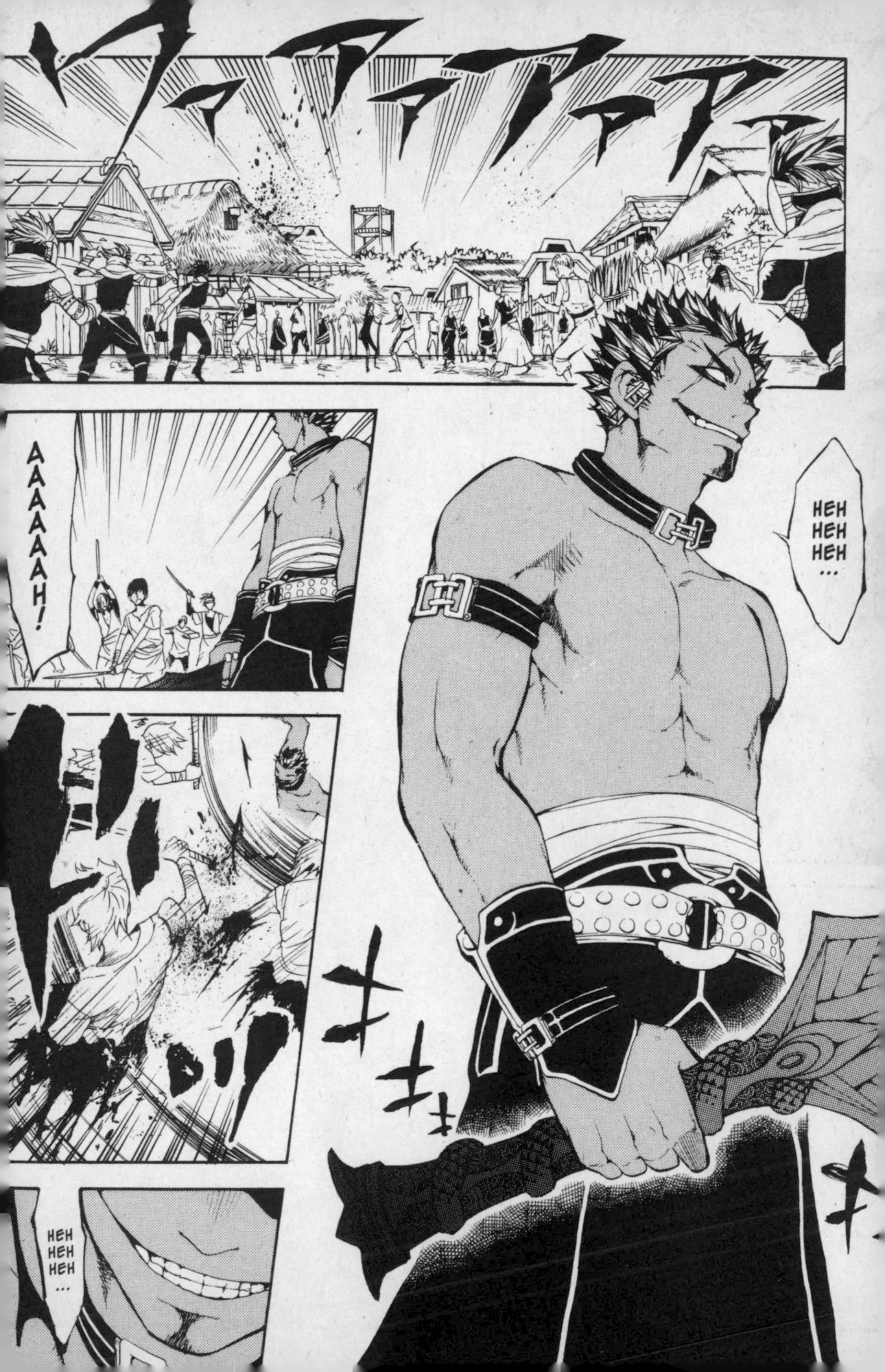
HEH HEH HEH...
AAAAAAH!
HEH HEH HEH...

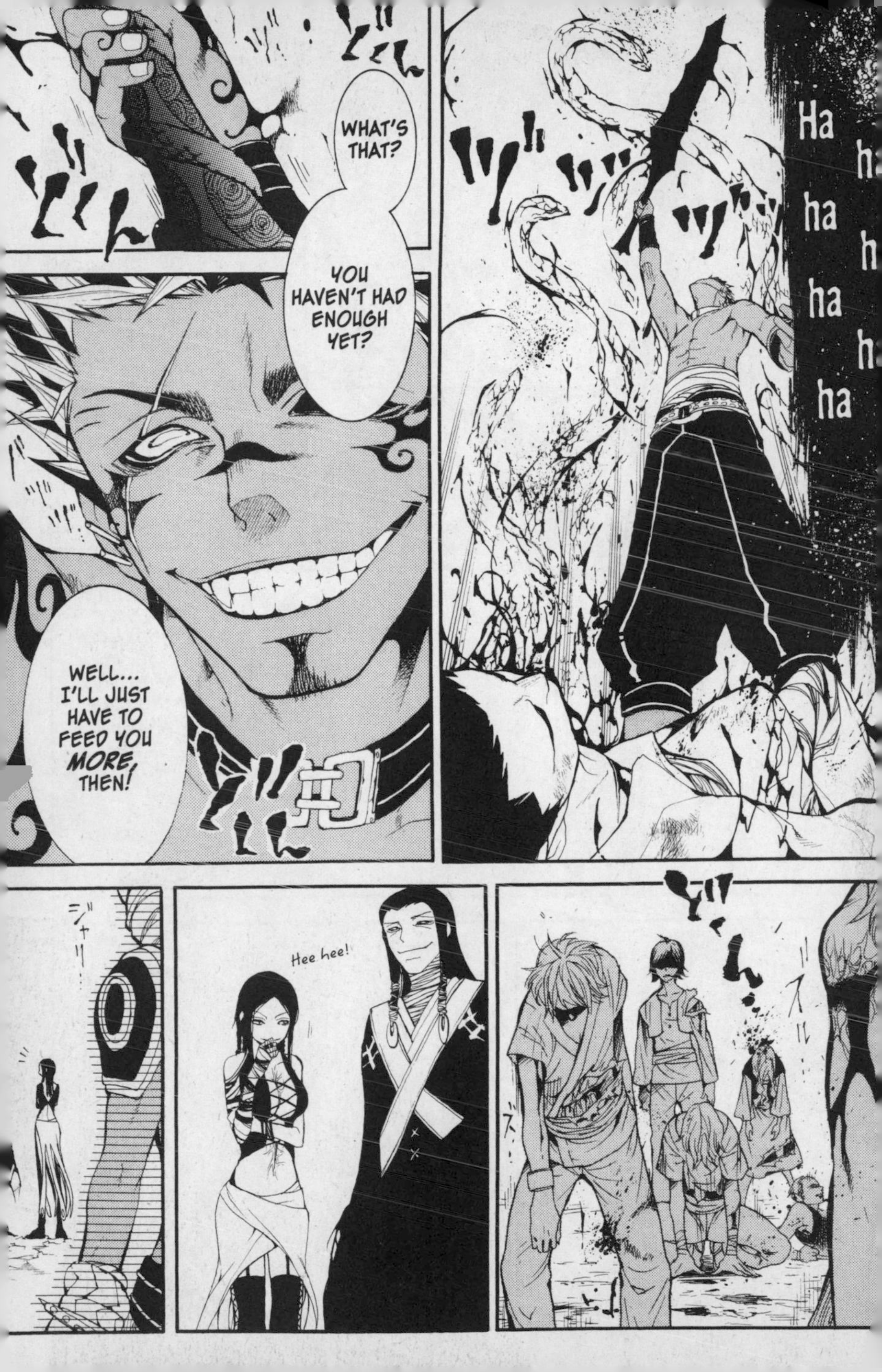
Ha ha ha ha
WHAT'S THAT?
YOU HAVEN'T HAD ENOUGH YET?
WELL... I'LL JUST HAVE TO FEED YOU MORE, THEN!
Hee hee!

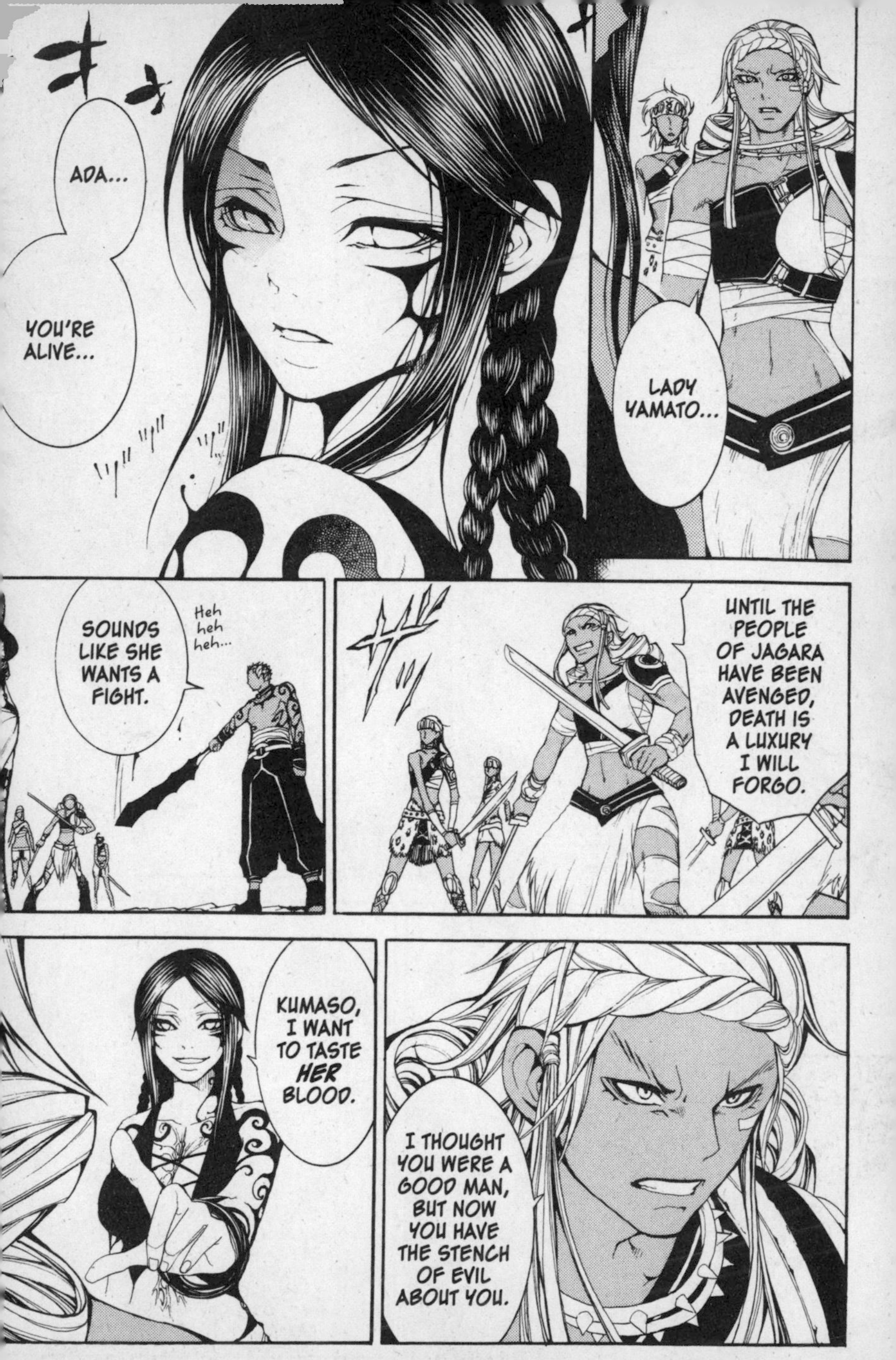
LADY YAMATO...
ADA...
YOU'RE ALIVE...
UNTIL THE PEOPLE OF JAGARA HAVE BEEN AVENGED, DEATH IS A LUXURY I WILL FORGO.
SOUNDS LIKE SHE WANTS A FIGHT.
Heh heh heh...
I THOUGHT YOU WERE A GOOD MAN, BUT NOW YOU HAVE THE STENCH OF EVIL ABOUT YOU.
KUMASO, I WANT TO TASTE *HER* BLOOD.

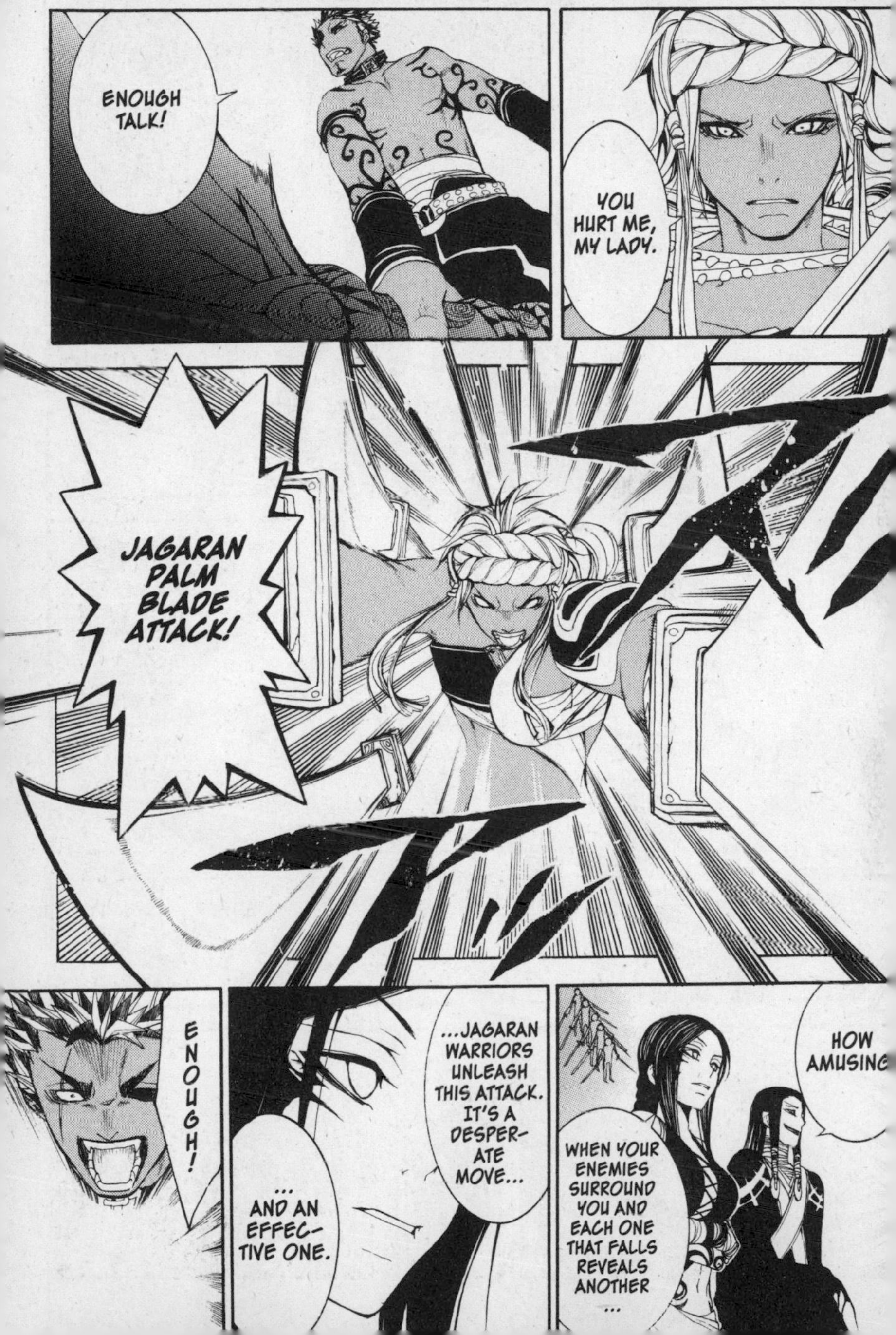
YOU HURT ME, MY LADY.
ENOUGH TALK!
JAGARAN PALM BLADE ATTACK!
HOW AMUSING
WHEN YOUR ENEMIES SURROUND YOU AND EACH ONE THAT FALLS REVEALS ANOTHER ...
...JAGARAN WARRIORS UNLEASH THIS ATTACK. IT'S A DESPERATE MOVE...
... AND AN EFFECTIVE ONE.
ENOUGH!

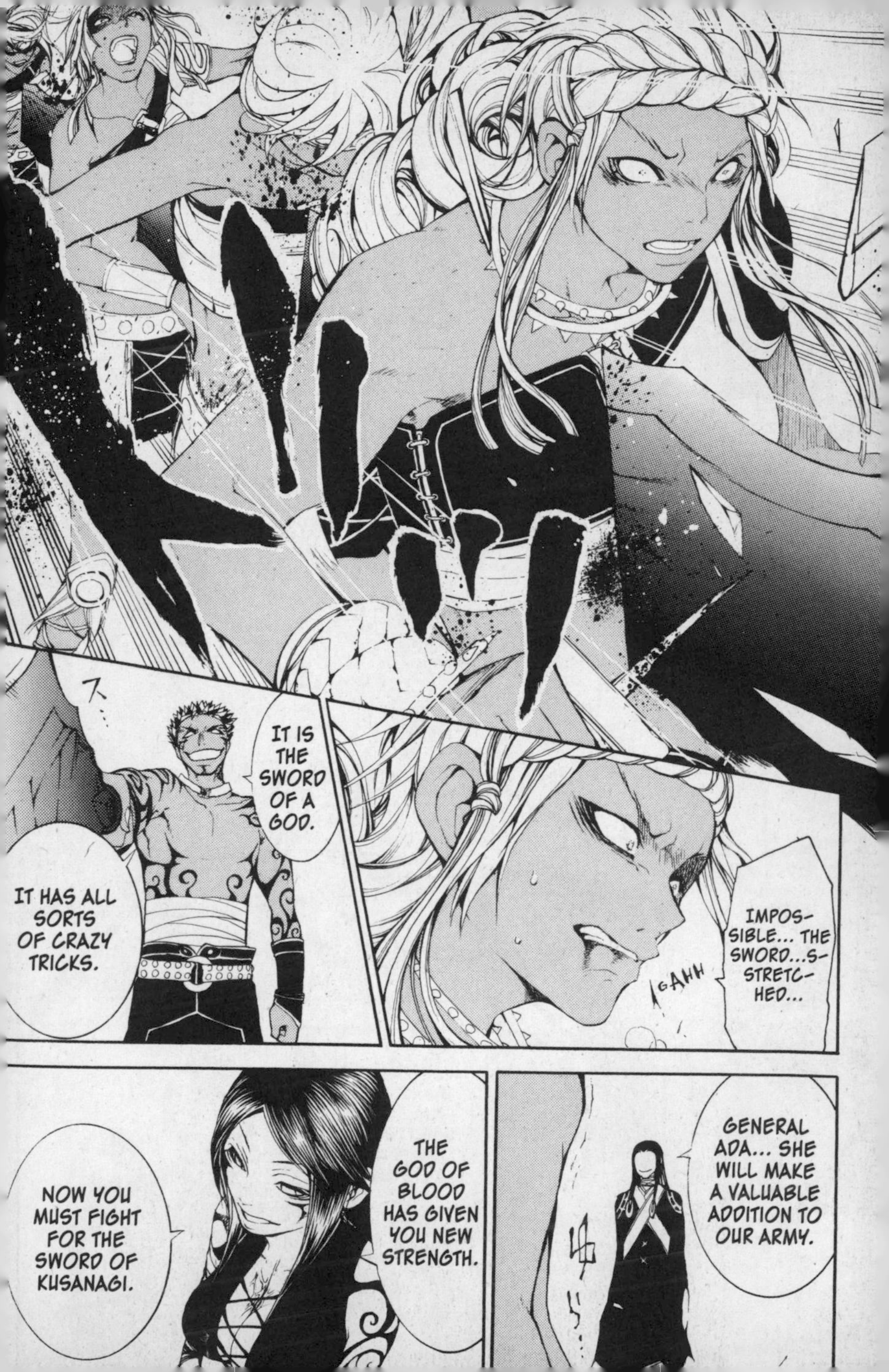
IMPOSSIBLE... THE SWORD...S-STRETCHED...
GAHH
IT IS THE SWORD OF A GOD.
IT HAS ALL SORTS OF CRAZY TRICKS.
GENERAL ADA... SHE WILL MAKE A VALUABLE ADDITION TO OUR ARMY.
THE GOD OF BLOOD HAS GIVEN YOU NEW STRENGTH.
NOW YOU MUST FIGHT FOR THE SWORD OF KUSANAGI.

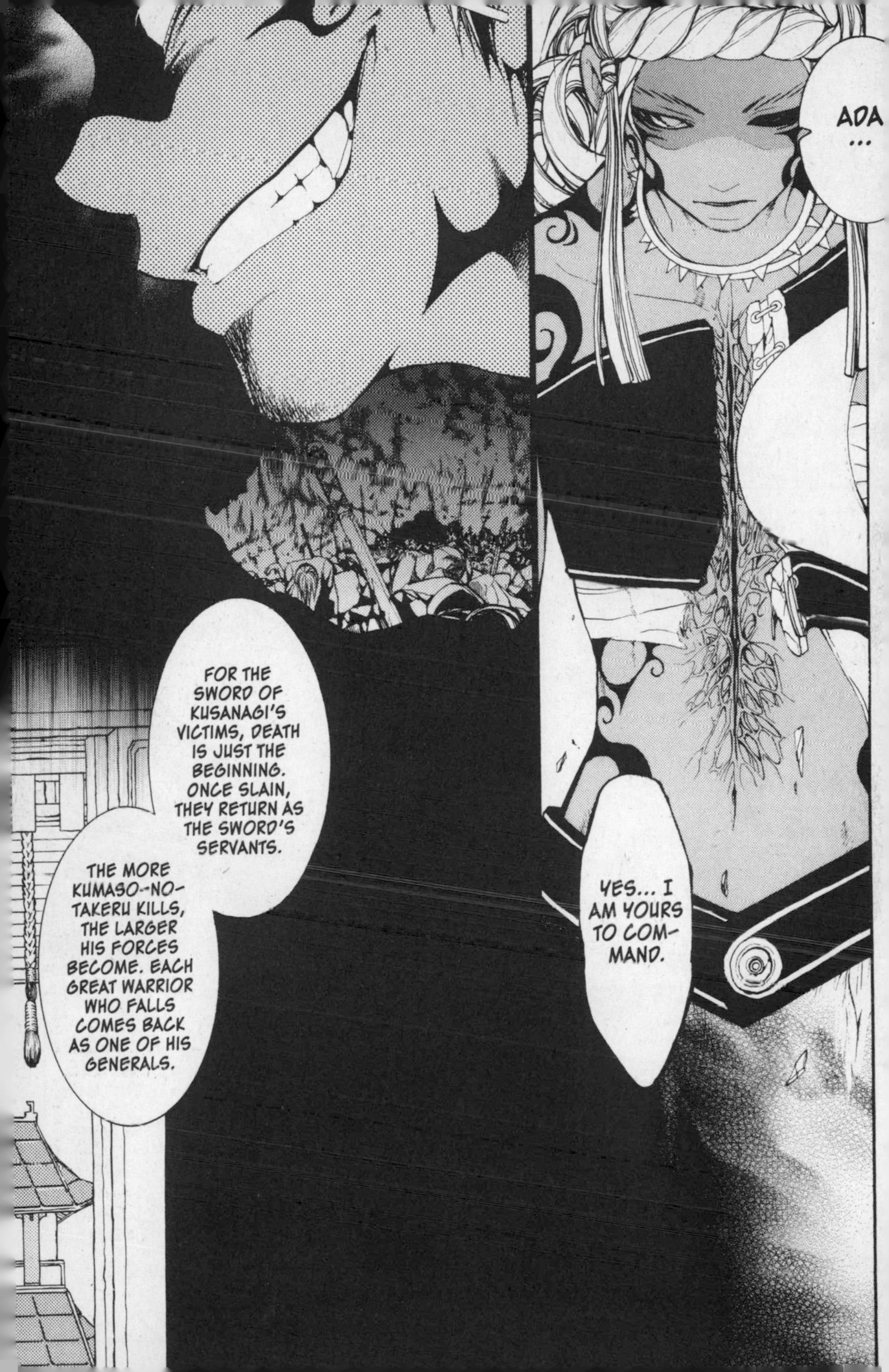
ADA ...
YES... I AM YOURS TO COMMAND.
FOR THE SWORD OF KUSANAGI'S VICTIMS, DEATH IS JUST THE BEGINNING. ONCE SLAIN, THEY RETURN AS THE SWORD'S SERVANTS.
THE MORE KUMASO-NO-TAKERU KILLS, THE LARGER HIS FORCES BECOME. EACH GREAT WARRIOR WHO FALLS COMES BACK AS ONE OF HIS GENERALS.

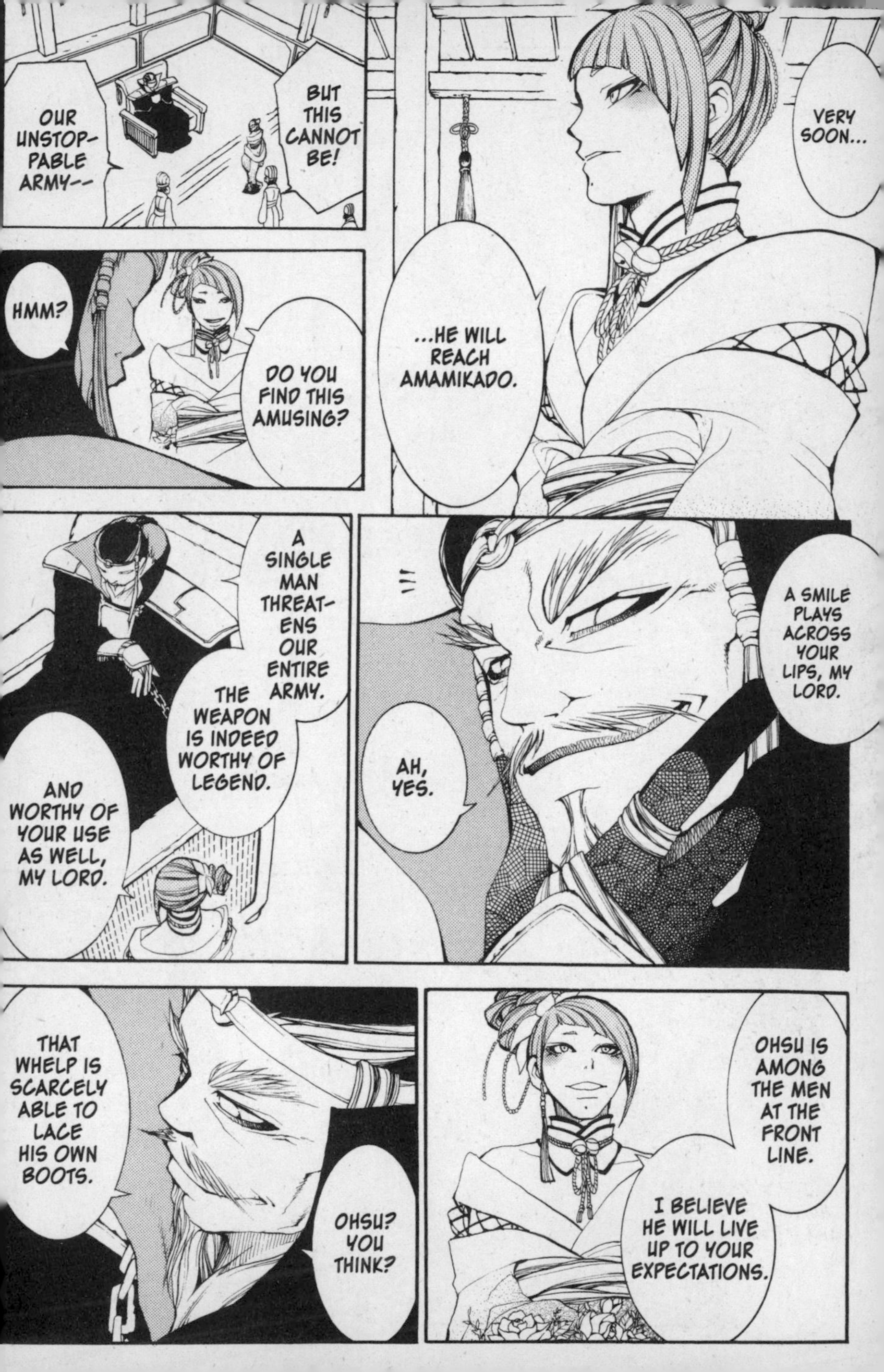
VERY SOON...
...HE WILL REACH AMAMIKADO.
BUT THIS CANNOT BE!
OUR UNSTOPPABLE ARMY--
DO YOU FIND THIS AMUSING?
HMM?
A SMILE PLAYS ACROSS YOUR LIPS, MY LORD.
AH, YES.
A SINGLE MAN THREATENS OUR ENTIRE ARMY.
THE WEAPON IS INDEED WORTHY OF LEGEND.
AND WORTHY OF YOUR USE AS WELL, MY LORD.
OHSU IS AMONG THE MEN AT THE FRONT LINE.
I BELIEVE HE WILL LIVE UP TO YOUR EXPECTATIONS.
OHSU? YOU THINK?
THAT WHELP IS SCARCELY ABLE TO LACE HIS OWN BOOTS.

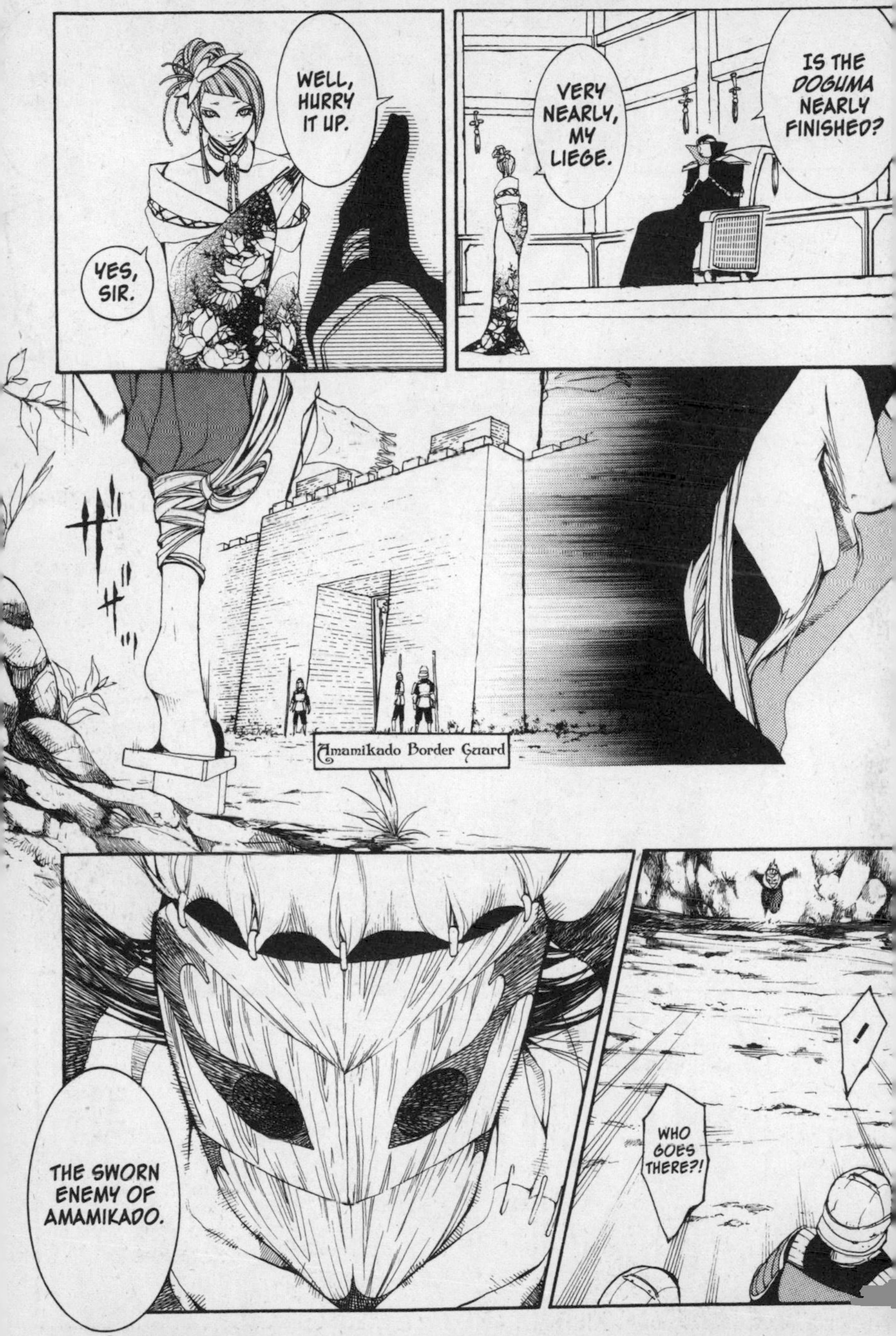
IS THE DOGUMA NEARLY FINISHED?
VERY NEARLY, MY LIEGE.
WELL, HURRY IT UP.
YES, SIR.
Amamikado Border Guard
!
WHO GOES THERE?!
THE SWORN ENEMY OF AMAMIKADO.

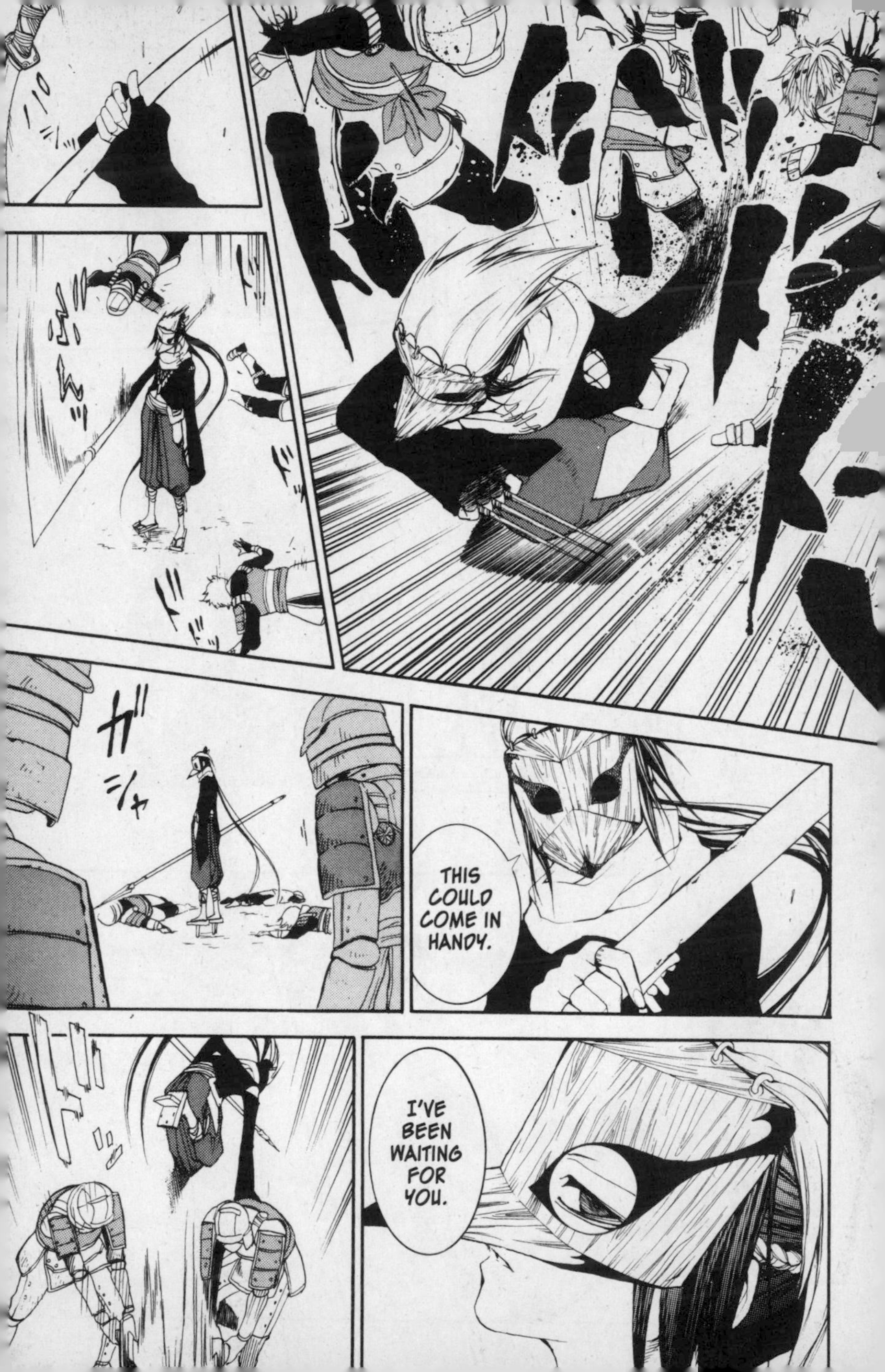
THIS COULD COME IN HANDY.
I'VE BEEN WAITING FOR YOU.

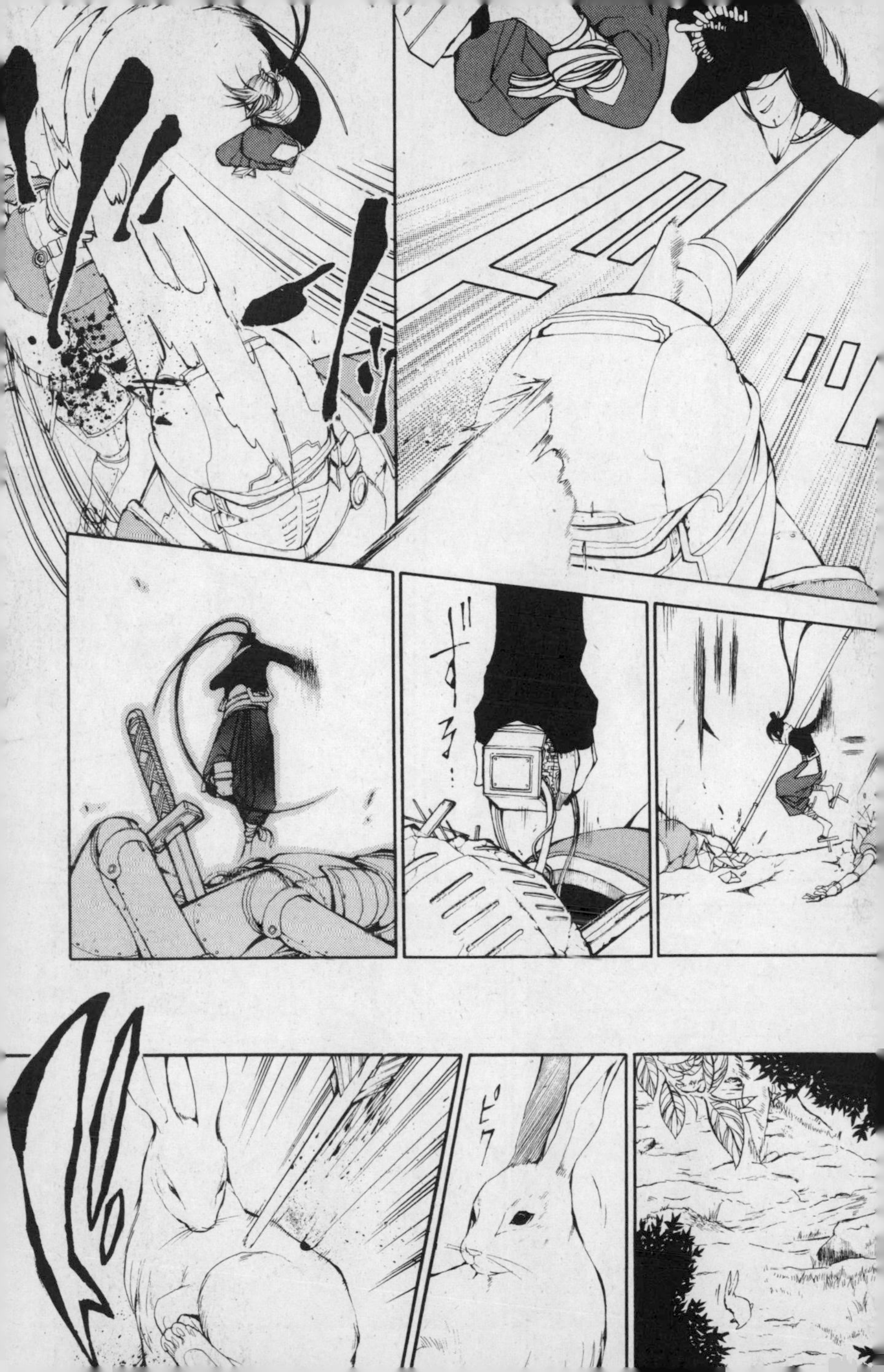
ずる…
ピク

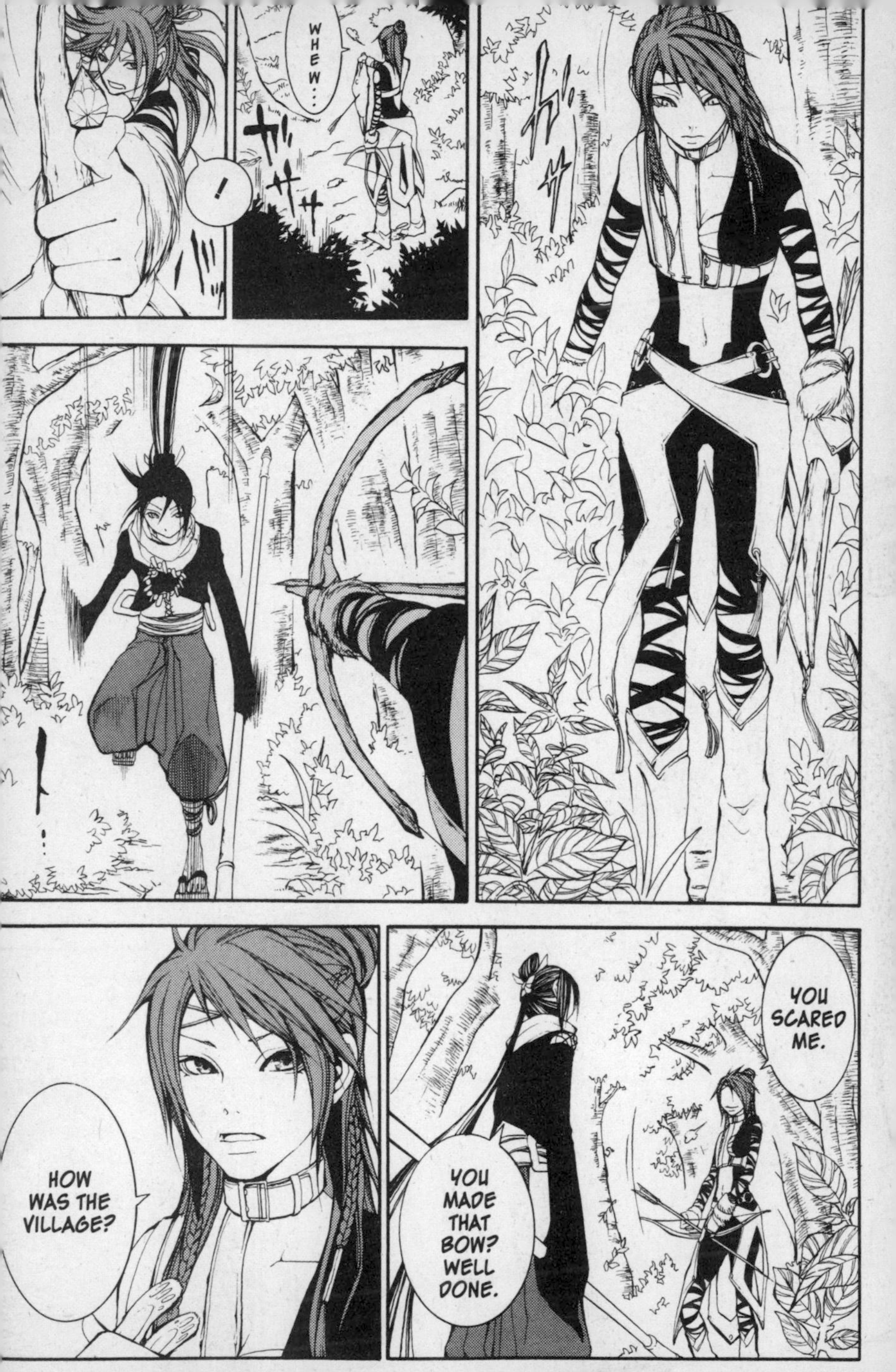
WHEW...
!
YOU SCARED ME.
YOU MADE THAT BOW? WELL DONE.
HOW WAS THE VILLAGE?

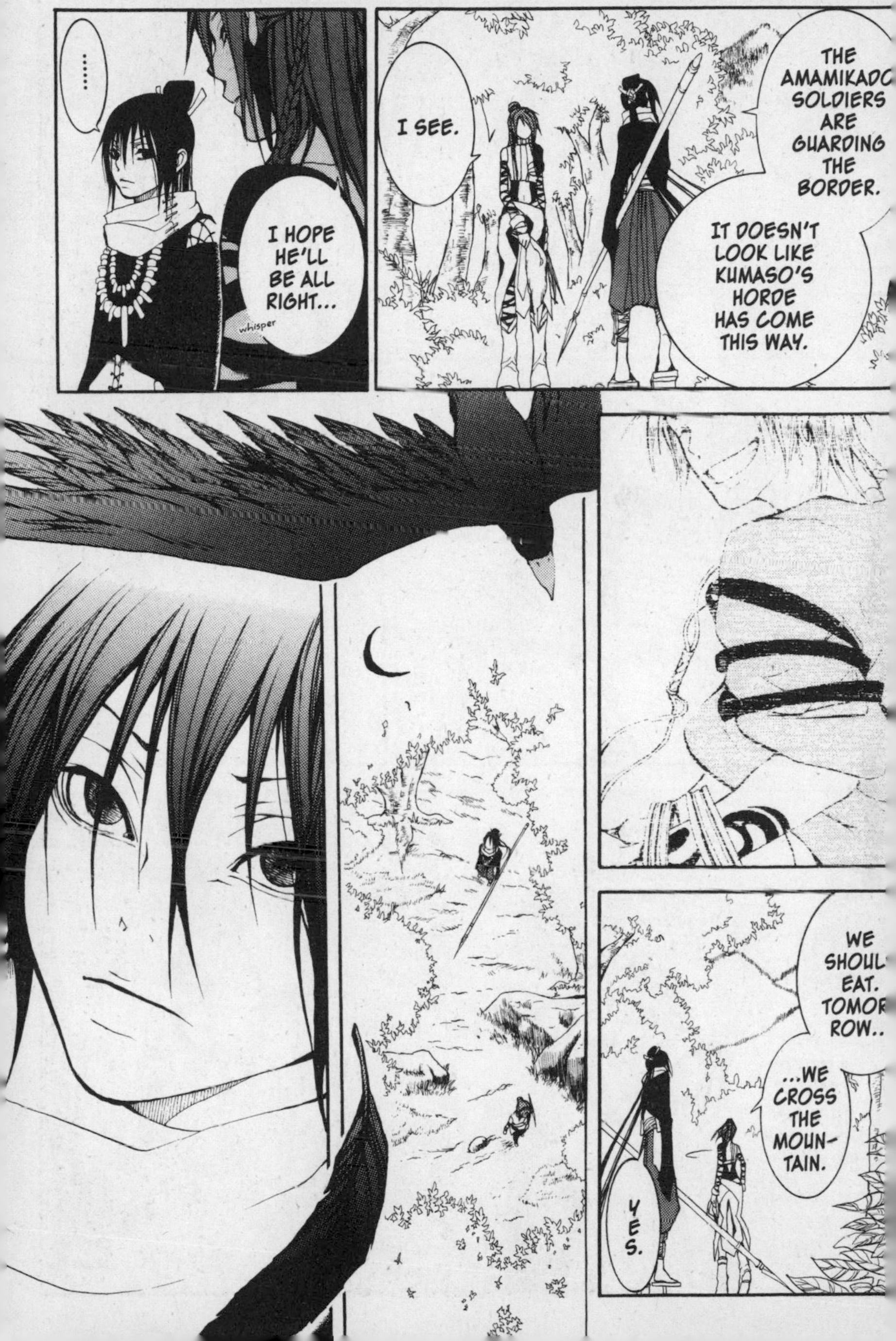
THE AMAMIKADC SOLDIERS ARE GUARDING THE BORDER.
IT DOESN'T LOOK LIKE KUMASO'S HORDE HAS COME THIS WAY.
I SEE.
......
I HOPE HE'LL BE ALL RIGHT...
whisper
WE SHOUL EAT. TOMOR ROW..
...WE CROSS THE MOUNTAIN.
YES.

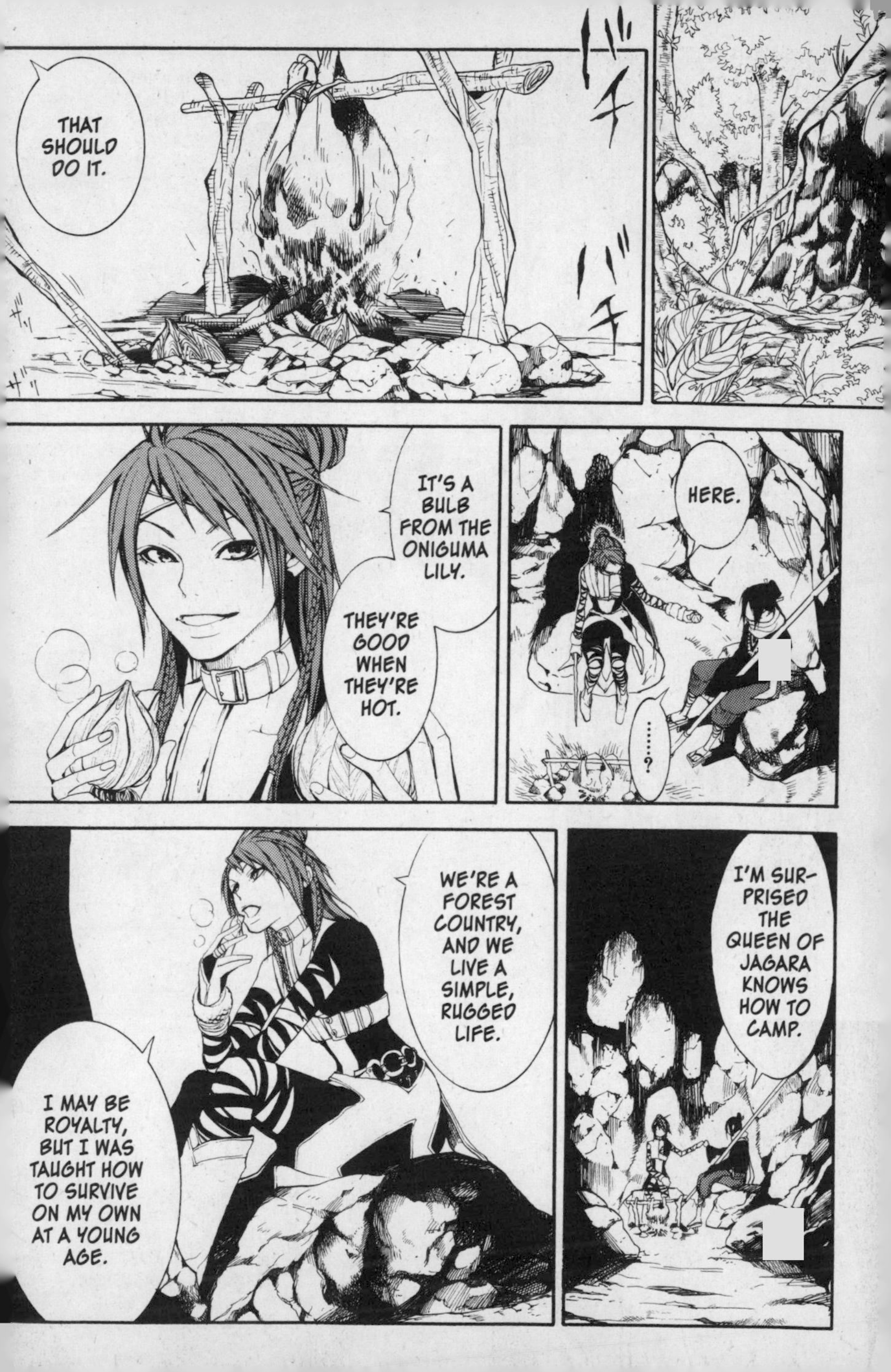
THAT SHOULD DO IT.
HERE.
......?
IT'S A BULB FROM THE ONIGUMA LILY.
THEY'RE GOOD WHEN THEY'RE HOT.
I'M SUR-PRISED THE QUEEN OF JAGARA KNOWS HOW TO CAMP.
WE'RE A FOREST COUNTRY, AND WE LIVE A SIMPLE, RUGGED LIFE.
I MAY BE ROYALTY, BUT I WAS TAUGHT HOW TO SURVIVE ON MY OWN AT A YOUNG AGE.

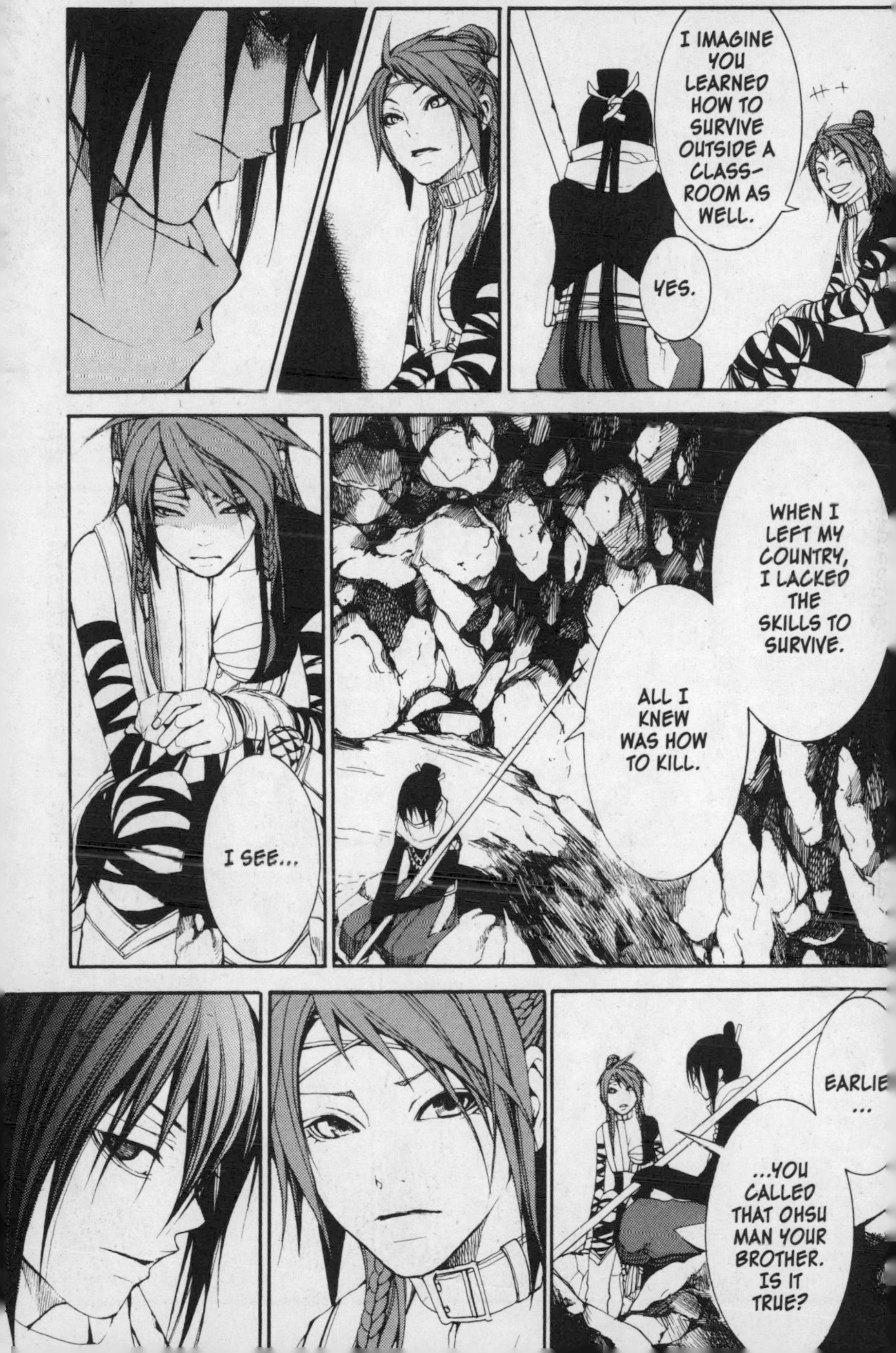
I IMAGINE YOU LEARNED HOW TO SURVIVE OUTSIDE A CLASS-ROOM AS WELL.
YES.
WHEN I LEFT MY COUNTRY, I LACKED THE SKILLS TO SURVIVE.
ALL I KNEW WAS HOW TO KILL.
I SEE...
EARLIE...
...YOU CALLED THAT OHSU MAN YOUR BROTHER. IS IT TRUE?

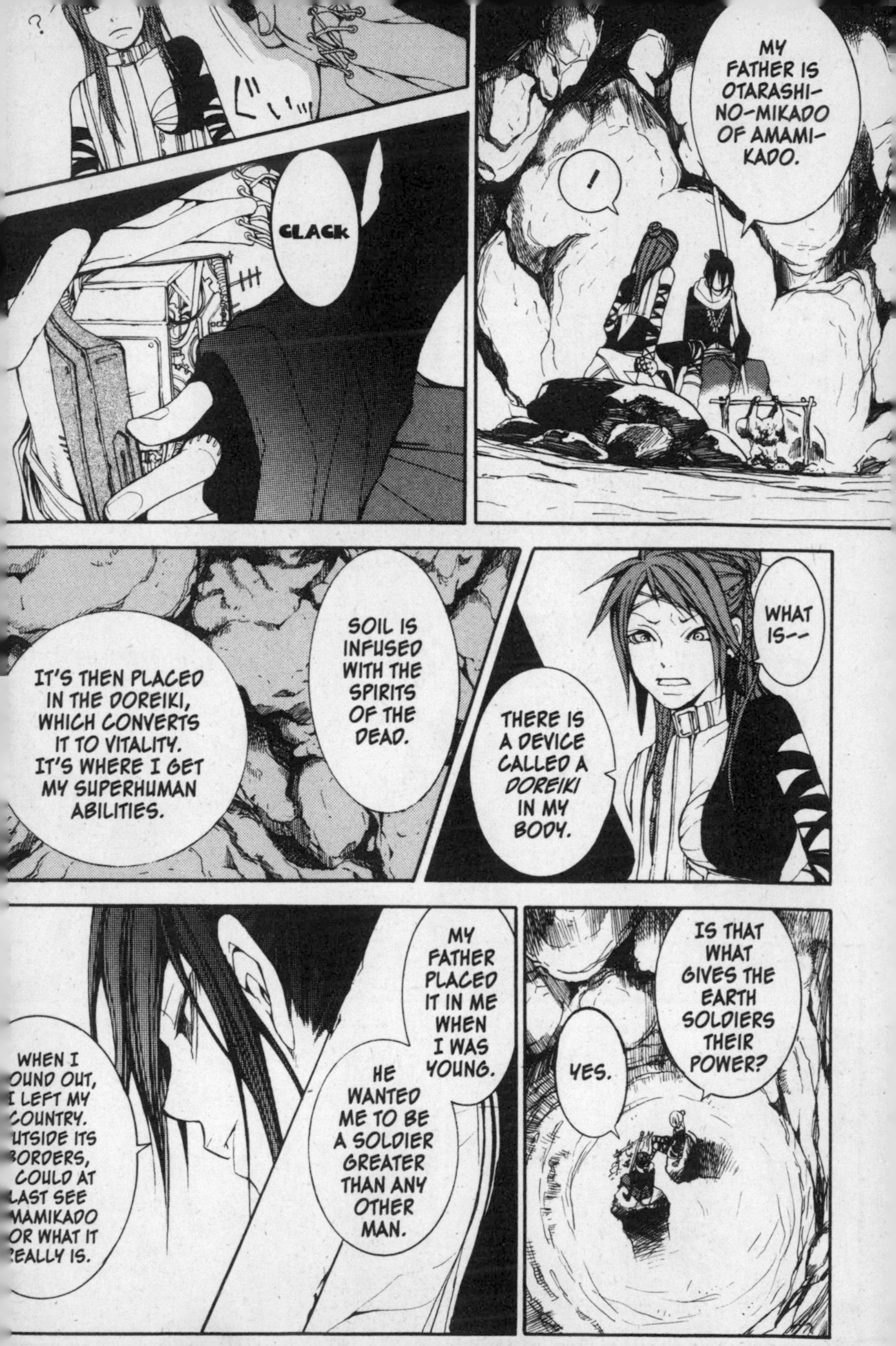
MY FATHER IS OTARASHI-NO-MIKADO OF AMAMI-KADO.
!
?
CLACK
WHAT IS--
THERE IS A DEVICE CALLED A *DOREIKI* IN MY BODY.
SOIL IS INFUSED WITH THE SPIRITS OF THE DEAD.
IT'S THEN PLACED IN THE DOREIKI, WHICH CONVERTS IT TO VITALITY. IT'S WHERE I GET MY SUPERHUMAN ABILITIES.
IS THAT WHAT GIVES THE EARTH SOLDIERS THEIR POWER?
YES.
MY FATHER PLACED IT IN ME WHEN I WAS YOUNG.
HE WANTED ME TO BE A SOLDIER GREATER THAN ANY OTHER MAN.
WHEN I OUND OUT, I LEFT MY COUNTRY. UTSIDE ITS BORDERS, COULD AT LAST SEE MAMIKADO OR WHAT IT EALLY IS.

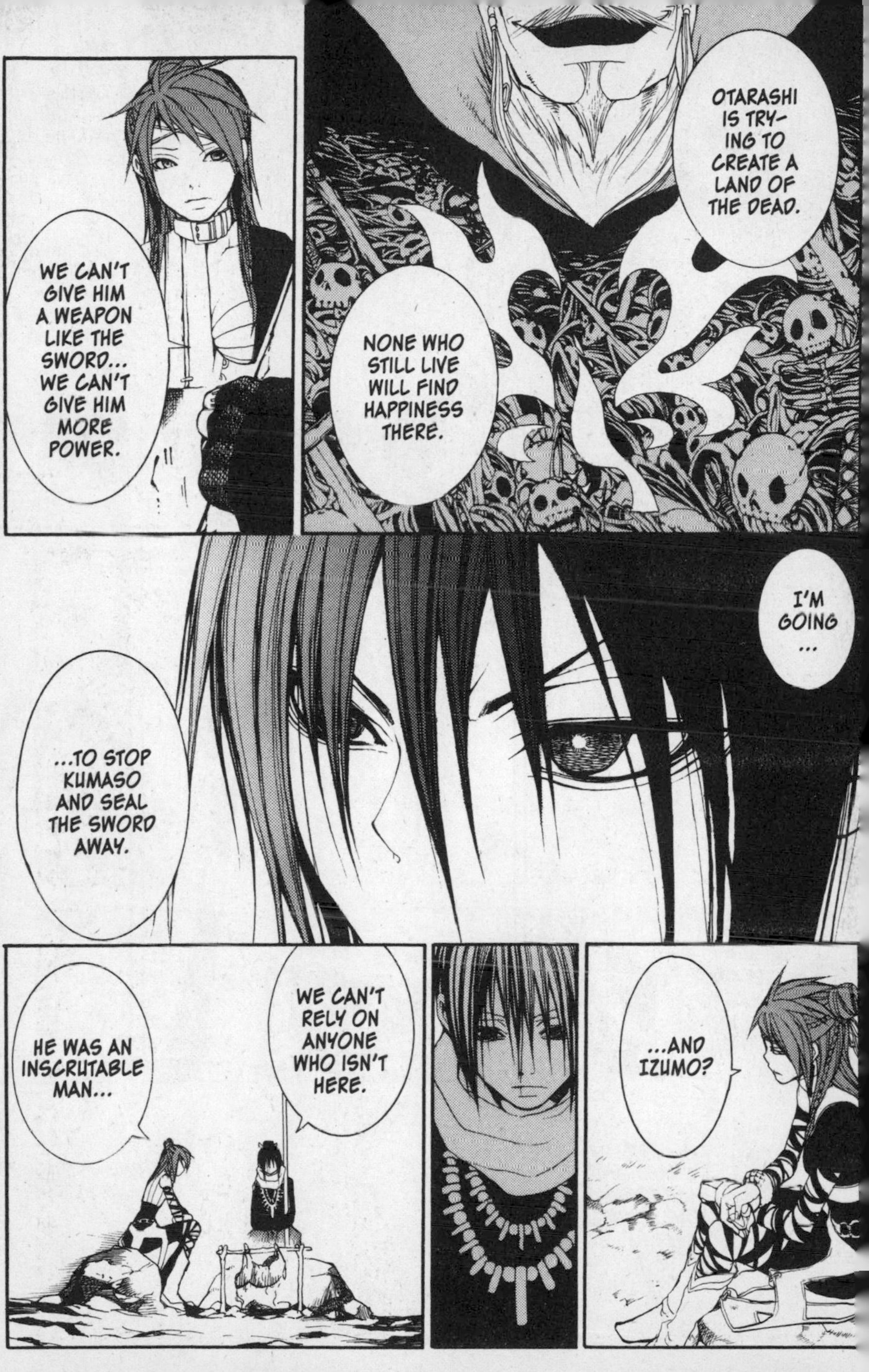
OTARASHI IS TRY-ING TO CREATE A LAND OF THE DEAD.
NONE WHO STILL LIVE WILL FIND HAPPINESS THERE.
WE CAN'T GIVE HIM A WEAPON LIKE THE SWORD... WE CAN'T GIVE HIM MORE POWER.
I'M GOING ...
...TO STOP KUMASO AND SEAL THE SWORD AWAY.
...AND IZUMO?
WE CAN'T RELY ON ANYONE WHO ISN'T HERE.
HE WAS AN INSCRUTABLE MAN...

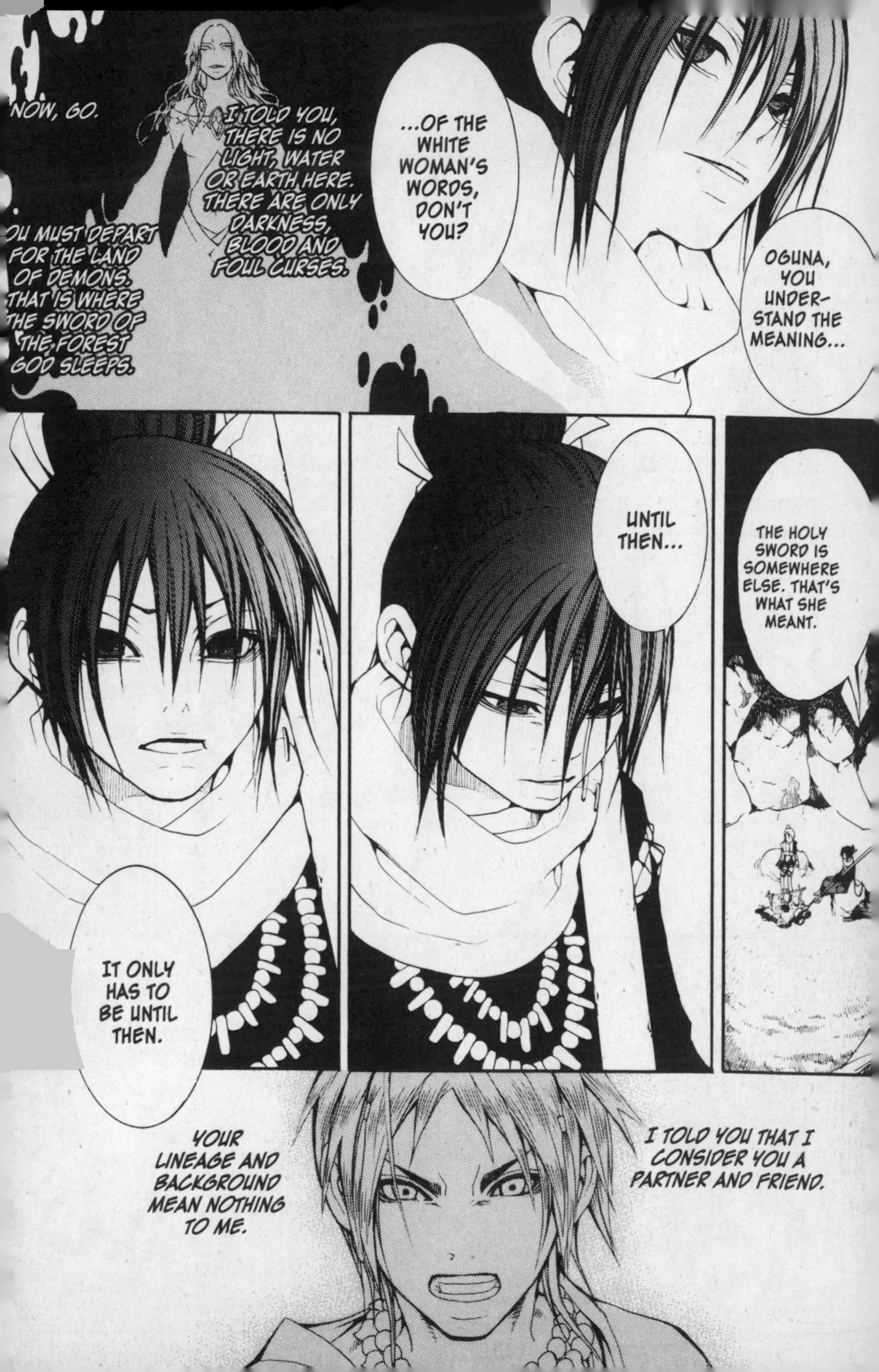
OGUNA, YOU UNDERSTAND THE MEANING...
...OF THE WHITE WOMAN'S WORDS, DON'T YOU?
I TOLD YOU, THERE IS NO LIGHT, WATER OR EARTH HERE. THERE ARE ONLY DARKNESS, BLOOD AND FOUL CURSES.
NOW, GO.
OU MUST DEPART FOR THE LAND OF DEMONS. THAT IS WHERE THE SWORD OF THE FOREST GOD SLEEPS.
THE HOLY SWORD IS SOMEWHERE ELSE. THAT'S WHAT SHE MEANT.
UNTIL THEN...
IT ONLY HAS TO BE UNTIL THEN.
I TOLD YOU THAT I CONSIDER YOU A PARTNER AND FRIEND.
YOUR LINEAGE AND BACKGROUND MEAN NOTHING TO ME.

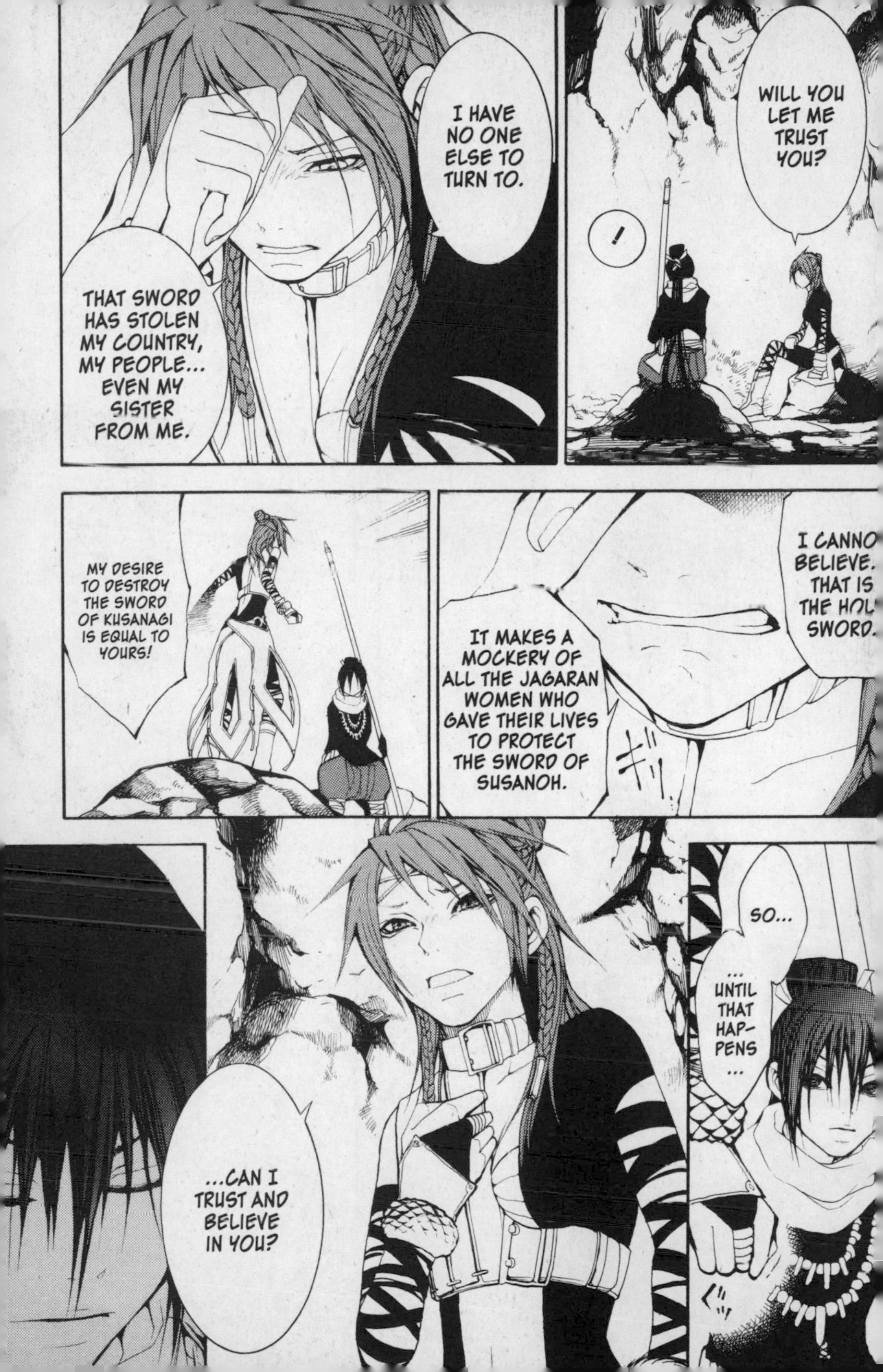
WILL YOU LET ME TRUST YOU?
!
I HAVE NO ONE ELSE TO TURN TO.
THAT SWORD HAS STOLEN MY COUNTRY, MY PEOPLE... EVEN MY SISTER FROM ME.
I CANNO BELIEVE. THAT IS THE HOL SWORD.
IT MAKES A MOCKERY OF ALL THE JAGARAN WOMEN WHO GAVE THEIR LIVES TO PROTECT THE SWORD OF SUSANOH.
ギリ
MY DESIRE TO DESTROY THE SWORD OF KUSANAGI IS EQUAL TO YOURS!
SO...
...UNTIL THAT HAP-PENS...
ぐッ
...CAN I TRUST AND BELIEVE IN YOU?

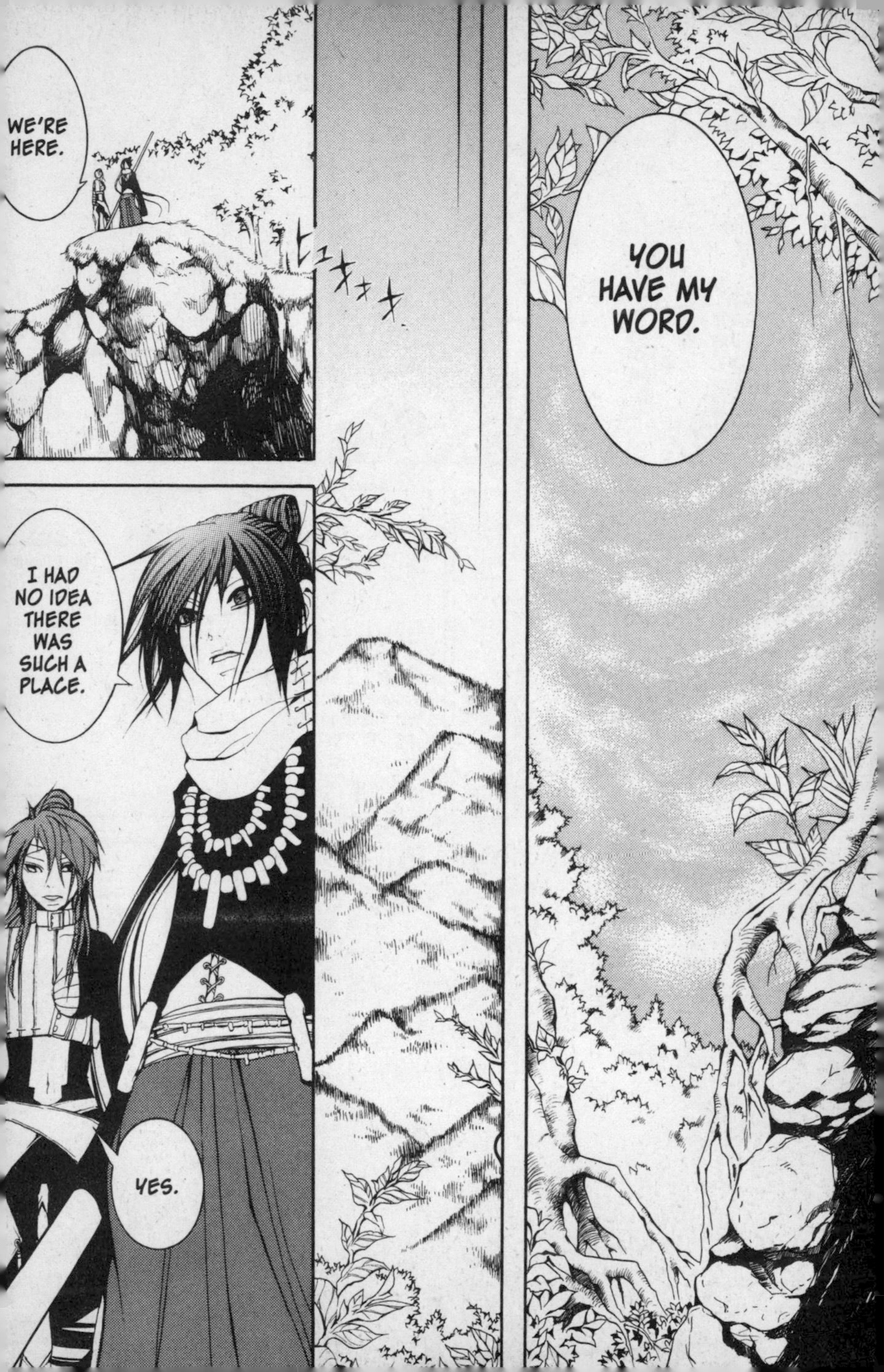
YOU HAVE MY WORD.
WE'RE HERE.
I HAD NO IDEA THERE WAS SUCH A PLACE.
YES.

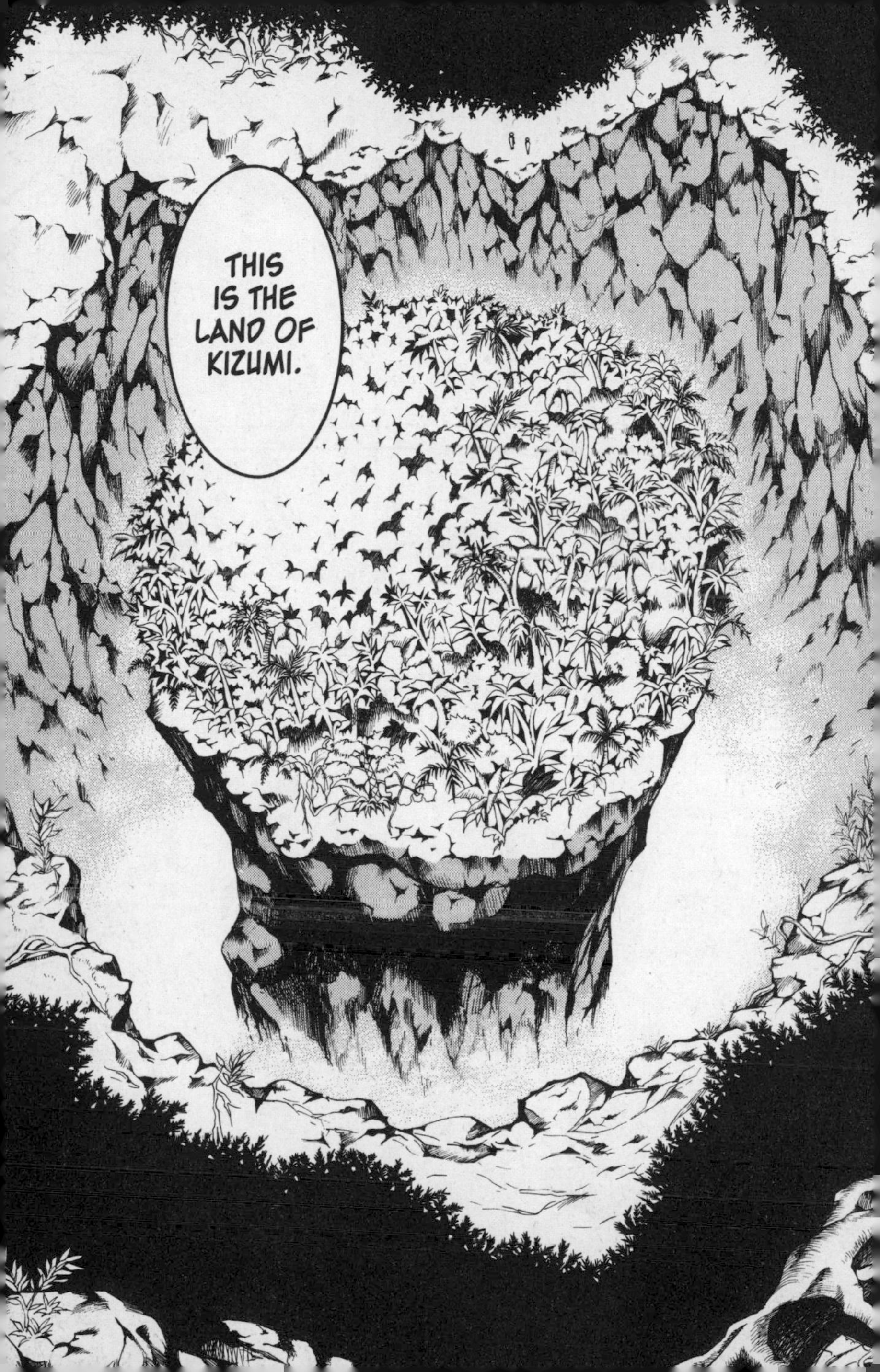
THIS IS THE LAND OF KIZUMI.

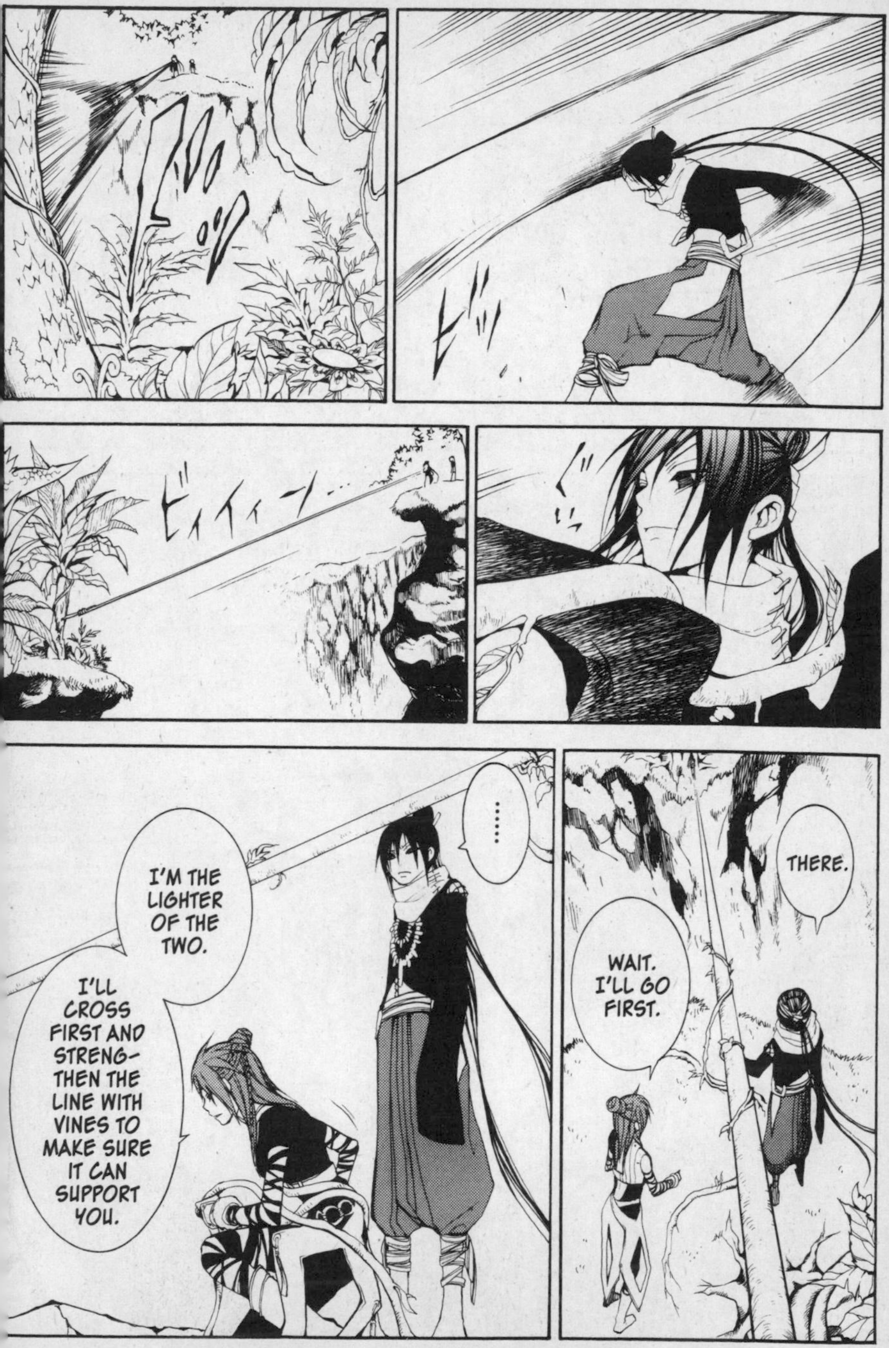
THERE.
WAIT. I'LL GO FIRST.
......
I'M THE LIGHTER OF THE TWO.
I'LL CROSS FIRST AND STRENG- THEN THE LINE WITH VINES TO MAKE SURE IT CAN SUPPORT YOU.

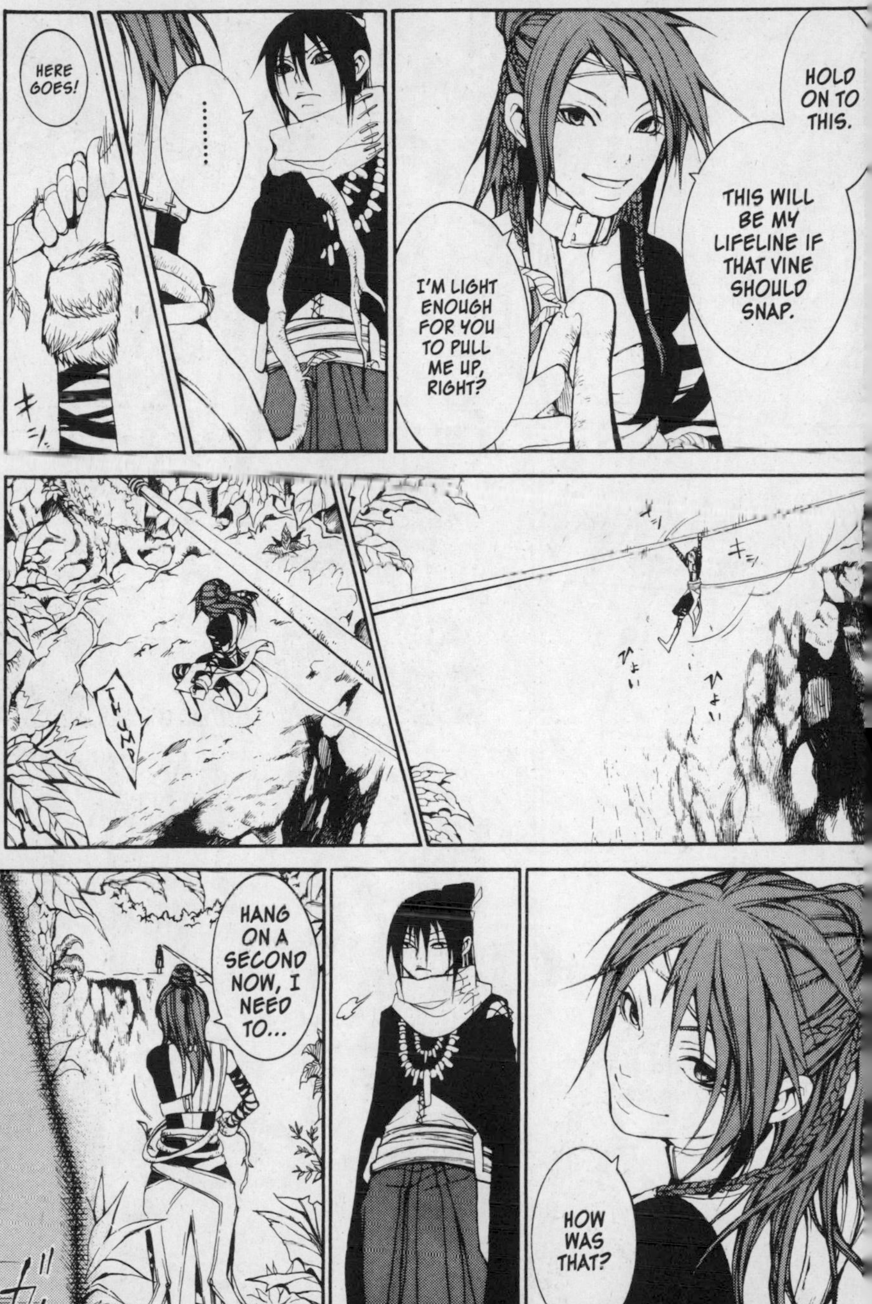
HOLD ON TO THIS.
THIS WILL BE MY LIFELINE IF THAT VINE SHOULD SNAP.
I'M LIGHT ENOUGH FOR YOU TO PULL ME UP, RIGHT?
....
HERE GOES!
ひょい
ひょい
THUMP
HOW WAS THAT?
HANG ON A SECOND NOW, I NEED TO...

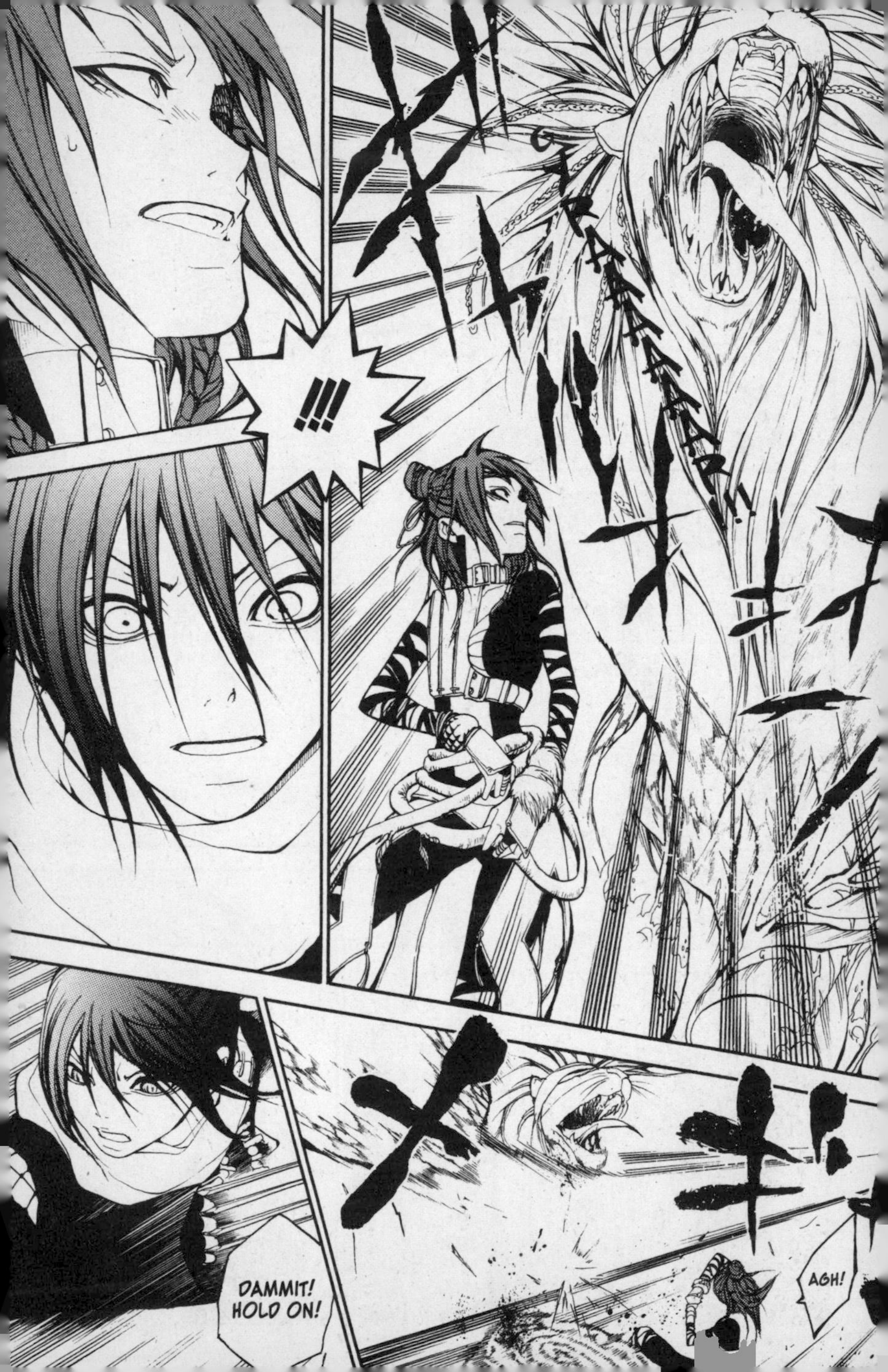
GRAAAAAAR!!
!!!!
AGH!
DAMMIT! HOLD ON!

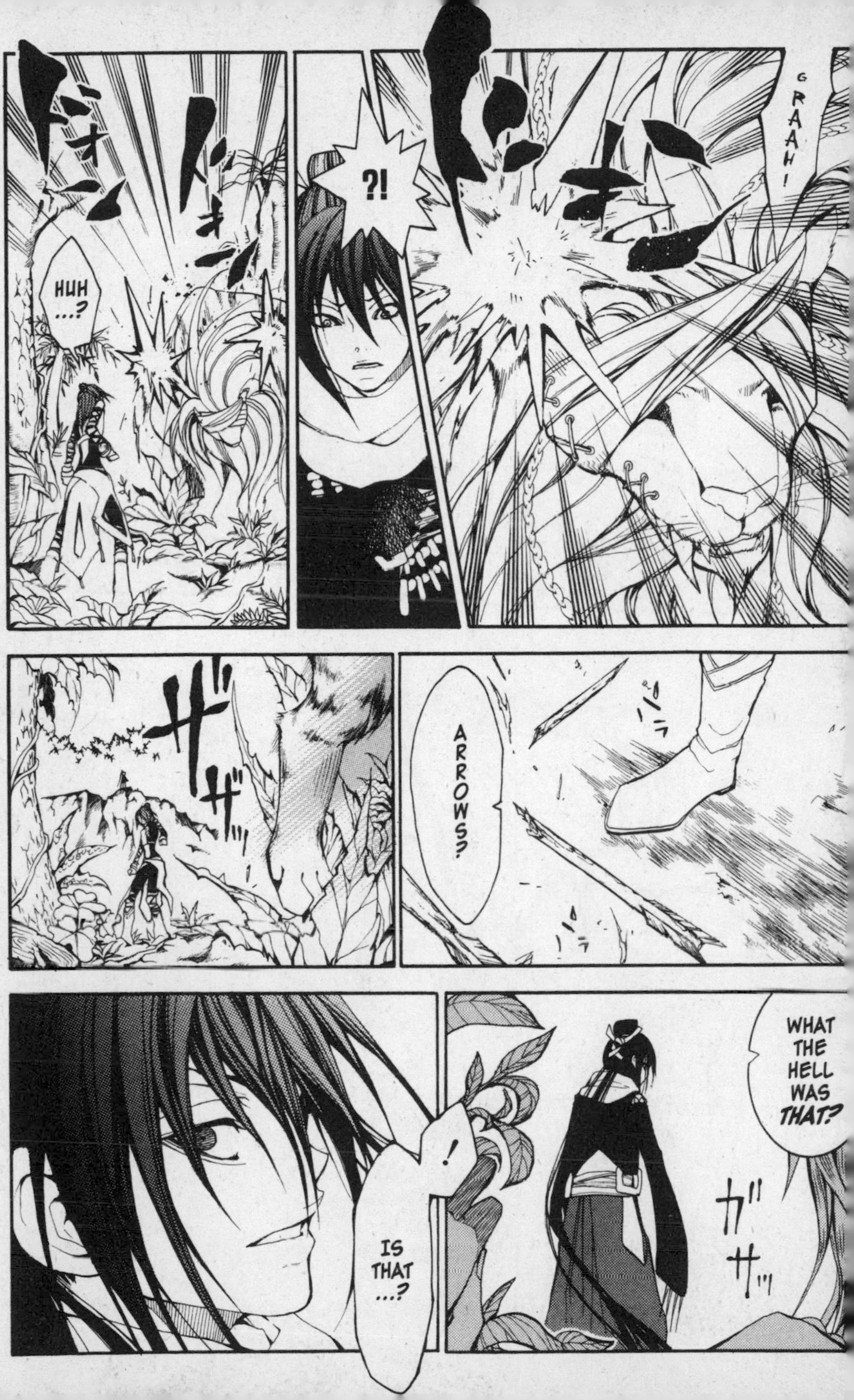
GRAAH!
?!
HUH ...?
ARROWS?
WHAT THE HELL WAS *THAT?*
!
IS THAT ...?

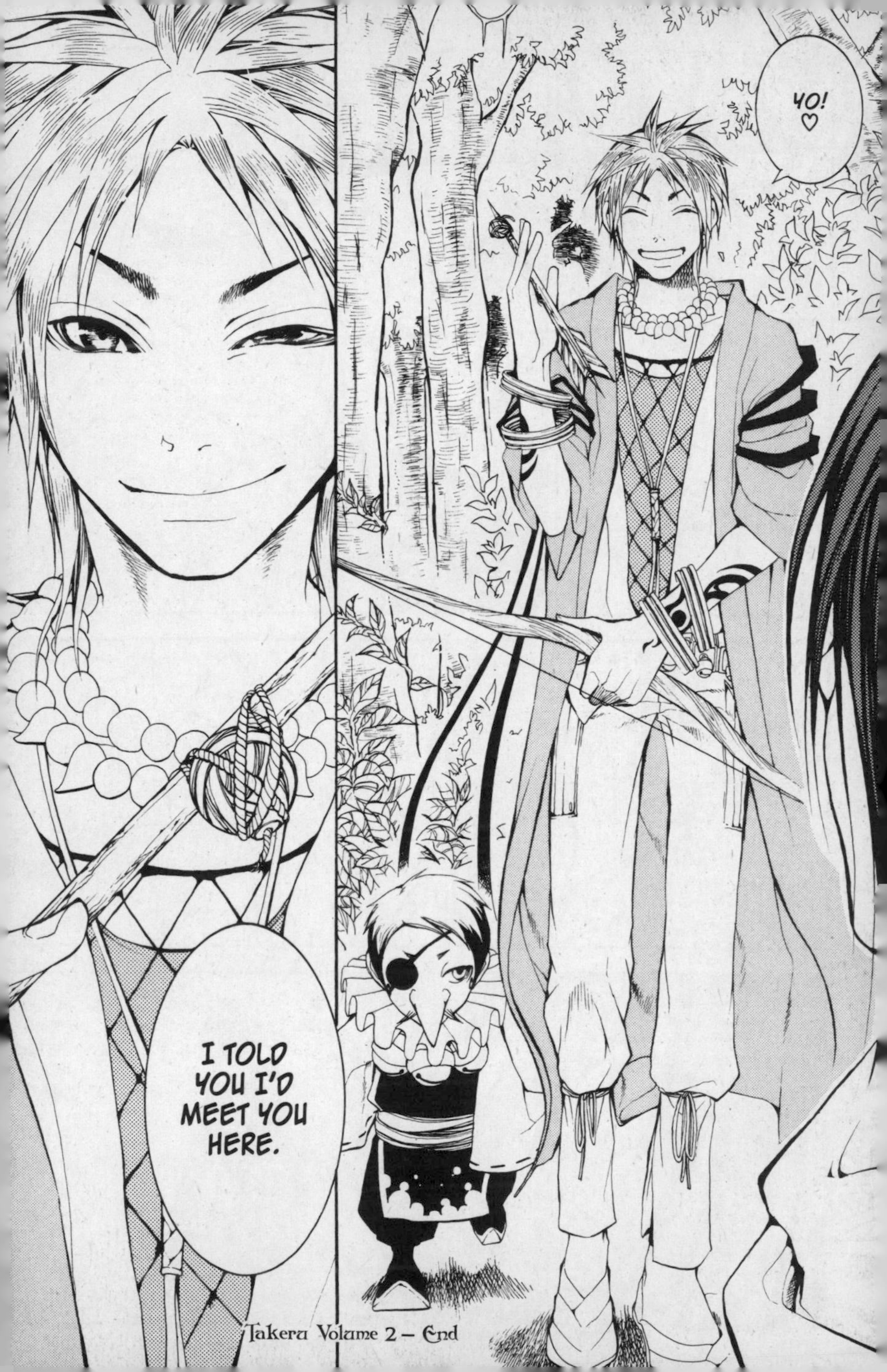
YO! ♡
I TOLD YOU I'D MEET YOU HERE.
Takeru Volume 2 – End

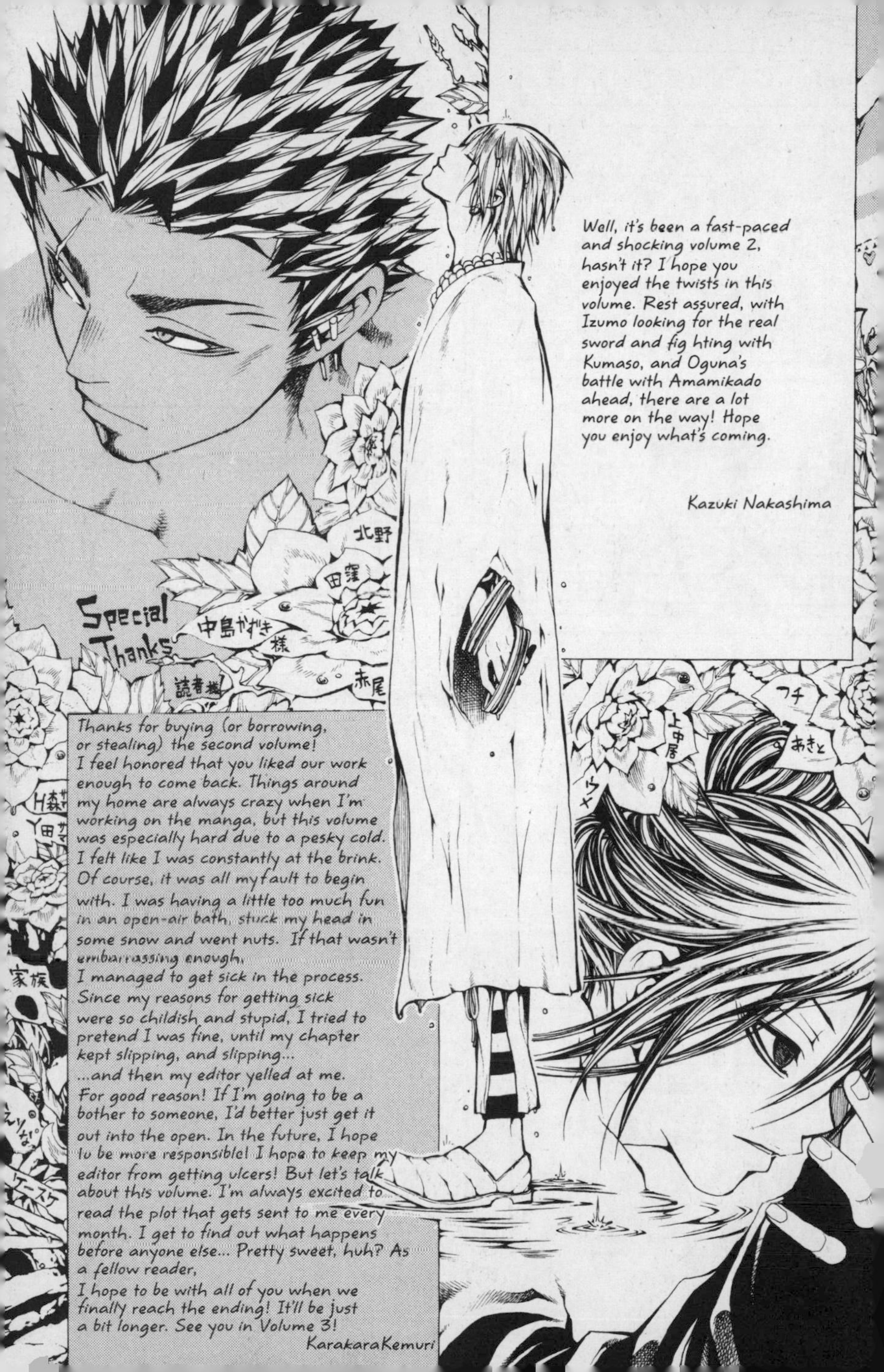
Special Thanks
北野
田窪
中島かずき 様
赤尾
読者様!
家族
ケースケ
フチ
上中居
あきと

Well, it's been a fast-paced and shocking volume 2, hasn't it? I hope you enjoyed the twists in this volume. Rest assured, with Izumo looking for the real sword and fig hting with Kumaso, and Oguna's battle with Amamikado ahead, there are a lot more on the way! Hope you enjoy what's coming.

Kazuki Nakashima

Thanks for buying (or borrowing, or stealing) the second volume! I feel honored that you liked our work enough to come back. Things around my home are always crazy when I'm working on the manga, but this volume was especially hard due to a pesky cold. I felt like I was constantly at the brink. Of course, it was all my fault to begin with. I was having a little too much fun in an open-air bath, stuck my head in some snow and went nuts. If that wasn't embarrassing enough, I managed to get sick in the process. Since my reasons for getting sick were so childish and stupid, I tried to pretend I was fine, until my chapter kept slipping, and slipping... ...and then my editor yelled at me. For good reason! If I'm going to be a bother to someone, I'd better just get it out into the open. In the future, I hope to be more responsible! I hope to keep my editor from getting ulcers! But let's talk about this volume. I'm always excited to read the plot that gets sent to me every month. I get to find out what happens before anyone else... Pretty sweet, huh? As a fellow reader, I hope to be with all of you when we finally reach the ending! It'll be just a bit longer. See you in Volume 3!

KarakaraKemuri

Dream

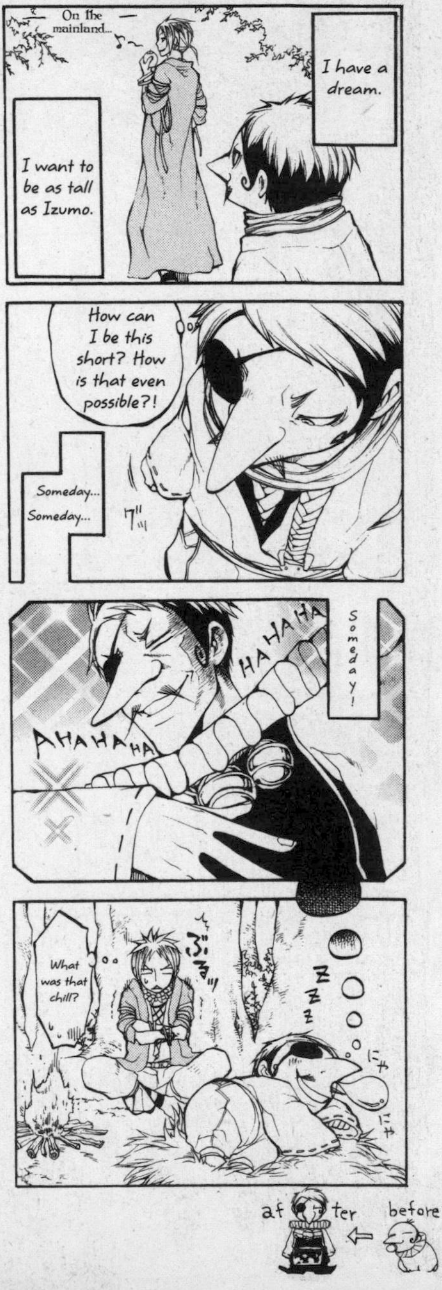
On the mainland...
I have a dream.
I want to be as tall as Izumo.
How can I be this short? How is that even possible?!
Someday... Someday...
Someday!
HA HA HA HA
AHAHAHAHA
What was that chill?
after
before

Chapter 7 Behind the Scenes

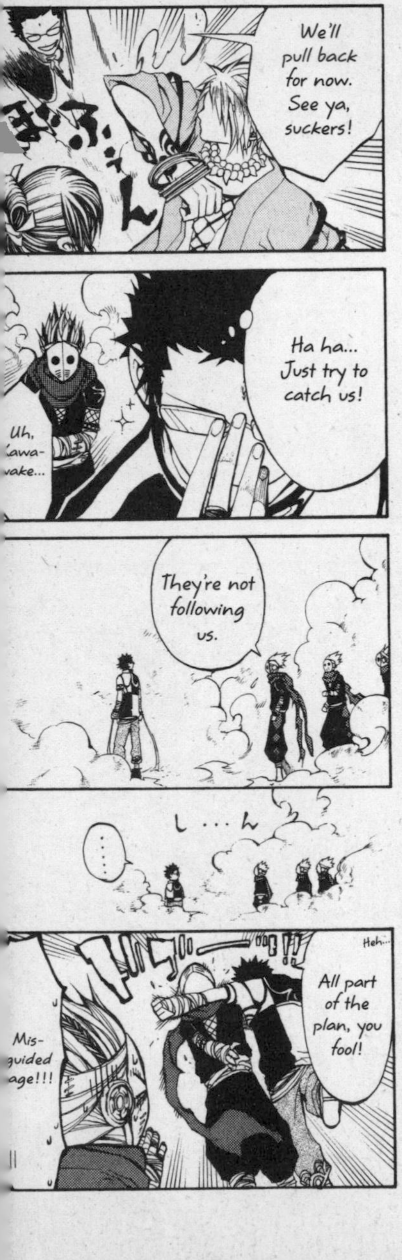
We'll pull back for now. See ya, suckers!
Ha ha... Just try to catch us!
Uh, Kawa- wake...
They're not following us.
......
Heh...
All part of the plan, you fool!
Mis- guided age!!!

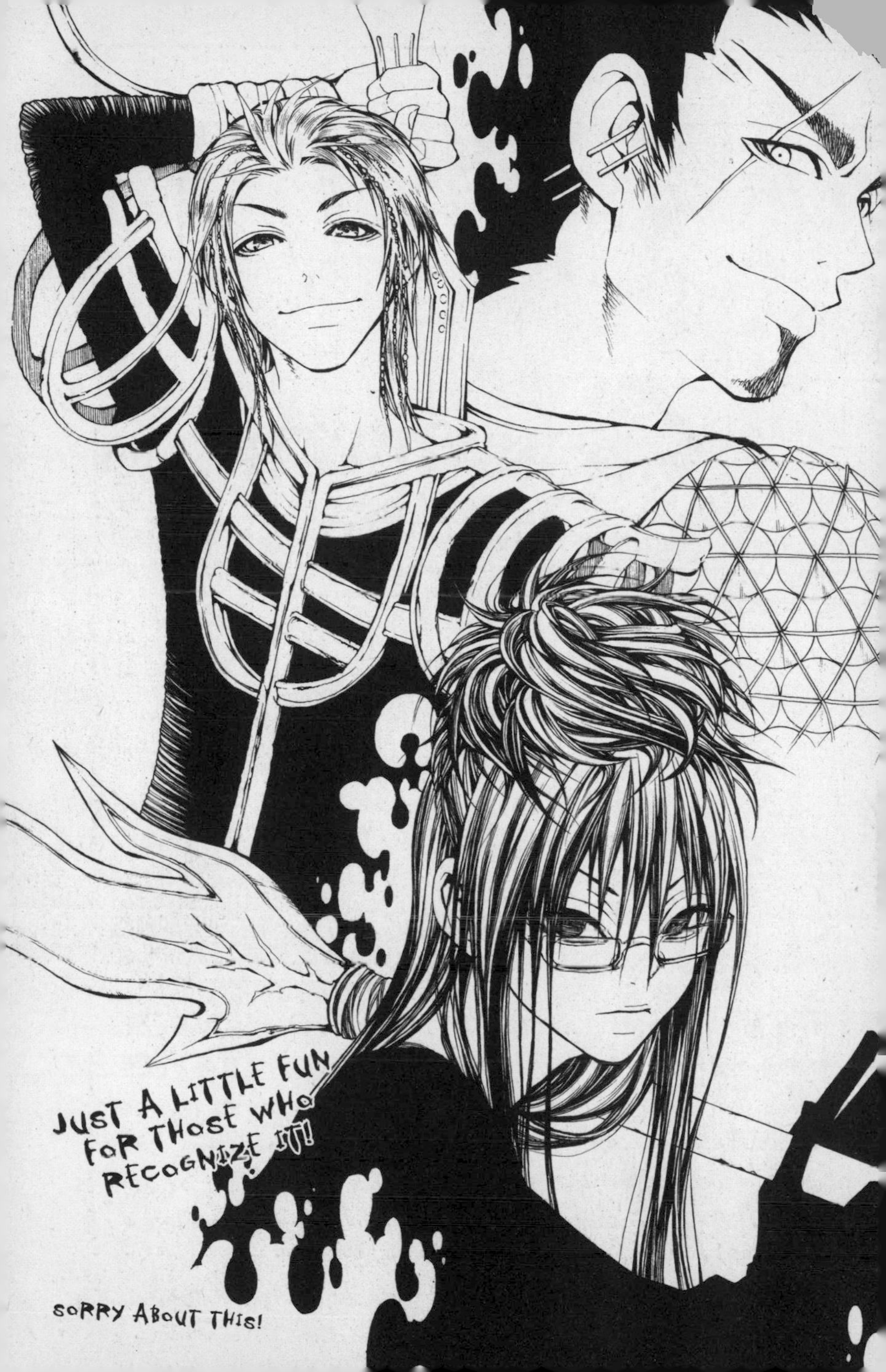
JUST A LITTLE FUN FOR THOSE WHO RECOGNIZE IT!
SORRY ABOUT THIS!

STORY BY
ART BY

Takeru
Opera Susanoh
Sword of the Devil™

SUSANOH～魔性の剣 （劇団☆新感線）より

KAZUKI NAKASHIMA
KARAKARAKEMURI

3

The kingdom of Jagara lies in ruins. Queen Yamato,
along with the hero Kumaso, is now under the control
of the evil Sword of Kusanagi and its army of puppets.
Queen Azuma has turned traitor and joined the empire
of Amamikado, which seeks to bring the sword under its
control. And Queen Miyazu, the eldest, has traveled to
the land of Kizumi with Izumo and Oguna in the hopes
of finding another holy sword that can stop Kusanagi...

EVERY TEXT COULD BE YOUR LAST

FUTURE DIARY ™

Yukiteru has a secret that nobody knows about—his cellphone can tell the future! Now he's entered a vicious game of survival among twelve future diary holders— with the winner crowned god of a new world!

"ESUNO'S ART IS SPRIGHTLY, SWEET AND DECEPTIVELY INNOCENT."
—*Publishers Weekly*

© 2006 Sakae ESUNO /KADOKAWA SHOTEN Publishing Co. Ltd.

BE SURE TO VISIT WWW.TOKYOPOP.COM/SHOP FOR
EVERYTHING YOU COULD EVER WANT!

A dark, Gothic tale from the artist of *Trinity Blood*

A mysterious drug, known only as "Zone-00," seems to be causing demons all over Tokyo to lose control and revert to their old, violent ways. Enter two young students who stand o opposite sides of an ageless conflict. One a demon, the othe an exorcist, they must now join forces to uncover the secret of "Zone-00" before it's too late!

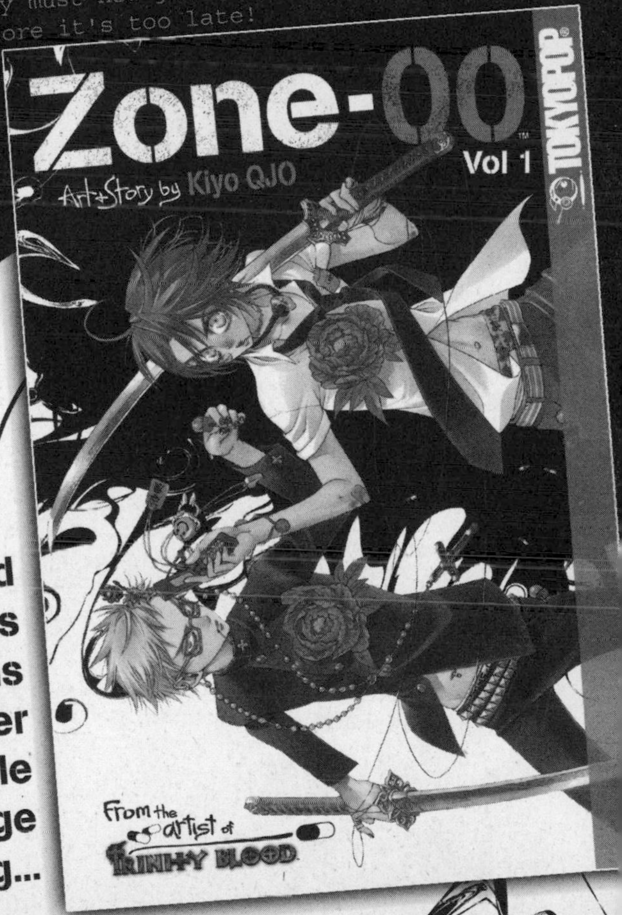
Zone-00™
Vol 1
Art+Story by Kiyo QJO
TOKYOPOP
From the artist of
TRINITY BLOOD

In a world where humans and demons coexist under a fragile peace, change is coming...

BE SURE TO VISIT WWW.TOKYOPOP.COM/SHOP FOR EVERYTHING YOU COULD EVER WANT!

TOKYOPOP MANGA SUPPLEMENT

TSUBASA
THOSE WITH WINGS

FROM THE CREATOR OF
FRUITS BASKET!

All ex-thief Kotobuki and her ex-military commander boyfriend Raimon want is a quiet, peaceful life together. But if those seeking a legendary wish-granting wing have anything to say about it, they won't be in retirement for long!

Available wherever books are sold!

FANTASY

OT OLDER TEEN AGE 16+

"I highly recommend this!"
-Sequential Tart

TSUBASA WO MOTSU MONO © 1995 Natsuki Takaya / HAKUSENSHA, Inc.

FOR MORE INFORMATION VISIT: WWW.TOKYOPOP.COM/NATSUKITAKAYA

TOKYOPOP MANGA SUPPLEMENT

Phantom Dream

new manga from **fruits basket** creator **natsuki takaya!**

Tamaki Otoya, the last in an ancient line of summoners, battles evil forces threatening mankind. When this fight turns against the love of his life, will he choose his passion or his destiny?

Available wherever books are sold!

Read *Phantom Dream* online at TOKYOPOP.com/PhantomDream

"Fans of Takaya's hit shojo series Fruits Basket will gladly welcome this." ~Publishers Weekly

 ROMANCE

 TEEN AGE 13+

GENEIMUSOU: © 1994 Natsuki Takaya / HAKUSEN

FOR MORE INFORMATION VISIT: www.TOKYOPOP.com/NatsukiTakaya

TOKYOPOP MANGA SUPPLEMENT

Animal ACADEMY
HAKOBUNE HAKUSHO
はこぶね白書

FEATURING THE CUTEST, MOST ORIGINAL CAST OF CHARACTERS SINCE +Anima!

1 · MOYAMU FUJINO

CAN YOU PLEDGE SECRECY WHEN YOU ARE...A HUMAN BEING?

When fifteen-year-old Neko is accepted to the mysterious Morimori school, she immediately senses that something is a little off about her classmates... It turns out that all the other students are magical animals who can transform into human form. Now Neko must pretend to be an animal—before the cat's out of the bag!

FANTASY

T
TEEN
AGE 13+

© MOYAMU FUJINO/MAG Garden

BE SURE TO VISIT WWW.TOKYOPOP.COM/SHOP FOR EVERYTHING YOU COULD EVER WANT!

The class president has a little secret she's keeping from the sexy bad boy in school...

It's love at first fight in this shojo romantic comedy—with a hilarious spin on geek culture and... student government?!

As President of the Student Council, the overachieving feminist Misaki really socks it to the boys in an attempt to make the former all-boys' school attract a more female student body. But what will she do when the hottest boy in class finds out Misaki's after-school gig is in a maid café?!

© 2005 Hiro Fujiwara / HAKUSENSHA, INC

BE SURE TO VISIT WWW.TOKYOPOP.COM/SHOP FOR EVERYTHING YOU COULD EVER WANT!

Nobody ever said
finding a soul mate
would be easy!

Maria✝Holic

Because of her phobia of men,
Kanako enrolls in an all-girls school
to find her one true love.
When she meets a captivating freshman
named Mariya who fits her criteria,
it turns out that her seemingly
ideal mate happens to be a
cross-dressing sadistic boy!

Can things get any worse?!

From Minari ENDOU,
creator of the
fan favorite Dazzle!

BE SURE TO VISIT WWW.TOKYOPOP.COM/SHOP FOR
EVERYTHING YOU COULD EVER WANT!

KARAKURI ODETTE

カラクリ オデット

SHE'S A HOT ROBOT IN HIGH SCHOOL
WHAT'S THE WORST THAT COULD HAPPEN?

KARAKURI ODETTE

カラクリ オデット

1

JULIETTA SUZUKI

KARAKURI ODETTO © 2005 Julietta Suzuki / HAKUSENSHA, Inc.

From the creator of *Akuma to Dolce*

Odette is an android created by the young, talented Dr. Yoshizawa. Wanting to find the ultimate difference between humans and androids, she decides to enroll in high school. Follow Odette's adventures, as she ventures through her school's hallowed halls, in search of the true meaning of being a human!

BE SURE TO VISIT WWW.TOKYOPOP.COM/SHOP FOR EVERYTHING YOU COULD EVER WANT!

STOP!

This is the back of the book.
You wouldn't want to spoil a great ending!

This book is printed "manga-style," in the authentic Japanese right-to-left format. Since none of the artwork has been flipped or altered, readers get to experience the story just as teh creater intended. You've been asking for it, so TOKYOPOP® delivered: authentic, hot-off-the-press, and far more fun!

1
2
3
4
5
6
7
8
9
10

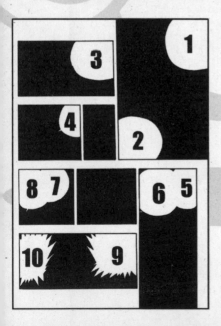

DIRECTIONS

If this is your first time reading manga-style, here's a quick guide to help you understand how it works.

It's easy... just start in the top right panel and follow the numbers. Have fun, and look for more 100% authentic manga from TOKYOPOP®!

THE MANGA REVOLUTION · LEADING THE MANGA REVOLUTION · LEADING

漫画革命

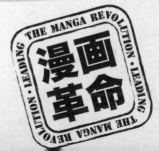